Computational Intelligence: Advances and Applications

Computational Intelligence: Advances and Applications

Edited by
Gabriele Cox

www.willfordpress.com

Published by Willford Press,
118-35 Queens Blvd., Suite 400,
Forest Hills, NY 11375, USA

ISBN: 978-1-68285-616-1

Cataloging-in-Publication Data

Computational intelligence : advances and applications / edited by Gabriele Cox.
    p. cm.
Includes bibliographical references and index.
ISBN 978-1-68285-616-1
1. Computational intelligence. 2. Artificial intelligence. I. Cox, Gabriele.
Q342 .C66 2019
006.3--dc23

For information on all Willford Press publications
visit our website at www.willfordpress.com

Contents

Preface

Computational intelligence is a set of methodologies designed to solve complex problems that cannot be solved using classical methods of mathematics or modeling. It operates using the techniques of fuzzy logic, artificial neural networks, evolutionary computing, learning theory and probabilistic methods. Computational intelligence provides solutions for real-world problems that cannot be put into binary code. Some popular approaches of this domain are artificial immune systems and swarm intelligence. The field of computational intelligence has applications in engineering, computer science, data analysis and biomedicine. The objective of this book is to give a general view of the different areas of computational intelligence and their applications. It aims to present researches that have transformed this discipline and aided its advancement. Students, researchers, experts and all associated with this field will benefit alike from this book.

The researches compiled throughout the book are authentic and of high quality, combining several disciplines and from very diverse regions from around the world. Drawing on the contributions of many researchers from diverse countries, the book's objective is to provide the readers with the latest achievements in the area of research. This book will surely be a source of knowledge to all interested and researching the field.

In the end, I would like to express my deep sense of gratitude to all the authors for meeting the set deadlines in completing and submitting their research chapters. I would also like to thank the publisher for the support offered to us throughout the course of the book. Finally, I extend my sincere thanks to my family for being a constant source of inspiration and encouragement.

Editor

Deep Learning in Visual Computing and Signal Processing

Danfeng Xie, Lei Zhang, and Li Bai

Department of Electrical and Computer Engineering, Temple University, Philadelphia, PA 19121, USA

Correspondence should be addressed to Danfeng Xie; danfeng.xie@temple.edu

Academic Editor: Francesco Carlo Morabito

Deep learning is a subfield of machine learning, which aims to learn a hierarchy of features from input data. Nowadays, researchers have intensively investigated deep learning algorithms for solving challenging problems in many areas such as image classification, speech recognition, signal processing, and natural language processing. In this study, we not only review typical deep learning algorithms in computer vision and signal processing but also provide detailed information on how to apply deep learning to specific areas such as road crack detection, fault diagnosis, and human activity detection. Besides, this study also discusses the challenges of designing and training deep neural networks.

1. Introduction

Deep learning methods are a group of machine learning methods that can learn features hierarchically from lower level to higher level by building a deep architecture. The deep learning methods have the ability to automatically learn features at multiple levels, which makes the system be able to learn complex mapping function $f : X \rightarrow Y$ directly from data, without help of the human-crafted features. This ability is crucial for high-level feature abstraction since high-level features are difficult to be described directly from raw training data. Moreover, with the sharp growth of data, the ability to learn high-level features automatically will be even more important.

The most characterizing feature of deep learning methods is that their models all have deep architectures. A deep architecture means it has multiple hidden layers in the network. In contrast, a shallow architecture has only few hidden layers (1 to 2 layers). Deep architectures are loosely inspired by mammal brain. When given an input percept, mammal brain processes it using different area of cortex which abstracts different levels of features. Researchers usually describe such concepts in hierarchical ways, with many levels of abstraction. Furthermore, mammal brains also seem to process information through many stages of transformation and representation. A very clear example is that the information in the primate visual system is processed in a sequence of stages: edge detection, primitive shapes, and more complex visual shapes.

Inspired by the deep architecture of mammal brain, researchers investigated deep neural networks for two decades but did not find effective training methods before 2006: researchers only obtained good experimental results of neural network with one or two hidden layers but could not get good results of neural network with more hidden layers. In 2006, Hinton et al. proposed deep belief networks (DBNs) [1], with a learning algorithm that uses unsupervised learning algorithm to greedily train deep neural network layer by layer. This training method, which is called deep learning, turns out to be very effective and efficient in training deep neural networks.

Many other deep architectures, that is, autoencoder, deep convolutional neural networks, and recurrent neural networks, are successfully applied in various areas. Regression [2], classification [3–9], dimensionality reduction [10, 11], modeling motion [12, 13], modeling textures [14], information retrieval [15–17], natural language processing [18–20], robotics [21], fault diagnosis [22], and road crack detection [23] have seen increasing deep learning-related research studies. There are mainly three crucial reasons for the rapid development of deep learning applications nowadays: the big leap of deep learning algorithms, the significantly increased computational abilities, and the sharp drop of price in hardware.

This survey provides an overview of several deep learning algorithms and their emerging applications in several specific areas, featuring face recognition, road crack detection, fault diagnosis, and falls detection. As complementarity to existing review papers [24, 25], we not only review the state-of-the-art deep learning methods but also provide detailed information on how to apply deep learning to specific problems. The reminder of this paper is organized as follows. In Section 2, the two categories of deep learning algorithms are introduced: restricted Boltzmann machines (RBMs) and convolutional neural networks (CNNs). The training strategies are discussed in Section 3. In Section 4, we describe several specific deep learning applications, that is, face recognition, road crack detection, fault diagnosis, and human activity detection. In Section 5, we discuss several challenges of training and using the deep neural networks. In Section 6, we conclude the paper.

2. Deep Learning Algorithms

Deep learning algorithms have been extensively studied in recent years. As a consequence, there are a large number of related approaches. Generally speaking, these algorithms can be grouped into two categories based on their architectures: restricted Boltzmann machines (RBMs) and convolutional neural networks (CNNs). In the following sections, we will briefly review these deep learning methods and their developments.

2.1. Deep Neural Network. This section introduces how to build and train RBM-based deep neural networks (DNNs). The building and training procedures of a DNN contain two steps. First, build a deep belief network (DBN) by stacking restricted Boltzmann machines (RBMs) and feed unlabeled data to pretrain the DBN. The pretrained DBN provides initial parameters for the deep neural network. In the second step, labeled data is fed to train the DNN using backpropagation. After two steps of training, a trained DNN is obtained. This section is organized as follows. Section 2.1.1 introduces RBM, which is the basic component of DBN. In Section 2.1.2, RBM-based DNN is introduced.

2.1.1. Restricted Boltzmann Machines. RBM is an energy-based probabilistic generative model [26–29]. It is composed of one layer of visible units and one layer of hidden units. The visible units represent the input vector of a data sample and the hidden units represent features that are abstracted from the visible units. Every visible unit is connected to every hidden unit, whereas no connection exists within the visible layer or hidden layer. Figure 1 illustrates the graphical model of restricted Boltzmann machine.

As a result of the lack of hidden-hidden and input-input interactions, the energy function of a RBM is

$$\text{Energy}(\mathbf{v}, \mathbf{h}; \theta) = -\mathbf{b}^T\mathbf{v} - \mathbf{c}^T\mathbf{h} - \mathbf{h}^T\mathbf{W}\mathbf{v}, \quad (1)$$

where $\theta = \{\mathbf{W}, \mathbf{b}, \mathbf{c}\}$ are the parameters of RBM and they need to be learned during the training procedure; $\mathbf{W}$ denotes the weights between the visible layer and hidden layer; $\mathbf{b}$ and $\mathbf{c}$

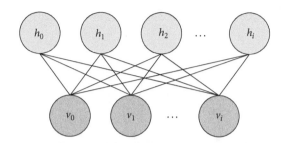

FIGURE 1: Restricted Boltzmann machine.

are the bias of the visible layer and hidden layer, respectively; this model is called binary RBM because the vectors $\mathbf{v}$ and $\mathbf{h}$ only contain binary values (0 or 1).

We can obtain a tractable expression for the conditional probability $P(h \mid v)$ [30]:

$$\begin{aligned} P(h \mid v) &= \frac{\exp\left(\mathbf{b}^T\mathbf{v} + \mathbf{c}^T\mathbf{h} + \mathbf{h}^T\mathbf{W}\mathbf{v}\right)}{\sum_{\widetilde{\mathbf{h}}} \exp\left(\mathbf{b}^T\mathbf{v} + \mathbf{c}^T\widetilde{\mathbf{h}} + \widetilde{\mathbf{h}}^T\mathbf{W}\mathbf{v}\right)} \\ &= \frac{\prod_i \exp\left(\mathbf{c}_i\mathbf{h}_i + \mathbf{h}_i\mathbf{W}_i\mathbf{v}\right)}{\prod_i \sum_{\widetilde{\mathbf{h}}_i} \exp\left(\mathbf{c}_i\widetilde{\mathbf{h}}_i + \widetilde{\mathbf{h}}_i\mathbf{W}_i\mathbf{v}\right)} \qquad (2) \\ &= \prod_i \frac{\exp\left(\mathbf{h}_i\left(\mathbf{c}_i + \mathbf{W}_i\mathbf{v}\right)\right)}{\sum_{\widetilde{\mathbf{h}}_i} \exp\left(\widetilde{\mathbf{h}}_i\left(\mathbf{c}_i + \mathbf{W}_i\mathbf{v}\right)\right)} = \prod_i P\left(\mathbf{h}_i \mid v\right). \end{aligned}$$

For binary RBM, where $h_i \in \{0, 1\}$, the equation for a hidden unit's output given its input is

$$P\left(h_i = 1 \mid v\right) = \frac{e^{c_i + W_i v}}{1 + e^{c_i + W_i v}} = \text{sigm}\left(c_i + W_i v\right). \quad (3)$$

Because v and h play a symmetric role in the energy function, the following equation can be derived:

$$P(v \mid h) = \prod_i P\left(v_i \mid h\right), \quad (4)$$

and for the visible unit $v_j \in \{0, 1\}$, we have

$$P\left(v_j = 1 \mid h\right) = \text{sigm}\left(b_j + W_{\cdot j}^T h\right), \quad (5)$$

where $W_{\cdot j}$ is the jth column of W.

Although binary RBMs can achieve good performance when dealing with discrete inputs, they have limitations to handle continuous-valued inputs due to their structure. Thus, in order to achieve better performance on continuous-valued inputs, Gaussian RBMs are utilized for the visible layer [4, 31]. The energy function of a Gaussian RBM is

$$\text{Energy}(\mathbf{v}, \mathbf{h}) = \sum_i \frac{\left(v_i - a_i\right)^2}{2\sigma_i^2} - \sum_{ij} w_{ij} h_j \frac{v_i}{\sigma_i} - \sum_j c_j h_j, \quad (6)$$

where a_i and σ_i are the mean and the standard deviation of visible unit i. Note here that only the visible layer v is continuous-valued and hidden layer h is still binary. In practical situation, the input data is normalized, which makes $a_i = 0$ and $\sigma_i = 1$. Therefore, (6) becomes

$$\text{Energy}(\mathbf{v}, \mathbf{h}) = \frac{1}{2}\mathbf{v}^T\mathbf{v} - \mathbf{c}^T\mathbf{h} - \mathbf{h}^T\mathbf{W}\mathbf{v}. \quad (7)$$

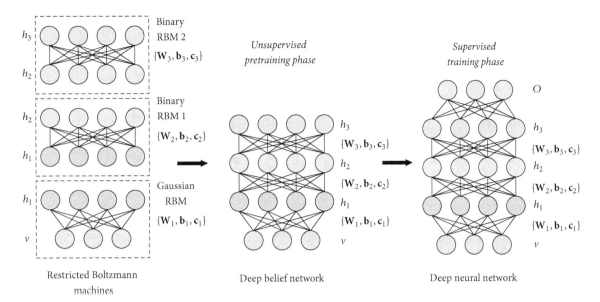

FIGURE 2: Deep belief network structure.

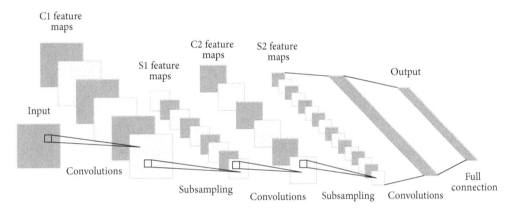

FIGURE 3: The architecture of convolution neural network.

2.1.2. Deep Neural Network. Hinton et al. [1] showed that RBMs can be stacked and trained in a greedy manner to form so-called deep belief networks (DBNs) [32]. DBNs are graphical models which learn to extract deep hierarchical representation of the training data. A DBN model with *l* layers models the joint distribution between observed vector *v* and ℓ hidden layers h^k as follows [30]:

$$P\left(v, h^1, \ldots, h^\ell\right) = \left(\prod_{k=0}^{\ell-2} P\left(h^k \mid h^{k+1}\right)\right) P\left(h^{\ell-1}, h^\ell\right), \quad (8)$$

where $v = h^0$, $P(h^{k-1} \mid h^k)$ is a conditional distribution for the visible units conditioned on the hidden units of the RBM at level *k* and $P(h^{\ell-1}, h^\ell)$ is the visible-hidden joint distribution in the top-level RBM. This is illustrated in Figure 2.

As Figure 2 shows, the hidden layer of low-level RBM is the visible layer of high-level RBM, which means that the output of low-level RBM is the input of high-level RBM. By using this structure, the high-level RBM is able to learn high-level features from low-level features generated from the low-level RBM. Thus, DBN allows latent variable space in its

hidden layers. In order to train a DBN effectively, we need to train its RBM from low level to high level successively.

After the unsupervised pretraining step for DBN, the next step is to use parameters from DBN to initialize the DNN and do supervised training for DNN using back-propagation. The parameters of the *N*-layer DNN are initialized as follows: parameters $\{W_n, c_n\}$ $(l = 1, \ldots, N)$ except the top layer parameters are set the same as the DBN, and the top layer weights $\{W_N, c_N\}$ are initialized stochastically. After that, the whole network can be fine-tuned by back-propagation in a supervised way using labeled data.

2.2. Convolutional Neural Network. Convolutional neural network is one of the most powerful classes of deep neural networks in image processing tasks. It is highly effective and commonly used in computer vision applications [33]. The convolution neural network contains three types of layers: convolution layers, subsampling layers, and full connection layers. The whole architecture of convolutional neural network is shown in Figure 3. A brief introduction to each type of layer is provided in the following paragraphs.

3	15	64	22	55	62
92	213	7	32	145	34
17	178	86	33	12	21
231	87	48	5	23	234
59	56	55	45	3	218
82	97	94	33	238	44

1	1	1
1	0	2
1	0	1

FIGURE 4: Digital image representation and convolution matrix.

2.2.1. Convolution Layer.
As Figure 4 shows, in convolution layer, the left matrix is the input, which is a digital image, and the right matrix is a convolution matrix. The convolution layer takes the convolution of the input image with the convolution matrix and generates the output image. Usually the convolution matrix is called filter and the output image is called filter response or filter map. An example of convolution calculation is demonstrated in Figure 5. Each time, a block of pixels is convoluted with a filter and generates a pixel in a new image.

2.2.2. Subsampling Layer.
The subsampling layer is an important layer to convolutional neural network. This layer is mainly to reduce the input image size in order to give the neural network more invariance and robustness. The most used method for subsampling layer in image processing tasks is max pooling. So the subsampling layer is frequently called max pooling layer. The max pooling method is shown in Figure 6. The image is divided into blocks and the maximum value of each block is the corresponding pixel value of the output image. The reason to use subsampling layer is as follows. First, the subsampling layer has fewer parameters and it is faster to train. Second, a subsampling layer makes convolution layer tolerate translation and rotation among the input pattern.

2.2.3. Full Connection Layer.
Full connection layers are similar to the traditional feed-forward neural layer. They make the neural network fed forward into vectors with a predefined length. We could fit the vector into certain categories or take it as a representation vector for further processing.

3. Training Strategy

Compared to conventional machine learning methods, the advantage of the deep learning is that it can build deep architectures to learn more multiscale abstract features. Unfortunately, the large amount of parameters of the deep architectures may lead to overfitting problem.

3.1. Data Augmentation.
The key idea of data augmentation is to generate additional data without introducing extra labeling costs. In general, the data augmentation is achieved by deforming the existing ones. Mirroring, scaling, and rotation are the most common methods for data augmentation [34–36]. Wu et al. extended the deforming idea to color space, the provided color casting, vignetting, and lens distortion

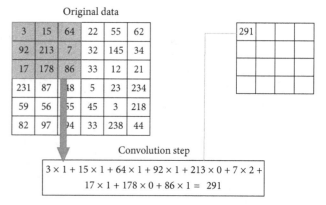

Original data

Convolution step

$$3 \times 1 + 15 \times 1 + 64 \times 1 + 92 \times 1 + 213 \times 0 + 7 \times 2 +$$
$$17 \times 1 + 178 \times 0 + 86 \times 1 = 291$$

FIGURE 5: An example of convolution calculation.

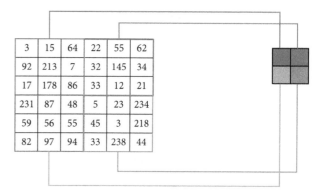

FIGURE 6: The example of the subsampling layer.

techniques in their work, which enlarged the training set significantly [37].

3.2. Pretraining and Fine-Tuning.
Training a deep learning architecture is a time-consuming and nontrivial task. On one hand, it is difficult to obtain enough well-labeled data to train the deep learning architecture in real application, although the data augmentation can help us obtain more training data.

For visual tasks, when it is hard to get sufficient data, a recommendable way is to fine-tune the pretrained CNN by natural images (e.g., ImageNet) and then use specific data set to fine-tune the CNN [36, 38, 39]. Tajbakhsh et al. showed that, for medical applications, the use of a pretrained CNN with adequate fine-tuning outperformed or, in the worst case, performed as well as a CNN trained from scratch [38].

On the other hand, the deep learning architecture contains hundreds of thousands of parameters to be initialized even with sufficient data. Erhan et al. provided the evidence to explain that the pretraining step helps train deep architectures such as deep belief networks and stacked autoencoders [40]. Their experiments supported a regularization explanation for the effect of pretraining, which helps the deep-learned model obtain better generalization from the training data set.

4. Applications

Deep learning has been widely applied in various fields, such as computer vision [25], signal processing [24], and speech recognition [41]. In this section, we will briefly review several recently developed applications of deep learning (all the results are referred from the original papers).

4.1. CNN-Based Applications in Visual Computing. As we know, convolutional neural networks are very powerful tools for image recognition and classification. These different types of CNNs are often tested on well-known ImageNet Large-Scale Visual Recognition Challenge (ILSVRC) data set and achieved state-of-the-art performance in recent years [42–44]. After winning the ImageNet competition in 2012 [42], the CNN-based methods have brought about a revolution in computer vision. CNNs have been applied with great success to the object detection [35, 45, 46], object segmentation [47, 48], and recognition of objects and regions in images [49–54]. Compared with hand-crafted features, for example, Local Binary Patterns (LBP) [55] and Scale Invariant Feature Transform (SIFT) [56], which need additional classifiers to solve vision problems [57–59], the CNNs can learn the features and the classifiers jointly and provide superior performance. In next subsection, we review how the deep-learned CNN is applied to recent face recognition and road crack detection problem in order to provide an overview for applying the CNN to specific problems.

4.1.1. CNN for Face Recognition. Face recognition has been one of the most important computer vision tasks since the 1970s [60]. Face recognition systems typically consist of four steps. First, given an input image with one or more faces, a face detector locates and isolates faces. Then, each face is preprocessed and aligned using either 2D or 3D modeling methods. Next, a feature extractor extracts features from an aligned face to obtain a low-dimensional representation (or embedding). Finally, a classifier makes predictions based on the low-dimensional representation. The key to get good performances for face recognition systems is obtaining an effective low-dimensional representation. Face recognition systems using hand-crafted features include [61–64]. Lawrence et al. [65] first proposed using CNNs for face recognition. Currently, the state-of-the-art performance of face recognition systems, that is, Facebook's DeepFace [66] and Google's FaceNet [67], are based on CNNs. Other notable CNN-based face recognition systems are lightened convolutional neural networks [68] and Visual Geometry Group (VGG) Face Descriptor [69].

Figure 7 shows the logic flow of CNN-based face recognition systems. Instead of using hand-crafted features, CNNs are directly applied to RGB pixel values and used as a feature extractor to provide a low-dimensional representation characterizing a person's face. In order to normalize the input image to make the face robust to different view angles, DeepFace [66] models a face in 3D and aligns it to appear as a frontal face. Then, the normalized input is fed to a single convolution-pooling-convolution filter. Next, 3 locally connected layers and 2 fully connected layers are used to make

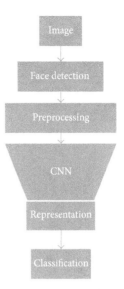

FIGURE 7: Logic flow of CNN based face recognition [70].

TABLE 1: Experiment results on LFW benchmark [70].

Technique	Accuracy
Human-level (cropped) [74]	0.9753
FaceNet [67]	0.9964 ± 0.009
DeepFace-ensemble [66]	0.9735 ± 0.0025
OpenFace [70]	0.9292 ± 0.0134

final predictions. The architecture of DeepFace is shown in Figure 8. Though DeepFace achieves the best performance on face recognition up to date, its representation is difficult to interpret and use because the faces of the same person are not clustered necessarily during the training process. In contrast, FaceNet defines a triplet loss function directly on the representation, which makes the training procedure learn to cluster face representation of the same person [70]. It should also be noted that OpenFace uses a simple 2D affine transformation to align face input.

Nowadays, face recognition in mobile computing is a very attractive topic [71, 72]. While DeepFace and FaceNet remain private and are of large size, OpenFace [70] offers a lightweighted, real-time, and open-source face recognition system with competitive accuracy, which is suitable for mobile computing. OpenFace implements FaceNet's architecture but it is one order of magnitude smaller than DeepFace and two orders of magnitude smaller than FaceNet. Their performances are compared on Labeled Faces in the Wild data set (LFW) [73], which is a standard benchmark in face recognition. The experiment results are demonstrated in Table 1. Though the accuracy of OpenFace is slightly lower than the state of the art, its smaller size and fast execution time show great potential in mobile face recognition scenarios.

4.1.2. CNN for Road Crack Detection. Automatic detection of pavement cracks is an important task in transportation maintenance for driving safety assurance. Inspired by recent success in applying deep learning to computer vision and

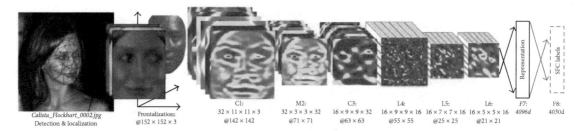

FIGURE 8: Outline of DeepFace architecture [66].

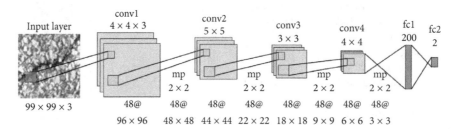

FIGURE 9: Illustration of the architecture of the proposed ConvNet [23].

medical problems, a deep learning based method for crack detection is proposed [23].

Data Preparation. A data set with more than 500 pavement pictures of size 3264×2448 is collected at the Temple University campus by using a smartphone as the data sensor. Each image is annotated by multiple annotators. Patches of size 99×99 are used for training and testing the proposed method. 640,000 patches, 160,000 patches, and 200,000 patches are selected as training set, validation set, and testing set, respectively.

Design and Train the CNN. A deep learning architecture is designed, which is illustrated in Figure 9 and *conv*, *mp*, and *fc* represent convolutional, max pooling, and fully connected layers, respectively. The CNNs are trained using the stochastic gradient descent (SGD) method on GPU with a batch size of 48 examples, momentum of 0.9, and weight decay of 0.0005. Less than 20 epochs are needed to reach a minimum on the validation set. The dropout method is used between two fully connected layers with a probability of 0.5 and the rectified linear units (ReLU) as the activation function.

Evaluate the Performance of the CNN. The proposed method is compared against the support vector machine (SVM) and the Boosting methods. The features for training the SVM and the Boosting method are based on color and texture of each patch which are associated with a binary label indicating the presence or absence of cracked pavement. The feature vector is 93-dimensional and is composed of color elements, histograms of textons, and LBP descriptor within the patch.

The Receiver Operating Characteristic (ROC) curves of the proposed method, the SVM, and the Boosting method are shown in Figure 10. Both the ROC curve and Area under the Curve (AUC) of the proposed method indicate that the proposed deep learning based method can outperform

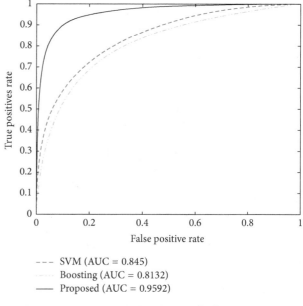

--- SVM (AUC = 0.845)
...... Boosting (AUC = 0.8132)
— Proposed (AUC = 0.9592)

FIGURE 10: ROC curves [23].

the shallow structure learned from hand-crafted features. In addition, more comprehensive experiments are conducted on 300×300 scenes as shown in Figure 11.

For each scene, each row shows the original image with crack, ground truth, and probability maps generated by the SVM and the Boosting methods and that by the ConvNet. The pixels in green and in blue denote the crack and the noncrack, respectively, and higher brightness means higher confidence. The SVM cannot distinguish the crack from the background, and some of the cracks have been misclassified. Compared to the SVM, the Boosting method can detect the cracks with a higher accuracy. However, some of the background

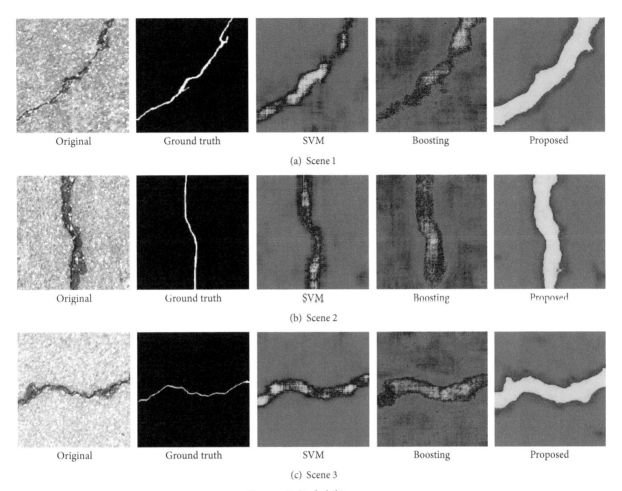

(a) Scene 1

(b) Scene 2

(c) Scene 3

FIGURE 11: Probability maps.

patches are classified as cracks, resulting in isolated green parts in Figure 11. In contrast to these two methods, the proposed method provides superior performance in correctly classifying crack patches from background ones.

4.2. DBN-Based Applications in Signal Processing

4.2.1. DNN for Fault Diagnosis. Plant faults may cause abnormal operations, emergency shutdowns, equipment damage, or even casualties. With the increasing complexity of modern plants, it is difficult even for experienced operators to diagnose faults fast and accurately. Thus, designing an intelligent fault detection and diagnose system to aid human operators is a critical task in process engineering. Data-driven methods for fault diagnosis are becoming very popular in recent years, since they utilize powerful machine learning algorithms. Conventional supervised learning algorithms used for fault diagnosis are Artificial Neural Networks [76–81] and support vector machines [82–84]. As one of emerging machine learning techniques, deep learning techniques are investigated for fault diagnosis in a few current studies [22, 85–88]. This subsection reviews a study which uses Hierarchical Deep Neural Network (HDNN) [22] to diagnose faults in a well-known data set called Tennessee Eastman Process (TEP).

TEP is a simulation model that simulates a real industry process. The model was first created by Eastman Chemical Company [75]. It consists of five units: a condenser, a compressor, a reactor, a separator, and a stripper. Two liquid products G and H are produced from the process with the gaseous inputs A, C, D, and E and the inert component B. The flowsheet of TEP is shown in Figure 12.

Data Preparation. The TEP is monitored by a network of M sensors that collect measurement at the same sampling time. At the ith sample, the state of mth sensor is represented by a scalar x_i^m. By combining all M sensors, the state of the whole process in ith sampling interval is represented as a row vector $x_i = [x_i^1, x_i^2, \ldots, x_i^M]$. The fault occurring at the ith sampling interval is indicated with class label $y_i \in \{1, 2, \ldots, C\}$, where value 1 to C represents one of C fault types. There are total N historical observations collected from all M sensors to form a data set $D = \{(x_i, y_i), i = 1, 2, \ldots, N, y_i \in \{1, 2, \ldots, C\}\}$. The objective of fault diagnosis is to train a classification $h : x_i \rightarrow y_i$ given data set $D = \{(x_i, y_i), i = 1, 2, \ldots, N\}$.

For each simulation run, the simulation starts without faults and the faults are introduced at sample 1. Each run collects a total of 1000 pieces of sample data. Each single fault type has 5 independent simulation runs. The Tennessee Eastman Process has 20 different predefined faults but faults

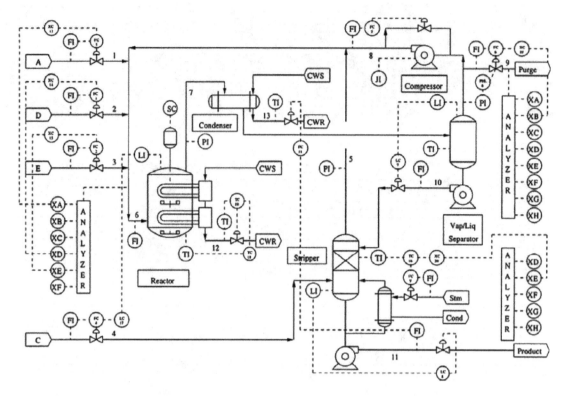

FIGURE 12: Tennessee Eastman Process [75].

3, 9, and 15 are excluded for fault diagnosis due to no effect or subtle effect on all the sensors [82, 84]. Thus, the training data set has a total of $N = 5 \times 17 \times 1000 = 85000$ data samples; that is, $D_{\text{train}} = \{(x_i, y_i), i = 1, 2, \ldots, N, y_i \in \{0, 1, \ldots, C\}\}$, $N = 85000$, $C = 17$. Then, test data is generated using the same method. Because only fault diagnosis methods are investigated in this work, normal operation data is not considered. Data normalization and data augmentation techniques are used to achieve better performance.

Design and Train the HDNN. The general diagnosis scheme of HDNN [22] is as follows. The symptom data generated by simulation is transmitted to a supervisory DNN. The supervisory DNN then classifies symptom data into different groups and triggers the DNN which is specially trained for that group to do further fault diagnosis. Figure 13 illustrates the fault diagnosis scheme of the HDNN, where each agent represents a DNN.

Evaluate the Performance of the DNN. The experiment result of the HDNN is compared to single neural network and Duty-Oriented Hierarchical Artificial Neural Network (DOHANN) [76] and is shown in Figure 14. 7 out of 17 faults have been diagnosed with 90% accuracy. The highest Correct Classification Rate (CCR) is 99.6% from fault 4, while the lowest CCR is 50.4% from fault 13. The average CCR of our method is 80.5%, while the average of CCRs of SNN and DOHANN is 49.7% and 70.7%, respectively. It demonstrates that the DNN-based algorithm outperforms other conventional NN-based algorithms.

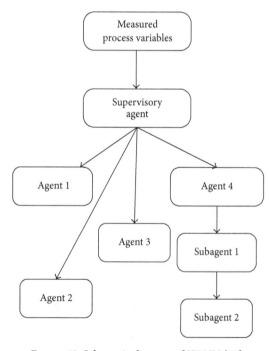

FIGURE 13: Schematic diagram of HDNN [22].

4.2.2. DNN for Human Activity Detection. Human activity detection has drawn much attention from researchers due to high demands for security, law enforcement, and health care [90–93]. In contrast to using cameras to detect human

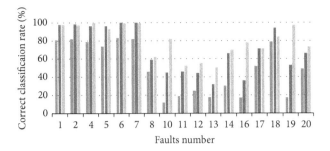

FIGURE 14: Correct classification rate of SNN, DOHANN [76], and HDNN [22].

activity, sensors such as worn accelerometers or in-home radar which use signals to detect human activities are robust to environmental conditions such as weather conditions and light variations [94–99]. Nowadays, there are a few emerging research works that focus on using deep learning technologies to detect human activities based on signals [89, 92, 100].

Fall detection is one of the very important human activity detection scenarios for researchers, since falls are a main cause of both fatal and nonfatal injuries for the elderly. Khan and Taati [100] proposed a deep learning method for falls detection based on signals collected from wearable devices. They propose an ensemble of autoencoders to extract features from each channel of sensing data. Unlike wearable devices which are intrusive and easily broken and must be carried, in-home radars which are safe, nonintrusive, and robust to lighting conditions show their advantages for fall detection. Jokanovic et al. [89] proposed a method that uses deep learning to detect fall motion through in-home radar. The procedure is demonstrated in Figure 15. They first denoise and normalize the spectrogram as input. Then, stacked autoencoders are performed as a feature extractor. On top of the stacked autoencoders, a softmax regression classifier is used to make predictions. The whole model is compared with a SVM model. Experiment results show that the overall correct classification rate for deep learning approach is 87%, whereas the overall correct classification rate for SVM is 78%.

5. Challenges

Though deep learning techniques achieve promising performance on multiple fields, there are still several big challenges as research articles indicate. These challenges are described as follows.

5.1. Training with Limited Data. Training deep neural network usually needs large amounts of data as larger training data set can prevent deep learning model from overfitting. Limited training data may severely affect the learning ability of a deep neural network. Unfortunately, there are many applications that lack sufficient labeled data to train a DNN.

Thus, how to train DNN with limited data effectively and efficiently becomes a hot topic.

Recently, two possible solutions draw attention from researchers. One of the solutions is to generalize new training data from original training data using multiple data augmentation methods. Traditional ones include rotation, scaling, and cropping. In addition to these, Wu et al. [37] adopted vignetting, color casting, and lens distortion techniques. These techniques can further produce more different training examples. Another solution is to obtain more training data using weak learning algorithms. Song et al. [101] proposed a weakly supervised method that can label image-level object-presence. This method helps to reduce laborious bounding box annotation costs while generating training data.

5.2. Time Complexity. Training deep neural network is very time-consuming in early years. It needs a large amount of computational resources and is not suitable for real-time applications. By default, GPUs are used to accelerate training of large DNNs with the help of parallel computing technique. Thus, it is important to make the most of GPU computing ability when training DNNs. He and Sun [102] investigated training CNN under time cost constrains and proposed fast training methods for real-world applications while having similar performance as existing CNN models. Li et al. [103] remove all the redundant computations during training CNNs for pixel wise classification, which leads to a speedup of 1500 times.

5.3. Theoretical Understanding. Though deep learning algorithms achieve promising results on many tasks, the underlying theory is still not very clear. There are many questions that need to be answered. For instance, which architecture is better than other architectures in certain task? How many layers and how many nodes in each layer should be chosen in a DNN? Besides, there are a few hyperparameters such as learning rate, dropout rate, and the strength of regularizer which need to be tuned with specific knowledge.

Several approaches are developed to help researchers to get better understanding in DNN. Zeiler and Fergus [43] proposed a visualization method that illustrates features in intermediate layers. It displays intermediate features in interpretable patterns, which may help design better architectures for future DNNs. In addition to visualizing features, Girshick et al. [49] tried to discover the learning pattern of CNN by testing the performance layer by layer during the training process. It demonstrates that convolutional layers can learn more generalized features.

Although there is progress in understanding the theory of deep learning, there is still large room to improve in deep learning theory aspect.

6. Conclusion

This paper gives an overview of deep learning algorithms and their applications. Several classic deep learning algorithms such as restricted Boltzmann machines, deep belief networks, and convolutional neural networks are introduced. In addition to deep learning algorithms, their applications are

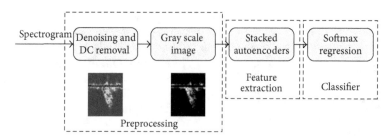

FIGURE 15: Block diagram of the deep learning based fall detector [89].

reviewed and compared with other machine learning methods. Though deep neural networks achieve good performance on many tasks, they still have many properties that need to be investigated and justified. We discussed these challenges and pointed out several new trends in understanding and developing deep neural networks.

Competing Interests

The authors declare that there is no conflict of interests regarding the publication of this paper.

References

[1] G. E. Hinton, S. Osindero, and Y.-W. Teh, "A fast learning algorithm for deep belief nets," *Neural Computation*, vol. 18, no. 7, pp. 1527–1554, 2006.

[2] R. Salakhutdinov and G. E. Hinton, "Using deep belief nets to learn covariance kernels for Gaussian processes," in *Proceedings of the 21st Annual Conference on Neural Information Processing Systems (NIPS '07)*, Vcancouver, Canada, December 2007.

[3] A. Ahmed, K. Yu, W. Xu, Y. Gong, and E. Xing, "Training hierarchical feed-forward visual recognition models using transfer learning from pseudo-tasks," in *Proceedings of the in European Conference on Computer Vision*, pp. 69–82, Springer, Marseille, France, October 2008.

[4] Y. Bengio, P. Lamblin, D. Popovici, and H. Larochelle, "Greedy layer-wise training of deep networks," in *Advances in Neural Information Processing Systems 19 (NIPS '06)*, pp. 153–160, MIT Press, 2007.

[5] H. Larochelle, D. Erhan, A. Courville, J. Bergstra, and Y. Bengio, "An empirical evaluation of deep architectures on problems with many factors of variation," in *Proceedings of the 24th International Conference on Machine Learning (ICML '07)*, pp. 473–480, ACM, Corvalis, Ore, USA, June 2007.

[6] H. Lee, R. Grosse, R. Ranganath, and A. Y. Ng, "Convolutional deep belief networks for scalable unsupervised learning of hierarchical representations," in *Proceedings of the 26th Annual International Conference on Machine Learning (ICML '09)*, pp. 609–616, ACM, Quebec, Canada, June 2009.

[7] M. Ranzato, Y.-L. Boureau, and Y. LeCun, "Sparse feature learning for deep belief networks," in *Advances in Neural Information Processing Systems*, pp. 1185–1192, 2008.

[8] M. Ranzato, C. Poultney, S. Chopra, and Y. LeCun, "Efficient learning of sparse representations with an energy-based model," in *Proceedings of the 20th Annual Conference on Neural Information Processing Systems (NIPS '06)*, pp. 1137–1144, Vancouver, Canada, December 2006.

[9] P. Vincent, H. Larochelle, Y. Bengio, and P.-A. Manzagol, "Extracting and composing robust features with denoising autoencoders," in *Proceedings of the 25th International Conference on Machine Learning*, pp. 1096–1103, ACM, Helsinki, Finland, July 2008.

[10] G. E. Hinton and R. R. Salakhutdinov, "Reducing the dimensionality of data with neural networks," *Science*, vol. 313, no. 5786, pp. 504–507, 2006.

[11] R. Salakhutdinov and G. E. Hinton, "Learning a nonlinear embedding by preserving class neighbourhood structure," in *Proceedings of the 8th International Conference on Artificial Intelligence and Statistics (AISTATS '07)*, pp. 412–419, San Juan, Puerto Rico, March 2007.

[12] G. W. Taylor and G. E. Hinton, "Factored conditional restricted Boltzmann machines for modeling motion style," in *Proceedings of the 26th Annual International Conference on Machine Learning(ICML '09)*, pp. 1025–1032, ACM, Quebec, Canada, June 2009.

[13] G. W. Taylor, G. E. Hinton, and S. T. Roweis, "Modeling human motion using binary latent variables," in *Advances in Neural Information Processing Systems*, pp. 1345–1352, 2006.

[14] S. Osindero and G. E. Hinton, "Modeling image patches with a directed hierarchy of Markov random fields," in *Advances in Neural Information Processing Systems*, pp. 1121–1128, 2008.

[15] M. Ranzato and M. Szummer, "Semi-supervised learning of compact document representations with deep networks," in *Proceedings of the 25th International Conference on Machine Learning*, pp. 792–799, ACM, Helsinki, Finland, July 2008.

[16] R. Salakhutdinov and G. Hinton, "Semantic hashing," *International Journal of Approximate Reasoning*, vol. 50, no. 7, pp. 969–978, 2009.

[17] P. E. Utgoff and D. J. Stracuzzi, "Many-layered learning," *Neural Computation*, vol. 14, no. 10, pp. 2497–2529, 2002.

[18] R. Collobert and J. Weston, "A unified architecture for natural language processing: deep neural networks with multitask learning," in *Proceedings of the 25th International Conference on Machine Learning*, pp. 160–167, ACM, Helsinki, Finland, July 2008.

[19] A. Mnih and G. Hinton, "A scalable hierarchical distributed language model," in *Proceedings of the 22nd Annual Conference on Neural Information Processing Systems (NIPS '08)*, pp. 1081–1088, British Columbia, Canada, December 2008.

[20] J. Weston, F. Ratle, H. Mobahi, and R. Collobert, "Deep learning via semi-supervised embedding," in *Neural Networks: Tricks of the Trade*, pp. 639–655, Springer, Berlin, Germany, 2012.

[21] R. Hadsell, A. Erkan, P. Sermanet, M. Scoffier, U. Muller, and Y. LeCun, "Deep belief net learning in a long-range vision system for autonomous off-road driving," in *Proceedings of the*

IEEE/RSJ International Conference on Intelligent Robots and Systems (IROS '08), pp. 628–633, Nice, France, September 2008.

[22] D. Xie and L. Bai, "A hierarchical deep neural network for fault diagnosis on Tennessee-Eastman process," in *Proceedings of the IEEE 14th International Conference on Machine Learning and Applications (ICMLA '15)*, pp. 745–748, IEEE, Miami, Fla, USA, December 2015.

[23] L. Zhang, F. Yang, Y. Daniel Zhang, and Y. J. Zhu, "Road crack detection using deep convolutional neural network," in *Proceedings of the IEEE International Conference on Image Processing (ICIP '16)*, pp. 3708–3712, Phoenix, Ariz, USA, September 2016.

[24] D. Yu and L. Deng, "Deep learning and its applications to signal and information processing," *IEEE Signal Processing Magazine*, vol. 28, no. 1, pp. 145–154, 2011.

[25] Y. Guo, Y. Liu, A. Oerlemans, S. Lao, S. Wu, and M. S. Lew, "Deep learning for visual understanding: a review," *Neurocomputing*, vol. 187, pp. 27–48, 2016.

[26] P. Smolensky, "Information processing in dynamical systems: foundations of harmony theory," Tech. Rep. DTIC Document, 1986.

[27] D. H. Ackley, G. E. Hinton, and T. J. Sejnowski, "A learning algorithm for boltzmann machines," *Cognitive Science*, vol. 9, no. 1, pp. 147–169, 1985.

[28] Y. LeCun, S. Chopra, R. Hadsell, M. Ranzato, and F. Huang, "A tutorial on energy-based learning," in *Predicting Structured Data*, vol. 1, MIT Press, 2006.

[29] Y. LeCun and F. J. Huang, "Loss functions for discriminative training of energy-based models," in *Proceedings of the 10th International Workshop on Artificial Intelligence and Statistics (AISTATS '05)*, January 2005.

[30] Y. Bengio, "Learning deep architectures for AI," *Foundations and Trends in Machine Learning*, vol. 2, no. 1, pp. 1–27, 2009.

[31] M. Welling, M. Rosen-Zvi, and G. E. Hinton, "Exponential family harmoniums with an application to information retrieval," in *Advances in Neural Information Processing Systems*, pp. 1481–1488, 2004.

[32] G. Hinton, "Deep belief networks," *Scholarpedia*, vol. 4, no. 5, article no. 5947, 2009.

[33] Y. LeCun and Y. Bengio, "Convolutional networks for images, speech, and time series," *The Handbook of Brain Theory and Neural Networks*, vol. 3361, no. 10, p. 1995, 1995.

[34] D. C. Cireşan, A. Giusti, L. M. Gambardella, and J. Schmidhuber, "Deep neural networks segment neuronal membranes in electron microscopy images," in *Proceedings of the 26th Annual Conference on Neural Information Processing Systems (NIPS '12)*, pp. 2843–2851, December 2012.

[35] H. R. Roth, L. Lu, J. Liu et al., "Improving computer-aided detection using convolutional neural networks and random view aggregation," *IEEE Transactions on Medical Imaging*, vol. 35, no. 5, pp. 1170–1181, 2016.

[36] S. Xie and Z. Tu, "Holistically-nested edge detection," in *Proceedings of the 15th IEEE International Conference on Computer Vision (ICCV '15)*, pp. 1395–1403, IEEE, Santiago, Chile, December 2015.

[37] R. Wu, S. Yan, Y. Shan, Q. Dang, and G. Sun, "Deep image: scaling up image recognition," https://arxiv.org/abs/1501.02876.

[38] N. Tajbakhsh, J. Y. Shin, S. R. Gurudu et al., "Convolutional neural networks for medical image analysis: full training or fine tuning?" *IEEE Transactions on Medical Imaging*, vol. 35, no. 5, pp. 1299–1312, 2016.

[39] H.-C. Shin, H. R. Roth, M. Gao et al., "Deep convolutional neural networks for computer-aided detection: CNN architectures, dataset characteristics and transfer learning," *IEEE Transactions on Medical Imaging*, vol. 35, no. 5, pp. 1285–1298, 2016.

[40] D. Erhan, Y. Bengio, A. Courville, P.-A. Manzagol, P. Vincent, and S. Bengio, "Why does unsupervised pre-training help deep learning?" *Journal of Machine Learning Research*, vol. 11, pp. 625–660, 2010.

[41] O. Abdel-Hamid, A.-R. Mohamed, H. Jiang, and G. Penn, "Applying convolutional neural networks concepts to hybrid NN-HMM model for speech recognition," in *Proceedings of the IEEE International Conference on Acoustics, Speech, and Signal Processing (ICASSP '12)*, pp. 4277–4280, IEEE, Kyoto, Japan, March 2012.

[42] A. Krizhevsky, I. Sutskever, and G. E. Hinton, "ImageNet classification with deep convolutional neural networks," in *Proceedings of the 26th Annual Conference on Neural Information Processing Systems (NIPS '12)*, pp. 1097–1105, December 2012.

[43] M. D. Zeiler and R. Fergus, "Visualizing and understanding convolutional networks," in *Computer Vision—ECCV 2014: 13th European Conference, Zurich, Switzerland, September 6–12, 2014, Proceedings, Part I*, vol. 8689 of *Lecture Notes in Computer Science*, pp. 818–833, Springer, 2014.

[44] P. Sermanet, D. Eigen, X. Zhang, M. Mathieu, R. Fergus, and Y. LeCun, "Overfeat: integrated recognition, localization and detection using convolutional networks," https://arxiv.org/abs/1312.6229.

[45] X. Wang, L. Zhang, L. Lin, Z. Liang, and W. Zuo, "Deep joint task learning for generic object extraction," in *Proceedings of the 27th International Conference on Neural Information Processing Systems (NIPS '14)*, pp. 523–531, ACM, Montreal, Canada, December 2014.

[46] J. Liu, N. Lay, Z. Wei et al., "Colitis detection on abdominal CT scans by rich feature hierarchies," in *Medical Imaging 2016: Computer-Aided Diagnosis*, vol. 9785 of *Proceedings of SPIE*, San Diego, Calif, USA, February 2016.

[47] G. Luo, R. An, K. Wang, S. Dong, and H. Zhang, "A deep learning network for right ventricle segmentation in short-axis mri," in *Proceedings of the Computing in Cardiology Conference (CinC '16)*, pp. 224–227, Vancouver, Canada, September 2016.

[48] H. R. Roth, L. Lu, A. Farag, A. Sohn, and R. M. Summers, "Spatial aggregation of holistically-nested networks for automated pancreas segmentation," https://arxiv.org/abs/1606.07830.

[49] R. Girshick, J. Donahue, T. Darrell, and J. Malik, "Rich feature hierarchies for accurate object detection and semantic segmentation," in *Proceedings of the 27th IEEE Conference on Computer Vision and Pattern Recognition (CVPR '14)*, pp. 580–587, IEEE, Columbus, Ohio, USA, June 2014.

[50] R. Girshick, "Fast R-CNN," in *Proceedings of the 15th IEEE International Conference on Computer Vision (ICCV '15)*, pp. 1440–1448, December 2015.

[51] J. Liu, C. Gao, D. Meng, and W. Zuo, "Two-stream contextualized CNN for fine-grained image classification," in *Proceedings of the 30th AAAI Conference on Artificial Intelligence*, pp. 4232–4233, Phoenix, Ariz, USA, February 2016.

[52] K. Wang, L. Lin, W. Zuo, S. Gu, and L. Zhang, "Dictionary pair classifier driven convolutional neural networks for object detection," in *Proceedings of the IEEE Conference on Computer Vision and Pattern Recognition (CVPR '16)*, pp. 2138–2146, Las Vegas, Nev, USA, June 2016.

[53] L. Lin, K. Wang, W. Zuo, M. Wang, J. Luo, and L. Zhang, "A deep structured model with radius-margin bound for 3D human

activity recognition," *International Journal of Computer Vision*, vol. 118, no. 2, pp. 256–273, 2016.

[54] K. He, X. Zhang, S. Ren, and J. Sun, "Delving deep into rectifiers: surpassing human-level performance on imagenet classification," in *Proceedings of the 15th IEEE International Conference on Computer Vision (ICCV '15)*, pp. 1026–1034, IEEE, Santiago, Chile, December 2015.

[55] T. Ojala, M. Pietikäinen, and T. Mäenpää, "Multiresolution gray-scale and rotation invariant texture classification with local binary patterns," *IEEE Transactions on Pattern Analysis and Machine Intelligence*, vol. 24, no. 7, pp. 971–987, 2002.

[56] D. G. Lowe, "Distinctive image features from scale-invariant keypoints," *International Journal of Computer Vision*, vol. 60, no. 2, pp. 91–110, 2004.

[57] W. Lu, M. Li, and L. Zhang, "Palm vein recognition using directional features derived from local binary patterns," *International Journal of Signal Processing, Image Processing and Pattern Recognition*, vol. 9, no. 5, pp. 87–98, 2016.

[58] D. Xie, Z. Huang, S. Wang, and H. Liu, "Moving objects segmentation from compressed surveillance video based on motion estimation," in *Proceedings of the 21st International Conference on Pattern Recognition (ICPR '12)*, pp. 3132–3135, IEEE, Tsukuba, Japan, November 2012.

[59] S. Wang, H. Liu, D. Xie, and B. Zeng, "A novel scheme to code object flags for video synopsis," in *Proceedings of the IEEE Visual Communications and Image Processing (VCIP '12)*, pp. 1–5, November 2012.

[60] T. Kanade, *Picture processing system by computer complex and recognition of human faces [Ph.D. thesis]*, Kyoto University, 3952, 1973.

[61] D. Chen, X. Cao, F. Wen, and J. Sun, "Blessing of dimensionality: high-dimensional feature and its efficient compression for face verification," in *Proceedings of the 26th IEEE Conference on Computer Vision and Pattern Recognition (CVPR '13)*, pp. 3025–3032, June 2013.

[62] X. Cao, D. Wipf, F. Wen, G. Duan, and J. Sun, "A practical transfer learning algorithm for face verification," in *Proceedings of the 14th IEEE International Conference on Computer Vision (ICCV '13)*, pp. 3208–3215, December 2013.

[63] T. Berg and P. N. Belhumeur, "Tom-vs-Pete classifiers and identity-preserving alignment for face verification," in *Proceedings of the 23rd British Machine Vision Conference (BMVC '12)*, BMVA Press, September 2012.

[64] D. Chen, X. Cao, L. Wang, F. Wen, and J. Sun, "Bayesian face revisited: a joint formulation," in *Computer Vision—ECCV 2012: 12th European Conference on Computer Vision, Florence, Italy, October 7-13, 2012, Proceedings, Part III*, vol. 7574 of *Lecture Notes in Computer Science*, pp. 566–579, Springer, Berlin, Germany, 2012.

[65] S. Lawrence, C. L. Giles, A. C. Tsoi, and A. D. Back, "Face recognition: a convolutional neural-network approach," *IEEE Transactions on Neural Networks*, vol. 8, no. 1, pp. 98–113, 1997.

[66] Y. Taigman, M. Yang, M. Ranzato, and L. Wolf, "DeepFace: closing the gap to human-level performance in face verification," in *Proceedings of the 27th IEEE Conference on Computer Vision and Pattern Recognition (CVPR '14)*, pp. 1701–1708, June 2014.

[67] F. Schroff, D. Kalenichenko, and J. Philbin, "FaceNet: a unified embedding for face recognition and clustering," in *Proceedings of the IEEE Conference on Computer Vision and Pattern Recognition (CVPR '15)*, pp. 815–823, IEEE, Boston, Mass, USA, June 2015.

[68] X. Wu, R. He, Z. Sun, and T. Tan, "A light CNN for deep face representation with noisy labels," https://arxiv.org/abs/1511.02683.

[69] O. M. Parkhi, A. Vedaldi, and A. Zisserman, "Deep face recognition," in *Proceedings of the British Machine Vision Conference*, vol. 1, p. 6, 2015.

[70] B. Amos, B. Ludwiczuk, and M. Satyanarayanan, "Openface: a general-purpose face recognition library with mobile applications," Tech. Rep. CMU-CS-16-118, CMU School of Computer Science, 2016.

[71] T. Soyata, R. Muraleedharan, C. Funai, M. Kwon, and W. Heinzelman, "Cloud-vision: real-time face recognition using a mobile-cloudlet-cloud acceleration architecture," in *Proceedings of the 17th IEEE Symposium on Computers and Communication (ISCC '12)*, pp. 59–66, July 2012.

[72] H.-J. Hsu and K.-T. Chen, "Face recognition on drones: issues and limitations," in *Proceedings of the 1st Workshop on Micro Aerial Vehicle Networks, Systems, and Applications for Civilian Use (DroNet '15)*, pp. 39–44, ACM, Florence, Italy, 2015.

[73] G. B. Huang, M. Ramesh, T. Berg, and E. Learned-Miller, "Labeled faces in the wild: a database for studying face recognition in unconstrained environments," Tech. Rep. 07-49, University of Massachusetts, Amherst, Mass, USA, 2007.

[74] N. Kumar, A. C. Berg, P. N. Belhumeur, and S. K. Nayar, "Attribute and simile classifiers for face verification," in *Proceedings of the 12th International Conference on Computer Vision (ICCV '09)*, pp. 365–372, IEEE, Kyoto, Japan, October 2009.

[75] J. J. Downs and E. F. Vogel, "A plant-wide industrial process control problem," *Computers & Chemical Engineering*, vol. 17, no. 3, pp. 245–255, 1993.

[76] R. Eslamloueyan, "Designing a hierarchical neural network based on fuzzy clustering for fault diagnosis of the Tennessee-Eastman process," *Applied Soft Computing Journal*, vol. 11, no. 1, pp. 1407–1415, 2011.

[77] V. Venkatasubramanian and K. Chan, "A neural network methodology for process fault diagnosis," *AIChE Journal*, vol. 35, no. 12, pp. 1993–2002, 1989.

[78] K. Watanabe, I. Matsuura, M. Abe, M. Kubota, and D. M. Himmelblau, "Incipient fault diagnosis of chemical processes via artificial neural networks," *AIChE Journal*, vol. 35, no. 11, pp. 1803–1812, 1989.

[79] J. Y. Fan, M. Nikolaou, and R. E. White, "An approach to fault diagnosis of chemical processes via neural networks," *AIChE Journal*, vol. 39, no. 1, pp. 82–88, 1993.

[80] K. Watanabe, S. Hirota, L. Hou, and D. M. Himmelblau, "Diagnosis of multiple simultaneous fault via hierarchical artificial neural networks," *AIChE Journal*, vol. 40, no. 5, pp. 839–848, 1994.

[81] R. Eslamloueyan, M. Shahrokhi, and R. Bozorgmehri, "Multiple simultaneous fault diagnosis via hierarchical and single artificial neural networks," *Scientia Iranica*, vol. 10, no. 3, pp. 300–310, 2003.

[82] L. H. Chiang, M. E. Kotanchek, and A. K. Kordon, "Fault diagnosis based on Fisher discriminant analysis and support vector machines," *Computers and Chemical Engineering*, vol. 28, no. 8, pp. 1389–1401, 2004.

[83] M. Ge, R. Du, G. Zhang, and Y. Xu, "Fault diagnosis using support vector machine with an application in sheet metal stamping operations," *Mechanical Systems and Signal Processing*, vol. 18, no. 1, pp. 143–159, 2004.

[84] M. Grbovic, W. Li, P. Xu, A. K. Usadi, L. Song, and S. Vucetic, "Decentralized fault detection and diagnosis via sparse PCA

based decomposition and maximum entropy decision fusion," *Journal of Process Control*, vol. 22, no. 4, pp. 738–750, 2012.

[85] W. Sun, S. Shao, R. Zhao, R. Yan, X. Zhang, and X. Chen, "A sparse auto-encoder-based deep neural network approach for induction motor faults classification," *Measurement*, vol. 89, pp. 171–178, 2016.

[86] M. Gan, C. Wang, and C. Zhu, "Construction of hierarchical diagnosis network based on deep learning and its application in the fault pattern recognition of rolling element bearings," *Mechanical Systems and Signal Processing*, vol. 72-73, pp. 92–104, 2016.

[87] P. Jiang, Z. Hu, J. Liu, S. Yu, and F. Wu, "Fault diagnosis based on chemical sensor data with an active deep neural network," *Sensors*, vol. 16, no. 10, p. 1695, 2016.

[88] H. J. Steinhauer, A. Karlsson, G. Mathiason, and T. Helldin, "Root-cause localization using restricted Boltzmann machines," in *Proceedings of the 19th International Conference on Information Fusion (FUSION '16)*, pp. 248–255, ISIF, 2016.

[89] B. Jokanovic, M. Amin, and F. Ahmad, "Radar fall motion detection using deep learning," in *Proceedings of the IEEE Radar Conference (RadarConf '16)*, IEEE, Philadelphia, Pa, USA, May 2016.

[90] L. M. Frazier, "MDR for law enforcement," *IEEE Potentials*, vol. 16, no. 5, pp. 23–26, 1997.

[91] E. F. Greneker, "Radar flashlight for through the wall detection of humans," in *SPIE Proceedings of the Targets and Backgrounds: Characterization and Representation IV*, pp. 280–285, SPIE, Orlando, Fla, USA, April 1998.

[92] J. Park, R. Javier, T. Moon, and Y. Kim, "Micro-doppler based classification of human aquatic activities via transfer learning of convolutional neural networks," *Sensors*, vol. 16, no. 12, p. 1990, 2016.

[93] J. Sung, C. Ponce, B. Selman, and A. Saxena, "Unstructured human activity detection from RGBD images," in *Proceedings of the IEEE International Conference on Robotics and Automation (ICRA '12)*, pp. 842–849, St Paul, Minn, USA, May 2012.

[94] J. R. Smith, K. P. Fishkin, B. Jiang et al., "RFID-based techniques for human-activity detection," *Communications of the ACM*, vol. 48, no. 9, pp. 39–44, 2005.

[95] P. Van Dorp and F. C. A. Groen, "Human walking estimation with radar," *IEE Proceedings: Radar, Sonar and Navigation*, vol. 150, no. 5, pp. 356–366, 2003.

[96] R. J. Javier and Y. Kim, "Application of linear predictive coding for human activity classification based on micro-doppler signatures," *IEEE Geoscience and Remote Sensing Letters*, vol. 11, no. 10, pp. 1831–1834, 2014.

[97] Y. Kim and H. Ling, "Human activity classification based on micro-doppler signatures using a support vector machine," *IEEE Transactions on Geoscience and Remote Sensing*, vol. 47, no. 5, pp. 1328–1337, 2009.

[98] R. Igual, C. Medrano, and I. Plaza, "Challenges, issues and trends in fall detection systems," *BioMedical Engineering Online*, vol. 12, no. 1, article 66, 2013.

[99] P. Rashidi and A. Mihailidis, "A survey on ambient-assisted living tools for older adults," *IEEE Journal of Biomedical and Health Informatics*, vol. 17, no. 3, pp. 579–590, 2013.

[100] S. S. Khan and B. Taati, "Detecting unseen falls from wearable devices using channel-wise ensemble of autoencoders," https://arxiv.org/abs/1610.03761.

[101] H. O. Song, Y. J. Lee, S. Jegelka, and T. Darrell, "Weakly-supervised discovery of visual pattern configurations," in *Proceedings of the 28th Annual Conference on Neural Information Processing Systems (NIPS '14)*, pp. 1637–1645, Québec, Canada, December 2014.

[102] K. He and J. Sun, "Convolutional neural networks at constrained time cost," in *Proceedings of the IEEE Conference on Computer Vision and Pattern Recognition (CVPR '15)*, pp. 5353–5360, Boston, Mass, USA, June 2015.

[103] H. Li, R. Zhao, and X. Wang, "Highly efficient forward and backward propagation of convolutional neural networks for pixelwise classification," https://arxiv.org/abs/1412.4526.

Differential Evolution with Novel Mutation and Adaptive Crossover Strategies for Solving Large Scale Global Optimization Problems

Ali Wagdy Mohamed[1,2] and Abdulaziz S. Almazyad[1,3]

[1]*College of Computer and Information Systems, Al-Yamamah University, P.O. Box 45180, Riyadh 11512, Saudi Arabia*
[2]*Operations Research Department, Institute of Statistical Studies and Research, Cairo University, Giza 12613, Egypt*
[3]*College of Computer and Information Sciences, King Saud University, Riyadh, Saudi Arabia*

Correspondence should be addressed to Ali Wagdy Mohamed; aliwagdy@gmail.com

Academic Editor: Miin-Shen Yang

This paper presents Differential Evolution algorithm for solving high-dimensional optimization problems over continuous space. The proposed algorithm, namely, ANDE, introduces a new triangular mutation rule based on the convex combination vector of the triplet defined by the three randomly chosen vectors and the difference vectors between the best, better, and the worst individuals among the three randomly selected vectors. The mutation rule is combined with the basic mutation strategy DE/rand/1/bin, where the new triangular mutation rule is applied with the probability of 2/3 since it has both exploration ability and exploitation tendency. Furthermore, we propose a novel self-adaptive scheme for gradual change of the values of the crossover rate that can excellently benefit from the past experience of the individuals in the search space during evolution process which in turn can considerably balance the common trade-off between the population diversity and convergence speed. The proposed algorithm has been evaluated on the 20 standard high-dimensional benchmark numerical optimization problems for the IEEE CEC-2010 Special Session and Competition on Large Scale Global Optimization. The comparison results between ANDE and its versions and the other seven state-of-the-art evolutionary algorithms that were all tested on this test suite indicate that the proposed algorithm and its two versions are highly competitive algorithms for solving large scale global optimization problems.

1. Introduction

In general, global numerical optimization problem can be expressed as follows (without loss of generality minimization problem is considered here):

$$\min \quad f(x),$$
$$\vec{x} = [x_1, x_2, \ldots, x_D] \in \mathbb{R}^D; \quad (1)$$
$$x_j \in \left[x_j^L, x_j^U\right], \quad \forall j = 1, 2, \ldots, D,$$

where f is the objective function, $\vec{x}$ is the decision vector $\in \mathbb{R}^D$ space consisting of D variables, D is the problem dimension, that is, the number of variables to be optimized, and

x_j^L and x_j^U are the lower and upper bounds for each decision variable, respectively.

The optimization of the large scale problems of this kind (i.e., $D = 1000$) is considered a challenging task since the solution space of a problem often increases exponentially with the problem dimension and the characteristics of a problem may change with the scale [1]. Generally speaking, there are different types of real-world large scale global optimization (LSGO) problems in engineering, manufacturing, and economy applications (biocomputing, data or web mining, scheduling, vehicle routing, etc.). In order to draw more attention to this challenge of optimization, the first competition on LSGO was held in CEC 2008 [2]. Consequently, In the recent few years, LSGO has gained considerable attention and has attracted much interest from Operations Research and

Computer Science professionals, researchers, and practitioners as well as mathematicians and engineers. Therefore, the challenges mentioned above have motivated the researchers to design and improve many kinds of efficient, effective, and robust various kinds of metaheuristics algorithms that can solve (LSGO) problems with high quality solution and high convergence performance with low computational cost. Evolutionary algorithms (EAs) have been proposed to meet the global optimization challenges. The structure of EAs has been inspired from the mechanisms of natural evolution. Due to their adaptability and robustness, EAs are especially capable of solving difficult optimization problems, such as highly nonlinear, nonconvex, nondifferentiable, and multimodal optimization problems. Generally, the process of EAs is based on the exploration and the exploitation of the search space through selection and reproduction operators [3]. Similar to other evolutionary algorithms (EAs), Differential Evolution (DE) is a stochastic population-based search method, proposed by Storn and Price [4]. The advantages are its simplicity of implementation, ease of use, speed, and robustness. Due to these advantages, it has been successfully applied for solving many real-world applications, like admission capacity planning in higher education [5, 6], financial markets dynamic modeling [7], solar energy [8], and many others. In addition, many recent studies prove that the performance of DE is highly competitive with and in many cases superior to other EAs in solving unconstrained optimization problems, constrained optimization problems, multiobjective optimization problems, and other complex optimization problems [9]. However, DE has many weaknesses as all other evolutionary search techniques. Generally, DE has a good global exploration ability that can reach the region of global optimum, but it is slow at exploitation of the solution [10]. Additionally, the parameters of DE are problem dependent and it is difficult to adjust them for different problems. Moreover, DE performance decreases as search space dimensionality increases [11]. Finally, the performance of DE deteriorates significantly when the problems of premature convergence and/or stagnation occur [11, 12]. The performance of DE basically depends on the mutation strategy and the crossover operator. Besides, the intrinsic control parameters (population size NP, scaling factor F, and the crossover rate CR) play a vital role in balancing the diversity of population and convergence speed of the algorithm. For the original DE, these parameters are user-defined and kept fixed during the run. However, many recent studies indicate that the performance of DE is highly affected by the parameter setting and the choice of the optimal values of parameters is always problem dependent. Moreover, prior to an actual optimization process, the traditional time-consuming trial-and-error method is used for fine-tuning the control parameters for each problem. Alternatively, in order to achieve acceptable results even for the same problem, different parameter settings along with different mutation schemes at different stages of evolution are needed. Therefore, some techniques have been designed to adjust control parameters in adaptive or self-adaptive manner instead of trial-and-error procedure plus new mutation rules have been developed to improve the search capability of DE [13–22]. Based on the above considerations, in this paper, we present a novel

DE, referred to as ANDE, including two novel modifications: triangular mutation rule and self-adaptive scheme for gradual change of CR values. In ANDE, a novel triangular mutation rule can balance the global exploration ability and the local exploitation tendency and enhance the convergence rate of the algorithm. Furthermore, a novel adaptation scheme for CR is developed that can benefit from the past experience of the individuals in the search space during evolution process. Scaling factors are produced according to a uniform distribution to balance the global exploration and local exploitation during the evolution process. ANDE has been tested on 20 benchmark test functions developed for the 2010 IEEE Congress on Evolutionary Computation (IEEE CEC 2010) [1]. The experimental results indicate that the proposed algorithm and its two versions are highly competitive algorithms for solving large scale global optimization problems. The remainder of this paper is organized as follows. Section 2 briefly introduces DE and its operators. Section 3 reviews the related work. Then, ANDE is presented in Section 4. The experimental results are given in Section 5. Section 6 discusses the effectiveness of the proposed modifications. Finally, the conclusions and future works are drawn in Section 7.

2. Differential Evolution (DE)

This section provides a brief summary of the basic Differential Evolution (DE) algorithm. In simple DE, generally known as DE/rand/1/bin [4, 23], an initial random population consists of NP vectors $\vec{X}_i$, $\forall i = 1, 2, \ldots, \text{NP}$, and is randomly generated according to a uniform distribution within the lower and upper boundaries (x_j^L, x_j^U). After initialization, these individuals are evolved by DE operators (mutation and crossover) to generate a trial vector. A comparison between the parent and its trial vector is then done to select the vector which should survive to the next generation [9]. DE steps are discussed below.

2.1. Initialization. In order to establish a starting point for the optimization process, an initial population must be created. Typically, each decision variable in every vector of the initial population is assigned a randomly chosen value from the boundary constraints:

$$x_{ij}^0 = x_j^L + \text{rand}_j \cdot \left(x_j^U - x_j^L \right), \tag{2}$$

where rand_j denotes a uniformly distributed number between $[0, 1]$, generating a new value for each decision variable.

2.2. Mutation. At generation G, for each target vector x_i^G, a mutant vector v_i^{G+1} is generated according to the following:

$$v_i^{G+1} = x_{r_1}^G + F * \left(x_{r_2}^G - x_{r_3}^G \right), \quad r_1 \neq r_2 \neq r_3 \neq i \tag{3}$$

with randomly chosen indices $r_1, r_2, r_3 \in \{1, 2, \ldots, \text{NP}\}$. F is a real number to control the amplification of the difference vector $(x_{r_2}^G - x_{r_3}^G)$. According to Price et al. [24], the range of

F is in $[0, 2]$. In this work, if a component of a mutant vector violates search space, the value of this component is generated newly using (2).

2.3. Crossover. There are two main crossover types, binomial and exponential. In the binomial crossover, the target vector is mixed with the mutated vector, using the following scheme, to yield the trial vector u_i^{G+1}.

$$u_{ij}^{G+1} = \begin{cases} v_{ij}^{G+1}, & \text{rand}\,(j) \leq \text{CR or } j = \text{randn}\,(i)\,, \\ x_{ij}^{G}, & \text{rand}\,(j) > \text{CR and } j \neq \text{randn}\,(i)\,, \end{cases} \quad (4)$$

where $j = 1, 2, \ldots, D$; $\text{rand}(j) \in [0, 1]$ is the jth evaluation of a uniform random generator number. $\text{CR} \in [0, 1]$ is the crossover rate; $\text{randn}(i) \in \{1, 2, \ldots, D\}$ is a randomly chosen index which ensures that u_i^{G+1} gets at least one element from v_i^{G+1}; otherwise no new parent vector would be produced and the population would not alter.

In an exponential crossover, an integer value l is randomly chosen within the range $\{1, D\}$. This integer value acts as a starting point in $\vec{x}_{j,G}$, from where the crossover or exchange of components with $\vec{V}_{i,G+1}$ starts. Another integer value L (denotes the number of components) is also chosen from the interval $\{1, D - l\}$. The trial vector $(\vec{u}_{i,G+1})$ is created by inheriting the values of variables in locations l to $l + L$ from $\vec{V}_{i,G+1}$ and the remaining ones from $\vec{x}_{j,G}$.

2.4. Selection. DE adapts a greedy selection strategy. If and only if the trial vector u_i^{G+1} yields fitness function value as good as or a better than x_i^{G}, then u_i^{G+1} is set to x_i^{G+1}. Otherwise, the old vector x_i^{G} is retained. The selection scheme is as follows (for a minimization problem):

$$x_i^{G+1} = \begin{cases} u_i^{G+1}, & f\left(u_i^{G+1}\right) \leq f\left(x_i^{G}\right) \\ x_i^{G}, & \text{otherwise.} \end{cases} \quad (5)$$

A detailed description of standard DE algorithm is given in Algorithm 1.

3. Related Work

As previously mentioned, during the past few years, LSGO has attracted much attention by the researches due to its significance as many real-world problems and applications are high-dimensional problems in nature. Basically, the current EA-based LSGO research can be classified into two categories:

(i) Cooperative Coevolution (CC) framework algorithms or divide-and-conquer methods

(ii) Noncooperative Coevolution (CC) framework algorithms or no divide-and-conquer methods

Cooperative Coevolution (CC) has become a popular and effective technique in evolutionary algorithms (EAs) for large scale global optimization since its initiation in the publication of Potter and Jong [25]. The main idea of CC is to partition the LSGO problem into a number of subproblems; that is, the decision variables of the problem are divided into smaller subcomponents, each of which is optimized using a separate EA. By using this divide-and-conquer method, the classical EAs are able to effectively solve many separable problems [25]. CC show better performance on separable problems but deteriorated on nonseparable problems because the interacting variables could not be grouped in one subcomponent. Recently, different versions of CC-based EAs have been developed and shown excellent performance. Yang et al. [26] proposed a new decomposition strategy called random grouping as a simple way of increasing the probability of grouping interacting variables in one subcomponent. According to this strategy, without any prior knowledge of the nonseparability of a problem, subdivide n-dimensional decision vector into m s-dimensional subcomponents. Later, Omidvar et al. [27] proposed DECC-DML algorithm which is a Differential Evolution algorithm adopting CC frame. They suggested a new decomposition strategy called delta grouping. The central idea of this technique was that the improvement interval of interacting variables would be limited if they were in different subcomponents. Delta method measures the averaged difference in a certain variable across the entire population and uses it for identifying interacting variables. The experimental results show that this new method is more effective than the existing random grouping method. However, DECC-DML is less efficient on nonseparable functions with more than one group of rotated variables. Likewise, Wang and Li [28] proposed another CC-based technique, named EOEA, to handle LSGO problems, in which the search procedure is divided into two stages: (1) the global shrinking stage and (2) the local exploitation stage. The objective of the first stage is to shrink the searching scope to the promising area as quickly as possible by using an EDA based on mixed Gaussian and Cauchy models (MUEDA) [29], while, to achieve the second objective, CC-based algorithm, different from the previous CC- based methods, is adopted to explore the limited area extensively to find solution as better as possible. Compared with some previous LSGO algorithms, EOEA demonstrates better performance. Many CC-based algorithms have been developed during the past decade such as FEPCC [30], DECC-I, DECC-II [31], MLCC [32], DEwSaCC [33], and CPSO [34]. On the other hand, there are many other approaches that optimize LSGO problems as a whole; that is, no divide-and-conquer methods was used. Actually, it is considered a challenging task as it needs to develop novel evolutionary operators that can promote and strengthen the capability of the algorithms to improve the overall optimization process in high-dimensional search space. In [35], Korošec et al. proposed an Ant-Colony Optimization- (ACO-) based algorithm for solving LSGO problems with continuous variables, labeled Differential Ant-Stigmergy Algorithm (DASA). The DASA transforms a real-parameter optimization problem into a graph-search problem, where the parameters' differences assigned to the graph vertices are used to navigate through the search space. Brest et al. [36] presented self-adaptive Differential Evolution algorithm (jDElsgo). In this approach, self-adaptive F and Cr control parameters and

```
(01) Begin
(02)  G = 0
(03)  Create a random initial population $\vec{x}_i^G$ $\forall i, i = 1, \ldots, NP$
(04)  Evaluate $f(\vec{x}_i^G)$ $\forall i, i = 1, \ldots, NP$
(05)  For G = 1 to GEN Do
(06)       For i = 1 to NP Do
(07)            Select randomly $r1 \neq r2 \neq r3 \neq i \in [1, NP]$
(08)            $j_{rand} = randint(1, D)$
(09)       For j = 1 to D Do
(10)       If ($rand_j[0, 1] < CR$ or $j = j_{rand}$) Then
(11)            $u_{i,j}^{G+1} = x_{r1,j}^G + F \cdot (x_{r2,j}^G - x_{r3,j}^G)$
(12)       Else
(13)            $u_{i,j}^{G+1} = x_{i,j}^G$
(14)       End If
(15)       End For
(16)       If ($f(\vec{u}_i^{G+1}) \leq f(\vec{x}_i^G)$) Then
(17)            $\vec{x}_i^{G+1} = \vec{u}_i^{G+1}$
(18)       Else
(19)            $\vec{x}_i^{G+1} = \vec{x}_i^G$
(20)       End If
(21)       End For
(22)   G = G + 1
(23)  End For
(24) End
```

ALGORITHM 1: Description of standard DE algorithm. rand[0, 1) is a function that returns a real number between 0 and 1. randint(min, max) is a function that returns an integer number between min and max. NP, GEN, CR, and F are user-defined parameters. D is the dimensionality of the problem.

"rand/1/bin" strategy along with population size reduction mechanism are used. Similarly, Wang et al. [37] introduced a sequential Differential Evolution (DE) enhanced by neighborhood search (SDENS), where hybrid crossover strategy "rand/1/bin" and "rand/1/exp" are used. In order to search the neighbors of each individual, two trial individuals by local and global neighborhood search strategies are created. Then, the fittest one among the current individual and the two created trial individuals is selected as a new current individual. Molina et al. [38] put forward a memetic algorithm based on local search chains, named MA-SW-CHAINS, which assigned local search intensity to each individual depending on its features by changing different local search applications. Zhao et al. [39] proposed a hybrid approach called (DMS-PSO-SHS) by combining the dynamic multiswarm particle swarm optimizer (DMS-PSO) with a subregional harmony search (SHS). A modified multitrajectory search (MTS) algorithm is also applied frequently on several selected solutions. In addition, an external memory of selected past solutions is used to enhance the diversity of the swarm. Generally, the proposed ANDE algorithm belongs to this category.

4. ANDE Algorithm

In this section, we outline a novel DE algorithm, ANDE, and explain the steps of the algorithm in detail.

4.1. Triangular Mutation Scheme. Storn and Price [4, 24] proposed the basic mutation scheme DE/rand/1. In fact, from the literature [9], it is considered as the most successful and widely used operator. Virtually, the main idea behind this strategy is that the three vectors are randomly selected from the population to form the mutation and the base vector is then chosen at random among the three. The difference vector is formed using the other two vectors added to the base vector. Obviously, it can be seen that the basic mutation scheme has excellent ability to maintain population diversity and global search capability as it is not directed to any specific search direction. However, the convergence speed of DE algorithms significantly slows down [15]. In the same context, DE/rand/2 strategy, which is similar to the basic scheme with another difference vector that is formed by extra two vectors, has better perturbation than original mutation with one difference vector [15]. Consequently, it is better than the

DE/rand/1/bin strategy as it can provide much more various differential trial vectors. On the other hand, there is another type of mutations which is called greedy strategies such as DE/best/1, DE/best/2, and DE/current-to-best/1. Actually, in order to increase the local search tendency that improves the convergence behavior of the algorithm, this type is based on benefits from the best solution found so far in the evolutionary process by incorporating it into the mutation operator. Nonetheless, the population diversity and exploration capability of the algorithm may be deteriorated or may be completely lost at the early stage of the optimization process that causes problems such stagnation and/or premature convergence. Accordingly, the recent studies proposed a strategy candidate pool that includes many mutation schemes that are different in structure and have distinct optimization capabilities to overcome the shortcomings of both types of mutation strategies. Then, it is combined with different control parameter adaptation rules to deal with various types of problems with different features at different stages of evolution [15, 17, 40]. Contrarily, taking into consideration the weakness of existing greedy strategies, Mohamed [16] introduced a new Differential Evolution (DE) algorithm, named JADE, to improve optimization performance by implementing a new mutation strategy "DE/current-to-pbest" with optional external archive and by updating control parameters in an adaptive manner. Simulation results show that JADE was better than, or at least competitive to, other classic or adaptive DE algorithms such as particle swarm and other evolutionary algorithms from the literature in terms of convergence performance. Consequently, from the literature, there are a few attempts in developing new mutations rule. Therefore, in this paper, a new triangular mutation rule is introduced. The proposed mutation can significantly balance both the global exploration ability and the local exploitation tendency that in turn will improve the convergence rate of the algorithm. The proposed mutation strategy is based on the convex combination vector of the triplet defined by the three randomly chosen vectors and three difference vectors between the tournament best, better, and worst selected vectors. The proposed mutation vector is generated in the following manner:

$$v_i^{G+1} = \overline{x}_c^G + F1 \cdot \left(x_{\text{best}}^G - x_{\text{better}}^G\right) + F2 \cdot \left(x_{\text{best}}^G - x_{\text{worst}}^G\right)$$
$$+ F3 \cdot \left(x_{\text{better}}^G - x_{\text{worst}}^G\right), \quad (6)$$

where $\overline{x}_c^G$ is a convex combination vector of the triangle and $F1$, $F2$, and $F3$ are the mutation factors that are associated with x_i and are independently generated according to uniform distribution in (0, 1) and x_{best}^G, x_{better}^G, and x_{worst}^G are the three tournament best, better, and worst randomly selected vectors, respectively. The convex combination vector $\overline{x}_c^G$ of the triangle is a linear combination of the three randomly selected vectors and is defined as follows:

$$\overline{x}_c^G = w_1 \cdot x_{\text{best}} + w_2 \cdot x_{\text{better}} + w_3 \cdot x_{\text{worst}}, \quad (7)$$

where the real weights w_i satisfy $w_i \geq 0$ and $\sum_{i=1}^{3} w_i = 1$, where the real weights w_i are given by $w_i = p_i / \sum_{i=1}^{3} p_i$,

$i = 1, 2, 3$, where $p_1 = 1$, $p_2 = \text{rand}(0.75, 1)$, and $p_3 = \text{rand}(0.5, p(2))$, $\text{rand}(a, b)$ is a function that returns a real number between a and b, where a and b are not included. For unconstrained optimization problems at any generation $g > 1$, for each target vector, three vectors are randomly selected; then sort them in ascending according to their objective function values and assign w_1, w_2, and w_3 to x_{best}^G, x_{better}^G, and x_{worst}^G, respectively. Without loss of generality, we only consider minimization problem.

Obviously, from mutation equation (6), it can be observed that the incorporation of the objective function value in the mutation scheme has two benefits. Firstly, the perturbation part of the mutation is formed by the three sides of the triangle in the direction of the best vector among the three randomly selected vectors. Therefore, the directed perturbations in the proposed mutation resembles the concept of gradient as the difference vectors are directed from the worst to the better to the best vectors [41]. Thus, it is considerably used to explore the landscape of the objective function being optimized in different subregion around the best vectors within search space through optimization process. Secondly, the convex combination vector $\overline{x}_c^G$ is a weighted sum of the three randomly selected vectors where the best vector has the significant contribution. Therefore, $\overline{x}_c^G$ is extremely affected and biased by the best vector more than the remaining two vectors. Consequently, the global solution can be easily reached if all vectors follow the direction of the best vectors; besides they also follow the opposite direction of the worst vectors among the randomly selected vectors. Indeed, the new mutation process exploits the nearby region of each $\overline{x}_c^G$ in the direction of $(x_{\text{best}}^G - x_{\text{worst}}^G)$ for each mutated vector. In a nutshell, it concentrates the exploitation of some subregions of the search space. Thus, it has better local search tendency so it accelerates the convergence speed of the proposed algorithm. Besides, the global exploration ability of the algorithm is significantly enhanced by forming many different sizes and shapes of triangles in the feasible region through the optimization process. Thus, the proposed directed mutation balances both global exploration capability and local exploitation tendency.

Thus, since the proposed directed mutation balances both global exploration capability and local exploitation tendency while the basic mutation favors exploration only, the probability of using the proposed mutation is twice as much the probability of applying the basic rule. The new mutation strategy is embedded into the DE algorithm and combined with the basic mutation strategy DE/rand/1/bin as follows.

If $(u(0, 1) \leq (2/3))$ then

$$v_i^{G+1} = \overline{x}_c^G + F1 \cdot \left(x_{\text{best}}^G - x_{\text{better}}^G\right) + F2 \cdot \left(x_{\text{best}}^G - x_{\text{worst}}^G\right)$$
$$+ F3 \cdot \left(x_{\text{better}}^G - x_{\text{worst}}^G\right). \quad (8)$$

Else

$$v_{i,j}^{G+1} = x_{r_1,j}^G + F \cdot \left(x_{r_1,j}^G - x_{r_3,j}^G\right), \quad (9)$$

where F is a uniform random variable in $[(-1, 0) \cup (0, 1)]$, $u(0, 1)$ returns a real number between 0 and 1 with uniform random probability distribution. From the abovementioned scheme, it can be realized that for each vector only one of the two strategies is used for generating the current trial vector, depending on a uniformly distributed random value within the range $(0, 1)$. For each vector, if the random value is greater than 2/3, then the basic mutation is applied. Otherwise, the proposed one is performed. It is noteworthy mentioning that the proposed triangular mutation and the trigonometric mutation proposed by Fan and Lampinen [23] use three randomly selected vectors but they are completely different in the following two main points.

(1) The proposed mutation strategy is based on the convex combination vector (weighted mean) of the triplet defined by the three randomly chosen vectors (as a donor) and three difference vectors between the tournament best, better, and worst selected vectors (they are directed difference, i.e., resembling the concept of gradient as the difference vectors are directed from the worst to the better to the best vectors). However, the trigonometric mutation is based on the center point (the mean) of the hypergeometric triangle defined by the three randomly chosen vectors. The perturbation to be imposed to the donor is then made up with a sum of three weighted vector differentials that are randomly constructed (not directed).

(2) With respect to the scaling factors in the proposed algorithm, at each generation G, the scale factors $F1$, $F2$, and $F3$ of each individual target vector are independently generated according to uniform distribution in $(0, 1)$ to enrich the search behavior. However, the scaling factors in the trigonometric mutation are constants; at each generation G, the scale factors of each individual target vector are computed as the ratio of the objective function value of each vector divided by the sum of the objective function values of the three vectors (sum equals 1). Therefore, it is obviously deduced that the trigonometric mutation operation is a rather greedy operator since it biases the new trial solution strongly in the direction where the best one of three individuals chosen for the mutation is. Therefore, the trigonometric mutation can be viewed as a local search operator and the perturbed individuals are produced only within a trigonometric region that is defined by the triangle used for a mutation operation [23]. Consequently, it is easily trapped in local points with multimodal problems and it may be also stagnated as it has not an exploration capability to seek the whole search space. However, the proposed triangular mutation has both the exploration capability and the exploitation tendency because directed perturbation in the proposed mutation resembles the concept of gradient as the difference vectors are directed from the worst to the better to the best vectors. Thus, it is considerably used to explore the landscape of the objective function being optimized in different subregion around the best vectors outside the trigonometric region that is defined by the triangle used for a mutation operation within search space through optimization process. Secondly, the convex combination vector $\overline{x}_c^G$ is a weighted sum of the three randomly selected vectors where the best vector has the significant contribution. Therefore, $\overline{x}_c^G$ is extremely affected and biased by the best vector more than the remaining two vectors. Consequently,

the global solution can be easily reached if all vectors follow the direction of the best vectors; besides they also follow the opposite direction of the worst vectors among the randomly selected vectors. Indeed, the new mutation process exploits the nearby region of each $\overline{x}_c^G$ in the direction of $(x_{\text{best}}^G - x_{\text{worst}}^G)$ for each mutated vector. In a nutshell, it concentrates the exploitation of some subregions of the search space. Thus, it has better local search tendency so it accelerates the convergence speed of the proposed algorithm. Besides, the global exploration ability of the algorithm is significantly enhanced by forming many different sizes and shapes of triangles in the feasible region through the optimization process.

4.2. Parameter Adaptation Schemes in ANDE. The successful performance of DE algorithm is significantly dependent upon the choice of its three control parameters: the scaling factor F and crossover rate CR and population size NP [4, 24]. In fact, they have a vital role because they greatly influence the effectiveness, efficiency, and robustness of the algorithm. Furthermore, it is difficult to determine the optimal values of the control parameters for a variety of problems with different characteristics at different stages of evolution. In the proposed ANDE algorithm, NP is kept as a user-specified parameter since it highly depends on the problem complexity. Generally speaking, F is an important parameter that controls the evolving rate of the population; that is, it is closely related to the convergence speed [15]. A small F value encourages the exploitation tendency of the algorithm that makes the search focus on neighborhood of the current solutions; hence it can enhance the convergence speed. However, it may also lead to premature convergence [41]. On the other hand, a large F value improves the exploration capability of the algorithm that can make the mutant vectors distributed widely in the search space and can increase the diversity of the population [40]. However, it may slow down the search [41]. With respect to the scaling factors in the proposed algorithm, at each generation G, the scale factors $F1$, $F2$, and $F3$ of each individual target vector are independently generated according to uniform distribution in $(0, 1)$ to enrich the search behavior. The constant crossover (CR) reflects the probability with which the trial individual inherits the actual individual's genes, that is, which and how many components are mutated in each element of the current population [17, 41]. The constant crossover CR practically controls the diversity of the population [40]. As a matter of fact, if CR is high, this will increase the population diversity. Nevertheless, the stability of the algorithm may reduce. On the other hand, small values of CR increase the possibility of stagnation that may weaken the exploration ability of the algorithm to open up new search space. Additionally, CR is usually more sensitive to problems with different characteristics such as unimodality and multimodality, separable and nonseparable problems. For separable problems, CR from the range $(0, 0.2)$ is the best while for multimodal parameter dependent problems CR in the range $(0.9, 1)$ is suitable [42]. On the other hand, there are wide varieties of approaches for adapting or self-adapting control parameters values through optimization process. Most of these methods are based on generating random values from uniform, normal, or Cauchy distributions or by generating different values from predefined parameter candidate pool. Besides, they use the previous experience (of generating better solutions) to guide the adaptation of these parameters [11, 15–17, 19, 40, 43–46]. The presented work proposed a novel self-adaptation scheme for CR.

The core idea of the proposed self-adaptation scheme for the crossover rate CR is based on the following fundamental principle. In the initial stage of the search process, the difference among individual vectors is large because the vectors in the population are completely dispersed or the population diversity is large due to the random distribution of the individuals in the search space that requires a relatively smaller crossover value. Then, as the population evolves through generations, the diversity of the population decreases as the vectors in the population are clustered because each individual gets closer to the best vector found so far. Consequently, in order to maintain the population diversity and improve the convergence speed, crossover should be gradually utilized with larger values along with the generations of evolution increased to preserve well genes in so far as possible and promote the convergence performance. Therefore, the population diversity can be greatly enhanced through generations. However, there is no appropriate CR value that balance both the diversity and convergence speed when solving a given problem during overall optimization process. Consequently, to address this problem and following the SaDE algorithm [15], in this paper, a novel adaptation scheme for CR is developed that can benefit from the past experience through generations of evolutionary.

Crossover Rate Adaptation. At each generation G, the crossover probability CR_i of each individual target vector is independently generated randomly from pool A according to uniform distribution and Procedure 1 exists through generations.

In Procedure 1, A is the pool of values of crossover rate CR that changes during and after the learning period LP; we set LP = 10% of GEN, G is the current generation number; GEN is the maximum number of generations. The lower and upper limits of the ranges for (G) are experimentally determined; $CR\_Flag\_List[i]$ is the list that contains one of two binary values $(0, 1)$ for each individual i through generation G, where 0 represents failure, no improvement, when the target vector is better than the trial vector during and after the learning period and 1 represents success, improvement, when the trial vector is better than the target vector during and after the learning period, the $failure\_counter\_list[i]$ is the list that monitors the working of individuals in terms of fitness function value during generations after completion of the learning period, and if there is no improvement in fitness, then the failure counter of this target vector is increased by unity. This process is repeated until it achieves prespecified value of Max_failure_counter which assigned a value 20 that is experimentally determined; $CR\_Ratio\_List[k]$ is the list that records the relative change improvement ratios between the trial and target objective function values with respect to each value k of the pool of values A of CR through generation G. It can be clearly seen from procedure 1 that, at $G = 1$, CR = 0.05

for each target vector and then, at each generation G, if the generated trial vector produced is better than the target vector, the relative change improvement ratio (RCIR) associated with this CR value is computed and the correspondence ratio is updated. On the other hand, during the learning period, if the target vector is better than the trial vector, then the CR value is chosen randomly from the associated pool A of CR values, that is, gradually added more values, according to generation number and hence, for this CR value, there is no improvement and its ratio remains unchanged. However, after termination of the learning period, if the target vector is better than the trial vector, that is, if there is no improvement in fitness, then the failure_counter is increased by one in each generation till this value achieves a prespecified value of Max_failure_counter which assigned a value 20; then this CR value should change to a new value that is randomly selected from the pool A of CR values that is taken in range 0.1–0.9 in steps of 0.1 and 0.05 and 0.95 are also included as lower and upper values, respectively. Note that the RCIR is only updated if there is an improvement. Otherwise, it remains constant. Thus, the CR value with maximum ratio is continuously changing according to the evolution process at each subsequent generation. In fact, although all test problems included in this study have optimum of zero, the absolute value is used in calculating RCIR as a general rule in order to deal with positive, negative, or mixed values of objective function.

Concretely, Procedure 1 shows that, during the first half of the learning period, the construction of pool A of CR values ensures the diversity of the population such that the crossover probability for ith individual target increases gradually in staircase along with the generations of evolution process increased, taking into consideration that the probability of chosen small CR values is greater than the probability of chosen larger CR values as the diversity of the population is still large. Additionally, in the second half of the learning period, larger values of 0.9 and 0.95 are added to the pool as it favors nonseparable functions. However, all the values have an equally likely chance of occurrence to keep on the diversity with different values of CR. Consequently, the successful CR values with high relative change improvement ratio in this period will survive to be used in the next generations of the optimization process until it fails to achieve improvement for a specific value of 20; then it must be changed randomly by a new value. Thus, the value of CR is adaptively changed as the diversity of the population changes through generations. Distinctly, it varies from one individual to another during generations, and also it is different from one function to another one being optimized. Generally, adaptive control parameters with different values during the optimization process in successive generations enrich the algorithm with controlled-randomness which enhances the global optimization performance of the algorithm in terms of exploration and exploitation capabilities. Therefore, it can be concluded that the proposed novel adaptation scheme for gradual change of the values of the crossover rate can excellently benefit from the past experience of the individuals in the search space during evolution process which in turn can considerably balance the common trade-off between the population diversity and

If ((CR_Flag_List[i] = 0) and (G <= LP)), If the target vector is better than the trial vector during the learning period, then:

$$
Cr_i = \begin{cases}
\text{Randomly select one value from } A, \quad A = [0.05], & 0 \le G < \left(\frac{1}{6}\right) * (LP) \\[6pt]
\text{Randomly select one value from } A, \quad A = [0.05, 0.1, 0.2], & \left(\frac{1}{6}\right) * (LP) \le G < \left(\frac{1}{4}\right) * (LP) \\[6pt]
\text{Randomly select one value from } A, \quad A = [0.05, 0.1, 0.2, 0.3, 0.4], & \left(\frac{1}{4}\right) * (LP) \le G < \left(\frac{1}{3}\right) * (LP) \\[6pt]
\text{Randomly select one value from } A, \quad A = [0.05, 0.1, 0.2, 0.3, 0.4, 0.5, 0.6], & \left(\frac{1}{3}\right) * (LP) \le G < \left(\frac{5}{12}\right) * (LP) \\[6pt]
\text{Randomly select one value from } A, \quad A = [0.05, 0.1, 0.2, 0.3, 0.4, 0.5, 0.6, 0.7, 0.8], & \left(\frac{5}{12}\right) * (LP) \le G < \left(\frac{1}{2}\right) * (LP) \\[6pt]
\text{Randomly select one value from } A, \quad A = [0.05, 0.1, 0.2, 0.3, 0.4, 0.5, 0.6, 0.7, 0.8, 0.9, 0.95], & \left(\frac{1}{2}\right) * (LP) \le G < (1) * (LP)
\end{cases}
$$

Else If ((CR_Flag_List[i] = 0) and (G > LP)), If the target vector is better than the trial vector after the learning period, then:
   If the failure_counter_list[i] = Max_failure_counter,
   Randomly select one value from list A, $A = [0.05, 0.1, 0.2, 0.3, 0.4, 0.5, 0.6, 0.7, 0.8, 0.9, 0.95]$.
   else
   failure_counter_list[i]= *failure_counter_list*[i] + 1;
   End If
Else ((CR_Flag_List[i] = 1)), If the trial vector is better than the target vector through generations, then:
   Select the CR value from A with maximum relative change improvement ratio (RCIR) from CR_Ratio_List[k].
End IF

PROCEDURE 1

convergence speed. The pseudocode of ANDE is presented in Algorithm 2.

It is worth noting that although this work is an extension and modification of our previous work in [47], there are significant differences as follows: (1) Previous work in [47] is proposed for solving small scale unconstrained problems (i.e., 10, 30, and 50 dimensions), whereas this work is proposed for solving large scale unconstrained problems with 1000 dimensions. (2) The crossover rate in [47] is given by a dynamic nonlinear increased probability scheme, but in this work a novel self-adaptation scheme for CR is developed that can benefit from the past experience through generations of evolutionary. (3) In [47], only one difference vector between the best and the worst individuals among the three randomly selected vectors with one scaling factor, uniformly random number in (0, 1), is used in the mutation, but in this work three difference vectors between the tournament best, better, and worst selected vectors with corresponding three scaling factors, which are independently generated according to uniform distribution in (0, 1), are used in the mutation scheme. (4) The triangular mutation rule is only used in this work, but in the previous work [47], the triangular mutation strategy is embedded into the DE algorithm and combined with the basic mutation strategy DE/rand/1/bin through a nonlinear decreasing probability rule. (5) In previous work [47] a restart mechanism based on Random Mutation and modified BGA mutation is used to avoid stagnation or premature convergence, whereas this work does not.

5. Experimental Study

5.1. Benchmark Functions. The performance of the proposed ANDE algorithm has been tasted on 20 scalable optimization functions for the CEC 2010 special session and competition on large scale in global optimization. A detailed description of these test functions can be found in [1]. These 20 test functions can be divided into four classes:

(1) Separable functions F_1-F_3

(2) Partially separable functions, in which a small number of variables are dependent while all the remaining ones are independent ($m = 50$) F_4-F_8

(3) Partially separable functions that consist of multiple independent subcomponents, each of which is m-nonseparable ($m = 50$) F_9-F_{18}

(4) Fully nonseparable functions F_{19}-F_{20},

where the sphere function, the rotated elliptic function, *Schwefels* Problem 1.2, Rosenbrock function, the rotated Rastrigin function, and the rotated Ackley function are used as the basic functions. The control parameter used to define the degree of separability of a given function in the given test suite is set as $m = 50$. The dimensions (D) of functions are 1000.

5.2. Parameter Settings and Involved Algorithms. To evaluate the performance of algorithm, experiments were conducted on the test suite. We adopt the solution error measure $f((x) - (x^*))$, where x is the best solution obtained by algorithms in one run and x^* is well-known global optimum of each benchmark function and is recorded after $1.2e + 05$, $6.0e + 05$, and $3.0e + 06$ function evaluations (FEs), all experiments for each function run 25 times independently, and statistical results are provided including the best, median, mean, worst results and the standard deviation. The population size in ANDE was set to 50. The learning period (LP) and the maximum

(01) Begin

(02) $G = 0$

(03) Create a random initial population $\vec{x}_i^G \; \forall i, i = 1, \ldots, \text{NP}$,
set the Learning Period (LP) = 10% GEN, set the Max_failure_counter = 20.
For each $\vec{x}_i^G$, set the failure_counter_list[i] = 0, set the CR_Flag_List[i] = 0,
For each CR values in the list, set the CR_Ratio_List[k] = 0 $\forall k, k = 1, \ldots, 11$.

(04) Evaluate $f(\vec{x}_i^G) \; \forall i, i = 1, \ldots, \text{NP}$

(05) **For** $G = 1$ to GEN **Do**

(06)   **For** $i = 1$ to NP **Do**

(07)   Select randomly $r1 \neq r2 \neq r3 \neq i \in [1, \text{NP}]$

(08) $j_{\text{rand}} = \text{randint}(1, D)$

(11)   Compute the (crossover rate) Cr_i according to Procedure 1.

(12)   **For** $j = 1$ to D **Do**

(13)   **If** $(\text{rand}_j[0, 1] < \text{CR}$ **or** $j = j_{\text{rand}})$ **Then**

(14)   **If** $(\text{rand}[0, 1] <= (2/3))$ **Then** (Use New Triangular Mutation Scheme)

(15)   Determine the tournament x_{best}^G, x_{better}^G and x_{worst}^G based on $f(\vec{x}_i^G), i = 1, 2, 3$
(three randomly selected vectors) and compute $\overline{x}_c^G$ according to eq. (2).

(16) $u_{i,j}^{G+1} = \overline{x}_{c,j}^G + F_1(x_{\text{best},j}^G - x_{\text{better},j}^G) + F_2(x_{\text{best},j}^G - x_{\text{worst},j}^G) + F_3(x_{\text{better},j}^G - x_{\text{worst},j}^G)$

(17)   **Else**

(18) $u_{i,j}^{G+1} = x_{r1,j}^G + F \cdot (x_{r2,j}^G - x_{r3,j}^G)$

          End If

(15)   **Else**

(16) $u_{i,j}^{G+1} = x_{i,j}^G$

(17)   **End If**

(18)   **End For**

(19)   **If** $(f(\vec{u}_i^{G+1}) \leq f(\vec{x}_i^G))$ **Then**

(20) $\vec{x}_i^{G+1} = \vec{u}_i^{G+1}, (f(\vec{x}_i^{G+1}) = f(\vec{u}_i^{G+1}))$
      If $(f(\vec{u}_i^{G+1}) \leq f(\vec{x}_{\text{best}}^G))$ **Then**
      $\vec{x}_{\text{best}}^{G+1} = \vec{u}_i^{G+1}, (f(\vec{x}_{\text{best}}^{G+1}) = f(\vec{u}_i^{G+1}))$
      End
      CR_Flag_List[i]= 1
      The relative change improvement ratio (RCIR) is updated

(21) $CR\_Ratio\_List[k] = CR\_Ratio\_List[k] + (1 - \min(|f(\vec{u}_i^{G+1})|, |f(\vec{x}_i^G)|)/\max(|f(\vec{u}_i^{G+1})|, |f(\vec{x}_i^G)|)).$
      Else

(22) $\vec{x}_i^{G+1} = \vec{x}_i^G$
      CR_Flag_List[i] = 0

(23)   **End If**

(24)   **End For**

(25) $G = G + 1$

(26) **End For**

(27) **End**

ALGORITHM 2: Description of ANDE algorithm.

failure counter (MFC) are set to 10% of total generations and 20 generations, respectively. For separable functions F_1–F_3, CR is chosen to be 0.05 as they are separable functions. ANDE was compared to population-based algorithms that were all tested on this test suite in this competition. These algorithms are

(i) DE Enhanced by Neighborhood Search for Large Scale Global Optimization (SDENS) [37],

(ii) Large Scale Global Optimization using Self-Adaptive Differential Evolution algorithm (jDElsgo) [36],

(iii) Cooperative Coevolution with Delta Grouping for Large Scale Nonseparable Function Optimization (DECC-DML) [27],

(iv) the Differential Ant-Stigmergy Algorithm for Large Scale Global Optimization (DASA) [35],

(v) two-stage based Ensemble Optimization for Large Scale Global Optimization (EOEA) [28],

(vi) Memetic Algorithm Based on Local Search Chains for Large Scale Continuous Global Optimization (MA-SW-CHAINS) [38],

(vii) Dynamic Multiswarm Particle Swarm Optimizer with Subregional Harmony Search (DMS-PSO-SHS) [39].

Note that since paper [48] was not accepted (based on private communication with the author) so it was excluded from this comparison. To compare the solution quality from a statistical angle of different algorithms and to check the behavior of the stochastic algorithms [38, 49], the results are compared using multiproblem Wilcoxon signed-rank test at a significance level 0.05. Wilcoxon signed-rank Test is a nonparametric statistical test that allow us to judge the difference between paired scores when it cannot make the assumption required by the paired-samples t-test; for example, the population should be normally distributed, where R^+ denotes the sum of ranks for the test problems in which the first algorithm performs better than the second algorithm (in the first column), and R^- represents the sum of ranks for the test problems in which the first algorithm performs worse than the second algorithm (in the first column). Larger ranks indicate larger performance discrepancy. The numbers in better, equal, and worse columns denote the number of problems in which the first algorithm is better than, equal to, or worse than the second algorithm. As a null hypothesis, it is assumed that there is no significance difference between the mean results of the two samples. Whereas the alternative hypothesis is that there is significance in the mean results of the two samples, the number of test problems $N = 20$ for $1.25e + 05$, $6.00e + 05$, and $3.00e + 006$ function evaluations and 5% significance level. Use the smaller values of the sums as the test value and compare it with the critical value or use the p value and compare it with the significance level. Reject the null hypothesis if the test value is less than or equal to the critical value or if the p value is less than or equal to the significance level (5%). Based on the result of the test, one of three signs ($+$, $-$, and $\approx$) is assigned for the comparison of any two algorithms (shown in the last column), where ($+$) sign means the first algorithm is significantly better than the second, ($-$) sign means the first algorithm is significantly worse than the second, and ($\approx$) sign means that there is no significant difference between the two algorithms. To perform comprehensive evaluation, the presentation of the experimental results is divided into three subsections. At first, the effectiveness of the proposed self-adaptive crossover rate scheme, modified basic differential evolution, and new triangular mutation scheme are evaluated. Second, overall performance comparisons between ANDE, ANDE-1, and ANDE-2 and other state-of-the-art DEs and non-DEs approaches are provided. Finally, the effectiveness of the proposed modifications and parameter settings on the performance of ANDE algorithm is discussed.

5.3. Experimental Results and Discussions. Firstly, some trials have been performed to evaluate the benefits and effectiveness of the proposed new triangular mutation and self-adaptive crossover rate on the performance of ANDE. Two different versions of ANDE have been tested and compared against the proposed one denoted as ANDE-1 and ANDE-2.

(1) ANDE-1, which is same as ANDE except that the new triangular mutation scheme is only used

(2) ANDE-2, which is same as ANDE except that the basic mutation scheme is only used

The solution error of ANDE and the two variants ANDE-1 and ANDE-2 algorithms are recorded in $1.2e + 05$, $6.0e + 05$, and $3.0e + 06$ function evaluations (FEs); all experiments for each function run 25 times independently and statistical results are provided including the best, median, mean, and worst results and the standard deviation in the supplemental file.

In this section, we compare directly the mean results obtained by ANDE, ANDE-1, and ANDE-2.

Tables S1, S2, and S3 contain the results obtained by ANDE, ANDE-1, and ANDE-2 in $1.2e + 05$, $6.0e + 05$, and $3.0e+06$ function evaluations (FEs), respectively. For remarking the best algorithm, best median and mean for each function are highlighted in boldface. The following characteristics can be clearly observed:

(i) In the majority of the functions, the differences between mean and median are small even in the cases when the final results are far away from the optimum, regardless of the number of function evaluations. That implies the ANDE and its versions are robust algorithms

(ii) In many functions, results with FEs = $3.0E + 06$ are significantly better than with FEs = $6.0E + 05$ and also results with FEs = $6.0E + 05$ are significantly better than with FEs = $1.2E + 05$. Therefore, ANDE, ANDE-1, and ANDE-2 benefit from desired FEs and there are continual improvements until the maximum FEs are achieved.

From Table S1, we can see that all algorithms perform well and there is no significant difference between them. However, it can be clearly seen from Table S2 that ANDE-2 performs significantly better than ANDE and ANDE-1 algorithms on separable functions (F_1, F_2). For F_3 and single-group m-nonseparable functions (F_4–F_8), the performance of the three algorithms are almost similar with the exception of test function F_6 where ANDE-2 performs better than HDE and ANDE-2 algorithms. Regarding $D/2m$-group m-nonseparable functions (F_9–F_{13}), the performance of the three algorithms is almost similar for F_9. ANDE-2 outperforms ANDE and ANDE-1 on F_{10}, F_{11} while for F_{12}, it loses to them. For F_{13}, ANDE outperforms other two algorithms. For D/m-group m-nonseparable functions (F_{14}–F_{18}), ANDE and ANDE-1 perform best but ANDE-2 only performs better than ANDE and ANDE-1 on F_{16}. But results of ANDE-1 on F_{13} and F_{17} are relatively better than results of ANDE. As for fully nonseparable functions (F_{19}-F_{20}), it is obvious that ANDE and ANDE-1 perform better than ANDE-2. As for F_{20}, ANDE performs significantly better than ANDE-1 and ANDE-2 algorithms. As can be seen from Table S3, ANDE, ANDE-1, and ANDE-2 algorithms were able to nearly reach the global optimal solution with high consistency of the separable F_1 (unimodal) and F_3 (multimodal) functions. However, ANDE-2 performs better than ANDE and ANDE-1 on separable multimodal function F_2. Besides, ANDE, ANDE-1, and ANDE-2 got close to the optimum single-group m-nonseparable functions multimodal function F_6 while only ANDE and ANDE-1 were also very close to the optimal solution of unimodal function F_7. As for F_4, F_5, and F_8, ANDE-1 outperforms ANDE and ANDE-2. Regarding the

TABLE 1: Results of multiple-problem Wilcoxon's test for ANDE, ANDE-1, and ANDE-2 over all functions at a significance level 0.05 (with $1.25E + 05$ FEs).

Algorithm	R^+	R^-	p value	Better	Equal	Worse	Dec.
ANDE versus ANDE-1	114	76	0.445	12	1	7	$\approx$
ANDE versus ANDE-2	107	83	0.629	10	1	9	$\approx$
ANDE-1 versus ANDE-2	117	93	0.654	10	0	10	$\approx$

TABLE 2: Results of the multiple-problem Wilcoxon's test for ANDE, ANDE-1, and ANDE-2 over all functions at a significance level 0.05 (with $6.00E + 05$ FEs).

Algorithm	R^+	R^-	p value	Better	Equal	Worse	Dec.
ANDE versus ANDE-1	92	118	0.627	12	0	8	$\approx$
ANDE versus ANDE-2	170	40	0.015	12	0	8	+
ANDE-1 versus ANDE-2	165	45	0.025	11	0	9	+

TABLE 3: Results of multiple-problem Wilcoxon's test for ANDE, ANDE-1, and ANDE-2 over all functions at a significance level 0.05 (with $3.00E + 06$ FEs).

Algorithm	R^+	R^-	p value	Better	Equal	Worse	Dec.
ANDE versus ANDE-1	85	124	0.467	12	0	8	$\approx$
ANDE versus ANDE-2	171	39	0.014	14	0	6	+
ANDE-1 versus ANDE-2	165	45	0.025	11	0	9	+

remaining problems, the performance of ANDE and ANDE-1 is almost similar and they outperform ANDE-2 while ANDE-2 performs some better that ANDE and ANDE-1 on F_{10}, F_{15}, F_{16}, and F_{20}. On the other hand, convergence behavior is another important factor that must be considered in comparison among all proposed algorithms. Therefore, in order to analyze the convergence behavior of each algorithm compared, the convergence graph of the median run has been plotted for each test problem. Figure S1 presents the convergence characteristics of all algorithms. From Figure S1, it can be observed that the convergence behavior supports the abovementioned analysis and discussions. Finally, it is clearly deduced that the remarkable performance of ANDE and ANDE-1 algorithms is due to the proposed mutation scheme that has both exploration ability and exploitation tendency. Additionally, it also visible that the proposed self-adaptive crossover procedure enhances the performance of the basic DE algorithm and it significantly promotes the performance of ANDE and ANDE-1 algorithms. In order to investigate and compare the performance of the proposed algorithms ANDE, ANDE-1, and ANDE-2 at statistical level, multiproblem Wilcoxon signed-rank test at a significance level 0.05 is performed on mean errors of all problems (with $1.25E + 05$ FEs, $6.00E + 05$ FEs, and $3.00E + 06$ FEs) and the results are presented in Tables 1, 2, and 3, respectively. From Table 1, it can be obviously seen that there is no significant difference between ANDE-1, ANDE-2, and ANDE. Besides, it can be obviously seen from Tables 2 and 3 that ANDE and ANDE-1 are significantly better than ANDE-2. Besides, there is no significant difference between ANDE-1 and ANDE. Although ANDE-2 achieved good performance in the initial phase of the search, it cannot keep the same performance during the rest of the optimization phases as expected because

it depends only on the basic mutation which has a lack of exploitation capability. On the other hand, ANDE and ANDE-1 have almost the same excellent performance due to the new triangular mutation.

In this section, we compare directly the mean results obtained by ANDE, ANDE-1, and ANDE-2 with the ones obtained by SDENS [37], jDElsgo [36], DECC-DML [27], DASA [35], EOEA [28], MA-SW-CHAINS [38], and DMS-PSO-SHS [39]. Tables S4–S6 contain the results obtained by ANDE, ANDE-1, and ANDE-2 in $1.2e + 05$, $6.0e + 05$, and $3.0e + 06$ function evaluations (FEs), respectively. For remarking the best algorithm, best median and mean for each function are highlighted in boldface. From these tables we have highlighted the following direct comparisons and conclusions.

(i) For many test functions, the worst results obtained by the proposed algorithms are better than the best results obtained by other algorithms with all FEs.

(ii) For many test functions, there is continuous improvement in the results obtained by our proposed algorithms, especially ANDE and ANDE-1, with all FEs while the results with FEs = $6.0E + 05$ are very close to the results with FEs = $3.0E + 06$ obtained by some of the compared algorithms which indicate that our proposed approaches are scalable enough and can balance greatly the exploration and exploitation abilities for solving high-dimensional problems until the maximum FEs are reached.

(iii) For many functions, the remarkable performance of ANDE and its two versions with FEs = $1.20E + 05$ and FEs = $6.0E + 05$ compared to the performance of other algorithms shows its fast convergence behavior.

TABLE 4: Results of multiple-problem Wilcoxon's test for ANDE, ANDE-1, and ANDE-2 versus SDENS, jDElsgo, DECC-DML, DASA, EOEA, MA-SW-CHAINS, and DMS-PSO-SHS over all functions at a significance level 0.05 (with $1.25E + 05$ FEs).

Algorithm	R^+	R^-	p value	Better	Equal	Worse	Dec.
ANDE versus SDENS	203	7	0.000	19	0	11	+
ANDE versus jDElsgo	210	0	0.000	20	0	0	+
ANDE versus DECC-DML	162	48	0.033	14	0	6	+
ANDE versus DASA	44	166	0.023	6	0	14	−
ANDE versus EOEA	26	184	0.003	2	0	18	−
ANDE versus MA-SW-CHAINS	30	180	0.005	2	0	18	−
ANDE versus DMS-PSO-SHS	104	106	0.970	12	0	8	≈
ANDE-1 versus SDENS	210	0	0.000	20	0	0	+
ANDE-1 versus jDElsgo	210	0	0.000	20	0	0	+
ANDE-1 versus DECC-DML	149	61	0.100	13	0	7	≈
ANDE-1 versus DASA	44	166	0.023	6	0	14	−
ANDE-1 versus EOEA	61	149	0.100	4	0	16	≈
ANDE-1 versus MA-SW-CHAINS	19	191	0.001	2	0	18	−
ANDE-1 versus DMS-PSO-SHS	110	100	0.852	12	0	8	≈
ANDE-2 versus SDENS	185	25	0.003	17	0	3	+
ANDE-2 versus jDElsgo	194	16	0.001	18	0	2	+
ANDE-2 versus DECC-DML	157	53	0.052	15	0	5	≈
ANDE-2 versus DASA	45	165	0.025	6	0	14	−
ANDE-2 versus EOEA	37	173	0.011	3	0	17	−
ANDE-2 versus MA-SW-CHAINS	31	179	0.006	4	0	16	−
ANDE-2 versus DMS-PSO-SHS	105	105	1	13	0	7	≈

Thus, our proposed algorithms can perform well and achieve good results within limited number of function evaluations which is very important issue when dealing with real-world problems.

(iv) ANDE and its two versions got very close to the optimum of single-group m-nonseparable multimodal functions F_6 in all statistical results with $1.20E + 05$ FEs.

(v) ANDE-1, among all other algorithms, got very close to the optimum of single-group m-nonseparable multimodal functions F_8 in the best and median results with $3.0E + 06$ FEs.

(vi) The performance of ANDE and ANDE-1 is well in all types of problems indicating that it is less affected than the most of other algorithms by the characteristics of the problems.

Furthermore, compared to the complicated structures and number of methods and number of control parameters used in other algorithms such as EOEA that uses three EAs optimizers within CC framework plus estimation of distribution algorithm (EDA), we can see that our proposed three ANDEs are very simple and easy to be implemented and programmed in many programming languages. They only use very simple self-adaptive crossover rate with two parameters and a free parameters novel triangular mutation rule and basic mutation. Thus, they neither increase the complexity of the original DE algorithm nor increase the number of control parameters. In order to investigate and compare the performance of the proposed algorithms ANDE, ANDE-1, and ANDE-2 against other algorithms in statistical sense, multiproblem Wilcoxon signed-rank test at a significance level 0.05 is performed on mean errors of all problems (with $1.25E + 05$ FEs, $6.00E + 05$ FEs, and $3.00E + 06$ FEs) and the results are presented in Tables 4, 5, and 6, respectively, where R^+ is the sum of ranks for the functions in which first algorithm outperforms the second algorithm in the row, and R^- is the sum of ranks for the opposite.

From Table 4, it can be obviously seen that ANDE is significantly better than SDENS, jDElsgo, and DECC-DML algorithms; ANDE is significantly worse than DASA, EOEA, and MA-SW-CHAINS algorithms. Besides, there is no significant difference between DMS-PSO-SHS and ANDE. Besides, it can be obviously seen that ANDE-1 is significantly better than SDENS and jDElsgo algorithms; ANDE-1 is significantly worse than DASA and MA-SW-CHAINS algorithms. However, there is no significant difference between DMS-PSO-HA, DECC-DML, EOEA, and ANDE-1. Regarding ANDE-2, it is significantly better than SDENS and jDElsgo algorithms; ANDE-2 is significantly worse than DASA, EOEA, and MA-SW-CHAINS algorithms. Besides, there is no significant difference between ANDE-2 and DMS-PSO-SHS and DECC-DML.

On the other hand, from Table 5, it can be obviously seen that ANDE is significantly better than SDENS, jDElsgo, and DECC-DML algorithms; ANDE is significantly worse than MA-SW-CHAINS algorithms. Besides, there is no significant difference between DMS-PSO-HA, DASA, EOEA, and ANDE. Besides, ANDE-1 is significantly better than

TABLE 5: Results of multiple-problem Wilcoxon's test for ANDE, ANDE-1, and ANDE-2 versus SDENS, jDElsgo, DECC-DML, DASA, EOEA, MA-SW-CHAINS, and DMS-PSO-SHS over all functions at a significance level 0.05 (with $6.00E + 05$ FEs).

Algorithm	R^+	R^-	p value	Better	Equal	Worse	Dec.
ANDE versus SDENS	210	0	0.000	20	0	0	+
ANDE versus jDElsgo	192	18	0.001	18	0	2	+
ANDE versus DECC-DML	178	32	0.006	15	0	5	+
ANDE versus DASA	77	133	0.296	8	0	12	≈
ANDE versus EOEA	67	143	0.156	6	0	14	≈
ANDE versus MA-SW-CHAINS	38	172	0.012	1	0	15	+
ANDE versus DMS-PSO-SHS	78	132	0.313	8	0	12	≈
ANDE-1 versus SDENS	210	0	0.000	20	0	0	+
ANDE-1 versus jDElsgo	172	38	0.012	15	0	5	+
ANDE-1 versus DECC-DML	162	48	0.033	12	0	8	+
ANDE-1 versus DASA	87	123	0.502	8	0	12	≈
ANDE-1 versus EOEA	61	149	0.100	4	0	16	≈
ANDE-1 versus MA-SW-CHAINS	41	169	0.017	4	0	16	−
ANDE-1 versus DMS-PSO-SHS	93	117	0.654	9	0	11	≈
ANDE-2 versus SDENS	187	23	0.002	18	0	2	+
ANDE-2 versus jDElsgo	154	56	0.067	15	0	5	≈
ANDE-2 versus DECC-DML	154	56	0.067	14	0	6	≈
ANDE-2 versus DASA	60	150	0.093	7	0	13	≈
ANDE-2 versus EOEA	52	158	0.048	5	0	15	−
ANDE-2 versus MA-SW-CHAINS	43	167	0.021	6	0	14	−
ANDE-2 versus DMS-PSO-SHS	61	149	0.100	7	0	13	≈

TABLE 6: Results of multiple-problem Wilcoxon's test for ANDE, ANDE-1, and ANDE-2 versus SDENS, jDElsgo, DECC-DML, DASA, EOEA, MA-SW-CHAINS, and DMS-PSO-SHS over all functions at a significance level 0.05 (with $3.00E + 06$ FEs).

Algorithm	R^+	R^-	p value	Better	Equal	Worse	Dec.
ANDE versus SDENS	187	23	0.002	17	0	3	+
ANDE versus jDElsgo	31	179	0.006	4	0	16	−
ANDE versus DECC-DML	185	25	0.003	16	0	4	+
ANDE versus DASA	103	107	0.940	12	0	8	≈
ANDE versus EOEA	88	122	0.526	9	0	11	≈
ANDE versus MA-SW-CHAINS	66	144	0.145	8	0	12	≈
ANDE versus DMS-PSO-SHS	54	156	0.057	7	0	13	≈
ANDE-1 versus SDENS	187	23	0.002	17	0	3	+
ANDE-1 versus jDElsgo	50	160	0.040	5	0	15	−
ANDE-1 versus DECC-DML	164	26	0.005	13	1	6	+
ANDE-1 versus DASA	122	88	0.526	12	0	8	≈
ANDE-1 versus EOEA	100	110	0.852	9	0	11	≈
ANDE-1 versus MA-SW-CHAINS	85	125	0.455	9	0	11	≈
ANDE-1 versus DMS-PSO-SHS	87	123	0.502	8	0	12	≈
ANDE-2 versus SDENS	155	55	0.062	15	0	5	≈
ANDE-2 versus jDElsgo	19	191	0.001	4	0	16	−
ANDE-2 versus DECC-DML	131	79	0.332	10	0	10	≈
ANDE-2 versus DASA	64	146	0.126	8	0	12	≈
ANDE-2 versus EOEA	41	169	0.017	5	0	15	−
ANDE-2 versus MA-SW-CHAINS	40	170	0.015	5	0	15	−
ANDE-2 versus DMS-PSO-SHS	21	189	0.002	16	0	4	−

SDENS, DECC-DML, and jDElsgo algorithms; ANDE-1 is significantly worse than MA-SW-CHAINS algorithms. Besides, there is no significant difference between DASA, EOEA, DMS-PSO-SHS, and ANDE-1. Besides, ANDE-2 is significantly better than SDENS algorithm; ANDE-2 is significantly worse than EOEA and MA-SW-CHAINS algorithms. Besides, there is no significant difference between jDElsgo, DECC-DML, DASA, DMS-PSO-SHS, and ANDE-2.

Finally, from Table 6, it can be obviously seen that HDE is significantly better than SDENS and DECC-DML algorithms; HDE is significantly worse than jDElsgo algorithm. Besides, there is no significant difference between DMS-PSO-SHS, DASA, EOEA, MA-SW-CHAINS, and HDE.

Additionally, it can be obviously seen that HDE-1 is significantly better than SDENS and DECC-DML algorithms; HDE-1 is significantly worse than jDElsgo algorithm. Besides, there is no significant difference between DMS-PSO-SHS, DASA, EOEA, MA-SW-CHAINS, and ANDE-1. However, it can be obviously seen that ANDE-2 is significantly worse than jDElsgo, EOEA, MA-SW-CHAINS, and DMS-PSO-SHS algorithms. Besides, there is no significant difference between SDENS, DECC-DML, DASA, and ANDE-2.

From Tables 4 and 5, it is noteworthy that ANDE-2 is better than all DEs algorithms (SDENS, jDElsgo, and DECC-DML) which indicate that the proposed self-adaptive crossover strategy improves the performance of the exploration capability of the basic DE in the earlier search stages. However, from Table 6, the poor performance of ANDE-2 algorithm in the remaining function evaluations is due to the fact that it has great global exploration ability with weak local exploitation tendency leading to inability of finding promising subregions that may deteriorate the overall performance as well as cause stagnation with almost benchmark problems. However, it is still statistically equal to SDENS, DECC-DML, and DASA algorithms. Therefore, taking into consideration the results obtained by a very simple version ANDE-2 plus remarkable performance of ANDE and ANDE-1 in the majority of the problems, it can be obviously concluded from direct and statistical results that ANDE and its versions are powerful algorithms and they are competitive with, and in some cases superior to, other existing algorithms in terms of the quality, efficiency, and robustness of the final solution.

6. A Parametric Study on ANDE

In this section, as the performance of ANDE and ANDE-1 is almost similar but ANDE converged to better solutions faster than ANDE-1 in many problems and ANDE explicitly includes both ANDE-1 and ANDE-2 versions, some experiments are carried out so as to identify the key parameters that significantly lead to the perfect performance of our proposed approach by studying the effects of the self-adaptive crossover rate scheme and the learning period as well as the maximum failure counter on the performance of ANDE algorithm. Note that in this study we do not try to find the optimal values for these parameters but to verify that the improved performance obtained after combining the proposed self-adaptive crossover rate into basic and proposed mutation schemes.

6.1. Efficacy of Parameter Adaptation and Setting. In the following three subsections, we investigate the effectiveness of the self-adaptive crossover scheme and we experimentally determine the appropriate values of the learning period and maximum failure counter parameters. Since they are not associated with the hybridization process and they have approximately the same effect with different number of function evaluations (FEs), the solution errors of all variants of ANDE are only recorded in $6.0E + 05$ function evaluations (FEs) as a median value of number of function evaluations; all experiments for each function run 25 times independently and statistical results are provided including the best, median, mean, and worst results and the standard deviation. Besides, since the adaptation scheme of crossover is not used with problems F_1–F_3, they are excluded from comparison.

6.1.1. Effectiveness of the Crossover Adaptation Procedure. In this subsection, some trials have been performed to evaluate the benefits and effectiveness of the proposed crossover rate adaptation scheme on the performance on the ANDE algorithm. Since all problems with exception to F_1–F_3 are partially or fully separable problems in nature, it is preferred to evaluate HDE algorithm with three different values of CR such as 0.1, 0.5, and 0.9. The following versions were implemented for comparisons:

(1) $ANDE_{CR=0.1}$, which is the same as ANDE except that the crossover rate CR is set to a constant number 0.1

(2) $ANDE_{CR=0.5}$, which is the same as ANDE except that the crossover rate CR is set to a constant number 0.5

(3) $ANDE_{CR=0.9}$, which is the same as ANDE except that the crossover rate CR is set to a constant number 0.9

On the other hand, in order to show the efficacy of the construction of the learning period of the self-adaptive crossover rate, Procedure 1 has been modified such that it uses only one list that contains all possible values of CR from the beginning of the learning period (LP) and, hence, all the values have an equally likely chance of occurrence instead of using it in the second half of the learning period (LP). The procedure with the proposed modification is explained in Procedure 2.

The new version of ANDE algorithm is called ANDE with one fixed list of CR values during the LP and it is abbreviated (ANDE-OFL).

The statistical results including the best, median, mean, and worst results and the standard deviation over 25 independent runs of these algorithms are summarized in Table S7.

It can be obviously seen from Table 7 that ANDE is significantly better than $ANDE_{CR=0.5}$, $ANDE_{CR=0.9}$, and ANDE-OFL algorithms. Besides, there is no significant difference between $ANDE_{CR=0.1}$ and ANDE. However, although no significant difference exists between ANDE and $ANDE_{CR=0.1}$, we can still say that ANDE performs better than $ANDE_{CR=0.1}$ because the R^+ value of ANDE is much larger than the R^- one. Moreover, ANDE outperforms $ANDE_{CR=0.1}$ in 10 problems out of 17 problems while losing to $ANDE_{CR=0.1}$ in 7 problems which are F_6, F_8, F_{11}, F_{13}, F_{16}, F_{18}, and F_{20} (Ackley and

---

If ((CR_Flag_List[i] = 0) and (G <= LP)), If the target vector is better than the trial vector during the learning period, then:
Cr$_i$ = Randomly select one value from A, $A = [0.05, 0.1, 0.2, 0.3, 0.4, 0.5, 0.6, 0.7, 0.8, 0.9, 0.95]$, $0 \le G \le$ LP
Else If ((CR_Flag_List[i] = 0) and ($G >$ LP)), If the target vector is better than the trial vector after the learning period, then:
    If the failure_counter_list[i] = Max_failure_counter,
    Randomly select one value from list A, $A = [0.05, 0.1, 0.2, 0.3, 0.4, 0.5, 0.6, 0.7, 0.8, 0.9, 0.95]$.
    else
    failure_counter_list[i]= *failure_counter_list*[i] + 1;
    End If
Else ((CR_Flag_List[i] = 1)), If the trial vector is better than the target vector through generations, then:
    Select the value from A with maximum CR ratio from CR_Ratio_List[k].
End IF

PROCEDURE 2

TABLE 7: Results of the multiple-problem Wilcoxon's test for ANDE, ANDE$_{CR=0.1}$, ANDE$_{CR=0.5}$, ANDE$_{CR=0.9}$, and ANDE-OFL over all functions at a significance level 0.05 (with $6.00E + 05$ FEs).

Algorithm	R^+	R^-	p value	Better	Equal	Worse	Dec.
ANDE versus ANDE$_{CR=0.1}$	117	36	0.055	10	0	7	$\approx$
ANDE versus ANDE$_{CR=0.5}$	144	9	0.001	15	0	2	+
ANDE versus ANDE$_{CR=0.9}$	146	7	0.001	16	0	1	+
ANDE versus ANDE-OFL	145	8	0.001	16	0	1	+

Rosenbrock) with all types of modality and nonseparability. This proves that the proposed triangular mutation with small value of CR performs well on some unimodal, multimodal, and nonseparable problems. Regarding the remaining problems, ANDE can perform well with the unknown optimal CR value that is appropriate for these types of problems. Additionally, it also shows the effectiveness of our proposed novel idea about the gradual increase of the crossover rate during the initial stage of the search process. In fact, the main idea behind this comparison is to prove that the proposed ANDE algorithm can achieve the same results on some of the problems but when CR is tuned manually. Therefore, it proves that the proposed mutation scheme has well exploration and exploitation abilities with associated appropriate CR values for each problem. Besides, it also proves that the proposed self-adaptive scheme of CR plays a vital role in determining the optimal CR values for all problems during the optimization process. Therefore, the statistical analysis on the results in Table 7 confirms that ANDE with the proposed self-adaptive crossover scheme outperforms the other compared ANDE versions with constant CR value and with one fixed list of CR values.

6.1.2. Parametric Study on the Learning Period Parameter.
The crossover (CR) practically controls the diversity of the population and it is directly affected by the value of the learning period parameter. In this subsection, some trials have been performed to determine the suitable values of learning period (LP). Thus, the performance of ANDE has been investigated under two different LP values (5% GEN and 20% GEN) and the results have been compared to those obtained by the value of 10% GEN. To analyze the sensitivity of this parameter, we further tested two extra configurations:

(1) ANDE$_{LP=5\%}$, which is the same as ANDE except that the leaning period was set to LP = 5% GEN

(2) ANDE$_{LP=20\%}$, which is the same as ANDE except that the leaning period was set to LP = 20% GEN

The statistical results including the best, median, mean, and worst results and the standard deviation over 25 independent runs of these algorithms are summarized in Table S8.

It can be obviously seen from Table 8 that ANDE is significantly better than ANDE$_{LP=20\%}$ algorithm. Besides, there is no significant difference between ANDE$_{LP=5\%}$ and ANDE. However, Table 8 shows that ANDE obtains higher R^+ value, which means that ANDE is overall better than ANDE$_{LP=5\%}$. Moreover, from Table 8, ANDE outperforms ANDE$_{LP=5\%}$ and ANDE$_{LP=20\%}$ in 13 problems out of 17 problems while losing to ANDE$_{LP=5\%}$ and ANDE$_{LP=20\%}$ in 4 problems which indicate that the performance of ANDE with the value of LP 10% is better than the performance of ANDE with the other two learning periods. However, this is not meaning that the LP of 10% is suitable for all problems with all function evaluations. Indeed, by a closer look at Tables 2 and 3, it can be seen that the solution of F_6 obtained by the three algorithms using $6.00E+5$ FEs is better than the solution achieved using $3.00E + 06$. The main reason of this case can be obviously deduced from the convergence performance for F_6 presented in Figure S1. It shows very fast convergence of all algorithms in the first $2.0E + 05$ evaluations which is considered to be premature convergence, meaning that, in the rest of the given time interval, the algorithms are slowly moving in the neighborhood of a local optimum. This is due to the delay in finding the suitable crossover value during the learning period which is 6000 generations. Practically, we applied the same learning period of $6.00E + 05$ FEs which is

TABLE 8: Results of the multiple-problem Wilcoxon's test for ANDE, $HDE_{LP=5\%}$, and $HDE_{LP=20\%}$ over all functions at a significance level 0.05 (with $6.00E + 05$ FEs).

Algorithm	R^+	R^-	p value	Better	Equal	Worse	Dec.
ANDE versus $HDE_{LP=5\%}$	103.5	49.5	0.201	13	0	4	$\approx$
ANDE versus $HDE_{LP=20\%}$	126	27	0.019	13	0	4	$+$

TABLE 9: Results of the multiple-problem Wilcoxon's test for ANDE, $ANDE_{MFC=0}$, $ANDE_{MFC=10}$, and $ANDE_{MFC=30}$ over all functions at a significance level 0.05 (with $6.00E + 05$ FEs).

Algorithm	R^+	R^-	p value	Better	Equal	Worse	Dec.
ANDE versus $ANDE_{MFC=0}$	123	30	0.028	13	0	4	$+$
ANDE versus $ANDE_{MFC=10}$	81	55	0.501	9	1	7	$\approx$
ANDE versus $ANDE_{MFC=30}$	127	26	0.017	13	0	4	$+$

1200 generations with $3.0E + 06$ FEs; the same results were achieved and another premature convergence or stagnation occurred again in another point as the $6.0E + 05$ case. The new best, median, worst, mean, standard deviation results obtained by ANDE were $2.44E + 00$, $3.07E + 00$, $7.27E + 00$, $4.19E + 00$, and $1.82E + 00$. The new convergence figure of the new median run compared to ANDE-1 and ANDE-2 is presented in Figure S2. Therefore, the learning period plays a vital role in optimization process and it is surely varied from one problem to another. Really, future research will focus on how to control the learning period. Overall, the learning period is suitable for all other problems as explained.

6.1.3. Parametric Study on the Maximum Failure Counter. In this subsection, some trials have been performed to determine the appropriate values of maximum failure counter (MFC). The crossover (CR) practically controls the diversity of the population and it is directly affected by the value of the maximum failure counter parameter. Thus, the performance of ANDE has been investigated under three different maximum failure counter values (0, 10, and 30) and the results have been compared to those obtained by the value of 10. To analyze the sensitivity of this parameter, we further tested three extra configurations:

(1) $ANDE_{MFC=0}$, which is the same as ANDE except that the maximum failure counter was set to MFC = 0

(2) $ANDE_{MFC=10}$, which is the same as ANDE except that the maximum failure counter was set to MFC = 10

(3) $ANDE_{MFC=30}$, which is the same as ANDE except that the maximum failure counter was set to MFC = 30

The statistical results including the best, median, mean, and worst results and the standard deviation over 25 independent runs of these algorithms are summarized in Table S9.

It can be obviously seen from Table 9 that ANDE is significantly better than $ANDE_{MFC=0}$ algorithm which shows the vital role and benefits of introducing (MFC) in the proposed self-adaptive CR scheme. Besides, there is no significant difference between $ANDE_{MFC=10}$ and ANDE. Moreover, ANDE outperforms $ANDE_{MFC=10}$ in 9 problems out of 17 problems while it loses to $ANDE_{MFC=10}$ in 7 problems and ties in 1 problem indicating that the performance of ANDE with the value of MFC = 10 is almost similar to the performance of ANDE with MFC = 20. However, ANDE is significantly better than $ANDE_{MFC=30}$ deducing that the increasing of MFC value has negative effect that could lead to significant deterioration in the performance of ANDE algorithm. From the above statistical analysis, it can be concluded that ANDE with self-adaptive crossover rate and with learning period LP of 5% or 10% and maximum failure counter (MFC) of 10–20 generations performs well in the majority of the problems.

7. Conclusion

In order to efficiently concentrate the exploitation tendency of some subregion of the search space and to significantly promote the exploration capability in whole search space during the evolutionary process of the conventional DE algorithm, a Differential Evolution (ANDE) algorithm for solving large scale global numerical optimization problems over continuous space was presented in this paper. The proposed algorithm introduced a new triangular mutation rule based on the convex combination vector of the triplet defined by the three randomly chosen vectors and the difference vectors between the best, better, and the worst individuals among the three randomly selected vectors. The mutation rule is combined with the basic mutation strategy DE/rand/1/bin, where only one of the two mutation rules is applied with the probability of 2/3 since it has both exploration ability and exploitation tendency. Furthermore, we propose a novel self-adaptive scheme for gradual change of the values of the crossover rate that can excellently benefit from the past experience of the individuals in the search space during evolution process which in turn can considerably balance the common trade-off between the population diversity and convergence speed. The proposed mutation rule was shown to enhance the global and local search capabilities of the basic DE and to increase the convergence speed. The algorithm has been evaluated on the standard high-dimensional benchmark problems. The comparison results between ANDE and its versions and the other seven state-of-the-art evolutionary algorithms that were all tested on this test suite on the IEEE congress on evolutionary competition in 2010 indicate that the proposed algorithm and its two versions are highly competitive algorithms for solving large scale global optimization problem. The experimental results and comparisons showed that the ANDE algorithm performed better in large scale global optimization problems with different types and complexity; it performed better with regard to the search process efficiency, the final solution quality, the convergence rate, and robustness, when compared with other algorithms. Finally, the performance of the ANDE algorithm was statistically superior to and competitive with other recent and well-known DEs and non-DEs algorithms. The effectiveness and benefits of the proposed modifications used in ANDE were experimentally investigated and compared. It was found that the two proposed algorithms ANDE and ANDE-1 are competitive in terms of quality of solution, efficiency, convergence rate, and robustness. They were statistically superior to the state-of-the-art DEs and non-DEs algorithms. Besides, they perform better than ANDE-2 algorithm in many cases. Although the remarkable performance of ANDE-2 was competitive with some of the compared algorithms, several current and future works can be developed from this study. Firstly, current research effort focuses on how to control the scaling factors by self-adaptive mechanism and develop another self-adaptive mechanism for crossover rate. Additionally, the new version of ANDE combined with Cooperative Coevolution (CC) framework is being developed and will be experimentally investigated soon. Moreover, future research will investigate the performance of the ANDE algorithm in solving constrained and multiobjective optimization problems as well as real-world applications such as data mining and clustering problems. In addition, large scale combinatorial optimization problems will be taken into consideration. Another possible direction is integrating the proposed triangular mutation scheme with all compared and other self-adaptive DE variants plus combining the proposed self-adaptive crossover with other DE mutation schemes. Additionally, the promising research direction is joining the proposed triangular mutation with evolutionary algorithms, such as genetic algorithms, harmony search, and particle swarm optimization, as well as foraging algorithms such as artificial bee colony, bees algorithm, and Ant-Colony Optimization.

Competing Interests

The authors declare that they have no competing interests.

References

[1] K. Tang, X. Li, P. N. Suganthan, Z. Yang, and T. Weise, "Benchmark functions for the CEC 2010 special session and competition on large scale global optimization," Tech. Rep., Nature Inspired Computation and Applications Laboratory, USTC, Hefei, China, 2009.

[2] K. Tang, X. Yao, P. N. Suganthan et al., "Benchmark functions for the CEC2008 special session and competition on large scale global optimization," Technical Report for CEC 2008 special issue, 2007.

[3] A. P. Engelbrecht, *Computational Intelligence: An Introduction*, Wiley-Blackwell, 2002.

[4] R. Storn and K. Price, "Differential evolution—a simple and efficient heuristic for global optimization over continuous spaces,"

Journal of Global Optimization, vol. 11, no. 4, pp. 341–359, 1997.

[5] S. A. El-Quliti, A. H. Ragab, R. Abdelaal et al., "A nonlinear goal programming model for university admission capacity planning with modified differential evolution algorithm," *Mathematical Problems in Engineering*, vol. 2015, Article ID 892937, 13 pages, 2015.

[6] S. A. El-Qulity and A. W. Mohamed, "A generalized national planning approach for admission capacity in higher education: a nonlinear integer goal programming model with a novel differential evolution algorithm," *Computational Intelligence and Neuroscience*, vol. 2016, Article ID 5207362, 14 pages, 2016.

[7] N. Hachicha, B. Jarboui, and P. Siarry, "A fuzzy logic control using a differential evolution algorithm aimed at modelling the financial market dynamics," *Information Sciences*, vol. 181, no. 1, pp. 79–91, 2011.

[8] S. A. El-Quliti and A. W. Mohamed, "A large-scale nonlinear mixed-binary goal programming model to assess candidate locations for solar energy stations: an improved binary differential evolution algorithm with a case study," *Journal of Computational and Theoretical Nanoscience*, vol. 13, no. 11, pp. 7909–7921, 2016.

[9] S. Das and P. N. Suganthan, "Differential evolution: a survey of the state-of-the-art," *IEEE Transactions on Evolutionary Computation*, vol. 15, no. 1, pp. 4–31, 2011.

[10] N. Noman and H. Iba, "Accelerating differential evolution using an adaptive local search," *IEEE Transactions on Evolutionary Computation*, vol. 12, no. 1, pp. 107–125, 2008.

[11] S. Das, A. Abraham, U. K. Chakraborty, and A. Konar, "Differential evolution using a neighborhood-based mutation operator," *IEEE Transactions on Evolutionary Computation*, vol. 13, no. 3, pp. 526–553, 2009.

[12] J. Lampinen and I. Zelinka, "On stagnation of the differential evolution algorithm," in *Proceedings of the Mendel 6th International Conference on Soft Computing*, pp. 76–83, Brno, Czech Republic, June 2000.

[13] A. W. Mohamed and H. Z. Sabry, "Constrained optimization based on modified differential evolution algorithm," *Information Sciences*, vol. 194, pp. 171–208, 2012.

[14] A. W. Mohamed, H. Z. Sabry, and M. Khorshid, "An alternative differential evolution algorithm for global optimization," *Journal of Advanced Research*, vol. 3, no. 2, pp. 149–165, 2012.

[15] A. K. Qin, V. L. Huang, and P. N. Suganthan, "Differential evolution algorithm with strategy adaptation for global numerical optimization," *IEEE Transactions on Evolutionary Computation*, vol. 13, no. 2, pp. 398–417, 2009.

[16] A. W. Mohamed, "Solving stochastic programming problems using new approach to differential evolution algorithm," *Egyptian Informatics Journal*, 2016.

[17] R. Mallipeddi, P. N. Suganthan, Q. K. Pan, and M. F. Tasgetiren, "Differential evolution algorithm with ensemble of parameters and mutation strategies," *Applied Soft Computing*, vol. 11, no. 2, pp. 1679–1696, 2011.

[18] A. W. Mohamed, "An efficient modified differential evolution algorithm for solving constrained non-linear integer and mixed-integer global optimization problems," *International Journal of Machine Learning and Cybernetics*, 2015.

[19] A. W. Mohamed, "A new modified binary differential evolution algorithm and its applications," *Applied Mathematics & Information Sciences*, vol. 10, no. 5, pp. 1965–1969, 2016.

[20] A. Wagdy Mohamed, H. Z. Sabry, and A. Farhat, "Advanced differential evolution algorithm for global numerical optimization," in *Proceedings of the IEEE International Conference on Computer Applications and Industrial Electronics (ICCAIE '11)*, pp. 156–161, Penang, Malaysia, December 2011.

[21] A. W. Mohamed, H. Z. Sabry, and T. Abd-Elaziz, "Real parameter optimization by an effective differential evolution algorithm," *Egyptian Informatics Journal*, vol. 14, no. 1, pp. 37–53, 2013.

[22] A. W. Mohamed, "A novel differential evolution algorithm for solving constrained engineering optimization problems," *Journal of Intelligent Manufacturing*, pp. 1–34, 2017.

[23] H.-Y. Fan and J. Lampinen, "A trigonometric mutation operation to differential evolution," *Journal of Global Optimization*, vol. 27, no. 1, pp. 105–129, 2003.

[24] K. V. Price, R. M. Storn, and J. A. Lampinen, *Differential Evolution: A Practical Approach to Global Optimization*, Natural Computing Series, Springer, New York, NY, USA, 1st edition, 2005.

[25] A. M. Potter and K. A. D. Jong, "A cooperative co-evolutionary approach to function optimization," in *Proceedings of the 3rd International Conference on Parallel Problem Solving from the Nature*, pp. 249–257, Springer, October 1994.

[26] Z. Yang, K. Tang, and X. Yao, "Large scale evolutionary optimization using cooperative co-evolution," *Information Sciences*, vol. 178, no. 15, pp. 2985–2999, 2008.

[27] M. N. Omidvar, X. D. Li, and X. Yao, "Cooperative co-evolution with delta grouping for large scale non-separable function optimization," in *Proceedings of the IEEE Congress on Evolutionary Computation (CEC '10)*, pp. 1762–1769, 2010.

[28] Y. Wang and B. Li, "Two-stage based ensemble optimization for large-scale global optimization," in *Proceedings of the IEEE Congress on Evolutionary Computation (CEC '10)*, pp. 4488–4495, Barcelona, Spain, July 2010.

[29] Y. Wang and B. Li, "A self-adaptive mixed distribution based uni-variate estimation of distribution algorithm for large scale global optimization," in *Nature-Inspired Algorithms for Optimisation*, R. Chiong, Ed., vol. 193 of *Studies in Computational Intelligence*, pp. 171–198, Springer, Berlin, Germany, 2009.

[30] Y. Liu, X. Yao, Q. Zhao, and T. Higuchi, "Scaling up fast evolutionary porgramming with cooperative co-evolution," in *Proceedings of the IEEE World Congress on Computational Intelligence*, pp. 1101–1108, 2001.

[31] Z. Yang, K. Tang, and X. Yao, "Differential evolution for high-dimensional function optimization," in *Proceedings of the IEEE Congress on Evolutionary Computation (CEC '07)*, pp. 3523–3530, IEEE, Singapore, September 2007.

[32] Z. Yang, K. Tang, and X. Yao, "Multilevel cooperative coevolution for large scale optimization," in *Proceedings of the IEEE Congress on Evolutionary Computation (CEC '08)*, pp. 1663–1670, June 2008.

[33] A. Zamuda, J. Brest, B. Bošović, and V. Žumer, "Large scale global optimization using differential evolution with self-adaptation and cooperative co-evolution," in *Proceedings of the IEEE Congress on Evolutionary Computation (CEC '08)*, June 2008.

[34] F. van den Bergh and A. P. Engelbrecht, "A cooperative approach to participle swam optimization," *IEEE Transactions on Evolutionary Computation*, vol. 8, no. 3, pp. 225–239, 2004.

[35] K. Korošec, K. Tashkova, and J. Šilc, "The differential ant-stigmergy algorithm for large-scale global optimization," in *Proceedings of the IEEE Congress on Evolutionary Computation*, pp. 4288–4295, Barcelona, Spain, 2010.

[36] J. Brest, A. Zamuda, I. Fister, and M. S. Maučec, "Large scale global optimization using self-adaptive differential evolution algorithm," in *Proceedings of the IEEE Congress on Evolutionary Computation (CEC '10)*, pp. 3097–3104, July 2010.

[37] H. Wang, Z. Wu, S. Rahnamayan, D. Jiang, and D. E. Sequential, "Enhanced by neighborhood search for large scale global optimization," in *Proceedings of the IEEE Congress on Evolutionary Computation*, pp. 4056–4062, Barcelona, Spain, July 2010.

[38] D. Molina, M. Lozano, and F. Herrera, "MA-SW-Chains: memetic algorithm based on local search chains for large scale continuous global optimization," in *Proceedings of the 6th IEEE World Congress on Computational Intelligence (WCCI '10)—IEEE Congress on Evolutionary Computation (CEC '10)*, esp, July 2010.

[39] S.-Z. Zhao, P. N. Suganthan, and S. Das, "Dynamic multi-swarm particle swarm optimizer with sub-regional harmony search," in *Proceedings of the 6th IEEE World Congress on Computational Intelligence (WCCI '10)—IEEE Congress on Evolutionary Computation (CEC '10)*, July 2010.

[40] Y. Wang, Z. Cai, and Q. Zhang, "Differential evolution with composite trial vector generation strategies and control parameters," *IEEE Transactions on Evolutionary Computation*, vol. 15, no. 1, pp. 55–66, 2011.

[41] V. Feoktistov, *Differential Evolution, in Search of Solutions*, vol. 5, Springer, New York, NY, USA, 2006.

[42] J. Ronkkonen, S. Kukkonen, and K. V. Price, "Real parameter optimization with differential evolution," in *Proceedings of the IEEE Congress on Evolutionary Computation (CEC '05)*, pp. 506–513, Edinburgh, UK, 2005.

[43] J. Brest, S. Greiner, B. Bošković, M. Mernik, and V. Zumer, "Self-adapting control parameters in differential evolution: a comparative study on numerical benchmark problems," *IEEE Transactions on Evolutionary Computation*, vol. 10, no. 6, pp. 646–657, 2006.

[44] M. Weber, F. Neri, and V. Tirronen, "A study on scale factor in distributed differential evolution," *Information Sciences*, vol. 181, no. 12, pp. 2488–2511, 2011.

[45] R. A. Sarker, S. M. Elsayed, and T. Ray, "Differential evolution with dynamic parameters selection for optimization problems," *IEEE Transactions on Evolutionary Computation*, vol. 18, no. 5, pp. 689–707, 2014.

[46] S. M. Elsayed, R. A. Sarker, and D. L. Essam, "An improved self-adaptive differential evolution algorithm for optimization problems," *IEEE Transactions on Industrial Informatics*, vol. 9, no. 1, pp. 89–99, 2013.

[47] A. W. Mohamed, "An improved differential evolution algorithm with triangular mutation for global numerical optimization," *Computers and Industrial Engineering*, vol. 85, pp. 359–375, 2015.

[48] S. Chen, "Locust Swarms for Large Scale Global Optimization for Nonseparable Problems".

[49] S. García, D. Molina, M. Lozano, and F. Herrera, "A study on the use of non-parametric tests for analyzing the evolutionary algorithms' behaviour: a case study on the CEC'2005 special session on real parameter optimization," *Journal of Heuristics*, vol. 15, no. 6, pp. 617–644, 2009.

3

Data-Driven Machine-Learning Model in District Heating System for Heat Load Prediction

Fisnik Dalipi,[1] Sule Yildirim Yayilgan,[1] and Alemayehu Gebremedhin[2]

[1]Faculty of Computer Science and Media Technology, Norwegian University of Science and Technology, 2815 Gjøvik, Norway
[2]Faculty of Technology and Management, Norwegian University of Science and Technology, 2815 Gjøvik, Norway

Correspondence should be addressed to Fisnik Dalipi; fisnik.dalipi@ntnu.no

Academic Editor: Shyi-Ming Chen

We present our data-driven supervised machine-learning (ML) model to predict heat load for buildings in a district heating system (DHS). Even though ML has been used as an approach to heat load prediction in literature, it is hard to select an approach that will qualify as a solution for our case as existing solutions are quite problem specific. For that reason, we compared and evaluated three ML algorithms within a framework on operational data from a DH system in order to generate the required prediction model. The algorithms examined are Support Vector Regression (SVR), Partial Least Square (PLS), and random forest (RF). We use the data collected from buildings at several locations for a period of 29 weeks. Concerning the accuracy of predicting the heat load, we evaluate the performance of the proposed algorithms using mean absolute error (MAE), mean absolute percentage error (MAPE), and correlation coefficient. In order to determine which algorithm had the best accuracy, we conducted performance comparison among these ML algorithms. The comparison of the algorithms indicates that, for DH heat load prediction, SVR method presented in this paper is the most efficient one out of the three also compared to other methods found in the literature.

1. Introduction

As stated in the report of European Commission strategy for energy, the continuous growing of energy demand worldwide has made energy security a major concern for EU citizens. This demand is expected to increase by 27% by 2030, with important changes to energy supply and trade [1]. Being the largest energy and CO_2 emitter in the EU, the building sector is responsible for 40–50% of energy consumption in Europe and about 30–40% worldwide [2]. The North European countries have proved themselves as forerunners in the development and application of clean and sustainable energy solutions. Their excellent performance on adopting such solutions enables them to achieve ambitious national climate objectives and requirements and to serve as key players in the entire European energy system [3].

District heating (DH) system is an optimal way of supplying heat to various sectors of the society such as industrial, public, or private buildings. DH network offers functional, economic, and ecological advantages and is also instrumental in reducing the global and local CO_2 emissions. It offers an enormous adaptability to combine different types of energy sources efficiently [4]. Considering the recent technological trends of progressing to smart energy infrastructures, the development of the fourth generation of district heating implies meeting the objective of more energy-efficient buildings. Moreover, this also envisions DH networks to be as an integrated part of the operation of smart energy systems, that is, integrated smart electricity, gas, and thermal grids [5]. The application of new and innovative technology in district heating is therefore considered essential to improve energy efficiency [6].

The deregulation of the electricity market and the increasing share of energy-efficient buildings have put district heating in a more vulnerable position with regard to challenges in terms of cost effectiveness, supply security, and energy sustainability within the local heat market. With this background, it is therefore important for district heating sector to maintain an efficient and competitive district heating system which is able to meet the various requirements which characterize the heat market. In a flexible district heating system with multiple energy sources and production technologies, the need for accurate load forecasting has become more and more important. This is especially important in a district heating system with simultaneous production of heat, steam, and electricity.

In this paper, with the application of three different ML algorithms to predict heat consumption, we investigate the performance of *Support Vector Regression* (SVR), *Partial Least Squares* (PLS), and *random forest* (RF) approach to develop heat load forecasting models by making a comparative study. Our focus is on low error, high accuracy, and validating our approach with real data. We also compare the error analysis of each algorithm with existing techniques (models) and also find the most efficient one out of the three.

The rest of the paper is organized as follows: Section 2 outlines the related work, where we provide an overview of many approaches to load prediction that are found in the literature. In Section 3, we provide some background information about DH concepts. This is followed by a presentation of the system framework and related prediction models, given in Section 4. Further, in Section 5, we present and discuss the evaluation and results. Finally, Section 6 concludes the paper.

2. Related Work

The state of the art in the area of energy (heating, cooling, and electric energy) demand estimation in buildings is classified as *forward (classical)* and *data-driven (inverse)* approaches [7]. While the forward modelling approach generally uses equations with physical parameters that describe the building as input, the inverse modelling approach uses machine-learning techniques. Here, the model takes the monitored building energy consumption data as inputs, which are expressed in terms of one or more driving variables and a set of empirical parameters and are widely applied for various measurements and other aspects of building performance [8]. The main advantage of data-driven models is that they can also operate online, making the process very easily updatable based on new data. Considering the fact that ML models offer powerful tools for discovery of patterns from large volumes of data and their ability to capture nonlinear behavior of the heat demand, they represent a suitable technique to predict the energy demand at the consumer side.

Numerous ML models and methods have been applied for heat load prediction during the last decade. A good overview of some recent references is given by Mestekemper [6, 9]. The former also built his own prediction models using dynamic factor models. A simple model proposed by Dotzauer [10] uses the ambient temperature and a weekly pattern for prediction of the heat demand in DH. The author makes the social component equal to a constant value for all days of the week. There is another interesting model, which address the utilization of a grey box that combines physical knowledge with mathematical modelling [11]. Some approaches to predict the heat load discussed in the literature include artificial neural networks (ANN) [12–15]. In [12], a backpropagation three-layered ANN is used for the prediction of the heat demand of different building samples. The inputs of the network for training and testing are building

transparency ratio (%), orientation angles (degrees), and insulation thickness (cm) and the output is building heating energy needs (Wh). When ANN's outputs of this study are compared with numerical results, average 94.8–98.5% accuracy is achieved. The authors have shown that ANN is a powerful tool for prediction of building energy needs. In [13], the authors discuss the way self-organizing maps (SOMs) and multilayer perceptrons (MLP) can be used to develop a two-stage algorithm for autonomous construction of prediction models. The problem of heat demand prediction in a district heating company is used as a case study where SOM is used as a means of grouping similar customer profiles in the first stage and MLP is used for predicting heat demand in the second stage. However, the authors do not provide any information related to the error rates obtained during the predictions.

In [14], recurrent neural networks (RNNs) are used for heat load prediction in district heating and cooling systems. The authors compare their prediction results from RNN with the prediction results obtained from a three layered feed forward neural network (TLNN). The mean squared error between the TLNN and the stationary actual heat load is reported to be 21.05^2 whereas it is 11.82^2 between the RNN and the actual heat load data. In the nonstationary case, RNN still provides lower mean squared error. The use of RNNs rises the expectation to capture the trend of heat load since it uses heat load data for several days as the input.

In [15], time, historical consumption data, and ambient temperatures were used as input parameters to forecast heat consumption for one week in the future. The authors compared the performances of three black-box modelling techniques SVR, PLS, and ANN for the prediction of heat consumption in the Suseo DH network and analyzed the accuracy of each method by comparing forecasting errors. The authors report that in one-day-ahead overall average error of PLS is 3.87% while that of ANN and SVR is 6.54% and 4.95%, respectively. The maximum error of SVR is 9.82%, which is lower than that of PLS (16.47%) and ANN (13.20%). In terms of the overall error, the authors indicate that PLS exhibits better forecasting performance than ANN or SVR.

In [16], a multiple regression (MR) model is used for heat load forecasting. The reported MAE is 9.30. The model described in [17] uses an online machine-learning approach named Fast Incremental Model Trees with Drift Detection (FIMT-DD) for heat load prediction and hence allows the flexibility of updating the model when the distribution of target variable changes. The results of the study indicate that MAE and MAPE for FIMT-DD (using Bagging) have lower values in comparison to Adaptive Model Rules (AMRules) and Instance Based Learner on Streams (IBLStreams).

Authors in [18] compare the performance of four supervised ML algorithms (MLR, FFN, SVR, and Regression Tree (RT)) by studying the effect of internal and external factors. The external factors include outdoor temperature, solar radiation, wind speed, and wind direction. The internal factors are related to the district heating system and include supply and return water pressure, supply and return water temperature, the difference of supply and return temperature, and circular flow. Their study shows that SVR showed the best

TABLE 1: ML models for heat demand prediction in the literature.

Applied algorithms	[12]	[13]	[14]	[15]	[16]	[17]	[32]	[33]	[34]	[35]	[36]	Our work
ANN/FNN/SOM/RNN	+	+	+	+	−	−	+	−	−	+	−	−
MLR/MR/PLS	−	−	−	+	+	−	+	−	−	−	−	+
SVM/SVR	−	−	−	+	−	−	+	+	−	−	+	+
BN	−	−	−	−	−	−	−	−	+	−	−	−
DT/RF/RT	−	−	−	−	−	+	+	−	−	−	−	+
Ensembles	−	−	−	−	−	+	−	−	−	−	−	+

accuracy on heat load prediction for 1- to 24-hour horizons. However, the prediction accuracy decreases with the rise in horizon from 1 to 18 hours.

Wu et al. [19] discuss and implement SVR as a predictive model to the building's historical energy use. Their predictive model proved to approximate current energy use with some seasonal and customer-specific variations in the approximations. Another work [20] discusses the importance of prediction of load in a smart energy grid network. The authors propose a BN to predict the total consumer water heat consumption in households. Shamshirband et al. [21] construct an adaptive neurofuzzy inference system (ANFIS), which is a special case of the ANN family, to predict heat load for individual consumers in a DH system. Their result indicates that more improvements of the model are required for prediction horizons greater than 1 hour. Protić et al. [22] study the relevance of short-term heat load prediction for operation control in DH network. Here, authors apply SVR for heat load prediction for only one substation for time horizon of every 15 minutes. To improve the predictive model, authors also add a dummy variable to define the state of DH operation.

In literature, the research towards developing load forecasting models is also discussed from different perspectives and used in different energy related applications, such as head load in district heating, wind turbine reaction torque prediction [23], and wind power forecasting [24, 25].

In [23], SVR is employed for wind turbine torque prediction. The results show that an improvement in accuracy can be achieved and conclude that SVR can be considered as a suitable alternative for prediction. It can be also seen that the proposed SVR prediction models produce higher accuracy compared to ANN and ANFIS (adaptive neurofuzzy inference system). The work discussed in [24] considers the penetrations of renewable energies in electrical power systems by increasing the level of uncertainty. In such situations, traditional methods for forecasting of load demand cannot properly handle these uncertainties. Hence, they implement a neural network method for constructing prediction intervals by using a low upper bound estimation (LUBE) approach. The authors conduct a comparative analysis and show that this method can increase the prediction intervals quality for load and wind power generation predictions.

Bhaskar and Singh [25] perform a statistical based wind power prediction using numerical weather prediction (NWP). In order to validate the effectiveness of the proposed method, the authors compared it with benchmark models, such as persistence (PER) and new-reference (NR), and show

that the proposed model outperforms these benchmark models.

Additionally, due to innovations in the future sustainable and smart energy systems and recent technological trends with IoT (Internet of Things), many research works [5, 26] consider DH systems as being an integral part in Smart Grid, within the smart city concept. Moreover, such a DH system model will require high computation time and resources for knowledge representation, knowledge inference, and operational optimization problems. Thus, in response to this, researchers are continuously focusing on the development and use of fast and efficient algorithms for real-time processing of energy and behavior related data.

As a summary, previous research on heat load prediction points to various training algorithms: ANN including RNN, FFN (Feedforward Neural Network)/MLP, and SOM; MR including MLR and PLS; SVM including SVR; Bayesian networks (BN); decision trees (DT); ensemble methods [27]; FIMT-DD; AMRules; and IBLStreams.

In spite of the interest and the considerable efforts given by the research community so far, there is no consensus among researchers on neither selecting the most suitable training model for heat load prediction nor selecting an appropriate set of input parameters for training the model with [16] in order to achieve high level of prediction accuracy. This is due to the fact that superiority of one model over another in heat load prediction cannot be asserted in general because performance of each model rather depends on the structure of the prediction problem and the type of data available. The comparison in [15] pointed to the superior performance of SVR already; however, as our problem structure and inputs are different from theirs, we chose to do a comparison of several up-to-date models to find the most promising approach for our case. Table 1 lists models from the literature. The "plus" sign indicates that a particular algorithm has been applied, while "minus" means the opposite. Based on the table, we concluded that SVR, PLS, and RF provide us with a unique combination of models to compare with each other. Simplicity and efficiency of each model in our combination are preferred such that rapid and simple assessment of energy demand with high accuracy can be obtained.

3. District Heating Systems

District heating is a well-proven technology for heat supply from different energy sources through heat generation and distribution to heat consumers. DH systems are valuable

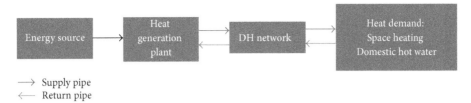

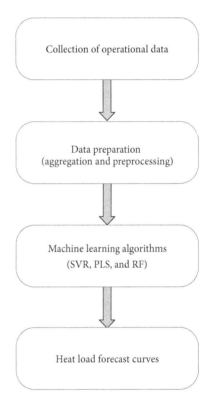

$\longrightarrow$ Supply pipe
$\longleftarrow$ Return pipe

FIGURE 1: District heating block diagram.

infrastructure assets, which enable effective resource utilization by incorporating the use of various energy sources. One of the main advantages of DH system is that it facilitates the use of combined heat and power (CHP) generation and thereby makes the overall system efficient.

District heating can play a crucial role in reaching some of the energy and environmental objectives by reducing CO_2 emissions and improve overall energy efficiency. In a district heating system, heat is distributed through a network of hot-water pipes from heat-supplying plants to end users. The heat is mostly used for space heating and domestic hot water. A simplified schematic picture of DH system is shown in Figure 1.

The main components of district heating system are heat generation units, distribution network, and customer substations. The heat generation unit may use heat-only boilers or CHP plants or a combination of these two for heat generation. Various types of energy sources, like biomass, municipal solid waste, and industrial waste heat, can be used for heat production. The heat is then distributed to different customers through a network of pipeline. In the customer substations, the heat energy from the network is transferred to the end users internal heating system.

The heat-supplying units are designed to meet the heat demand. The heat output to the network depends on the mass flow of the hot water and the temperature difference between the supply and the return line. The supply temperature of the hot water is controlled directly from the plant's control room based on the outdoor temperature and it follows mostly a given operation temperature curve. The return temperature, on the other hand, depends mainly on the customer's heat usage and also other network specific constraints. The level of the supply temperature differs from country to country. For instance, in Sweden, the temperature level varies between 70 and 120°C depending on season and weather [28].

The heat load in district heating systems is the sum of all heat loads that are connected to the network and distribution and other losses in the network.

With increased concerns about the environment, climate change, and energy economy, DH is an obvious choice to be used. Nowadays, district heating systems are equipped with advanced and cutting-edge technology systems and sensors that monitor and control production units from a control room remotely. From a smart city perspective, one of the future challenges that now remains is to integrate district heating with the electricity sector as well as the transport sector. Heat load forecasting models with high accuracy are

FIGURE 2: Workflow scenario of the proposed heat load approach.

important to keep up with the rapid development in this direction.

4. System Design and Application

As mentioned earlier, in this study, we perform short time prediction for heat consumption and evaluate the three ML methods. For the development of the heat load system presented in our previous work [6], in this section, we present and describe our heat load prediction approach in detail, as shown in Figure 2, which includes collection of operational data, data preparation, and the examined ML algorithms.

In this work, there are two main tasks, which are relevant in the system implementation: (a) data aggregation and preprocessing and (b) ML application, where the heal load prediction is approached with the supervised ML algorithms.

4.1. Operational Data Collection. The data we have used in this study is provided by Eidsiva Bioenergi AS which operates

TABLE 2: Typical data samples for one day from the Eidsiva dataset.

Time (h)	FT (°C)	RT (°C)	Flow (m³/h)	HL (MW)
1	100.9	60.4	316.5	14.6
2	99.4	57.5	279.1	13.4
3	99.6	58.3	228.3	13.2
4	100.3	59.8	261.9	15.1
5	100.5	59.6	276.9	14.9
6	100.1	58.9	270.5	12.8
⋮	⋮	⋮	⋮	⋮
⋮	⋮	⋮	⋮	⋮
20	98.7	59.7	353	14.8
21	101.4	58.9	330.9	16.1
22	101.1	59.1	250.8	14.2
23	100.8	59.8	260.2	15.4
24	101.9	59.3	247.9	14.1

one of Europe's most modern waste incineration plants located in the city of Hamar, Norway. The plant produces district heating, process steam, and electricity. These data are collected by regular measurements that are part of the control system in a DH plant. The measurements consist of 24 measurements per each day, that is, every hour. The dataset contains values of the parameters: time of day (tD), forward temperature (FT), return temperature (RT), flow rate (FR), and heat load (HL). The data are collected in the period between October 1st 2014 and April 30th 2015. In Table 2, we present a portion of typical data samples for one day.

4.2. Data Preparation. In this module, activities related to preparing the data to be compatible with the ML module are performed. The module includes data aggregation and preprocessing. During the process of data aggregation, we combine the sources of this data with the weather data (outdoor temperature), which is collected at the same interval with previous parameters. Consequently, we obtain from the aggregation process these output parameters: outdoor temperature (OT), heat load (HL), forward temperature (FT), time of day (tD), and the difference between forward temperature (FT) and return temperature (RT), namely, DT.

4.3. Machine-Learning Predictive Modelling. Machine learning (ML) is a very broad subject; it goes from very abstract theory to extreme practice. It turns out that even amongst machine-learning practitioners there is no very well accepted definition of what is machine learning. As a subfield of artificial intelligence, with its objective on building models that learn from data, machine learning has made tremendous improvements and applications in the last decade.

In general, ML can be clearly defined as a set of methods that can automatically detect and extract knowledge patterns in empirical data, such as sensor data or databases, and then use the discovered knowledge patterns to predict future data or execute other types of decision-making under uncertainty. ML is divided into three principal groups: supervised learning (predictive learning approach), unsupervised learning

(descriptive learning approach), and reinforcement learning [29]. In supervised learning, the algorithm is given data in which the "correct answer" for each example is told and the main property of the supervised learning is that the main criteria of the target function $y = f(x)$ are unknown. At the very high level, the two steps of supervised learning are as follows: (i) train a machine-learning model using labeled data that consist of N data pairs $(x_1, y_1), \ldots, (x_N, y_N)$, called instances, and (ii) make predictions on new data for which the label is unknown. Each instance is described by an input vector x_i which incorporates a set of attributes $A = \{A_1, A_2, \ldots, A_m\}$ and a label y_i of the target attribute that represents the wanted output. To summarize these two steps, the predictive model is learning from past examples made up of inputs and outputs and then applying what is learned to future inputs, in order to predict future outputs. Since we are making predictions on unseen data, which is data that is not used to train the model, it is often said that the primary goal of supervised learning is to build models that generalizes; that is, the built machine-learning model accurately predicts the future rather than the past. Therefore, the goal is to train a model that can afterwards predict the label of new instances and to figure out the target function.

Based on the type of output variable y_i, supervised learning tasks are further divided into two types, as classification and regression problems. In problems where the output variable y_i is categorical or nominal (or belongs to a finite set), the ML tasks are known as classification problems or pattern recognition, whereas in regression problems the output variable is a real valued scalar or takes continuous values.

4.3.1. Support Vector Regression (SVR). Support vector machines (SVM), as a set of supervised learning algorithms based on a statistical learning theory, are one of the most successful and widely applied machine-learning methods, for both solving regression and pattern recognition problems. Since the formulation of SVMs is based on structural risk minimization and not on empirical risk minimization, this algorithm shows better performance than the traditional ones. Support Vector Regression (SVR) is a method of SVM, specifically for regressions. In SVR, the objective function (e.g., the error function that may need to be minimized) is convex, meaning that the global optimum is always reached and satisfied. This is sharply in contrast to artificial neural networks (ANNs), where, for instance, the classical backpropagation learning algorithm is prone to convergence to "bad" local minima [30, 31], which makes them harder to analyze theoretically. In practice, SVR have greatly outperformed ANNs in a wide range of applications [31].

In SVR, the input x is mapped first into an m-dimensional feature space by using nonlinear mapping. As a subsequent step, we construct a linear model in that feature space. Mathematically, the linear model $f(x, w)$ is given by

$$f(x, w) = \sum_{j=1}^{m} w_j g_j(x) + b, \tag{1}$$

where $g_j(x)$, $j = 1, \ldots, m$, represents the set of nonlinear transformations, while b is the bias term, and most of the time is assumed to be zero; hence, we omit this term.

The model obtained by SVR depends exclusively on a subset of the training data; at the same time, SVR tries to reduce model complexity by minimizing $\|w\|^2$. Consequently, the objective of SVR is to minimize the following function [32]:

$$
\begin{aligned}
\min \quad & \frac{1}{2}\|w\|^2 + C\sum_{i=1}^{n}\left(\xi_i + \xi_i^*\right) \\
\text{such that} \quad & y_i - f(x_i, w) \le \varepsilon + \xi_i^* \\
& f(x_i, w) - y_i \le \varepsilon + \xi_i \\
& \xi_i, \xi_i^* \ge 0, \quad i = 1, \ldots, n.
\end{aligned}
\tag{2}
$$

In these equations, ε is a new type of (insensitive) loss function or a threshold, which denotes the desired error range for all points. The nonnegative variables ξ_i and ξ_i^* are called slack variables; they measure the deviation of training samples outside ε, that is, guaranteeing that a solution exists for all ε. The parameter $C > 0$ is a penalty term used to determine the tradeoff between data fitting and flatness, and w are the regression weights. In most cases, the optimization problem can be easily solved if transformed into a dual problem. By utilizing Lagrange multipliers, the dualization method is applied as follows:

$$
\begin{aligned}
L = {} & \frac{1}{2}\|w\|^2 + C\sum_{i=1}^{n}\left(\xi_i + \xi_i^*\right) \\
& - \sum_{i=1}^{n}\alpha_i^*\left(\varepsilon + \xi_i^* - y_i + f(x_i, w)\right) \\
& - \sum_{i=1}^{n}\alpha_i\left(\varepsilon + \xi_i + y_i - f(x_i, w)\right) \\
& - \sum_{i=1}^{n}\left(\lambda_i\xi_i + \lambda_i^*\xi_i^*\right),
\end{aligned}
\tag{3}
$$

where L is the Lagrangian and $\alpha_i, \alpha_i^*, \lambda_i, \lambda_i^* \ge 0$, are called the Lagrange multipliers.

Considering the saddle point condition, it follows that the partial derivatives of L in relation to variables (w, b, ξ_i, ξ_i^*) will disappear for optimality. By proceeding with similar steps, we end up with the dual optimization problem. Finally, the solution of the dual problem is given by

$$
f(x) = \sum_{i=1}^{n_{SV}}\left(\alpha_i - \alpha_i^*\right)K(x_i - x),
\tag{4}
$$

where $0 \le \alpha_i^* \le C$, $0 \le \alpha_i \le C$, n_{SV} is the number of space vectors, and K is the kernel function, which for given two vectors in input space will return, to a higher dimensional

feature space, the dot product of their images. The kernel is given by

$$
K(x, x_i) = \sum_{i=1}^{m} g_j(x) g_j(x_i).
\tag{5}
$$

In order to map the input data to a higher dimensional space and to handle nonlinearities between input vectors and their respective class, we use as a kernel the Gaussian radial basis function (RBF), which has γ as its kernel parameter. Once the kernel is selected, we used grid search to identify the best pair of the regularization parameters C and γ, that is, the pair with the best cross-validation accuracy.

4.3.2. Partial Least Squares (PLS). The Partial Least Squares (PLS) technique is a learning method based on multiple linear regression model that takes into account the latent structure in both datasets. The dataset consists of explanatory variables X_i and dependent variables Y_j. The model is linear, as can be seen in (6), that, for each sample n, the value y_{nj} is

$$
y_{nj} = \sum_{i=0}^{k}\beta_i x_{ni} + \varepsilon_{nj}.
\tag{6}
$$

The PLS model is similar to a model from a linear regression; however, the way of calculating β_i is different. The principle of PLS regression is that the data tables or matrices X and Y are decomposed into latent structure in an iterative process. The latent structure corresponding to the most variation of Y is extracted and explained by a latent structure of X that explains it the best.

The Partial Least Squares (PLS) technique is a learning method based on multivariate regression model, which can be used for correlating the information in one data matrix X to the information in another matrix Y. More specifically, PLS is used to find the fundamental relations between two matrices (X and Y), which are projected onto several key factors, such as T and U, and linear regression is performed for the relation between these factors. Factor U represents the most variations for Y whereas factor T denotes the variations for X, but it is not necessarily explaining the most variation in X.

The first results of PLS are the model equations showing the β coefficients that give the relationship between variables X and Y. These model equations are as follows:

$$
\begin{aligned}
Y &= X\beta + \varepsilon, \\
Y &= T_h C_h' + \varepsilon_h = X W_h^* C_h' + \varepsilon_h \\
&= X W_h \left(P_h' W_h\right)^{-1} C_h' + \varepsilon_h,
\end{aligned}
\tag{7}
$$

where Y is the matrix of dependent variables, X is the matrix of explanatory variables, T_h, C_h, W_h^*, W_h, and P_h are the matrices generated by the PLS algorithm, and ε_h is the matrix of residuals. Matrix β of the regression coefficients of Y on X, with h components generated by the PLS algorithm, is given by

$$
\beta = W_h \left(P_h' W_h\right)^{-1} C_h'.
\tag{8}
$$

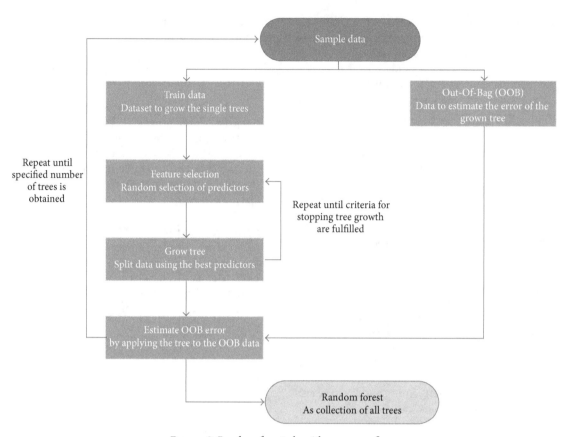

FIGURE 3: Random forest algorithm process flow.

The advantage of PLS is that this algorithm allows taking into account the data structure in both X and Y matrices. It also provides great visual results that help the interpretation of data. Finally, yet importantly, PLS can model several response variables at the same time taking into account their structure.

4.3.3. Random Forest (RF).

Random forest algorithm, proposed by Breiman [33], is an ensemble-learning algorithm consisting of three predictors where the trees are formulated based on various random features. It develops lots of decision trees based on random selection of data and random selection of variables, providing the class of dependent variable based on many trees.

This method is based on the combination of a large collection of decorrelated decision trees (i.e., Classification and Regression Trees (CART) [34]). Since all the trees are based on random selection of data as well as variables, these are random trees and many such random trees lead to a random forest. The name forest means that we use many decision trees to make a better classification of the dependent variable. The CART technique divides the learning sample using an algorithm known as binary recursive partitioning. This splitting or partitioning starts from the most important variable to the less important ones and it is applied to each of the new branches of the tree [35].

In order to increase the algorithm accuracy and reduce the generalization error of the ensemble trees, another technique called *Bagging* is incorporated. The estimation for the generalization error is performed with the Out-Of-Bag (OOB) method. Bagging is used on the training dataset to generate a lot of copies of it, where each one corresponds to a decision tree.

With the RF algorithm, each tree is grown as follows [36]:

(a) If the number of cases (observations) in the training set is N, sample N cases at random, but with replacement, from the original data, this sample will be the training set for the growing tree.

(b) If there are M input variables, a number $m \ll M$ is specified such that, at each node, m variables are selected at random out of the M and the best split on these m is used to split the node. This value m is held constant during the forest growing.

(c) Each tree is grown to the largest extent possible.

The process flow in the random forest models is shown in Figure 3.

The error rate of RF primarily depends on the correlation degree between any two trees and the prediction accuracy of an individual tree. The principal advantages of this method are the ease of parallelization, robustness, and indifference to noise and outliers in most of the dataset. Due to its unbiased nature of execution, this method avoids overfitting.

TABLE 3: Performance results for one week.

Algorithm	Training			Testing		
	MAE (%)	MAPE (%)	Correlation coefficient	MAE (%)	MAPE (%)	Correlation coefficient
SVR	64.91	3.11	0.90	70.32	3.43	0.91
PLS	265.24	12.73	0.81	238.68	10.42	0.79
RF	173.82	19.77	0.83	159.32	18.61	0.84

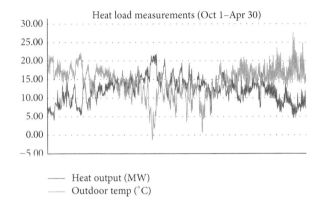

FIGURE 4: Hourly heat load pattern in relation to outdoor temperature in the DH network.

5. Performance Evaluation and Results

The proposed approach is implemented in MATLAB R2014a [37] and executed in a PC with Intel® Core i7 processor with 2.7 GHz speed and 8 GB of RAM. In this work, as training dataset, we select the data measured during the first 28 weeks, which consist of 4872 instances. As for prediction period, we choose the 29th week as test data, that is, 148 instances. In order to evaluate the performance of the proposed algorithms in terms of accuracy of the results, we use the mean absolute average (MAE), the mean average percentage error (MAPE), and the correlation coefficient, which measures the correlation between the actual and predicted heat load values. MAE and MAPE are defined as follows:

$$MAE = \frac{\sum_{i=1}^{n} |p_i - y_i|}{n},$$

$$MAPE = \frac{\sum_{i=1}^{n} |(p_i - y_i')/p_i|}{n},$$

(9)

where p_i is the actual value, y_i is the predicted value, and n is the number of samples in the training set.

We apply a 10-fold cross-validation for obtaining the valid evaluation metrics. Figure 4 presents the heat load in the network with respect to the outdoor temperature. We see that the higher values of the heat load occur during the days with lower outdoor temperature values, which in fact reflects the increased consumption of heat.

Figure 5(a) shows results of actual heat load and heat load prediction for one week, based on SVR algorithm. In Figure 5(b), results of heat prediction production for one week based on PLS are shown with data on actual heal load,

whereas results of heat load forecasting for one week based on RF are shown in Figure 5(c).

As can be seen from Figure 5, the predicted HL with SVR is closer to the actual energy consumption, with an MAPE value of about 3.43% and a correlation coefficient of 0.91. Correlation has been consistent throughout training and testing. On the other hand, graphs presented in Figures 5(b) and 5(c) for PLS and RF, respectively, are less accurate with higher errors. The performance of the PLS is significantly lower compared to SVR. Concerning RF, as the trees started to become progressively uncorrelated, the error rate also declined significantly. The best performance of the SVR over the other two methods is attributed to the efficient modelling of feature space and to the fact that SVR is less prone to overfitting, and that does not require any procedure to determine the explicit form as in ordinary regression analysis.

Table 3 outlines the results of the investigated ML algorithms for heat consumption prediction for both training phase (where we developed the models using supervised learning schemes) and testing phase (to generalize newly unseen data). From Table 3, it is evident that SVR shows the best prediction performance in terms of average errors and correlation coefficient, confirming the superiority of SVR over the other machine-learning methods. Therefore, based on the assumption that the number and type of the operating facilities should be determined, SVR can be effectively applied in the management of a DHS. The mean absolute percentage error value of 3.43% obtained in our approach with the SVR is lower than or equal to the mean absolute percentage error of state-of-the-art approaches for heat load prediction in DHS. Moreover, SVR is also better than PLS and RF in terms of mean average errors and correlation coefficient. Nevertheless, sometimes it is impossible to perform direct comparison with other works due to different system implementation and input data and different structure of the experimental setup.

5.1. Comparison with State-of-the-Art Methods. Some prior research work is carried out to predict and analyze the head demand in DH. However, due to different system design and input data and different architecture implementation or structure of the experimental setup, sometimes it is difficult to perform direct comparison. Our approach uses operational data from DHS to model the heat demand, and since the SVR exhibited the best prediction performance, we use this method to perform the comparison. In our case, we obtained smaller MAPE compared to [17], where the experimental results showed MAPE of 4.77% which is lower than or at least equal to the mean percentage error of state-of-the-art regression approaches that have been proposed for heat load forecasting in DH systems. Furthermore, reported results

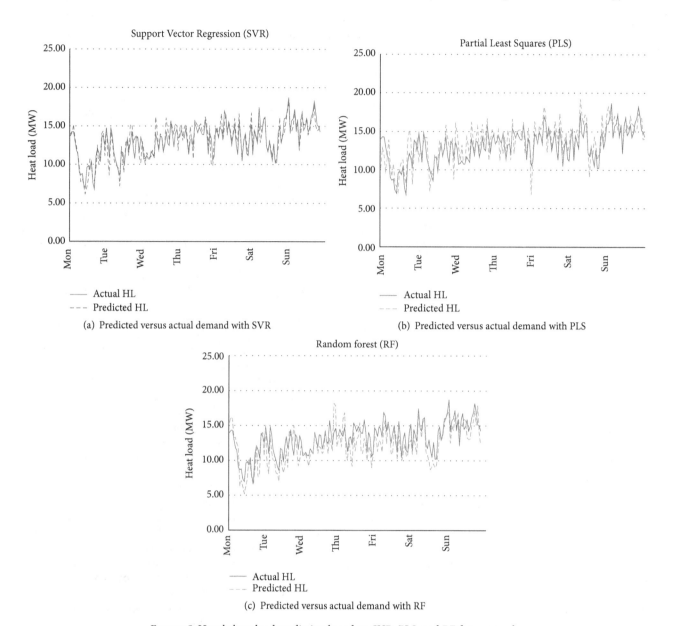

FIGURE 5: Hourly heat load prediction based on SVR, PLS, and RF for one week.

from our study are also superior compared to the results presented in [15, 32]. More specifically, the SVR method we apply shows better results in terms of MAPE and correlation coefficient compared to [32], where MAPE in this paper is 5.54% and the correlation coefficient is 0.87. As far as the comparison with work [15] is concerned, in terms of MAPE, our SVR method exhibits better hourly prediction performance, where the MAPE for one week is 5.63%. On the other hand, the PLS method performs better than in our case, having the MAPE value of about 8.99%.

6. Conclusion

District heating (DH) sector can play an indispensable role in the current and future sustainable energy system of the North European countries, where the share of DH in the total European heat market is significantly high. The innovations and emergence of new technology and the increasing focus on smart buildings impose energy systems to face a challenge in adapting to customers' more flexible and individual solutions. Consequently, one needs to know more about what drives customers' requirements, choices, and priorities. Therefore, the creation and application of innovative IT ecosystems in DH are considered essential to improve energy efficiency.

Heat load prediction in the past decade has attracted a lot of interest to the researchers, since it can assist in energy efficiency of the DHS, which also leads to cost reduction for heat suppliers and to many environmental benefits.

In this paper, three ML algorithms for heat load prediction in a DH network are developed and presented. The algorithms are SVR, PLS, and RF. The heat load prediction models were developed using data from 29 weeks. The predicted hourly results were compared with actual heat load data. Performances of these three different ML algorithms were studied, compared, and analyzed. SVR algorithm proved to be the most efficient one, producing the best performance in terms of average errors and correlation coefficient. Moreover, the prediction results were also compared against existing SVR and PLS methods in literature, showing that the SVR presented in this paper produces better accuracy.

In conclusion, the comparison results validate the notion that the developed SVR method is appropriate for application in heat load prediction or it can serve as a promising alternative for existing models.

As for the future work, apart from outdoor temperature, we intend to incorporate other meteorological parameters influencing the heat load, such as wind speed and humidity.

Competing Interests

The authors declare that they have no competing interests.

Acknowledgments

The authors would like to thank *Eidsiva Bioenergi AS*, Norway, which kindly provided the data for this research work.

References

[1] Report on European Energy Security Strategy, May 2014, Brussels, http://eur-lex.europa.eu/legal-content/EN/TXT/PDF/?uri=CELEX:52014DC0330&from=EN.

[2] A. R. Day, P. Ogumka, P. G. Jones, and A. Dunsdon, "The use of the planning system to encourage low carbon energy technologies in buildings," *Renewable Energy*, vol. 34, no. 9, pp. 2016–2021, 2009.

[3] IEA (International Energy Agency), *Nordic Energy Technology Perspectives*, OECD/IEA, Paris, France, 2013.

[4] A. Gebremedhin and H. Zinko, "Seasonal heat storages in district heating systems," in *Proceedings of the 11th International Thermal Energy Storage for Energy Efficiency and Sustainability Conference (Effstock '09)*, Stockholm, Sweden, June 2009.

[5] H. Lund, S. Werner, R. Wiltshire et al., "4th Generation District Heating (4GDH): integrating smart thermal grids into future sustainable energy systems," *Energy*, vol. 68, pp. 1–11, 2014.

[6] F. Dalipi, S. Y. Yayilgan, and A. Gebremedhin, "A machine learning approach to increase energy efficiency in district heating systems," in *Proceedings of the International Conference on Environmental Engineering and Computer Application (ICEECA '14)*, pp. 223–226, CRC Press, Hong Kong, December 2014.

[7] N. Fumo, "A review on the basics of building energy estimation," *Renewable and Sustainable Energy Reviews*, vol. 31, pp. 53–60, 2014.

[8] D. E. Claridge, "Using simulation models for building commissioning," in *Proceedings of the International Conference on Enhanced Building Operation*, Energy Systems Laboratory, Texas A&M University, October 2004.

[9] T. Mestekemper, *Energy demand forecasting and dynamic water temperature management [Ph.D. thesis]*, Bielefeld University, Bielefeld, Germany, 2011.

[10] E. Dotzauer, "Simple model for prediction of loads in district-heating systems," *Applied Energy*, vol. 73, no. 3-4, pp. 277–284, 2002.

[11] H. A. Nielsen and H. Madsen, "Modelling the heat consumption in district heating systems using a grey-box approach," *Energy and Buildings*, vol. 38, no. 1, pp. 63–71, 2006.

[12] B. B. Ekici and U. T. Aksoy, "Prediction of building energy consumption by using artificial neural networks," *Advances in Engineering Software*, vol. 40, no. 5, pp. 356–362, 2009.

[13] M. Grzenda and B. Macukow, "Demand prediction with multi-stage neural processing," in *Advances in Natural Computation and Data Mining*, pp. 131–141, 2006.

[14] K. Kato, M. Sakawa, K. Ishimaru, S. Ushiro, and T. Shibano, "Heat load prediction through recurrent neural network in district heating and cooling systems," in *Proceedings of the IEEE International Conference on Systems, Man and Cybernetics (SMC '08)*, pp. 1401–1406, Singapore, October 2008.

[15] T. C. Park, U. S. Kim, L.-H. Kim, B. W. Jo, and Y. K. Yeo, "Heat consumption forecasting using partial least squares, artificial neural network and support vector regression techniques in district heating systems," *Korean Journal of Chemical Engineering*, vol. 27, no. 4, pp. 1063–1071, 2010.

[16] T. Catalina, V. Iordache, and B. Caracaleanu, "Multiple regression model for fast prediction of the heating energy demand," *Energy and Buildings*, vol. 57, pp. 302–312, 2013.

[17] S. Provatas, N. Lavesson, and C. Johansson, "An online machine learning algorithm for heat load forecasting in district heating systems," in *Proceedings of the 14th International Symposium on District Heating and Cooling*, Stockholm, Sweden, September 2014.

[18] S. Idowu, S. Saguna, C. Åhlund, and O. Schelén, "Forecasting heat load for smart district heating systems: a machine learning approach," in *Proceedings of the IEEE International Conference on Smart Grid Communications (SmartGridComm '14)*, pp. 554–559, IEEE, Venice, Italy, November 2014.

[19] L. Wu, G. Kaiser, D. Solomon, R. Winter, A. Boulanger, and R. Anderson, *Improving Efficiency and Reliability of Building Systems Using Machine Learning and Automated Online Evaluation*, Columbia University Academic Commons, 2012, http://hdl.handle.net/10022/AC:P:13213.

[20] M. Vlachopoulou, G. Chin, J. C. Fuller, S. Lu, and K. Kalsi, "Model for aggregated water heater load using dynamic Bayesian networks," Tech. Rep., Pacific Northwest National Laboratory (PNNL), Richland, Wash, USA, 2012.

[21] S. Shamshirband, D. Petković, R. Enayatifar et al., "Heat load prediction in district heating systems with adaptive neuro-fuzzy method," *Renewable and Sustainable Energy Reviews*, vol. 48, pp. 760–767, 2015.

[22] M. Protić, S. Shamshirband, M. H. Anisi et al., "Appraisal of soft computing methods for short term consumers' heat load prediction in district heating systems," *Energy*, vol. 82, pp. 697–704, 2015.

[23] S. Shamshirband, D. Petković, A. Amini et al., "Support vector regression methodology for wind turbine reaction torque prediction with power-split hydrostatic continuous variable transmission," *Energy*, vol. 67, pp. 623–630, 2014.

[24] H. Quan, D. Srinivasan, and A. Khosravi, "Short-term load and wind power forecasting using neural network-based prediction intervals," *IEEE Transactions on Neural Networks and Learning Systems*, vol. 25, no. 2, pp. 303–315, 2014.

[25] K. Bhaskar and S. N. Singh, "AWNN-assisted wind power forecasting using feed-forward neural network," *IEEE Transactions on Sustainable Energy*, vol. 3, no. 2, pp. 306–315, 2012.

[26] Heat Pump Centre Newsletters, International Energy Agency (IEA) Heat Pumping Technologies, Vol. 30, Nr. 2/2012.

[27] T. G. Dietterich, "An experimental comparison of three methods for constructing ensembles of decision trees: bagging, boosting, and randomization," *Machine Learning*, vol. 40, no. 2, pp. 139–157, 2000.

[28] Swedish District Heating Association, 2016, http://www.svensk-fjarrvarme.se/.

[29] K. P. Murphy, *Machine Learning: A Probabilistic Perspective*, Adaptive Computation and Machine Learning Series, MIT Press, 2012.

[30] L. Wang, *Support Vector Machines: Theory and Applications*, Springer, New York, NY, USA, 2005.

[31] D. Basak, S. Pal, and D. C. Patranabis, "Support vector regressions," *Neural Information Processing—Letters and Reviews*, vol. 11, no. 10, pp. 203–224, 2007.

[32] R. E. Edwards, J. New, and L. E. Parker, "Predicting future hourly residential electrical consumption: a machine learning case study," *Energy and Buildings*, vol. 49, pp. 591–603, 2012.

[33] L. Breiman, "Random forests," *Machine Learning*, vol. 45, no. 1, pp. 5–32, 2001.

[34] L. Breiman, J. H. Friedman, R. A. Olshen, and C. J. Stone, *Classification and Regression Trees*, Wadsworth and Brooks, Monterey, Calif, USA, 1984.

[35] P. Vezza, C. Comoglio, M. Rosso, and A. Viglione, "Low flows regionalization in North-Western Italy," *Water Resources Management*, vol. 24, no. 14, pp. 4049–4074, 2010.

[36] L. Breiman and A. Cutler, "Random forests," January 2016, http://www.stat.berkeley.edu/users/breiman/RandomForests/.

[37] *MATLAB, Version 8.3.0*, MathWorks, Natick, Mass, USA, 2014.

4

Distributed Nonparametric and Semiparametric Regression on SPARK for Big Data Forecasting

Jelena Fiosina and Maksims Fiosins

Clausthal University of Technology, Clausthal-Zellerfeld, Germany

Correspondence should be addressed to Jelena Fiosina; jelena.fiosina@gmail.com

Academic Editor: Francesco Carlo Morabito

Forecasting in big datasets is a common but complicated task, which cannot be executed using the well-known parametric linear regression. However, nonparametric and semiparametric methods, which enable forecasting by building nonlinear data models, are computationally intensive and lack sufficient scalability to cope with big datasets to extract successful results in a reasonable time. We present distributed parallel versions of some nonparametric and semiparametric regression models. We used MapReduce paradigm and describe the algorithms in terms of SPARK data structures to parallelize the calculations. The forecasting accuracy of the proposed algorithms is compared with the linear regression model, which is the only forecasting model currently having parallel distributed realization within the SPARK framework to address big data problems. The advantages of the parallelization of the algorithm are also provided. We validate our models conducting various numerical experiments: evaluating the goodness of fit, analyzing how increasing dataset size influences time consumption, and analyzing time consumption by varying the degree of parallelism (number of workers) in the distributed realization.

1. Introduction

The most current methods of data analysis, data mining, and machine learning should deal with big databases. Cloud Computing technologies can be successfully applied to parallelize standard data mining techniques in order to make working with massive amounts of data feasible [1]. For this purpose, standard algorithms should often be redesigned for parallel environment to distribute computations among multiple computation nodes.

One such approach is to use Apache Hadoop, which includes MapReduce for job distribution [2] and distributed file system (HDFS) for data sharing among nodes.

Recently, a new and efficient framework called Apache SPARK [3] was built on top of Hadoop, which allows more efficient execution of distributed jobs and therefore is very promising for big data analysis problems [4]. However, SPARK is currently in the development stage, and the number of standard data analysis libraries is limited.

R software is a popular instrument for data analysts. It provides several possibilities for parallel data processing through the add-on packages [5]. It is possible also to use Hadoop and SPARK inside of R using SPARKR. This is an R package that provides a lightweight front-end to use Apache SPARK within R. SPARKR is still in the developing stage and supports only some features of SPARK but has a big potential for the future of data science [6].

There exist also alternative parallelization approaches, such as Message Passing Interface (MPI) [7]. However, in the present paper, we will concentrate on SPARK because of its speed, simplicity, and scalability [8].

In this study, we consider regression-based forecasting for the case where the data has a nonlinear structure, which is common in real-world datasets. This implies that linear regression cannot make accurate forecasts and, thus, we resort to nonparametric and semiparametric regression methods, which do not require linearity and are more robust to outliers. However, the main disadvantage of these methods is that they are very time-consuming, and therefore the term "big data" for such methods starts much earlier than with parametrical approaches. In the case of big datasets, traditional nonparallel realizations are not capable of processing all the available data. This makes it imperative to adapt to existing techniques and to develop new ones that overcome this disadvantage. The distributed parallel SPARK framework gives us the possibility of addressing this difficulty and increasing the scalability of nonparametric and semiparametric regression methods, allowing us to deal with bigger datasets.

There are some approaches in the current literature to address nonparametric or semiparametric regression models for parallel processing of big datasets [9], for example, using R add-on packages, MPI. Our study examines a novel, fast, parallel, and distributed realization of the algorithms based on the modern version of Apache SPARK, which is a promising tool for the efficient realization of different machine learning and data mining algorithms [3].

The main objective of this study is to enable a parallel distributed version of nonparametric and semiparametric regression models, particularly kernel-density-based and partial linear models to be applied on big data. To realize this, a SPARK MapReduce based algorithm has been developed, which splits the data and performs various algorithm processes in parallel in the map phase and then combines the solutions in the reduce phase to merge the results.

More specifically, the contribution of this study is (i) to design novel distributed parallel kernel density regression and partial linear regression algorithms over the SPARK MapReduce paradigm for big data and (ii) to validate the algorithms, analyzing their accuracy, scalability, and speedup by means of numerical experiments.

The remainder of this paper is organized as follows. Section 2 reviews the traditional regression models to be analyzed. Section 3 reviews the existent distributed computation frameworks for big datasets. In Section 4, we propose parallel versions of kernel-density-based and partial linear regression model algorithms, based on SPARK MapReduce paradigm. In Section 5, we present the experimental setup and in Section 6 we discuss the experimental framework and analysis. Section 7 concludes the paper and discusses future research opportunities.

2. Background: Regression Models

2.1. Linear Multivariate Regression. We start with linear regression, which is the only regression model realized in the current version of SPARK to compare the results of the proposed methods.

Let us first consider the classical multivariate linear regression model $E(Y \mid \mathbf{X}) = \mathbf{X}\boldsymbol{\beta}$ [10, 11]:

$$\mathbf{Y} = \mathbf{X}\boldsymbol{\beta} + \boldsymbol{\varepsilon}, \tag{1}$$

where n is a number of observations, d is the number of factors, $\mathbf{Y}_{n \times 1}$ is a vector of dependent variables, $\boldsymbol{\beta}_{d \times 1}$ is a vector of unknown parameters, $\boldsymbol{\varepsilon}_{n \times 1}$ is a vector of random errors, and $\mathbf{X}_{n \times d}$ is a matrix of explanatory variables. The rows of the matrix $\mathbf{X}$ correspond to observations and the columns correspond to factors. We suppose that $\{\varepsilon_i\}$ are mutually independent and have zero expectation and equal variances.

```
(1)  while not converged do
(2)      for all j ∈ 0,d̄ do
(3)          β̂_j ← β̂_j − α ∂/∂β̂_j J(β̂; X, Y)
(4)      end for
(5)  end while
```

ALGORITHM 1: Stochastic Gradient Descent algorithm.

The well-known least square estimator (LSE) $\widehat{\boldsymbol{\beta}}$ of $\boldsymbol{\beta}$ is

$$\widehat{\boldsymbol{\beta}} = \left(\mathbf{X}^T \mathbf{X}\right)^{-1} \mathbf{X}^T \mathbf{Y}. \tag{2}$$

Further, let $(\mathbf{x}_i, y_i)_{i=1}^n$ be the observations sampled from the distribution of $(\mathbf{X}, Y)$. After the estimation of the parameters $\boldsymbol{\beta}$, we can make a forecast for a certain kth (future) time moment as $E(Y_k) = \mathbf{x}_k \widehat{\boldsymbol{\beta}}$, where $\mathbf{x}_k$ is a vector of observed values of explanatory variables for the kth time moment.

For big data, it is a problem to perform the matrix operations in (2). For this purpose, other optimization techniques can be used. One effective option is to use the Stochastic Gradient Descent algorithm [12], which is realized in SPARK. The generalized cost function to be minimized is

$$J\left(\boldsymbol{\beta}; \mathbf{X}, \mathbf{Y}\right) = \frac{1}{2n} \left(\mathbf{X}\boldsymbol{\beta} - \mathbf{Y}\right)^T \left(\mathbf{X}\boldsymbol{\beta} - \mathbf{Y}\right). \tag{3}$$

Algorithm 1 presents the Stochastic Gradient Descent algorithm, where α is a learning rate parameter.

Algorithm 1 can be executed iteratively (incrementally) that is easy to parallelize.

2.2. Kernel Density Regression. The first alternative to the linear regression model we want to consider is the kernel density estimation-based regression, which is of big importance in the case when data have a nonlinear structure. This nonparametric approach for estimating a regression curve has four main purposes. First, it provides a versatile method for exploring a general relationship between two variables. Second, it can predict observations without a reference to a fixed parametric model. Third, it provides a tool for finding spurious observations by studying the influence of isolated points. Fourth, it constitutes a flexible method of substitution or interpolation between adjacent X-values for missing values [13].

Let us consider a nonparametric regression model, $m(x) = E(Y \mid X = x)$ [14], with the same Y, X, and ε as for a linear model

$$y = m(x) + \varepsilon. \tag{4}$$

The Nadaraya-Watson kernel estimator [15, 16] of $m(x)$ is

$$
\begin{aligned}
m_n(x) &= \frac{\sum_{i=1}^n K\left(\left(x - x_i\right)/h\right) y_i}{\sum_{i=1}^n K\left(\left(x - x_i\right)/h\right)} \\
&= \frac{\sum_{i=1}^n K_h\left(x - x_i\right) y_i}{\sum_{i=1}^n K_h\left(x - x_i\right)},
\end{aligned}
\tag{5}
$$

where $K(u)$ is the kernel function of R^d, which is a nonnegative real-valued integrable function satisfying the following two requirements: $\int_{-\infty}^{\infty} K(u)\,du = 1$ and $K(-u) = K(u)$ for all values of u; $h > 0$ is a smoothing parameter called bandwidth, $K_h(u) = (1/h)K(u/h)$. We can see that each value of the historical forecast, y_i, is taken with some weight of the corresponding independent variable value of the same observation, x_i.

In a multidimensional case $E(Y \mid \mathbf{X}) = m(\mathbf{X})$, the kernel function $K_{\mathbf{H}}(\mathbf{x}) = |\mathbf{H}|^{-1} K(\mathbf{H}^{-1}\mathbf{x})$, where $\mathbf{H}$ is a $d \times d$ matrix of smoothing parameters. The choice of the bandwidth matrix $\mathbf{H}$ is the most important factor affecting the accuracy of the estimator, since it controls the orientation and amount of smoothing induced. The simplest choice is $\mathbf{H} = h\mathbf{I}_d$, where h is a unidimensional smoothing parameter and $\mathbf{I}_d$ is $d \times d$ identity matrix. Then, we have the same amount of smoothing applied in all coordinate directions. Another relatively easy to manage choice is to take the bandwidth matrix equal to a diagonal matrix $\mathbf{H} = \text{diag}(h_1, h_2, \ldots, h_d)$, which allows for different amounts of smoothing in each of the coordinates. We implemented the latter in our experiments. The multidimensional kernel function, $K(\mathbf{u}) = K(u_1, u_2, \ldots, u_d)$, then is easy to present with univariate kernel functions as $K(\mathbf{u}) = K(u_1) \cdot K(u_2) \cdot \ldots \cdot K(u_d)$. We used the Gaussian kernel in our experiments. Then, (5) for the multidimensional case can be rewritten as

$$m_n(\mathbf{x}_k) = \frac{\sum_{i=1}^{n} K_{\mathbf{H}}(\mathbf{x}_k - \mathbf{x}_i)\, y_i}{\sum_{i=1}^{n} K_{\mathbf{H}}(\mathbf{x}_k - \mathbf{x}_i)} = \frac{\sum_{i=1}^{n} \prod_{j=1}^{d} K_{\mathbf{H}}(\mathbf{x}_{k,j} - \mathbf{x}_{i,j})\, y_i}{\sum_{i=1}^{n} \prod_{j=1}^{d} K_{\mathbf{H}}(\mathbf{x}_{k,j} - \mathbf{x}_{i,j})}. \tag{6}$$

An important problem in a kernel density estimation is the selection of the appropriate bandwidth, h. It has an influence on the structure of the neighborhood in (5): the bigger the value of h selected, the higher the significant influence that x_i points have on the estimator $m_n(\mathbf{x}_k)$. In the multidimensional case, $\mathbf{H}$ also regulates the balance between factors. The most popular heuristic methods of bandwidth selection are plug-in and resampling methods. However, those heuristics require a substantial amount of computations, which is not possible for big datasets. For our case, we used a well-known rule-of-thumb approach, proposed by Silverman [17], which works for Gaussian kernels. In the case of no correlation between explanatory variables, there is a simple and useful formula for bandwidth selection with Scott's rule [18]: $h_j = n^{-1/(d+4)} \sigma_j$, $j = 1, 2, \ldots, d$, where σ_j is a variance of the jth factor.

It is known [14] that the curse of dimensionality is one of the major problems that arises when using nonparametric multivariate regression techniques. For the practitioner, an additional problem is that, for more than two regressors, graphical illustrations or interpretations of the results are hard or even impossible. Truly multivariate regression models are often far too flexible and general for making a detailed inference.

A very suitable property of the kernel function is its additive nature. This property makes the kernel function easy

to use for distributed data [13]. Unfortunately, such models, even with current parallelization possibilities, remain very time-consuming.

2.3. Partial Linear Models. Another alternative to the linear regression model is a semiparametric partial linear regression model (PLM). Currently, several efforts have been allocated to developing methods that reduce the complexity of high dimensional regression problems [14]. The models allow easier interpretation of the effect of each variable and may be preferable to a completely nonparametric model. These refer to the reduction of dimensionality and provide an allowance for partly parametric modelling. On the other hand, PLMs are more flexible than the standard linear model because they combine both parametric and nonparametric components. It is assumed that the response variable $\mathbf{Y}$ depends on variable $\mathbf{U}$ in a linear way but is nonlinearly related to other independent variables $\mathbf{T}$ [19]. The resulting models can be grouped together as so called semiparametric models. PLM of regression consists of two additive components, a linear and a nonparametric part. PLM of regression is given as

$$E(Y \mid \mathbf{U}, \mathbf{T}) = \mathbf{U}\boldsymbol{\beta} + m(\mathbf{T}), \tag{7}$$

where $\boldsymbol{\beta}_{p \times 1}$ is a finite dimensional vector of parameters of a linear regression part and $m(\cdot)$ is a smooth function. Here, we assume the decomposition of the explanatory variables $\mathbf{X}$ into two vectors, $\mathbf{U}$ and $\mathbf{T}$. The vector $\mathbf{U}$ denotes a p-variate random vector which typically covers categorical explanatory variables or variables that are known to influence the index in a linear way. The vector, $\mathbf{T}$, is a q-variate random vector of continuous explanatory variables that is to be modelled in a nonparametric way, so $p + q = d$. Economic theory or intuition should ideally guide the inclusion of the regressors in $\mathbf{U}$ or $\mathbf{T}$, respectively.

An algorithm for the estimation of the PLMs was proposed in [13], which is based on the likelihood estimator and known as generalized Speckman [20] estimator. We reformulated this algorithm (Algorithm 2) in terms of functions and data structures, which can be easily parallelizable in Section 4.

PLM function is the primary function of Algorithm 2, which takes as parameters the training dataset $[\mathbf{Y}, \mathbf{U}, \mathbf{T}]$, bandwidth vector $\mathbf{h}$, and a test dataset, $[\mathbf{U}', \mathbf{T}']$. The first step in the estimation is to execute the function, *SmoothMatrix*, to compute a smoother matrix, $\mathbf{S}$, based on the training data of the nonlinear parts $\mathbf{T}$ and $\mathbf{h}$. This helps us to obtain the smoother matrix, which transforms the vector of observations into fitted values. Next, we estimate the linear coefficients of the linear part of the model with the *LinearCoefficients* function. First, we take into account the influence of the nonlinear part on the linear part of the independent variable, $\widetilde{\mathbf{U}} \leftarrow (\mathbf{I} - \mathbf{S})\mathbf{U}$, and on the dependent variable, $\widetilde{\mathbf{Y}} \leftarrow (\mathbf{I} - \mathbf{S})\mathbf{Y}$. Then, we use the ordinary equation (2) or Algorithm 1 to obtain the linear coefficients. With these coefficients, we calculate the linear part of the forecast. Next, we calculate the nonlinear part of the forecast, using Nadaraya-Watson estimator (6). Here, we recalculate a smoother matrix, taking into account the test-set data of the nonlinear part. We take also into account the influence

```
(1)  function SmoothMatrix(T, T', h)
(2)       n ← rows(T), n' ← rows(T')
(3)       for all i ∈ 1,n, j ∈ 1,n' do
(4)           W : Wᵢ,ⱼ ← K_H(Tᵢ - T'ⱼ), S : Sᵢ,ⱼ ← Wᵢ,ⱼ/∑ⁿᵢ₌₁ Wᵢ,ⱼ
(5)       end for
(6)       return S
(7)  end function
(8)
(9)  function LinearCoefficients(S, [Y, U, T])
(10)      Ũ ← (I - S)U, Ỹ ← (I - S)Y
(11)      return β ← (ŨᵀŨ)⁻¹ŨᵀỸ
(12) end function
(13)
(14) function KernelPart(β, [Y, U, T], h, T')
(15)      S ← SmoothMatrix(T, T', h)
(16)      return m(T') ← S(Y - Uβ)
(17) end function
(18)
(19) function PLM([Y, U, T], h, [U', T'])
(20)      Smooth matrix S ← SmoothMatrix(T, T, h)
(21)      β ← LinearCoefficients(S, [Y, U, T])
(22)      m(T') ← KernelPart(β, [Y, U, T], h, T')
(23)      return Y' ← U'β + m(T')
(24) end function
```

ALGORITHM 2: PLM estimation, training set: $[\mathbf{Y}, \mathbf{U}, \mathbf{T}]$, test set: $[\mathbf{Y}', \mathbf{U}', \mathbf{T}']$.

of the linear part, $\mathbf{Y} - \mathbf{U}\boldsymbol{\beta}$. Finally, we sum the linear and nonlinear part of the forecast to obtain the final result, $\mathbf{Y}' \leftarrow \mathbf{U}'\boldsymbol{\beta} + m(\mathbf{T}')$.

3. Background: MapReduce, Hadoop, and SPARK

MapReduce [2] is one of the most popular programming models to deal with big data. It was proposed by Google in 2004 and was designed for processing huge amounts of data using a cluster of machines. The MapReduce paradigm is composed of two phases: map and reduce. In general terms, in the map phase, the input dataset is processed in parallel producing some intermediate results. Then, the reduce phase combines these results in some way to form the final output. The most popular implementation of the MapReduce programming model is Apache Hadoop, an open-source framework that allows the processing and management of large datasets in a distributed computing environment. Hadoop works on top of the Hadoop Distributed File System (HDFS), which replicates the data files in many storage nodes, facilitates rapid data transfer rates among nodes, and allows the system to continue operating uninterruptedly in case of a node failure.

Another Apache project that also uses MapReduce as a programming model, but with much richer APIs in Java, Scala, Python, and R, is SPARK [3]. SPARK is intended to enhance, not replace, the Hadoop stack. SPARK is more than a distributed computational framework originally developed in the UC Berkeley AMP Lab for large-scale data processing that improves the efficiency by the use of intensive memory. It also provides several prebuilt components empowering users to implement applications faster and easier. SPARK uses more RAM instead of network and disk I/O and is relatively fast as compared to Hadoop MapReduce.

From an architecture perspective, Apache SPARK is based on two key concepts; Resilient Distributed Datasets (RDDs) and directed acyclic graph (DAG) execution engine. With regard to datasets, SPARK supports two types of RDDs: parallelized collections that are based on existing Scala collections and Hadoop datasets that are created from the files stored by the HDFS. RDDs support two kinds of operations: transformations and actions. Transformations create new datasets from the input (e.g., map or filter operations are transformations), whereas actions return a value after executing calculations on the dataset (e.g., reduce or count operations are actions). The DAG engine helps to eliminate the MapReduce multistage execution model and offers significant performance improvements.

RDDs [21] are distributed memory abstractions that allow programmers to perform in-memory computations on large clusters while retaining the fault tolerance of data flow models like MapReduce. RDDs are motivated by two types of applications that current data flow systems handle inefficiently: iterative algorithms, which are common in graph applications and machine learning, and interactive data mining tools. In both cases, keeping data in memory can improve performance by an order of magnitude. To achieve fault tolerance efficiently, RDDs provide a highly restricted form of shared memory; they are read-only datasets that can only be constructed through bulk operations on other RDDs. This in-memory processing is a faster process as there is

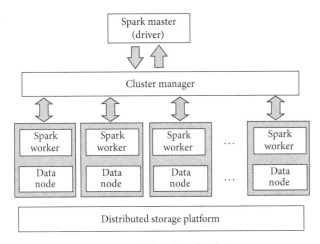

FIGURE 1: SPARK distributed architecture.

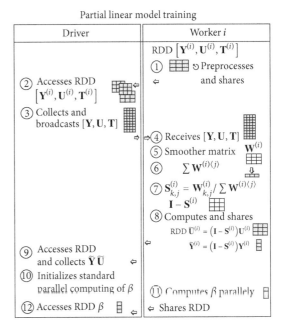

FIGURE 2: PLM parallel training.

no time spent in moving the data/processes in and out of the disk, whereas MapReduce requires a substantial amount of time to perform these I/O operations, thereby increasing latency.

SPARK uses a master/worker architecture. There is a driver that talks to a single coordinator, called the master, that manages workers in which executors run (see Figure 1).

SPARK uses HDFS and has high-level libraries for stream processing, machine learning, and graph processing, such as MLlib [22]. For this study, linear regression realization included in MLlib [23] was used to evaluate the proposed distributed PLM algorithm.

In this paper, Apache SPARK is used to implement the proposed distributed PML algorithm, as described in Section 4.

4. Distributed Parallel Partial Linear Regression Model

4.1. Distributed Partial Linear Model Estimation. In this section, we continue to discuss kernel-density-based and partial linear models (PLMs), described in Section 2. Next, we consider kernel-density-based regression as a specific case of PLM, when the parametric linear part is empty. The general realization of PLM algorithm allows us to conduct experiments with nonparametric kernel-density-based regression. We discuss how to distribute the computations of Algorithm 2 to increase the speed and scalability of the approach. As we can see from the previous subsection, PLM presupposes several matrix operations, which requires a substantial amount of computational demands [24] and, therefore, is not feasible for application to big datasets. In this section, we focus our attention on (1) how to organize matrix computations in a maximally parallel and effective manner and (2) how to parallelize the overall computation process of the PLM estimation. SPARK provides us with various types of parallel structures. Our first task is to select the appropriate SPARK data structures to facilitate the computation process. Next, we develop algorithms, which execute a PLM estimation (Algorithm 2) using MapReduce and SPARK principles.

Traditional methods of data analysis, especially based on matrix computations, must be adapted for running on a cluster, as we cannot readily reuse linear algebra algorithms that are available for single-machine situations. A key idea is to distribute operations, separating algorithms into portions that require matrix operations versus vector operations. Since matrices are often quadratically larger than vectors, a reasonable assumption is that vectors are stored in memory on a single machine, while for matrices it is not reasonable or feasible. Instead, the matrices are stored in blocks (rectangular pieces or some rows/columns), and the corresponding algorithms for block matrices are implemented. The most challenging of tasks here is the rebuilding of algorithms from single-core modes of computation to operate on distributed matrices in parallel [24].

Similar to a linear regression forecasting process, PLM forecasting, because of its parametric component, assumes training and estimating steps. Distributed architectures of Hadoop and SPARK assume one driver computer and several worker computers, which perform computations in parallel. We take this architecture into account while developing our algorithms.

Let us describe the training procedure with the purpose of computing the β parameter, presented in Figure 2. This part was very computationally intensive and could not be calculated without appropriate parallelization of computations.

First, the driver computer reads the training data, $[\mathbf{Y}, \mathbf{U}, \mathbf{T}]$, from a file or database, divides the data into various RDD partitions, and distributes among the workers, $[\mathbf{Y}^{(i)}, \mathbf{U}^{(i)}, \mathbf{T}^{(i)}]$. Next, the training process involves the following steps:

(1) Each worker makes an initial preprocessing and transformation of $[\mathbf{Y}^{(i)}, \mathbf{U}^{(i)}, \mathbf{T}^{(i)}]$, which include scaling and formatting.

Partial linear model forecasting

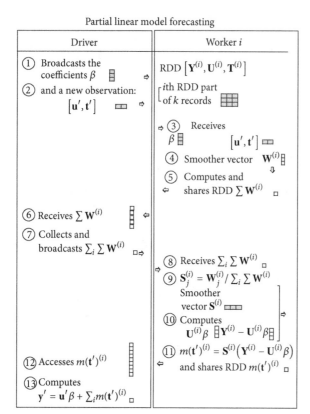

FIGURE 3: PLM parallel forecasting.

(2) The driver program accesses all preprocessed data.

(3) The driver program collects all the preprocessed data and broadcasts them to all the workers.

(4) Then, each worker makes its own copy of the training data $[\mathbf{Y}, \mathbf{U}, \mathbf{T}]$.

(5) A smoother matrix, $\mathbf{W}$, is computed in parallel. Since the rows of $\mathbf{W}$ are divided into partitions, each worker then computes its part $\mathbf{W}^{(i)}$.

(6) Each worker computes the sum of elements in each row within its partition $\mathbf{W}^{(i)}$: $\sum_j \mathbf{W}_j^{(i)}$, which is then saved as a RDD.

(7) We do not actually need the normalized matrix $\mathbf{S}$ itself, which could be computed as $\mathbf{W}_j^{(i)}/\sum_j \mathbf{W}_j^{(i)}$, but only $(\mathbf{I}-\mathbf{S})$ as RDD, which is the part directly computed by each worker: $(\mathbf{I}-\mathbf{S}^{(i)})$.

(8) Using the ith part of matrix $(\mathbf{I}-\mathbf{S})$, we multiply it from the right side with the corresponding elements of matrix $\mathbf{U}$. Thus, we obtain the ith part of transformed matrix $\widetilde{\mathbf{U}}^{(i)}$ as a RDD. The ith part of transformed matrix $\widetilde{\mathbf{Y}}^{(i)}$ as RDD is computed analogously.

(9) Finally, the driver program accesses and collects matrices $\widetilde{\mathbf{U}}$ and $\widetilde{\mathbf{Y}}$.

(10) The driver program initializes computing of the standard linear regression algorithm, *LinearRegressionModelWithSGD*, which is realized in SPARK.

(11) The parameters β are computed in parallel.

(12) Then, β are accessed by the driver computer.

Let us now describe the forecasting process (Figure 3), which occurs after the parametric part of the PLM has completed its estimation. Note that the kernel part of the model is nonparametric and is directly computed for each forecasted data point.

Since the forecasting is performed after the training process, then the preprocessed training set is already distributed among the workers and is available as a RDD. The PLM distributed forecasting procedure includes the following steps:

(1) The driver program broadcasts the estimated linear part coefficients, β, to the workers.

(2) Receiving new observation $[\mathbf{u}', \mathbf{t}']$, the driver program broadcasts it to all the workers.

(3) Each worker receives its copy of $[\mathbf{u}', \mathbf{t}']$ and β.

(4) We compute a smoother matrix $\mathbf{W}$, which is in a vector form. This computation is also partitioned among the workers (see (5)), so the ith worker computes $\mathbf{W}^{(i)}$ as particular columns of $\mathbf{W}$.

(5) Each worker computes partial sums of the rows of the matrix $\mathbf{W}^{(i)}$ elements and shares the partial sums with the driver program.

(6) The driver program accesses the partial sums and performs reducing step to obtain the final sum, $\sum_i \mathbf{W}^{(i)}$.

(7) The driver program broadcasts the final sum to all the workers.

(8) Each worker receives the final sum, $\sum_i \mathbf{W}^{(i)}$.

(9) Each worker computes its columns of the smoother matrix $\mathbf{S}^{(i)}$.

(10) Based on the RDD part $[\mathbf{Y}^{(i)}, \mathbf{U}^{(i)}, \mathbf{T}^{(i)}]$ (known from the training step), each worker computes the linear part of the forecast for training data. It was necessary to identify the kernel part of the forecast, performing subtraction of the linear part from the total forecast, the values of which were known from the training set.

(11) Each worker computes the kernel part of the forecast $m(\mathbf{t}')^{(i)}$ as RDD and shares with the driver program.

(12) The driver program accesses the partial kernel forecasts $m(\mathbf{t}')^{(i)}$.

(13) The driver program performs the reducing step to make the final forecast, combining the accessed kernel parts and computing the linear part: $\mathbf{y}' = \mathbf{u}'\beta + \sum_i m(\mathbf{t}')^{(i)}$.

4.2. Case Studies. We illustrate the distributed execution of PLM algorithm with a simple numerical example. First, the driver computer reads the training data, $[\mathbf{Y}, \mathbf{U}, \mathbf{T}]$:

$$[\mathbf{Y}, \mathbf{U}, \mathbf{T}] = \begin{pmatrix} \begin{array}{c|cc|cc} \mathbf{Y} & \multicolumn{2}{c|}{\mathbf{U}} & \multicolumn{2}{c}{\mathbf{T}} \\ \hline 1 & 1 & 2 & 1 & 2 \\ 2 & 2 & 3 & 2 & 3 \\ 3 & 2 & 1 & 2 & 1 \\ 4 & 2 & 2 & 1 & 1 \end{array} \end{pmatrix}. \tag{8}$$

We suppose that the algorithm is being executed in parallel on two workers. The driver accesses $[\mathbf{Y}, \mathbf{U}, \mathbf{T}]$ and creates the corresponding RDDs.

First, data preprocessing takes place. This job is shared between the workers in a standard way, and the result is returned to the driver. We do not change our data at this stage for illustrative purposes.

The goal of the training process is to compute the coefficients β of the linear part. First, the matrices $[\mathbf{Y}, \mathbf{U}, \mathbf{T}]$ are divided into the parts by rows:

$$[\mathbf{Y}, \mathbf{U}, \mathbf{T}] = \begin{pmatrix} \mathbf{Y}^{(1)}, \mathbf{U}^{(1)}, \mathbf{T}^{(1)} \\ \mathbf{Y}^{(2)}, \mathbf{U}^{(2)}, \mathbf{T}^{(2)} \end{pmatrix}$$

$$= \begin{pmatrix} \begin{array}{c|cc|cc} \mathbf{Y}^{(1)} & \multicolumn{2}{c|}{\mathbf{U}^{(1)}} & \multicolumn{2}{c}{\mathbf{T}^{(1)}} \\ \hline 1 & 1 & 2 & 1 & 2 \\ 2 & 2 & 3 & 2 & 3 \\ \hline \mathbf{Y}^{(1)} & \multicolumn{2}{c|}{\mathbf{U}^{(2)}} & \multicolumn{2}{c}{\mathbf{T}^{(2)}} \\ \hline 3 & 2 & 1 & 2 & 1 \\ 4 & 2 & 2 & 1 & 1 \end{array} \end{pmatrix}. \tag{9}$$

Each worker i accesses its part of data $[\mathbf{Y}^{(i)}, \mathbf{U}^{(i)}, \mathbf{T}^{(i)}]$, and it has access to the whole data.

Each worker computes its part of the smoother matrix $\mathbf{S}^{(i)}$, in particular:

$$\mathbf{S} = \begin{pmatrix} \mathbf{S}^{(1)} \\ \mathbf{S}^{(2)} \end{pmatrix} = \begin{pmatrix} SmoothMatrix\left(\mathbf{T}^{(1)}, \mathbf{T}\right) \\ SmoothMatrix\left(\mathbf{T}^{(2)}, \mathbf{T}\right) \end{pmatrix}. \tag{10}$$

The first worker obtains the elements of smoother matrix $\mathbf{S}^{(1)}$ (it gets directly matrix $\mathbf{I} - \mathbf{S}^{(i)}$); the corresponding elements of matrix $\mathbf{W}^{(1)}$ should be computed first. For example, to get the element $\mathbf{W}_{1,3}^{(1)}$ according to the function *SmoothMatrix*,

$$\mathbf{W}_{1,3}^{(1)} = K_H\left(\mathbf{T}_1^{(1)} - \mathbf{T}_3\right) = K_H\left((1, 2) - (2, 1)\right)$$

$$= K_H\left((-1, 1)\right) = K\left((-2, 2)\right) = 0.007. \tag{11}$$

Then, matrix $\mathbf{W}$ for both workers is the following:

$$\mathbf{W} = \begin{pmatrix} \mathbf{W}^{(1)} \\ \mathbf{W}^{(2)} \end{pmatrix} = \begin{pmatrix} 0.399 & 0.007 & 0.007 & 0.054 \\ 0.007 & 0.399 & 0.000 & 0.000 \\ \hline 0.007 & 0.000 & 0.399 & 0.054 \\ 0.054 & 0.000 & 0.054 & 0.399 \end{pmatrix}. \tag{12}$$

To get the element $(\mathbf{I} - \mathbf{S}^{(1)})_{1,3}$ knowing matrix $\mathbf{W}^{(1)}$ according to the function *SmoothMatrix*, we compute

$$\left(\mathbf{I} - \mathbf{S}^{(1)}\right)_{1,3} = -\frac{0.007}{(0.399 + 0.007 + 0.007 + 0.005)} \tag{13}$$

$$= -0.016.$$

Then, matrix $(\mathbf{I} - \mathbf{S})$ for both workers is the following:

$$(\mathbf{I} - \mathbf{S}) = \begin{pmatrix} (\mathbf{I} - \mathbf{S})^{(1)} \\ (\mathbf{I} - \mathbf{S})^{(2)} \end{pmatrix} \tag{14}$$

$$= \begin{pmatrix} 0.147 & -0.016 & -0.016 & -0.115 \\ -0.018 & 0.018 & -0.000 & -0.000 \\ \hline -0.016 & -0.000 & 0.133 & -0.117 \\ -0.106 & -0.000 & -0.107 & 0.213 \end{pmatrix}.$$

Then, the corresponding smoothed matrices $\widetilde{\mathbf{U}}$ and $\widetilde{\mathbf{Y}}$ computed by both workers are

$$\widetilde{\mathbf{U}} = \begin{pmatrix} \widetilde{\mathbf{U}}^{(1)} \\ \widetilde{\mathbf{U}}^{(2)} \end{pmatrix} = \begin{pmatrix} -0.147 & -0.000 \\ 0.018 & 0.019 \\ \hline 0.016 & -0.134 \\ 0.106 & 0.106 \end{pmatrix},$$

$$\tag{15}$$

$$\widetilde{\mathbf{Y}} = \begin{pmatrix} \widetilde{\mathbf{Y}}^{(1)} \\ \widetilde{\mathbf{Y}}^{(2)} \end{pmatrix} = \begin{pmatrix} -0.393 \\ 0.018 \\ \hline -0.085 \\ 0.426 \end{pmatrix}.$$

Matrices $\widetilde{\mathbf{U}}^{(1)}$ and $\widetilde{\mathbf{U}}^{(2)}$ are sent to the driver and collected into the matrix $\widetilde{\mathbf{U}}$, but $\widetilde{\mathbf{Y}}^{(1)}$ and $\widetilde{\mathbf{Y}}^{(2)}$ are collected into the vector $\widetilde{\mathbf{Y}}$.

The driver program calls the standard procedure of regression coefficient calculation, which is shared between workers in a standard way. The resulting coefficients β are collected on the driver:

$$\beta = \begin{pmatrix} \beta_0 \\ \beta_1 \\ \beta_2 \end{pmatrix} = \begin{pmatrix} -0.002 \\ 2.753 \\ 1.041 \end{pmatrix}. \tag{16}$$

At the forecasting stage, each worker receives a set of points for forecasting. Now, we illustrate the algorithm for a single point $[\mathbf{u}', \mathbf{t}'] = [(2, 1), (1, 1)]$ and two workers.

Each worker i accesses its part of training data $[\mathbf{Y}^{(i)}, \mathbf{U}^{(i)}, \mathbf{T}^{(i)}]$ and computes then the elements of matrix $\mathbf{S}^{(i)} = SmoothMatrix(\mathbf{T}^{(i)}, \mathbf{t}')$. First, smoother matrix $\mathbf{W}^{(i)}$ should be computed. For example, worker 1 computes the element

$$\mathbf{W}_{1,1}^{(1)} = K_H\left((1, 2) - (2, 1)\right) = K_H\left((-1, 1)\right) \tag{17}$$

$$= K\left((-2, 2)\right) = 0.007.$$

So, workers 1 and 2 obtain matrices

$$\mathbf{W} = \begin{pmatrix} \mathbf{W}^{(1)} \\ \mathbf{W}^{(2)} \end{pmatrix} = \begin{pmatrix} 0.007 & 0.000 \\ 0.399 & 0.054 \end{pmatrix}. \tag{18}$$

Now, each worker computes partial sums (so for worker 1, $\mathbf{W}_{1,1}^{(1)} + \mathbf{W}_{1,2}^{(1)} = 0.007 + 0.000 = 0.007$; for worker 2, $0.399 + 0.054 = 0.453$) and shares them to the driver program. The driver computes the total sum $0.007 + 0.453 = 0.46$ and sends it to the workers.

Now, each worker computes matrix $\mathbf{S}^{(i)}$. For example, worker 1 computes the element $\mathbf{S}_{1,1}^{(1)} = 0.007/0.46 = 0.016$.

Then, matrices $\mathbf{S}^{(i)}$ for both workers are

$$\mathbf{S} = \left(\frac{\mathbf{S}^{(1)}}{\mathbf{S}^{(2)}} \right) = \left(\begin{array}{cc} 0.016 & 0.000 \\ 0.867 & 0.117 \end{array} \right). \tag{19}$$

Now, each worker computes $\mathbf{U}^{(i)}\beta$ and the corresponding difference $\mathbf{Y} - \mathbf{U}^{(i)}\beta$:

$$\mathbf{U}\beta = \left(\frac{\mathbf{U}^{(1)}\beta}{\mathbf{U}^{(2)}\beta} \right) = \left(\begin{array}{c} 4.83 \\ 8.63 \\ 6.55 \\ 7.59 \end{array} \right),$$

$$\mathbf{Y} - \mathbf{U}\boldsymbol{\beta} = \left(\frac{\mathbf{Y}^{(1)} - \mathbf{U}^{(1)}\boldsymbol{\beta}}{\mathbf{Y}^{(2)} - \mathbf{U}^{(2)}\boldsymbol{\beta}} \right) = \left(\begin{array}{c} -3.83 \\ -6.63 \\ -3.55 \\ -3.59 \end{array} \right). \tag{20}$$

Each worker computes the smoothed value of the kernel part of the forecast:

$$m^{(i)}\left(\mathbf{t}'\right) = \mathbf{S}^{(i)}\left(\mathbf{Y}^{(i)} - \mathbf{U}^{(i)}\beta\right), \tag{21}$$

so $m^{(1)}(\mathbf{t}') = -0.0628$ and $m^{(2)}(\mathbf{t}') = -3.49$. These values are shared with the driver program. It computes their sum, which is considered as a kernel part of the prediction: $m(\mathbf{t}') = -3.56$.

The driver program computes the linear part of the prediction, $\mathbf{u}'\beta = 3.79$, and the final forecast, $\mathbf{y}' = \mathbf{u}'\beta + m(\mathbf{t}') = 0.236$.

In the next sections, we evaluate the performance of the proposed algorithms by various numerical experiments.

5. Experimental Setup

5.1. Performance Evaluation Metrics

5.1.1. Parameters.
In our study, we divided the available datasets into two parts: training dataset and test dataset. The training dataset was used to train the model and the test dataset was used to check the accuracy of the results. The sizes of the training and test datasets were the important parameters as they influenced accuracy, scalability, and speed-up metrics.

Another important parameter was the level of parallelism, which we considered in the number of cores used. We varied this parameter between 1 (no parallelism) and 48 cores.

We also considered processing (learning) time as an important parameter to compare the methods. In most of our experiments, we varied one parameter and fixed the remaining parameters.

We conducted three kinds of experiments.

5.1.2. Accuracy Experiments.
In the accuracy experiments, we evaluated the goodness of fit that depended on the sizes of training and test datasets. As the accuracy criterion, we used the coefficient of determination R^2, which is usually a quality metric for regression model. It is defined as a relative part of the sum of squares explained by the regression and can be calculated as

$$R^2 = 1 - \frac{SS_{\text{res}}}{SS_{\text{tot}}} = 1 - \frac{\sum_i \left(y_i - \widehat{y_i}\right)^2}{\sum_i \left(y_i - \overline{y}\right)^2}, \tag{22}$$

where $\overline{y} = \sum_{i=1}^{n} y_i/n$ and $\widehat{y_i}$ is the estimation (prediction) of y_i calculated by the regression model.

Note that we calculated R^2 using test dataset. Thus, the results were more reliable, because we trained our model on one piece of data (training set) but checked the accuracy of the model on the other one (test set).

5.1.3. Scalability Experiments.
Next, we tested the proposed methods on big data. We analyzed how increasing the size of the dataset influences the time consumption of the algorithm. First, we discussed how the execution time changed with the increasing of the size of the dataset. Then, we analyzed how methods accuracy depends on the execution (training) time under different conditions. Scalability was measured with the fixed number of cores.

5.1.4. Speed-Up Experiments.
Finally, we analyzed the relationship between time consumption and the degree of parallelism (number of cores) in the distributed realization. We varied the various parallelization degrees and compared the speed of work of various methods. The speed was measured with the fixed accuracy and scale.

5.2. Hardware and Software Used.
The experiments were carried out on a cluster of 16 computing nodes. Each one of these computing nodes had the following features: processors: 2x Intel Xeon CPU E5-2620, cores: 4 per node (8 threads), clock speed: 2.00 GHz, cache: 15 MB, network: QDR InfiniBand (40 Gbps), hard drive: 2TB, RAM: 16 GB per node.

Both Hadoop master processes the NameNode and the JobTracker were hosted in the master node. The former controlled the HDFS, coordinating the slave machines by means of their respective DataNode processes, while the latter was in charge of the TaskTrackers of each computing node, which executed the MapReduce framework. We used a standalone SPARK cluster, which followed a similar configuration, as the master process was located on the master node, and the worker processes were executed on the slave machines. Both frameworks shared the underlying HDFS file system.

These are the details of the software used for the experiments: MapReduce implementation: Hadoop version 2.6.0, SPARK version 1.5.2, operating system: CentOS 6.6.

5.3. Datasets.
We used three datasets: synthetic data, airlines data, and Hanover traffic data. The main characteristics of these datasets are summarized in Table 1. Table 2 presents sample records for each dataset.

TABLE 1: Characteristics of the datasets.

Dataset	Number of records	Number of factors
Synthetic data	10,000	2
Traffic data	6,500	7
Airlines delays	120,000,000 (13,000)	29 + 22 (10)

Synthetic Data. We started with synthetic data in order to check how the partially linear regression performs on partially linear data and to compute the basic performance characteristics that depended on training and test set sizes. We took the following model:

$$y = 0.5x^1 + x^2 \sin\left(x^2\right) + \varepsilon, \qquad (23)$$

where x^1 and x^2 were independently uniformly distributed in the interval $[0; 1000]$ and $\varepsilon \sim N(0; 50)$. The dependence on x^2 was clearly nonlinear and strictly fluctuating.

Hanover Traffic Data. In [25], we simulated a traffic network in the southern part of Hanover, Germany, on the base of real traffic data. In this study, we used this simulation data as a dataset. The network contained three parallel and five perpendicular streets, which formed 15 intersections with a flow of approximately 5000 vehicles per hour. For our experiments, 6 variables were used: y travel time (min), x^1 length of the route (km), x^2 average speed in the system (km/h), x^3 average number of stops in the system (units/min), x^4 congestion level of the flow (veh/h), x^5 traffic lights in the route (units), and x^6 left turns in the route (units).

For the Hanover traffic data, we solved the problem of travel time predictions. We did not filter the dataset and instead used the data in the original form. Principally, the analysis of outliers allows deleting suspicious observations to obtain more accurate results; however, some important information can be lost [26].

Taking different subsets of variables, we found that the following variable assignment to linear and kernel parts of PLM is optimal:

(i) Linear part **U**: x^4, x^6

(ii) Kernel part **T**: x^1, x^2, x^3, x^5

Airlines Data. The data consists of flight arrival and departure details for all commercial flights within the USA, from October 1987 to April 2008 [27]. This is a large dataset: there are nearly 120 million records in total, taking up 12 gigabytes. Every row in the dataset includes 29 variables. This data was used in various studies for analyzing the efficiency of methods proposed for big data processing, including regression [28]. In order to complement this data and to obtain a better prediction, we added weather average daily information, including daily temperatures (min/max), wind speed, snow conditions, and precipitation, which is freely available from the site https://www.wunderground.com/. This provided an additional 22 factors for each of the 731 days. The airlines and weather datasets were joined on the corresponding date.

For this data, we aimed to solve the problem of the departure delay prediction, which corresponded to the DepDelay column of data.

For test purposes, we selected the Salt Lake City International Airport (SLC). Our experiments showed that construction of a model for several airports resulted in poor results; this required special clustering [29] and could be the subject of future research.

Therefore, we selected two years (1995 and 1996) for our analysis. This yielded approximately 170,000 records.

An additional factor, which was added to this data, was the number of flights 30 minutes before and 30 minutes after the specific flight.

The initial analysis showed the heterogeneous structure of this data. Clustering showed that two variables are the most important for separating the data: departure time and travel distance. A very promising cluster with good prediction potential was short late flights (DepTime $\geq$ 21:45 and Distance $<$ 1000 Km). They could provide relatively good predictions; however, the distribution of delays did not significantly differ from the original dataset. This cluster contained approximately 13,000 records.

In subsequent experiments, we used subsets from this data in order to demonstrate the influence of dataset sizes on the prediction quality.

For the PLM algorithm, the first important issue was how to divide the variables for the linear and kernel parts of the regression. Taking different subsets of variables and including/excluding variables one by one, we found 10 most significant variables and the following optimal subsets:

(i) Linear part **U**: distance of the flight (Distance), average visibility distance (MeanVis), average wind speed (MeanWind), average precipitation (Precipitationmm), wind direction (WindDirDegrees), number of flights in 30-minute interval (Num), and departure time (DepTime)

(ii) Kernel part **T**: day of the week (DayOfWeek), thunderstorm (0 or 1), and destination (Dest)

Table 2 presents data fragments of 10 random records from each training dataset.

6. Experimental Framework and Analysis

6.1. Accuracy Experiments. We compared the goodness-of-fit metric (R^2) of the partially linear, linear, and kernel regression for the datasets by varying the size of the training dataset. Note that the accuracy did not depend on the size of the test set (which was taken equal to 1000). The results are presented in Figures 4, 5, and 6.

We observed very different results. For synthetic data, one variable was linear by definition and another one was nonlinear; the partially linear model was preferable as it produced R^2 with a value of 0.95 against 0.12 for both linear and kernel models. For the airlines dataset, partially linear model was also preferable, but the difference was not so significant. In contrast, for the Hanover data, the kernel model was preferable compared with the partially linear one

TABLE 2: Fragments of datasets.

(a) Synthetic dataset

y	x^1	x^2
2.31	0.87	1.26
1.45	1.27	−0.36
−0.5	0.47	−0.06
−1.9	−0.94	1.51
−1.51	0.33	1.72
−0.09	−0.1	−1.71
0.17	0.24	1.64
1.8	0.07	0.77
−0.5	0.45	−0.22
0.76	0.94	1.32

(b) Hanover dataset

y: travel time	x^1: length	x^2: speed	x^3: stops	x^4: congestion	x^5: tr. lights	x^6: left turns
256	2107.51	30.30	2.10	42.43	225	0
284	2349.74	22.36	4.89	85.56	289	4
162	1248.51	19.33	9.27	85.91	81	1
448	2346.80	20.58	8.39	86.60	289	1
248	352.67	19.33	9.27	85.91	25	1
327	907.30	23.54	3.96	86.95	100	0
443.5	1093.29	22.01	5.44	88.66	169	0
294	348.35	23.68	3.81	89.33	25	0
125.5	1236.62	18.97	10.65	85.21	81	1
511.5	357.23	19.96	7.66	84.85	25	1

(c) Airlines dataset

DepDelay	DayOfWeek	Distance	MeanVis	MeanWind	Thunderstorm	Precipitationmm	WindDirDegrees	Num	Dest	DepTime
0	3	588	24	14	0	12.7	333	18	SNA	2150
63	7	546	22	13	0	1.78	153	2	GEG	2256
143	5	919	24	18	0	9.14	308	27	MCI	2203
−4	6	599	22	16	0	11.68	161	23	SFO	2147
4	6	368	24	14	0	7.62	151	22	LAS	2159
19	5	188	20	35	0	1.02	170	23	IDA	2204
25	7	291	23	19	0	0	128	22	BOI	2200
1	6	585	17	10	0	6.6	144	25	SJC	2151
0	3	507	28	13	0	9.91	353	24	PHX	2150
38	2	590	28	23	0	0	176	7	LAX	2243

starting from some point. One possible explanation is that the dimension of traffic data was less than airlines data, so the kernel model worked better when it had sufficient data.

6.2. Scalability Experiments. We compared the speed (execution time) of the partially linear, linear, and kernel regression for the datasets by varying the size of training and test datasets. Note that both sizes of training and test datasets influenced the execution time. The results for airlines data are presented in Figures 7 and 8. Other datasets produced similar results.

For the partially linear regression, we could see quadratic relationship between execution time and the size of the training set and a linear dependence of execution time from the size of the test set. These results could be easily interpreted, because the computation of $\widetilde{U}$ and $\widetilde{Y}$ (steps (9) and (10) of PLM training, Figure 2) required a smoother matrix of size $n \times n$, where n is the size of the training dataset. On the other hand, the test set participated in the forecasting step only, and the complexity had a linear relationship with its size. For kernel and linear regressions, the relationship with execution time was linear for both training and test set sizes.

Next, we demonstrated how much resources (execution time) should be spent to reach some quality level (R^2) for the partially linear regression model. The results for synthetic data are presented in Figure 9. This graph was constructed

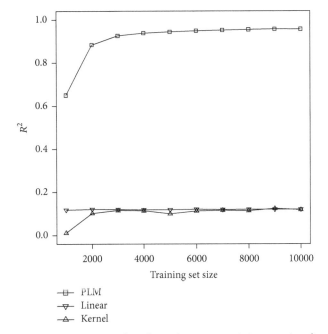

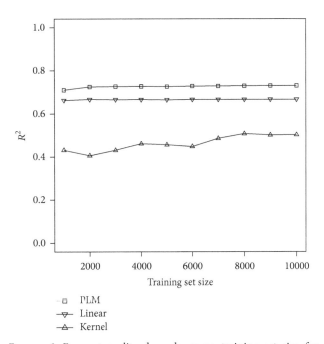

Figure 4: Forecast quality dependence on training set size for synthetic data.

Figure 6: Forecast quality dependence on training set size for airlines data.

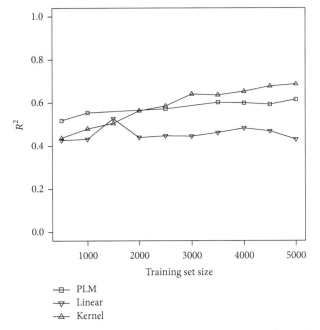

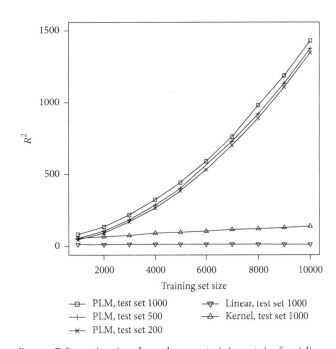

Figure 5: Forecast quality dependence on training set size for traffic data.

Figure 7: Execution time dependence on training set size for airlines data.

by fixing the test set size to 900, executing the algorithm for different training set sizes, obtaining the corresponding execution time and accuracy, and plotting them on the graph.

We could see relatively fast growth at the beginning, but it slowed towards the end, and successive execution time investments did not increase the goodness of fit, R^2.

6.3. Speed-Up Experiments. Finally, we examined how the execution time changes with the number of available cores.

The results for the Hanover traffic data are presented in Figure 10 and the remaining datasets produced similar results.

We could see that the execution time decreased until it reached a threshold of 5–10 cores and then slightly increased (this is true for the PLM and the kernel regression; for the linear regression, the minimum was reached with 2 cores). This is explained by the fact that data transfer among a large number of cores takes significantly more time than computations. This meant that SPARK still needed a better

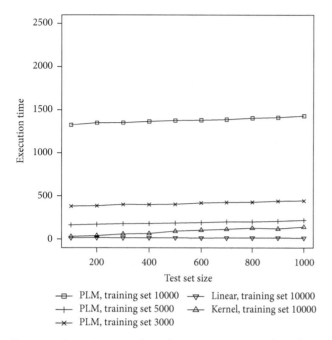

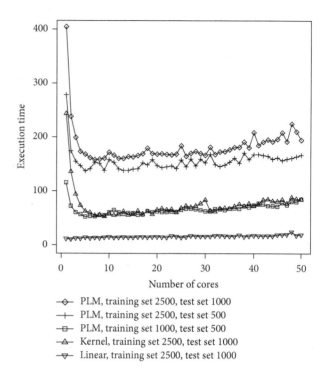

FIGURE 8: Execution time dependence on test set size for airlines data.

FIGURE 10: PLM algorithm execution time depending on the number of processing cores for traffic data.

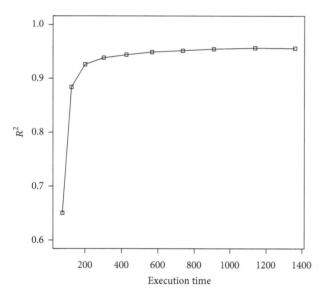

FIGURE 9: Forecast quality dependence on execution time of PLM algorithm for synthetic data.

optimization mechanism for parallel task execution. A similar issue has been reported by other researchers in [30] for clustering techniques.

7. Concluding Remarks

This paper presents distributed parallel versions of kernel-density-based and partially linear regression models, intended to process big datasets in a reasonable time. The algorithms deploy Apache SPARK, which is a well-known distributed computation framework. The algorithms were tested over three different datasets of approximately 10,000

records, which cannot be processed by a single computer in a reasonable time. Thus, it was tested over a cluster of 16 nodes. We conducted three kinds of experiments. First, in the *Accuracy Experiments,* the results indicated that they could not be well forecasted using the linear regression model. We conducted the experiments with a more common situation, when the structure of the data is not linear or partially linear. For all the datasets, (non)semiparametric models (kernel and PLM) showed better results, taking as an efficiency criterion coefficient of determination, R^2. As discussed, kernel regression experiences problem with increasing the dimensionality, because it is difficult to find the points in the neighborhood of the specified point in big dimensions. In our experiments, benchmark data and real-world data had many variables and we showed that semiparametric models gave more accurate results. We also conducted experiments by increasing the training set to show that it resulted in increased accuracy. Next, in the *Scalability Experiments,* we changed the sizes of training and test sets with the aim of analyzing the algorithms' computation time with the same fixed level of parallelism (number of working nodes/cores). All the experiments showed that the training set influenced the time nonlinearly (at most quadratically), but the test set influenced the time linearly. Finally, in the *Speed-Up Experiments,* our purpose was to show the importance of parallel realization of the algorithms to work with big datasets, taking into account the fact that nonparametric and semiparametric estimation methods are very computationally intensive. We demonstrated the feasibility of processing datasets of varying sizes that were otherwise not feasible to process with a single machine. An interesting aspect was that for each combination (dataset, algorithm) we could find the optimal amount of resources (number of cores) to minimize the algorithms execution time. For example, for the PLM regression of the airlines data, with the training set size equal to 2500 and test set size equal to 500, the optimal number of cores was 5 and with the same training set size and the test set size equal to 1000 the optimal number of cores was 9. After this optimal point, the execution time of the algorithm starts to increase. We could explain this phenomenon, as the distribution expenses in this case were more than the award from the parallel execution. Thus, we could conclude that it is important to find the optimal amount of the resources for each experiment.

Competing Interests

The authors declare that there are no competing interests regarding the publication of this paper.

References

[1] C. Long, Ed., *Data Science and Big Data Analytics: Discovering, Analyzing, Visualizing and Presenting Data*, John Wiley and Sons, Inc, New York, NY, USA, 2015.

[2] J. Dean and S. Ghemawat, "Map reduce: a flexible data processing tool," *Communications of the ACM*, vol. 53, no. 1, pp. 72–77, 2010.

[3] Spark. spark cluster computing framework, http://spark.apache .org/.

[4] D. Peralta, S. del Río, S. Ramírez-Gallego, I. Triguero, J. M. Benitez, and F. Herrera, "Evolutionary feature selection for big data classification: a MapReduce approach," *Mathematical Problems in Engineering*, vol. 2015, Article ID 246139, 11 pages, 2015.

[5] "CRAN task view: High-performance and parallel computing with R," https://cran.r-project.org/web/views/HighPerform anceComputing.html.

[6] SparkR(Ronspark), https://spark.apache.org/docs/latest/sparkr .html.

[7] P. D. Michailidis and K. G. Margaritis, "Accelerating kernel density estimation on the GPU using the CUDA framework," *Applied Mathematical Sciences*, vol. 7, no. 29-32, pp. 1447–1476, 2013.

[8] A. Fernández, S. del Río, V. López et al., "Big data with cloud computing: an insight on the computing environment, mapreduce, and programming frameworks," *Wiley Interdisciplinary Reviews: Data Mining and Knowledge Discovery*, vol. 4, no. 5, pp. 380–409, 2014.

[9] N. E. Helwig, "Semiparametric regression of big data in R," in *Proceedings of the CSE Big Data Workshop*, May 2014.

[10] N. Draper and H. Smith, *Applied Regression Analysis*, John Wiley & Sons, New York, NY, USA, 1986.

[11] M. S. Srivastava, *Methods of multivariate statistics*, Wiley Series in Probability and Statistics, Wiley-Interscience [John Wiley & Sons], NY, USA, 2002.

[12] L. Bottou, "Stochastic gradient descent tricks," *Lecture Notes in Computer Science (including subseries Lecture Notes in Artificial Intelligence and Lecture Notes in Bioinformatics)*, vol. 7700, pp. 421–436, 2012.

[13] W. Härdle, *Applied Nonparametric Regression*, Cambridge University Press, Cambridge, UK, 2002.

[14] W. Härdle, M. Müller, S. Sperlich, and A. Werwatz, *Nonparametric and Semiparametric Models*, Springer Series in Statistics, Springer-Verlag, New York, NY, USA, 2004.

[15] E. Nadaraya, "On estimating regression," *Theory of Probability and its Applications*, vol. 9, no. 1, pp. 141–142, 1964.

[16] G. S. Watson, "Smooth regression analysis," *The Indian Journal of Statistics. Series A*, vol. 26, pp. 359–372, 1964.

[17] B. W. Silverman, *Density Estimation for Statistics and Data Analysis*, Chapman & Hall, 1986.

[18] D. W. Scott, *Multivariate Density Estimation: Theory, Practice, and Visualization*, Wiley-Interscience, 1992.

[19] H. Liang, "Estimation in partially linear models and numerical comparisons," *Computational Statistics & Data Analysis*, vol. 50, no. 3, pp. 675–687, 2006.

[20] P. Speckman, "Kernel smoothing in partial linear models," *Journal of the Royal Statistical Society B*, vol. 50, no. 3, pp. 413–436, 1988.

[21] M. Zaharia, M. Chowdhury, T. Das et al., "Resilient distributed datasets: a fault-tolerant abstraction for in-memory cluster computing," in *Proceedings of the 9th USENIX Conference on Networked Systems Design and Implementation (NSDI '12)*, USENIX Association, Berkeley, Calif, USA, 2012.

[22] Mllib guide, http://spark.apache.org/docs/latest/mllib-guide .html.

[23] N. Pentreath, *Machine Learning with Spark*, Packt Publishing Ltd., Birmingham, UK, 2015.

[24] R. B. Zadeh, X. Meng, A. Ulanov et al., "Matrix computations and optimisation in apache spark," in *Proceedings of the 22nd ACM SIGKDD International Conference on Knowledge Discovery and Data Mining (KDD '16)*, 38, 31 pages, San Francisco, Calif, USA, August 2016.

[25] M. Fiosins, J. Fiosina, J. P. Müller, and J. Görmer, "Agent-based integrated decision making for autonomous vehicles in Urban traffic," *Advances in Intelligent and Soft Computing*, vol. 88, pp. 173–178, 2011.

[26] J. Fiosina and M. Fiosins, "Cooperative regression-based forecasting in distributed traffic networks," in *Distributed Network Intelligence, Security and Applications*, Q. A. Memon, Ed., chapter 1, p. 337, CRC Press, Taylor & Francis Group, 2013.

[27] Airline on-time performance data, asa sections on statistical computing statistical graphics, http://stat-computing.org/ dataexpo/2009/.

[28] Data science with hadoop: Predicting airline delays part 2, http://de.hortonworks.com/blog/data-science-hadoop-spark-scala-part-2/.

[29] J. Fiosina, M. Fiosins, and J. P. Müller, "Big data processing and mining for next generation intelligent transportation systems," *Jurnal Teknologi*, vol. 63, no. 3, 2013.

[30] J. Dromard, G. Roudire, and P. Owezarski, "Unsupervised network anomaly detection in real-time on big data," in *Communications in Computer and Information Science: ADBIS 2015 Short Papers and Workshops, BigDap, DCSA, GID, MEBIS, OAIS, SW4CH, WISARD, Poitiers, France, September 8–11, 2015. Proceedings*, vol. 539 of *Communications in Computer and Information Science*, pp. 197–206, Springer, Berlin, Germany, 2015.

5

Reidentification of Persons Using Clothing Features in Real-Life Video

Guodong Zhang,[1] **Peilin Jiang,**[2] **Kazuyuki Matsumoto,**[1] **Minoru Yoshida,**[1] **and Kenji Kita**[1]

[1]*Faculty of Engineering, Tokushima University, Tokushima 7708506, Japan*
[2]*Xian Jiao Tong University, No. 28, Xianning West Road, Xian, China*

Correspondence should be addressed to Guodong Zhang; zhang-g@hotmail.co.jp

Academic Editor: Qiushi Zhao

Person reidentification, which aims to track people across nonoverlapping cameras, is a fundamental task in automated video processing. Moving people often appear differently when viewed from different nonoverlapping cameras because of differences in illumination, pose, and camera properties. The color histogram is a global feature of an object that can be used for identification. This histogram describes the distribution of all colors on the object. However, the use of color histograms has two disadvantages. First, colors change differently under different lighting and at different angles. Second, traditional color histograms lack spatial information. We used a perception-based color space to solve the illumination problem of traditional histograms. We also used the spatial pyramid matching (SPM) model to improve the image spatial information in color histograms. Finally, we used the Gaussian mixture model (GMM) to show features for person reidentification, because the main color feature of GMM is more adaptable for scene changes, and improve the stability of the retrieved results for different color spaces in various scenes. Through a series of experiments, we found the relationships of different features that impact person reidentification.

1. Introduction

As public security technology has become increasingly intelligent, surveillance cameras have been set up in public places such as airports and supermarkets. These cameras provide huge amounts of nonoverlapping video data. It is often necessary to track an object or person of interest that appears on video from multiple cameras under different illumination conditions [1–3]. When searching for moving people in surveillance video data, object retrieval systems for intelligent video surveillance experience the following problems.

(1) Object retrieval results in video surveillance depend on motion segmentation and video analysis. Digital video is a series of images, constituted by frames that contain rich information. If an image frame contains moving objects, then object retrieval detection can be used to segment a moving target [4]. Object retrieval results depend on the object segmentation. If video analysis cannot separate the foreground and moving objects, the target object cannot be retrieved from the many irrelevant foreground objects. A good object retrieval system should adapt to various levels of video quality for foreground detection, which could eliminate unrelated objects and retrieve the target [5].

(2) Specific object retrieval in video surveillance faces technical limitations. The moving objects of interest in surveillance video are often persons and cars. Facial features are the most distinctive elements for person recognition, and relatively mature methods are available for this process. However, low camera resolution often makes it difficult to extract perceivable information about facial expression [6]. The mature technology of video object retrieval based on facial features should receive more technical exploration.

(3) External factors greatly influence objects appearance under video surveillance. A robust object retrieval system should be able to compensate for the following factors.

   (i) Person pose variation: a moving person may have arbitrary poses (Figure 1(a)).

(a)　　　　　　　　(b)　　　　　　　　(c)　　　　　　　　(d)

FIGURE 1: Images showing the same person in different camera views: (a) pose change, (b) illumination change, (c) occlusion, and (d) low resolution.

(ii) Varying illumination conditions: illumination conditions usually differ between camera views (Figure 1(b)).

(iii) Occlusion: a person body parts may be occluded by other subjects, such as a carried bag, in one camera view (Figure 1(c)).

(iv) Low image resolution: due to surveillance camera performance, images of a moving person often have low resolution (Figure 1(d)).

The color histogram is a tool used to describe the color composition of an image [7]. The histogram shows the appearance of different colors and the number of pixels for each color in an image. Colors possess better immunity to the noise jamming of images and are robust against image degradation and scaling. We selected a global color approach to body features for person reidentification in surveillance video. Extracting the color information of the person makes the method clear and simple. Because color statistic features lose information about color spatial distribution, we combined this approach with the spatial pyramid matching (SPM) model. We tested our method in the RGB, HSV, and UVW color spaces using real video images. We present related work on person reidentification and feature analysis in Section 2. We offer details on our proposed method in Section 3. We report and discuss the experimental results in Section 4, and we give conclusions and suggestions for future work in Section 5.

2. Related Works

For the past few years, object retrieval techniques using content-based video retrieval have received significant theoretical and technological support. Many researchers have examined person reidentification, and the related literature is extensive [8, 9]. This section discusses feature modeling and effective matching strategies, which are important methods for person reidentification.

2.1. Color Feature. Color features are one of the low-level feature types that have been widely used in content-based image retrieval (CBIR). Compared with other features, color exhibits little dependence on image rotation, translation,

scale change, and even the shape change. Color is thus thought of as almost independent of the images dimensions, direction, and view angles. Most representations in previous approaches are based on appearance. Gray and Tao [10] used a similarity function that was trained from a set of data. These authors focused on the problems of unknown viewpoint and pose. The method is robust to viewpoint change because it is based on the ensemble of localized features (ELF). Farenzena et al. [11] presented an appearance-based method based on the localization of perceptually relevant human parts. The information features contain three parts: overall chromatic content, the spatial arrangement of colors into stable regions, and the presence of recurrent local motifs with high entropy. The method is robust to pose, viewpoint, and illumination variations. Zhao et al. [12] transformed person reidentification into a distance learning problem. Using the relative distance comparison model to compute the distance of a pair of views, these authors considered a likely true match pair to have a smaller distance than that of a wrong match pair. These authors also used a new relative distance comparison model to measure the distance between pairs of person images and judge the pairs of true matches and wrong matches. Angela et al. proposed a new feature based on the definition of the probabilistic color histogram and trained fuzzy k-nearest neighbors (KNN) classifier based on an ad hoc dataset. The method is effective at discriminating and reidentifying people across two different video cameras regardless of viewpoint change. Metternich et al. [13] used a global color histogram and shape information to track people in real-life surveillance data, finding that the appearance of the subject impacted the tracking results. These authors also focused on the performance of matching techniques over cameras with different fields of view.

2.2. Metric Learning. Hirzer et al. [14] focused the matching method of metric learning on person reidentification. These authors accomplished metric learning from pairs of samples from different cameras. The method benefits from the advantages of metric learning and reduces the required computational effort. Good performance can be achieved even using less color and texture information. Khedher et al. [15] proposed a new automatic statistical method that could accept and reject SURF correspondence based on the

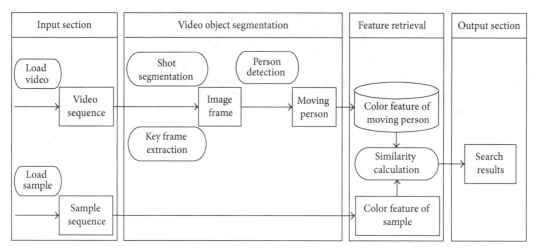

FIGURE 2: Overview of the system.

likelihood ratio of two Gaussian mixed models (GMMs) learned on a reference set. The method does not need to select the matching SURF pairs by empirical means. Instead, interest point matching over whole video sequences is used to judge the person identity. Matsukawa et al. [16] focused on the problem of overfitting and proposed a discriminative accumulation method of local histograms for person reidentification. The proposed method jointly learns pairs of a weight map for the accumulations and employs a distance metric that emphasizes discriminative histogram dimensions. This method can achieve better reidentification accuracy than other typical metric learning methods on various sizes of datasets.

3. System Description

3.1. An Overview of the Proposed System. The techniques of moving person retrieval information from a video database include shot segmentation, person detection, scene segmentation, feature extraction, and similarity calculation. As shown in Figure 2, shot segmentation refers to automatically segmenting video clips into shots as the basic unit for indexing. One second of video contains about 20–30 video frames, and neighboring frames are very similar to each other. There is no need to perform retrieval and matching for each frame, and frame differentiation is used to detect and extract the moving person. Frame differentiation relies on the change of pixel value between neighboring key frames. A change value greater than the established threshold value marks the pixel position of the moving person. This step is important in video parsing and directly affects the effectiveness of moving person retrieval.

The measurement method for similarity calculation influences the results ranking of object retrieval. Essentially, image similarity calculation computes the content of feature vectors from the objects. Each feature attribute selection can employ a different similarity computing method [17]. Frequently, image features are extracted in the form of feature vectors that can be regarded as points in multidimensional space.

The most common similarity measure method uses the distance between two spots in feature space. We also use distance measurement and correlativity calculation to scale the comparability between images.

Our proposed method is presented in Figure 3. We use traditional histogram and SPM histogram to retrieve the object. The traditional histogram method contains three parts, the color histogram feature extraction, color histogram distance computing, and outputting. The difference between SPM histogram and traditional histogram is the histogram distance computing part. The sample image and matching image are segmented into three parts, the upper, middle, and lower part. The three parts then separately computed the color histogram distance and use average distance to evaluate the results. Then the system uses GMM model to filter the top 20 results, extracts the GMM main color feature, and computes the similarity of them. Finally, the system outputs the rank of top 10 results.

3.2. Perception-Based Color Space Histogram Feature. Computations in the RGB and HSV color spaces cannot solve the problem of background illumination sensitivity. The color spaces always affect the computing accuracy of the color histogram [18]. We attempted to use perception-based color space, which exhibits good performance in image processing [19]. As the name suggests, the perception-based color space associated metric approximates perceived distances and color displacements, capturing relationships that are robust to spectral changes in illumination [20]. RGB color space can be transformed to perception-based color space through the following steps.

RGB color space can be transformed to perception-based color space through the following steps.

(1) Transform RGB to XYZ color space using the following formula (1):

$$
\begin{bmatrix} X \\ Y \\ Z \end{bmatrix} = \frac{1}{0.177} \begin{pmatrix} 0.49 & 0.361 & 0.20 \\ 0.177 & 0.0812 & 0.011 \\ 0.00 & 0.01 & 0.99 \end{pmatrix} \begin{bmatrix} G(R) \\ G(G) \\ G(B) \end{bmatrix}, \quad (1)
$$

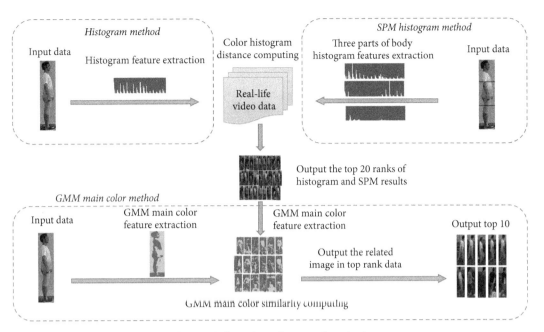

FIGURE 3: Overview of proposed method.

where $G(\ )$ is the gamma correction function and equals 2.0. The gamma correction function addresses color distortion and rediscovers the real environment to a certain extent.

(2) Transform XYZ to UVW color space. In UVW color space, the influence of lighting conditions is simulated by the tristimulus multiplication values and scale factor, as shown in the following formula (2):

$$\begin{bmatrix} X \\ Y \\ Z \end{bmatrix} \longrightarrow \begin{bmatrix} U \\ V \\ W \end{bmatrix} = B^{-1}DB \begin{bmatrix} X \\ Y \\ Z \end{bmatrix}, \tag{2}$$

where D is a diagonal matrix, accounting only for illumination, and independent of the material. B is the transfer matrix from the current color space coordinates to the base coordinates. The nonlinear transfer uses the following formula (3):

$$\begin{bmatrix} U \\ V \\ W \end{bmatrix} = A \left(\widehat{\ln} \left(B \begin{bmatrix} X \\ Y \\ Z \end{bmatrix} \right) \right), \tag{3}$$

where A and B are invertible 3×3 matrices and denote the component-wise natural logarithm. Matrix B transforms the color coordinates to the basis in which relighting best corresponds to multiplication by a diagonal matrix, while matrix A provides degrees of freedom that can be used to match perceptual distances. Based on similar color experiments in

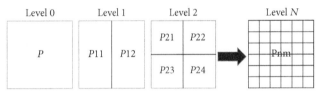

FIGURE 4: The method of SPM.

the database, A and B matrix-value formulas are shown as (4) and (5), respectively.

$$A = \begin{pmatrix} 27.07439 & -22.80783 & -1.806681 \\ -5.646736 & -7.722125 & 12.86503 \\ -4.163133 & -4.579428 & -4.576049 \end{pmatrix}, \tag{4}$$

$$B = \begin{pmatrix} 0.9465229 & 0.2946927 & -0.1313419 \\ -0.117917 & 0.9929960 & 0.007371554 \\ 0.0923046 & -0.046457 & 0.9946464 \end{pmatrix}. \tag{5}$$

3.3. SPM Model. Lazebnik et al. [21] proposed the Spatial Pyramid Matching (SPM) in 2006. SPM model contains broad space information, with which the color histogram information will be encoded orderly in space. The model divides the image into different levels, which can then be further refined. The SPM model space is shown in Figure 4. The level 0 image P is based on the original image feature information. But the image feature is based on the global unordered color information. Level 1 shows image separated as space geometry. $P11$ and $P12$ are expressed by a spatial order that contains simple space information.

P11 and P12, which also lack internal space information, are in level 1. If internal space information is necessary in P11 and P12, they must be separated using the same process. The level $i + 1$ feature is divided by level i. The levels of division are decided by the actual situation.

3.3.1. The SPM Histogram Feature. Image similarity is computed by the levels corresponding to parts in SPM model. For two images P and Q, the formula is as follows:

$$d(P, Q) = \sum k_{ij} d\left(p_{ij}, q_{ij}\right), \qquad (6)$$

where P_{ij} is the image P histogram feature of the part j in level i; $d(p_{ij}, q_{ij})$ is the feature similarity degree images P and Q; and K_{ij} is the weight of the similarity calculation. In this case, we focus on part j of level i. The weight of calculation should be set high.

3.4. Gaussian Color Model. Gaussian color model (GMM) is constantly used for color image segmentation according to the classification and clustering of image characteristics [22]. The image is divided into different parts based on pixel classification. We considered the main part of person identification to be based on minutia matching and ignored details. The retrieval of similar objects in a video system prioritizes the main part of similarity matching and does not emphasize accurate detail matching, so we considered the main colors as the features of the Gaussian color model.

3.4.1. Gaussian Distribution. The Gaussian distribution is a parametric probability density function that is a mean value and variance continuous distribution maximum information entropy [23]. As shown in (7), when distributing a unit value that fits the normal distribution random variable, the frequency of the variable that follows the Gaussian distribution is entirely determined by the mean value μ and variance σ^2. As x approaches μ, probability increases. σ means the dispersion, and the value of σ is a much greater degree of dispersion.

$$f(x) = \frac{1}{\sigma\sqrt{2\pi}} e^{-(x-\mu)^2/2\sigma^2}. \qquad (7)$$

For an image, the Gaussian distribution describes the distribution of specific pixel brightness that reflects the frequency of some gray numerical value [24]. A single-mode Gaussian distribution cannot represent a multicolored image. Therefore, we used a multiplicity of Gaussian models to show different pixel distributions that approximately simulate a multicolored image. Theoretically, we could increase the numbers of models to improve the descriptive ability.

Every pixel of the color image could be represented as a d dimensional vector x_i (color image $d = 3$ and gray image $d = 1$). The whole image could be represented as $X = (x_1^T, x_2^T, \ldots, x_N^T)$, where N is the sum of all pixels in a picture, X is represented as M states in GMM, and the value of M is usually restricted from 3 to 5. The linear stacking of the M Gaussian distributions could show the GMM of the

probability density function, as shown in (8): x is the pixel sampling of a picture.

$$P(x) = \sum_{k=1}^{M} p(k)\, p(x \mid k) = \sum_{k=1}^{M} \pi(k)\, N\left(x \mid \mu_k, \sum k\right). \qquad (8)$$

$N(x \mid \mu_k, \sum k)$ is the single Gaussian density function. As shown in (8), $k = 1, \ldots, M$ indicates the Gaussian density function of $No.k$. μ_k is the sample mean vector, $\sum k$ is sample covariance matrix, and π_k is the nonnegative coefficient of weight that describes the proportion of $No.k$ data in the total data.

3.5. Color Histogram Feature Extraction. The histogram of an image is related to the probability distribution function of the images pixel density. When this concept is extended to a color image, it is necessary to obtain the joint probability distribution value for multiple channels [25]. In general, a color histogram is defined by the following equation (9):

$$h_{A,B,C} = N \bullet \mathrm{Prob}\,(A = a,\ B = b,\ C = c), \qquad (9)$$

where A, B, and C indicate three color channels (R, G, and B or H, S, and V) and N is the sum of all pixels in the image. In terms of computing, the first step is to discretize the pixel values of the image, creating statistics for the number of pixels of each color for color histogram.

3.6. Histogram of Color Feature Similarity Measurement. Several methods exist to calculate and weigh the similarity measurement of the histogram. The distance formula of the similarity measure between images is based on the color content. Euclidean distance, histogram intersection, and histogram quadratic distance are widely used in image retrieval.

The Euclidean distance of the histogram between two images is given by the following equation (10):

$$d^2(h, g) = \sum_A \sum_B \sum_C (h(a, b, c) - g(a, b, c))^2, \qquad (10)$$

where h and g are two histograms and a, b, and c are the color channels. The formula subtracts the pixel value in the same bin of histograms h and g.

The formula for histogram intersection distance is as follows:

$$d(h, g) = \frac{\sum_A \sum_B \sum_C \min\left(h(a, b, c) - g(a, b, c)\right)}{\min\left(|h|, |g|\right)}, \qquad (11)$$

where $|h|$ and $|g|$ stand for the pixel values of image sampling in histograms h and g, respectively.

3.7. Evaluation Method. (1) We focused on the degree of search result accuracy using evaluation parameters for precision. Precision reflects the capability of filtering irrelevant content. These video retrieval system performance criteria reference the evaluation method for information search systems. For a retrieval object, the retrieval system returns a sort of search results. The precision rate expresses the number of correct relevant retrieval results divided by the number of total retrieval results.

$$\text{Precision} \ (\%) = \frac{A}{A + B} \times 100,$$

$$\text{AveragePrecision} \ (\%) = \frac{1}{n} \sum_{i=1}^{n} \text{Precision} \ (i).$$

(12)

In formula (12), A is the number of correct relevant retrieval examples, B is the number of irrelevant video retrieval examples, and C is the number of missing correct relevant retrieval examples.

(2) Cumulative Match Characteristic (CMC) curve is employed to evaluate the performance of the reidentification system. The CMC curve is used when the full gallery is available. It depicts the relationship between the accuracy and the threshold of rank. Most of the existing pedestrian reidentification algorithms use the CMC curve to evaluate the algorithm performance. Given a probe set and a pedestrian gallery set, the experimental result of CMC analysis describes what is the percentage of probe searches in the pedestrian dataset that returns the probes gallery mate within the top r rank-ordered results.

4. Experiment

We evaluate our reidentification method on three datasets, that is, the multicamera video data, the VIPeR data, and the SARC3D data. We examine our proposed SPM histogram + GMM main color method, the SPM histogram method, and the traditional histogram method on three datasets and further compare our method with the Symmetry-Driven Accumulation of Local Features (SDALF) method on the public VIPeR and SARC3D datasets. The code of SDALF could be downloaded on https://github.com/lorisbaz/sdalf. All the experiments are run on a desktop computer with an i7-3.4 GHz CPU.

4.1. Experiment on Multicamera Videos. We evaluated the performance of different color spaces for real-life video data. Uneven illumination distribution should affect person reidentification results in color images. Therefore, we created a video data set to test the validity and robustness of our method. We recorded the video data on a school campus. Six pedestrians walked from left to right in order under a surveillance camera, as shown in Figures 5 and 6. Our real-life video data consists of two videos that were recorded simultaneously at different locations. Location 1 was bright and location 2 was dark. The videos were recorded at 25 frames per second. Pictures of the side viewpoints of the six pedestrians were used as the retrieval samples, as shown in Figure 7. The six pedestrians were without a hat, bag, or other accessories. The RGB results are based on machine vision, while the HSV results are closer to human visual perception. As shown in Table 1, our proposed method outperforms the traditional histogram method and the SPM histogram method. We find that although the RGB color space reflects all sorts of colors from the images, the background color which is mixed in

TABLE 1: The average precision for persons retrieval in location 1.

Method	RGB	HSV	UVWS
Histogram	75	73.33	80
SPM histogram	71.66	75	70
GMM	86.66	85	88.33

TABLE 2: The average precision for persons retrieval in location 2.

Method	RGB	HSV	UVWS
Histogram	73.33	75	81.66
SPM histogram	83.33	85	80
GMM	81.66	83.33	85

these channels has affected the reidentification result. This problem is even severe in the SPM method, in which the lower part of the separated image contains a greater part of the background color than the body color. As shown in Table 2, the performance of UVW is better than HSV and RGB. The reason is that the results were affected mostly by the color transfer. In different illumination, the color histogram of one's clothes would be transferred to another color. For example, the red color in a dark environment seems like a black or gray color. The UVW color space is aimed at this problem. In the GMM color modeling, to solve the color transfer problem in low resolution images, we employ the primary colors of red, blue, and green as the dominant colors. However, for the dark background images, the GMM method generates a poor result.

4.2. Experiment on VIPeR Dataset. We examine the appearance model for person reidentification based on the VIPeR dataset, which consists of 632 pedestrian image pairs taken from arbitrary viewpoints under varying illumination conditions. Each image is scaled to 128×48 pixels.

As shown in Figure 8, our proposed method outperforms the histogram-based methods in the RGB color space, and the traditional histogram and the SPM histogram methods generate very similar results. We also observe that the proposed method in the HSV space performs better than in the RGB space, as shown in Figure 9. This is because that the image illumination in the VIPeR dataset varies significantly. The SDALF method renders a slightly better result than our proposed method, while our method has a great advantage on the calculation cost. Specifically, the SDALF takes about 3850 seconds to extract its features from 1264 images in the VIPeR dataset, while our proposed method takes only 40 seconds to extract and calculate the color histogram features. In addition, the SDALF method needs about 4260 seconds to compare all 399424 pairs of images, while our method needs only 610 seconds to calculate the GMM similarity for comparison in 1264 images. This result suggests that in terms of computational cost our approach significantly outperforms the SDALF method.

4.3. Experiment on SARC3D Dataset. The SARC3D dataset consists of short video clips of 50 people which have been

FIGURE 5: Location 1.

FIGURE 6: Location 2.

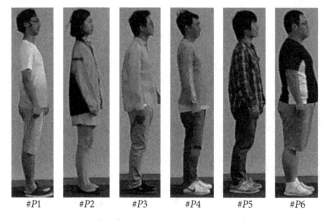

FIGURE 7: Example of placing a figure with experimental results.

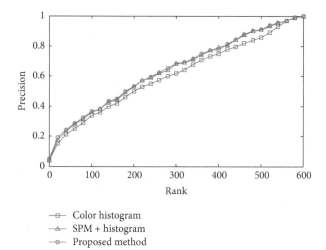

FIGURE 8: CMC curves on the VIPeR dataset for the proposed method and histogram methods in RGB space.

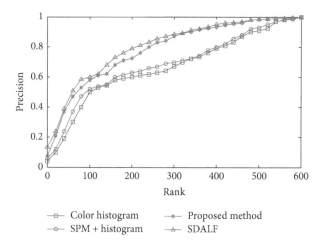

FIGURE 9: CMC curves on the VIPeR dataset for the proposed method and the other methods in HSV space.

captured with a calibrated camera. We employ the SARC3D dataset to effectively evaluate different person reidentification methods. To simplify the image alignment process, we manually select four frames for each clip which correspond to the predefined positions and postures, that is, back, front, left, and right, of these people. The selected dataset consists of 200 snapshots with four views for each person. For person reidentification, we randomly choose one of the four views for each person, calculate the similarity scores with all other images, and find the most similar images by sorting their similarities with the chosen image. The images of the same person

with different positions and postures should be ranked higher than the other images. In the dataset, 6 people are not fully visible in their images and 2 people are observed with the same dressing, that is, colors and combinations, except for the waling postures. We remove images of these people to avoid the different size of their masks form in the original images. All methods in the experiment are based on the RGB color space. Figure 10 shows the average CMC curves for the person reidentification under different methods. Our method significantly outperforms the SDALF method in recognition rate because the backward information in GMM matching has been filtered out given the people annotation template in the dataset. In the meantime, our method significantly outperforms the SDALF method in calculation cost, with only 30 seconds for color histogram feature extraction and image matching in 126 images, while the latter takes about 440 seconds for feature extraction and 70 more seconds for image matching.

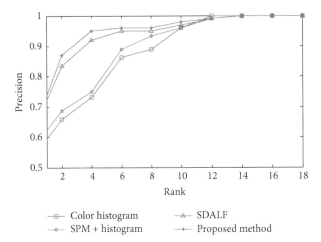

FIGURE 10: CMC curves on the VIPeR dataset for the proposed method and the other methods in RGB space.

5. Conclusion

Person reidentification in multicamera videos often has some problems that contain person pose variation, varying illumination, and low image resolution. We propose to solve two common problems in person reidentification, which are the varying illumination and low image resolution. Varying illumination conditions usually occur because of the difference between camera views. For example, the same people in different camera video have a color transfer. The low resolution image often contains high noise. It is difficult to extract the robust feature from the low resolution image. In order to improve the illumination problem in histogram methods, we introduce the perception-based color space which has been successfully employed in the image segmentation research into the person identification method. Secondly, for the low resolution images we incorporate spatial pyramid matching (SPM) method into the main color extraction method, which has shown great improvement in our experiment. In addition, our method has shown significant advantage in the computation cost compared with the traditional methods. In this paper we just extract the main color feature by the GMM model. We did not analyse the feature information from the mean value parameter and variance in the GMM. The main color feature also used the global object color; we could combine the SPM model with GMM main color local feature to retrieve the object from the video data.

Competing Interests

The authors declare that they have no competing interests.

Acknowledgments

This research was partially supported by JSPS KAKENHI Grant nos 15K00425 and 15K00309.

References

[1] R. Satta, "Appearance descriptors for person reidentification: a comprehensive review," https://arxiv.org/abs/1307.5748.

[2] A. Dangelo and J.-L. Dugelay, "People re-identification in camera networks based on probabilistic color histograms," in *Visual Information Processing and Communication II*, vol. 7882 of *Proceedings of SPIE*, January 2011.

[3] G. Doretto, T. Sebastian, P. Tu, and J. Rittscher, "Appearance-based person reidentification in camera networks: problem overview and current approaches," *Journal of Ambient Intelligence and Humanized Computing*, vol. 2, no. 2, pp. 127–151, 2011.

[4] M. A. Saghafi, A. Hussain, H. B. Zaman, and M. H. Md Saad, "Review of person re-identification techniques," *IET Computer Vision*, vol. 8, no. 6, pp. 455–474, 2014.

[5] S. Lee, N. Kim, K. Jeong, I. Paek, H. Hong, and J. Paik, "Multiple moving object segmentation using motion orientation histogram in adaptively partitioned blocks for high-resolution video surveillance systems," *Optik—International Journal for Light and Electron Optics*, vol. 126, no. 19, pp. 2063–2069, 2015.

[6] A. Bedagkar-Gala and S. K. Shah, "A survey of approaches and trends in person re-identification," *Image and Vision Computing*, vol. 32, no. 4, pp. 270–286, 2014.

[7] R. Vezzani, D. Baltieri, and R. Cucchiara, "People reidentification in surveillance and forensics: a survey," *ACM Computing Surveys*, vol. 46, no. 2, article no. 29, 2013.

[8] X. Wang and R. Zhao, "Person re-identification: system design and evaluation overview," in *Person Re-Identification*, pp. 351–370, Springer, 2014.

[9] B. Ma, Q. Li, and H. Chang, "Gaussian descriptor based on local features for person re-identification," in *Proceedings of the Asian Conference on Computer Vision (ACCV '14)*, pp. 505–518, Springer, Singapore, November 2014.

[10] D. Gray and H. Tao, "Viewpoint invariant pedestrian recognition with an ensemble of localized features," in *Computer Vision—ECCV 2008: 10th European Conference on Computer Vision, Marseille, France, October 12–18, 2008, Proceedings, Part I*, vol. 5302 of *Lecture Notes in Computer Science*, pp. 262–275, Springer, Berlin, Germany, 2008.

[11] M. Farenzena, L. Bazzani, A. Perina, V. Murino, and M. Cristani, "Person re-identification by symmetry-driven accumulation of local features," in *Proceedings of the IEEE Conference on Computer Vision and Pattern Recognition (CVPR '10)*, pp. 2360–2367, IEEE, San Francisco, Calif, USA, June 2010.

[12] R. Zhao, W. Ouyang, and X. Wang, "Unsupervised salience learning for person re-identification," in *Proceedings of the 26th IEEE Conference on Computer Vision and Pattern Recognition (CVPR '13)*, pp. 3586–3593, IEEE, Portland, Ore, USA, June 2013.

[13] M. J. Metternich, M. Worring, and A. W. M. Smeulders, "Color based tracing in real-life surveillance data," in *Transactions on Data Hiding and Multimedia Security V*, vol. 6010 of *Lecture Notes in Computer Science*, pp. 18–33, Springer, Berlin, Germany, 2010.

[14] M. Hirzer, P. M. Roth, M. Köstinger, and H. Bischof, "Relaxed pairwise learned metric for person re-identification," in *Proceedings of the European Conference on Computer Vision*, pp. 780–793, Springer, Florence, Italy, October 2012.

[15] M. I. Khedher, M. A. El-Yacoubi, and B. Dorizzi, "Probabilistic matching pair selection for SURF-based person re-identification," in *Proceedings of the International Conference of the Biometrics Special Interest Group (BIOSIG '12)*, pp. 1–6, Darmstadt, Germany, September 2012.

[16] T. Matsukawa, T. Okabe, and Y. Sato, "Person re-identification via discriminative accumulation of local features," in *Proceedings of the 22nd International Conference on Pattern Recognition*

(ICPR '14), pp. 3975–3980, IEEE, Stockholm, Sweden, August 2014.

[17] W.-S. Zheng, S. Gong, and T. Xiang, "Reidentification by relative distance comparison," *IEEE Transactions on Pattern Analysis and Machine Intelligence*, vol. 35, no. 3, pp. 653–668, 2013.

[18] H. Y. Chong, S. J. Gortler, and T. Zickler, "A perception-based color space for illumination-invariant image processing," *ACM Transactions on Graphics*, vol. 27, no. 3, article 61, 2008.

[19] K.-J. Yoon and I.-S. Kweon, "Human perception based color image quantization," in *Proceedings of the 17th International Conference on Pattern Recognition (ICPR '04)*, pp. 664–667, August 2004.

[20] L. Shamir, "Human perception-based color segmentation using fuzzy logic," *IPCV*, vol. 2, pp. 96–502, 2006.

[21] S. Lazebnik, C. Schmid, and J. Ponce, "Beyond bags of features: spatial pyramid matching for recognizing natural scene categories," in *Proceedings of the IEEE Computer Society Conference on Computer Vision and Pattern Recognition (CVPR '06)*, vol. 2, pp. 2169–2178, New York, NY, USA, June 2006.

[22] D. A. Reynolds, T. F. Quatieri, and R. B. Dunn, "Speaker verification using adapted Gaussian mixture models," *Digital Signal Processing*, vol. 10, no. 1, pp. 19–41, 2000.

[23] C. E. Rasmussen, "The infinite gaussian mixture model," *NIPS*, vol. 12, pp. 554–560, 1999.

[24] Z. Zivkovic, "Improved adaptive gaussian mixture model for background subtraction," in *Proceedings of the 17th International Conference on Pattern Recognition (ICPR '04)*, vol. 2, pp. 28–31, Cambridge, UK, August 2004.

[25] C. Liu, S. Gong, C. C. Loy, and X. Lin, "Person re-identification: what features are important?" in *Computer Vision—ECCV 2012. Workshops and Demonstrations: Florence, Italy, October 7–13, 2012, Proceedings, Part I*, vol. 7583 of *Lecture Notes in Computer Science*, pp. 391–401, Springer, Berlin, Germany, 2012.

6

Low-Rank Kernel-Based Semisupervised Discriminant Analysis

Baokai Zu,[1,2] Kewen Xia,[1,2] Shuidong Dai,[1,2] and Nelofar Aslam[1,2]

[1]School of Electronic and Information Engineering, Hebei University of Technology, Tianjin 300401, China
[2]Key Lab of Big Data Computation of Hebei Province, Tianjin 300401, China

Correspondence should be addressed to Kewen Xia; kwxia@hebut.edu.cn

Academic Editor: Yu Cao

Semisupervised Discriminant Analysis (SDA) aims at dimensionality reduction with both limited labeled data and copious unlabeled data, but it may fail to discover the intrinsic geometry structure when the data manifold is highly nonlinear. The kernel trick is widely used to map the original nonlinearly separable problem to an intrinsically larger dimensionality space where the classes are linearly separable. Inspired by low-rank representation (LLR), we proposed a novel kernel SDA method called low-rank kernel-based SDA (LRKSDA) algorithm where the LRR is used as the kernel representation. Since LRR can capture the global data structures and get the lowest rank representation in a parameter-free way, the low-rank kernel method is extremely effective and robust for kinds of data. Extensive experiments on public databases show that the proposed LRKSDA dimensionality reduction algorithm can achieve better performance than other related kernel SDA methods.

1. Introduction

For many real world data mining and pattern recognition applications, the labeled data are very expensive or difficult to obtain, while the unlabeled data are often copious and available. So how to use both labeled and unlabeled data to improve the performance becomes a significant problem [1, 2]. Recently, semisupervised dimensionality reduction has attracted considerable attention, which can be directly used in the whole database [3]. Illuminated by semisupervised learning (SSL), many methods have been put forward to relieve the so-called small sample size (SSS) problem of LDA [4, 5]. Semisupervised Discriminant Analysis (SDA) first is proposed by Cai et al. [2], which can easily resolve the out-of-sample problem [6] and is more suitable for the real world applications. In SDA algorithm, the labeled samples are used to maximize the different classes' separability and the unlabeled ones to estimate the data's intrinsic geometric information.

Semisupervised Discriminant Analysis may fail to discover the intrinsic geometry structure when the data manifold is highly nonlinear [2, 7]. The kernel trick [8] has been widely used to generalize linear dimensionality reduction

algorithms to nonlinear ones, which maps the original nonlinearly separable problem to an intrinsically larger dimensionality space where the classes are linearly separable. So the kernel SDA (KSDA) [2, 7] can discover the underlying subspace more exactly in the feature space, which brings a better subspace for the classification task by a nonlinear learning technique. Cai et al. discussed how to perform SDA in Reproducing Kernel Hilbert Space (RKHS), which gives rise to kernel SDA [2]. You et al. have presented the derivations of a first approach to optimize the parameters of a kernel. It can map the original class distributions to a space where these are optimally (with respect to Bayes) separated with a hyperplane [7]. A new kernel-based nonlinear discriminant analysis algorithm is proposed to solve the fundamental limitations in LDA [9]. A novel KFDA kernel parameters optimization criterion is presented for maximizing the uniformity of class-pair separabilities and class separability in kernel space simultaneously [10]. To overcome the nonlinear dimensionality reduction problems and adopting multiple features restrictions of LFDA, Wang and Sun proposed a new dimensionality reduction algorithm called multiple kernel local Fisher discriminant analysis (MKLFDA) based on the multiple kernel learning [11].

The kernelization of graph embedding applies the kernel trick on the linear graph embedding algorithm to handle data with nonlinear distributions [12]. Weinberger et al. described an algorithm for nonlinear dimensionality reduction based on semidefinite programming and kernel matrix factorization which learns a kernel matrix for high dimensional data that lies on or near a low-dimensional manifold [13].

Low-rank matrix decomposition and completion are recently becoming very popular since Yang et al. and Chen et al. proved that a robust estimation of an underlying subspace which can be obtained by decomposing the observations into a low-rank matrix and a sparse error matrix [14, 15]. Recently, Liu et al. propose a low-rank representation method which is robust to noise and data corruptions due to its ability to decompose noise from the data set [14]. More recently, low-rank representation [16, 17], as a promising method to capture the underlying low-dimensional structures of data, has attracted much attention in the pattern analysis and signal processing communities. LRR method [16–18] seeks the lowest rank representation of all data jointly, such that each data point can be represented as a linear combination of some bases.

The major problem of kernel methods is to find the proper kernel parameters. But all these kernel methods usually use fixed global parameters to determinate the kernel matrix, which are very sensitive to the parameters setting. In fact, the most suitable kernel parameters may vary greatly at different random distribution of the same data. Moreover, the kernel mapping of KSDA always analyze the relationship of the data using the mode one-to-others, which emphasizes local information and lacks global constraints on their solutions. These shortcomings limit the performance and efficiency of KSDA methods. To overcome the disadvantages of the traditional kernel methods, inspired by LRR, we proposed a novel kernel-based Semisupervised Discriminant Analysis called low-rank kernel-based SDA (LRKSDA) where the low-rank representation is used as the kernel method. Compared with other kernels, the low-rank kernel jointly obtains the representation of all the samples under a global low-rank constraint [19]. Thus it is better at capturing the global data structures and very robust to different random distribution of the data set. In addition, we can get the lowest rank representation in a parameter-free way, which is very convenient and robust for kinds of data. Extensive experiments on public databases show that our proposed LRKSDA dimensionality reduction algorithm can achieve better performance than other related methods.

The rest of the paper is organized as follows. We start by a brief review on an overview of SDA in Section 2. We then introduce the low-rank kernel-based SDA framework in Section 3. Then Section 4 reports the experiment results on real world database tasks. In Section 5, we conclude the paper.

2. Overview of SDA

Given a set of samples $[\mathbf{x}_1, \ldots, \mathbf{x}_m, \mathbf{x}_{m+1}, \ldots, \mathbf{x}_{m+l}]$, where $N = m + l$, the first m samples are labeled as $[\mathbf{y}_1, \ldots, \mathbf{y}_m]$, and the remaining l are unlabeled ones. They all belong to c classes. The SDA [2] hopes to find a rejection matrix $\mathbf{a}$, which motivates us to present the prior assumption of consistency by a regularizer term. The objective function is as follows:

$$\mathbf{a} = \max_{\mathbf{a}} \frac{\mathbf{a}^T \mathbf{S}_b \mathbf{a}}{\mathbf{a}^T \mathbf{S}_t \mathbf{a} + \alpha J(\mathbf{a})}, \tag{1}$$

where $\mathbf{S}_b$ and $\mathbf{S}_t$ are the between class scatter and total class scatter matrix. And $\mathbf{S}_w$ is defined as the within class scatter matrix

$$\mathbf{S}_w = \sum_{k=1}^{c} \left(\sum_{i=1}^{l_k} \left(\mathbf{x}_i^{(k)} - \mu^{(k)} \right) \left(\mathbf{x}_i^{(k)} - \mu^{(k)} \right)^T \right),$$

$$\mathbf{S}_b = \sum_{k=1}^{c} l_k \left(\mu^{(k)} - \mu \right) \left(\mu^{(k)} - \mu \right)^T, \tag{2}$$

$$\mathbf{S}_t = \sum_{i=1}^{l} \left(\mathbf{x}_i - \mu \right) \left(\mathbf{x}_i - \mu \right)^T,$$

where μ is the mean vector of the total sample, l_k is the number of samples in the kth class, $\mu^{(k)}$ is the average vector of the kth class, and $\mathbf{x}_i^{(k)}$ is the ith sample in the kth class.

The parameter α in (1) balances the model complexity and the empirical loss. The regularizer term supplies us with the flexibility to incorporate the prior knowledge in the applications. We aim at constructing $J(\mathbf{a})$ graph combining the manifold structure through the available unlabeled samples [2]. The key of SSL algorithm is the prior assumption of consistency. For classification, it means that the nearby samples are likely to have same label [20]. And for dimensionality reduction, it implicates that the nearby samples have similar embeddings (low-dimensional representations).

Given a set of samples $\{\mathbf{x}_i\}_{i=1}^m$, we can construct the graph $\mathbf{G}$ to represent the relationship between nearby samples by kNN algorithm. Then put an edge between k nearest neighbors of each other. The corresponding weight matrix $\mathbf{S}$ is defined as follows:

$$\mathbf{S}_{ij} = \begin{cases} 1, & \text{if } \mathbf{x}_i \in N_k\left(\mathbf{x}_j\right) \text{ or } \mathbf{x}_j \in N_k\left(\mathbf{x}_i\right) \\ 0, & \text{otherwise,} \end{cases} \tag{3}$$

where $N_k(\mathbf{x}_i)$ denotes the set of k nearest neighbors of $\mathbf{x}_i$. Then $J(\mathbf{a})$ term can be defined as follows:

$$J(\mathbf{a}) = \sum_{ij} \left(\mathbf{a}^T \mathbf{x}_i - \mathbf{a}^T \mathbf{x}_j \right)^2 \mathbf{S}_{ij}$$

$$= 2 \sum_i \mathbf{a}^T \mathbf{x}_i \mathbf{D}_{ii} \mathbf{x}_i^T \mathbf{a} - 2 \sum_{ij} \mathbf{a}^T \mathbf{x}_i \mathbf{S}_{ij} \mathbf{x}_j^T \mathbf{a} \tag{4}$$

$$= 2 \mathbf{a}^T \mathbf{X} \left(\mathbf{D} - \mathbf{S} \right) \mathbf{X}^T \mathbf{a} = 2 \mathbf{a}^T \mathbf{X} \mathbf{L} \mathbf{X}^T \mathbf{a},$$

where $\mathbf{D}$ is a diagonal matrix whose entries are column (or row since $\mathbf{S}$ is symmetric) sum of $\mathbf{S}$; that is, $\mathbf{D}_{ii} = \sum_j \mathbf{S}_{ij}$. The Laplacian matrix [21] is $\mathbf{L} = \mathbf{D} - \mathbf{S}$.

We can get the objective function of the SDA with regularizer term $J(\mathbf{a})$ [2]:

$$\mathbf{a} = \max_{\mathbf{a}} \frac{\mathbf{a}^T \mathbf{S}_b \mathbf{a}}{\mathbf{a}^T \left(\mathbf{S}_t + \alpha \mathbf{X} \mathbf{L} \mathbf{X}^T \right) \mathbf{a}}. \tag{5}$$

By maximizing the generalized eigenvalue problem, we can obtain the projective vector $\mathbf{a}$:

$$\mathbf{S}_b\mathbf{a} = \lambda\left(\mathbf{S}_t + \alpha\mathbf{XLX}^T\right)\mathbf{a}. \tag{6}$$

3. Low-Rank Kernel-Based SDA Framework

3.1. Low-Rank Representation. Yan and Wang [22] proposed sparse representation (SR) to construct l_1-graph [23] by solving l_1 optimization problem. However, l_1-graph lacks global constraints, which greatly reduce the performance when the data is grossly corrupted. To solve this drawback, Liu et al. proposed the low-rank representation and used it to construct the affinities of an undirected graph (here called LR-graph) [19]. It jointly obtains the representation of all the samples under a global low-rank constraint, and thus it is better at capturing the global data structures [24].

Let $\mathbf{X} = [\mathbf{x}_1, \mathbf{x}_2, \ldots, \mathbf{x}_n]$ be a set of samples; each column is a sample which can be represented by a linear combination of the dictionary $\mathbf{A}$ [19]. Here, we select the samples themselves $\mathbf{X}$ as the dictionary $\mathbf{A}$:

$$\mathbf{X} = \mathbf{AZ}, \tag{7}$$

where $\mathbf{Z} = [\mathbf{z}_1, \mathbf{z}_2, \ldots, \mathbf{z}_n]$ is the coefficient matrix with each $\mathbf{z}_i$ being the representation coefficient of $\mathbf{x}_i$. Different from the SR which may not capture the global structure of the data, LRR seeks the lowest rank solution by solving the following optimization problem [19]:

$$\begin{aligned} \min_{\mathbf{Z}} \quad & \operatorname{rank}(\mathbf{Z}) \\ \text{s.t.} \quad & \mathbf{X} = \mathbf{AZ}. \end{aligned} \tag{8}$$

The above optimization problem can be relaxed to the following convex optimization [25]:

$$\begin{aligned} \min_{Z} \quad & \|\mathbf{Z}\|_* \\ \text{s.t.} \quad & \mathbf{X} = \mathbf{AZ}. \end{aligned} \tag{9}$$

Here $\|\cdot\|_*$ denotes the nuclear norm (or trace norm) [26] of a matrix, that is, the sum of the matrix's singular values. By considering the noise or corruption in our real world applications, a more reasonable objective function is

$$\begin{aligned} \min_{\mathbf{Z},\mathbf{E}} \quad & \|\mathbf{Z}\|_* + \lambda\|\mathbf{E}\|_l \\ \text{s.t.} \quad & \mathbf{X} = \mathbf{AZ} + \mathbf{E}, \end{aligned} \tag{10}$$

where $\|\cdot\|_l$ can be $l_{2,1}$-norm or l_1-norm. In this paper we choose $l_{2,1}$-norm as the error term which is defined as $\|\mathbf{E}\|_{2,1} = \sum_{j=1}^{n}\sqrt{\sum_{i=1}^{n}([\mathbf{E}]_{ij})^2}$. The parameter λ is used to balance the effect of low rank and the error term. The optimal solution $\mathbf{Z}^*$ can be obtained via the inexact augmented Lagrange multipliers method [27, 28].

3.2. Kernel SDA. Semisupervised Discriminant Analysis may fail to discover the intrinsic geometry structure when the data

manifold is highly nonlinear. The kernel trick is a popular technique in machine learning which uses a kernel function to map samples to a high dimensional space [8, 29, 30]. By using the kernel trick, we can nonlinearly map the original data to the kernel feature space.

Let $Z, Z : R^m \rightarrow F$ be a nonlinear mapping from R^m into F feature space. For any two points $\mathbf{x}_i$ and $\mathbf{x}_j$, we use a kernel function $K(\mathbf{x}_i, \mathbf{x}_j) = \langle\Phi(\mathbf{x}_i), \Phi(\mathbf{x}_j)\rangle$ to map the data into a kernel feature space. Some commonly used kernels are including the Gaussian radial basis function (RBF) kernel $K(\mathbf{x}, \mathbf{y}) = \exp(-\|\mathbf{x} - \mathbf{y}\|^2/\sigma^2)$, polynomial kernel $K(\mathbf{x}, \mathbf{y}) = (c + \langle\mathbf{x}, \mathbf{y}\rangle)^d$, and sigmoid kernel $K(\mathbf{x}, \mathbf{y}) = \tanh(\langle\mathbf{x}, \mathbf{y}\rangle + \alpha)$ [2, 31].

Let ϕ denote the data matrix in the kernel space: $\Phi = [\phi, (\mathbf{x}_1)\phi(\mathbf{x}_2), \ldots, \phi(\mathbf{x}_m)]$. The projective vectors $\alpha_1, \alpha_2, \ldots, \alpha_c$ are the eigenvector problem in (6) and then we get $m \times c$ transformation matrix $\Theta = [\alpha_1, \alpha_2, \ldots, \alpha_c]$. The number of the feature dimensions c can be decided by us. Then a data point can be embedded into c dimensional feature space by

$$\mathbf{x} \longrightarrow \mathbf{y} = \Theta^T K(:, \mathbf{x}), \tag{11}$$

where $K(:, \mathbf{x}) = [K(\mathbf{x}_1, \mathbf{x}), \ldots, K(\mathbf{x}_m, \mathbf{x})]^T$.

Kernel SDA (KSDA) [2, 7] can discover the underlying subspace more exactly in the feature space. It results in a better subspace for the classification task by a nonlinear learning technique.

3.3. Low-Rank Kernel-Based SDA. The major problem of all these kernel methods is to find the proper kernel parameters. And they usually use fixed global parameters to determinate the kernel matrix, which is very sensitive to the parameters setting. In fact, the most proper kernel parameters may vary greatly at different random distribution even if they are for the same data. Moreover, the traditional kernel mapping always analyzes the relationship of the data using the mode one-to-others, which emphasizes local information and lacks global constraints on their solutions. These shortcomings limit the performance and efficiency of KSDA methods. To overcome these shortcomings mentioned above, inspired by low-rank representation, we propose a novel kernel-based Semisupervised Discriminant Analysis (LRKSDA) where LRR is used as the kernel representation.

Let $Z, Z : R^m \rightarrow F$ be a low-rank mapping from R^m into a low-rank kernel feature space F. For the database $\mathbf{X} = [\mathbf{x}_1, \mathbf{x}_2, \ldots, \mathbf{x}_n]$, a reasonable objective function is as follows:

$$\begin{aligned} \min_{\mathbf{Z},\mathbf{E}} \quad & \|\mathbf{Z}\|_* + \lambda\|\mathbf{E}\|_{2,1} \\ \text{s.t.} \quad & \mathbf{X} = \mathbf{AZ} + \mathbf{E}. \end{aligned} \tag{12}$$

The optimal solution $\mathbf{Z} = [\mathbf{z}_1, \mathbf{z}_2, \ldots, \mathbf{z}_n]$ is the coefficient matrix with each $\mathbf{z}_i$ being the low-rank representation coefficient of $\mathbf{x}_i$.

Let $\mathbf{Z} = [\mathbf{z}_1, \mathbf{z}_2, \ldots, \mathbf{z}_n]$ denote the data matrix in the kernel space. The projective vectors $\alpha_1, \alpha_2, \ldots, \alpha_c$ are the eigenvector problem in (6) and $m \times c$ transformation matrix is $\Theta = [\alpha_1, \alpha_2, \ldots, \alpha_c]$. The number of the feature dimensions

c can be decided by us. Then a data point can be embedded into c dimensional feature space by

$$\mathbf{x} \longrightarrow \mathbf{y} = \mathbf{\Theta}^T \mathbf{z}, \qquad (13)$$

where $\mathbf{z}$ is the low-rank representation of $\mathbf{x}$.

Since the low-rank representation jointly obtains the representation of all the samples under a global low-rank constraint to capture the global data structures, we can get the lowest rank representation in a parameter-free way, which is very convenient and robust for kinds of data. So low-rank kernel-based SDA algorithm can improve the performance to a very large extent. The step of the LRKSDA is as follows.

Firstly, map the labeled and unlabeled data to the LR-graph kernel space. Secondly, execute the SDA algorithm for dimensionality reduction. Finally execute the nearest neighbor method for the final classification in the derived low-dimensional feature subspace. The procedure of low-rank kernel-based SDA is described as follows.

Algorithm 1 (low-rank kernel-based SDA algorithm). *Input.* The whole data set $[\mathbf{x}_1, \ldots, \mathbf{x}_m, \mathbf{x}_{m+1}, \ldots, \mathbf{x}_{m+l}]$, where l samples are labeled and m are unlabeled ones.

Output. The classification results.

Step 1. Map the labeled and unlabeled data $\mathbf{X}$ to feature space by the LRR algorithm:

$$\begin{aligned} \min_{\mathbf{Z},\mathbf{E}} \quad & \|\mathbf{Z}\|_* + \lambda \|\mathbf{E}\|_{2,1} \\ \text{s.t.} \quad & \mathbf{X} = \mathbf{A}\mathbf{Z} + \mathbf{E}. \end{aligned} \qquad (14)$$

Step 2. Implement the SDA algorithm for dimensionality reduction.

Step 3. Execute the nearest neighbor method for final classification.

4. Experiments and Analysis

In this section, we conduct extensive experiments to examine the efficiency of low-rank kernel-based SDA algorithm. The simulation experiment is conducted in MATLAB7.11.0 (R2010b) environment on a computer with AMD Phenom(tn)II P960 1.79 GHz CPU and 2 GB RAM.

4.1. Experiment Overview

4.1.1. Databases. The proposed LRKSDA is tested on six real world databases, including three face databases and three University of California Irvine (UCI) databases. In these experiments, we normalize the sample to a unit norm.

(1) Extended Yale Face Database B [2]. This database has 38 individuals and around 64 near frontal images under different illuminations per individual. Each face image is resized to 32 × 32 pixels. And we select the first 20 persons and choose 20 samples of each subject.

(2) ORL Database [22]. The ORL database contains 10 different images of each for 40 distinct subjects. The images are taken at different times, varying the lighting, facial expressions, and facial details. Each face image is manually cropped and resized to 32 × 32 pixels, with 256 grey levels per pixel.

(3) CMU PIE Face Database [2]. It contains 68 subjects with 41,368 face images. The face images were captured under varying poses, illuminations, and expressions. The size of each image is resized to 32 × 32 pixels. We select the first 20 persons and choose 20 samples for per subject.

(4) Musk (Version 2) Data Set 2. This database contains 2 classes and 6598 instances with 166 features. Here, we randomly select 300 examples for the experiments.

(5) Seeds Data Set. It contains 210 instances for three different wheat varieties. A soft X-ray technique and GRAINS package were used to construct all seven, real-valued attributes.

(6) SPECT Heart Data Set. The database describes diagnosing of cardiac Single Proton Emission Computed Tomography (SPECT) images. Each of the patients is classified into two categories: normal and abnormal. The database of 267 SPECT image sets was processed to extract features that summarize the original SPECT images. The pattern was further processed to obtain 22 binary feature patterns.

4.1.2. Compared Algorithms. In order to demonstrate how the semisupervised dimensionality reduction performance can be improved by low-rank kernel-based SDA, we list out SDA, KSDA1, and KSDA2 algorithm for comparison. In all experiments, the number of the nearest neighbors in the kNN regularizer graph is set to 4.

(1) KSDA1 Algorithm. KSDA1 algorithm is the KSDA with Gaussian radial basis function (RBF) kernel $K(\mathbf{x}, \mathbf{y}) = \exp(-\|\mathbf{x} - \mathbf{y}\|^2 / \sigma^2)$.

(2) KSDA2 Algorithm. KSDA2 algorithm is the KSDA which uses polynomial kernel $K(\mathbf{x}, \mathbf{y}) = (c + \langle \mathbf{x}, \mathbf{y} \rangle)^d$. Here, $c = 1$.

The classification accuracy is influenced by the kernel parameters. So after comparing, we choose a proper kernel parameters σ and c for the KSDA1 and KSDA2 algorithm in each database in the following pairs, respectively, where $(0.9, 0.9)$ is for Extended Yale Face Database B, $(0.55, 1.5)$ is for ORL database, $(0.9, 0.9)$ is for CMU PIE database, $(0.65, 0.2)$ is for Musk database, $(0.05, 0.6)$ is for Seeds Data Set, and $(0.8, 0.3)$ is for SPECT Heart Data Set, respectively. Since the most suitable kernel parameters vary greatly at different random distribution even if they are for the same data, these kernel parameters are relatively suitable after comparing by many times' runs.

4.2. Experiment 1: Different Algorithms Performances. To examine the effectiveness of the proposed LRKSDA algorithm, we conduct experiments on the six public databases. In our experiments, we randomly select 30% samples from

TABLE 1: Classification accuracy of different SDA algorithms on six databases.

	Yale B	ORL	PIE	Musk	Seeds	SPECT Heart
LRKSDA	0.825769	0.815	0.578243	0.836667	0.90625	0.778378
KSDA1	0.691392	0.693025	0.541478	0.756849	0.825	0.683333
KSDA2	0.723549	0.681576	0.534542	0.755128	0.709814	0.694154
SDA	0.668397	0.687692	0.527715	0.757407	0.819122	0.69857

TABLE 2: Classification accuracy of different graphs on ORL, Yale, and USPS databases.

Database	Algorithm	The percentage of labeled samples				
		10%	20%	30%	40%	50%
Yale B	LRKSDA	0.711471	0.792667	0.825769	0.848636	0.877778
Yale B	KSDA1	0.316113	0.536868	0.691392	0.807183	0.856101
Yale B	KSDA2	0.33994	0.569484	0.723549	0.819317	0.877637
Yale B	SDA	0.325919	0.560259	0.668397	0.815348	0.855167
ORL	LRKSDA	0.615556	0.728125	0.815	0.873333	0.9
ORL	KSDA1	0.172412	0.448653	0.693167	0.868578	0.937414
ORL	KSDA2	0.172454	0.454899	0.681576	0.851755	0.930487
ORL	SDA	0.173478	0.442731	0.687692	0.877294	0.948035
PIE	LRKSDA	0.29	0.46	0.578243	0.701044	0.82734
PIE	KSDA1	0.195252	0.371027	0.541478	0.711166	0.827522
PIE	KSDA2	0.195345	0.37646	0.543015	0.712033	0.825519
PIE	SDA	0.195707	0.387806	0.527715	0.725264	0.82658

each class as the labeled samples to evaluate the performance with different numbers of selected features. The evaluations are conducted with 20 independent runs for each algorithm. We average them as the final results. First we utilize different kernel methods to get the kernel mapping, and then we implement the SDA algorithm for dimensionality reduction. Finally, the nearest neighbor approach is employed for the final classification in the derived low-dimensional feature subspace. For each database, the classification accuracy for different algorithms is shown in Figure 1. Table 1 shows the performance comparison of different algorithms. Note that the results are the best results of all these different selected features mentioned above. From these results, we can observe the following.

In most cases, our proposed low-rank kernel-based SDA algorithm consistently achieves the highest classification accuracy compared to the other algorithms. LRKSDA achieves the best performance when the dimensionality is larger than a certain low dimension. And the classification accuracy is much higher than the other kernel SDA algorithms. So it improves the classification performance to a large extent, which suggests that low-rank kernel is more informative and suitable for SDA algorithm.

Since the proper kernel parameters are the most important thing of these traditional algorithms and since the kernel parameters of KSDA1 and KSDA2 algorithm are fixed global parameters, the two algorithms are very sensitive to different data or different random distribution of the same data. The performance improvement of these KSDA methods is not obvious. More seriously, as a result of randomly select labeled samples, the random distribution in each run may not adapt

the so-called proper kernel parameters of KSDA1 and KSDA2 algorithm. Moreover, the traditional kernel mapping always analyzes the relationship of the data using the mode one-to-others, which emphasizes local information and lacks global constraints on their solutions. This situation may result in not good performance in some case, while the low-rank representation is better at capturing the global data structures. And we can get the lowest rank representation in a parameter-free way, which is very convenient and robust for kinds of data. So low-rank kernel-based SDA separates the different classes very well compared to other kernel SDA. And it can improve the performance to a very large extent, which means that our proposed low-rank kernel method is extremely effective.

4.3. Experiment 2: Influence of the Label Number. We evaluate the influence of the label number in this part. The experiments are conducted with 20 independent runs for each algorithm. We average them as the final results. The procedure is the same with experiment 1. For each database, we vary the percentage of labeled samples from 10% to 50% and the recognition accuracy is shown in Tables 2 and 3, from which we observe the following.

In most cases, our proposed low-rank kernel-based SDA algorithm consistently achieves the best results, which is robust to the label percentage variations. While some other compared algorithms are not as robust as our LRKSDA algorithm, we can see that the classification accuracy is very awful when the label rate is low. Thus, our proposed method has much superiority than the traditional KSDA and SDA algorithms. Sometimes these traditional methods

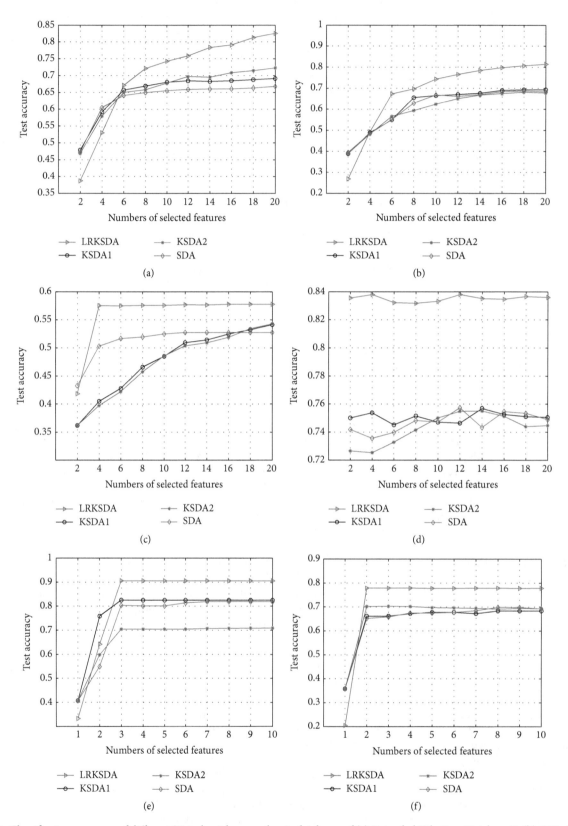

FIGURE 1: Classification accuracy of different SDA algorithms on the six databases of (a) Extended Yale Face Database B, (b) ORL database, (c) CMU PIE face database, (d) Musk (Version 2) Data Set 2, (e) Seeds Data Set, and (f) SPECT Heart Data Set.

TABLE 3: Classification accuracy of different graphs on Musk, Seeds, and SPECT Heart databases.

Database	Algorithm	The percentage of labeled samples				
		10%	20%	30%	40%	50%
Musk	LRKSDA	0.767778	0.827083	0.838095	0.838889	0.895125
Musk	KSDA1	0.356299	0.592578	0.756849	0.83253	0.883174
Musk	KSDA2	0.418741	0.607271	0.755128	0.817146	0.888439
Musk	SDA	0.352444	0.611676	0.757407	0.840006	0.894315
Seeds	LRKSDA	0.890323	0.893333	0.90625	0.90813	0.929608
Seeds	KSDA1	0.46676	0.654862	0.825	0.874946	0.914757
Seeds	KSDA2	0.410025	0.609322	0.709814	0.845034	0.890559
Seeds	SDA	0.503879	0.725435	0.819122	0.872932	0.929595
SPECT Heart	LRKSDA	0.778992	0.778378	0.776216	0.78038	0.826076
SPECT Heart	KSDA1	0.404513	0.622916	0.683333	0.786381	0.85786
SPECT Heart	KSDA2	0.398401	0.608538	0.702989	0.77983	0.869786
SPECT Heart	SDA	0.364647	0.556669	0.69857	0.759696	0.818995

TABLE 4: Classification accuracy of different graphs with varying noise on Yale B database.

Noise types	Algorithm	Variance or density of the three noises					
		0	0.02	0.04	0.06	0.08	0.1
Gaussian	LRKSDA	0.825769	0.816429	0.814286	0.807857	0.808214	0.807143
Gaussian	KSDA1	0.691392	0.555408	0.565422	0.562556	0.574249	0.579816
Gaussian	KSDA2	0.723549	0.585366	0.597015	0.602456	0.590576	0.59866
Gaussian	SDA	0.668397	0.543879	0.540266	0.542199	0.541947	0.543264
"Salt and pepper"	LRKSDA	0.825769	0.794643	0.7675	0.711786	0.643929	0.599286
"Salt and pepper"	KSDA1	0.691392	0.56888	0.509246	0.474557	0.450803	0.436003
"Salt and pepper"	KSDA2	0.723549	0.59498	0.522505	0.478096	0.446308	0.43581
"Salt and pepper"	SDA	0.668397	0.553305	0.498777	0.468533	0.452681	0.429647
Multiplicative	LRKSDA	0.825769	0.825357	0.821429	0.82	0.814286	0.793929
Multiplicative	KSDA1	0.691392	0.631297	0.619849	0.594597	0.584588	0.576168
Multiplicative	KSDA2	0.723549	0.641188	0.622062	0.616446	0.594529	0.594516
Multiplicative	SDA	0.668397	0.594035	0.588897	0.58513	0.582225	0.556328

may achieve good performances in some databases with high enough label rate. But they are not as stable as our proposed algorithm. Since the labeled data is very expensive and difficult, our proposed algorithm is much robust and suitable to the real word data.

As we mentioned in the previous part, since the low-rank kernel method gets the kernel matrix in a parameter-free way, it is robust for different kinds of data, while for the traditional kernel like Gaussian radial basis function kernel and polynomial kernel, if the data's structure does not fit the stable kernel parameters they used, they cannot obtain the good representation of the original data set. Therefore, the low-rank kernel method is much more stable for all the data sets we use. And the low-rank representation jointly obtains the representation of all the samples under a global low-rank constraint, which can capture the global data structures. So it is robust to the label percentage variations even though the label rate is low.

4.4. Experiment 3: Robustness to Different Types Noises. In this test we compare the performance of different algorithms in the noisy environment. Extended Yale Face Database B

and Musk database are randomly selected in this experiment. The Gaussian white noise, "salt and pepper" noise, and multiplicative noise are added to the data, respectively. The Gaussian white noise is with mean 0 and different variances from 0 to 0.1. The "salt and pepper" noise is added to the image with different noise densities from 0 to 0.1. And multiplicative noise is added to the data I, using the equation $J = I + n * I$, where I and J are the original and noised data and n is uniformly distributed random noise with mean 0 and varying variance from 0 to 0.1. The number of labeled samples in each class is 30%. The experiments are conducted with 20 runs for each algorithm. We average them as the final results. The procedure is the same with experiment 1. For each graph, we vary the parameter of different noise. The results are shown in Tables 4 and 5.

As we can see, our proposed low-rank kernel-based SDA algorithm always achieves the best results, which means that our method is stable for Gaussian noise, "salt and pepper" noise, and multiplicative noise. And because of the robustness of the low-rank representation to noise, our method LRKSDA is much more robust than other algorithms. With the different kinds of gradually increasing noise, the

TABLE 5: Classification accuracy of different graphs with varying noise on Musk database.

Noise types	Algorithm	Variance or density of the three noises					
		0	0.02	0.04	0.06	0.08	0.1
Gaussian	LRKSDA	0.838095	0.783333	0.810476	0.795238	0.789524	0.777619
Gaussian	KSDA1	0.756849	0.689112	0.705138	0.702206	0.699312	0.710083
Gaussian	KSDA2	0.755128	0.705054	0.695936	0.697523	0.695125	0.70306
Gaussian	SDA	0.757407	0.713289	0.699202	0.714286	0.676558	0.681785
"Salt and pepper"	LRKSDA	0.838095	0.785238	0.771429	0.772143	0.766429	0.761905
"Salt and pepper"	KSDA1	0.756849	0.683009	0.667079	0.656237	0.66388	0.653854
"Salt and pepper"	KSDA2	0.755128	0.705003	0.664427	0.658723	0.656934	0.652174
"Salt and pepper"	SDA	0.757407	0.70503	0.697131	0.681818	0.678207	0.666734
Multiplicative	LRKSDA	0.838095	0.832381	0.827143	0.809524	0.793333	0.784286
Multiplicative	KSDA1	0.756849	0.733777	0.723228	0.71144	0.716774	0.71115
Multiplicative	KSDA2	0.755128	0.737889	0.716812	0.710216	0.701506	0.68323
Multiplicative	SDA	0.757407	0.749432	0.738486	0.726044	0.703764	0.68799

traditional KSDA and SDA algorithms' performance falls a lot, while our method's performance is robust to these three noises and drops a few.

Notice that the noise is from a different model other than the original data's subspaces. LRR can well solve the low-rank representation problem. When the data corrupted by arbitrary errors, LRR can also approximately recover the original data with theoretical guarantees. In other words, LRR is robust in an efficient way. Therefore, our method is much more robust than other algorithms with the three noises mentioned above.

5. Conclusions

In this paper, we propose a novel low-rank kernel-based SDA (LRKSDA) algorithm, which largely improves the performance of KSDA and SDA. Since low-rank representation is better at capturing the global data structures, LRKSDA algorithm separates the different classes very well compared to other kernel SDA. Therefore, our proposed low-rank kernel method is extremely effective. Empirical studies on six real world databases show that our proposed low-rank kernel-based SDA is much robust and suitable to the real word applications.

Disclosure

Current affiliation for Baokai Zu is Computer Science Department, Worcester Polytechnic Institute, Worcester, MA 01609, USA.

Competing Interests

The authors declare that they have no competing interests.

Acknowledgments

This work was supported by the National Natural Science Foundation of China (no. 51208168), Tianjin Natural Science Foundation (no. 13JCYBJC37700), Hebei Province Natural Science Foundation (no. E2016202341), Hebei Province Natural Science Foundation (no. F2013202254 and no. F2013202102), and Hebei Province Foundation for Returned Scholars (no. C2012003038).

References

[1] D. Zhang, Z. H. Zhou, and S. Chen, *Semi-Supervised Dimensionality Reduction*, SDM, Minneapolis, Minn, USA, 2007.

[2] D. Cai, X. He, and J. Han, "Semi-supervised discriminant analysis," in *Proceedings of the IEEE 11th International Conference on Computer Vision (ICCV '07)*, pp. 1–7, Rio de Janeiro, Brazil, October 2007.

[3] Y. Zhang and D.-Y. Yeung, "Semi-supervised discriminant analysis using robust path-based similarity," in *Proceedings of the 26th IEEE Conference on Computer Vision and Pattern Recognition (CVPR '08)*, pp. 1–8, Anchorage, Alaska, USA, June 2008.

[4] M. Sugiyama, T. Idé, S. Nakajima, and J. Sese, "Semi-supervised local Fisher discriminant analysis for dimensionality reduction," *Machine Learning*, vol. 78, no. 1-2, pp. 35–61, 2010.

[5] Y. Song, F. Nie, C. Zhang, and S. Xiang, "A unified framework for semi-supervised dimensionality reduction," *Pattern Recognition*, vol. 41, no. 9, pp. 2789–2799, 2008.

[6] Y. Bengio, J. F. Paiement, P. Vincent et al., "Out-of-sample extensions for LLE, isomap, MDS, eigenmaps, and spectral clustering," in *Advances in Neural Information Processing Systems 16*, pp. 177–184, MIT Press, 2004.

[7] D. You, O. C. Hamsici, and A. M. Martinez, "Kernel optimization in discriminant analysis," *IEEE Transactions on Pattern Analysis and Machine Intelligence*, vol. 33, no. 3, pp. 631–638, 2011.

[8] K.-R. Müller, S. Mika, G. Rätsch, K. Tsuda, and B. Schölkopf, "An introduction to kernel-based learning algorithms," *IEEE Transactions on Neural Networks*, vol. 12, no. 2, pp. 181–201, 2001.

[9] W.-J. Zeng, X.-L. Li, X.-D. Zhang, and E. Cheng, "Kernel-based nonlinear discriminant analysis using minimum squared errors criterion for multiclass and undersampled problems," *Signal Processing*, vol. 90, no. 8, pp. 2333–2343, 2010.

[10] J. Liu, F. Zhao, and Y. Liu, "Learning kernel parameters for kernel Fisher discriminant analysis," *Pattern Recognition Letters*, vol. 34, no. 9, pp. 1026–1031, 2013.

[11] Z. Wang and X. Sun, "Multiple kernel local Fisher discriminant analysis for face recognition," *Signal Processing*, vol. 93, no. 6, pp. 1496–1509, 2013.

[12] S. Yan, D. Xu, B. Zhang, H.-J. Zhang, Q. Yang, and S. Lin, "Graph embedding and extensions: a general framework for dimensionality reduction," *IEEE Transactions on Pattern Analysis and Machine Intelligence*, vol. 29, no. 1, pp. 40–51, 2007.

[13] K. Q. Weinberger, B. D. Packer, and L. K. Saul, "Nonlinear dimensionality reduction by semidefinite programming and kernel matrix factorization," in *Proceedings of the 10th International Workshop on Artificial Intelligence and Statistics (AISTATS '05)*, pp. 381–388, January 2005.

[14] S. Yang, X. Wang, M. Wang, Y. Han, and L. Jiao, "Semisupervised low-rank representation graph for pattern recognition," *IET Image Processing*, vol. 7, no. 2, pp. 131–136, 2013.

[15] C.-F. Chen, C.-P. Wei, and Y.-C. F. Wang, "Low-rank matrix recovery with structural incoherence for robust face recognition," in *Proceedings of the IEEE Conference on Computer Vision and Pattern Recognition (CVPR '12)*, pp. 2618–2625, IEEE, Providence, RI, USA, June 2012.

[16] G. Liu, Z. Lin, S. Yan, J. Sun, Y. Yu, and Y. Ma, "Robust recovery of subspace structures by low-rank representation," *IEEE Transactions on Pattern Analysis and Machine Intelligence*, vol. 35, no. 1, pp. 171–184, 2013.

[17] G. Liu and S. Yan, "Latent low-rank representation for subspace segmentation and feature extraction," in *Proceedings of the IEEE International Conference on Computer Vision (IC-CV '11)*, pp. 1615–1622, IEEE, Barcelona, Spain, November 2011.

[18] X. Lu, Y. Wang, and Y. Yuan, "Graph-regularized low-rank representation for destriping of hyperspectral images," *IEEE Transactions on Geoscience and Remote Sensing*, vol. 51, no. 7, pp. 4009–4018, 2013.

[19] G. Liu, Z. Lin, and Y. Yu, "Robust subspace segmentation by low-rank representation," in *Proceedings of the 27th International Conference on Machine Learning (ICML '10)*, pp. 663–670, Haifa, Israel, June 2010.

[20] D. Zhou, O. Bousquet, N. T. La et al., "Learning with local and global consistency," *Advances in Neural Information Processing Systems*, vol. 16, no. 16, pp. 321–328, 2004.

[21] D. M. Cvetkovic and P. Rowlinson, "Spectral graph theory," in *Topics in Algebraic Graph Theory*, pp. 88–112, Cambridge University Press, 2004.

[22] S. Yan and H. Wang, "Semi-supervised learning by sparse representation," in *Proceedings of the 2009 SIAM International Conference on Data Mining*, pp. 792–801, SDM, 2009.

[23] J. Wright, A. Y. Yang, A. Ganesh, S. S. Sastry, and Y. Ma, "Robust face recognition via sparse representation," *IEEE Transactions on Pattern Analysis and Machine Intelligence*, vol. 31, no. 2, pp. 210–227, 2009.

[24] C. Cortes and M. Mohri, "On transductive regression," in *Advances in Neural Information Processing Systems 19*, pp. 305–312, 2007.

[25] E. J. Candès, X. Li, Y. Ma, and J. Wright, "Robust principal component analysis?" *Journal of the ACM*, vol. 58, no. 3, article 11, 2011.

[26] J.-F. Cai, E. J. Candès, and Z. Shen, "A singular value thresholding algorithm for matrix completion," *SIAM Journal on Optimization*, vol. 20, no. 4, pp. 1956–1982, 2010.

[27] Z. Lin, M. Chen, and Y. Ma, "The augmented lagrange multiplier method for exact recovery of corrupted low-rank matrices," https://arxiv.org/abs/1009.5055.

[28] G. Liu, Z. Lin, S. Yan, J. Sun, Y. Yu, and Y. Ma, "Robust recovery of subspace structures by low-rank representation," *IEEE Transactions on Pattern Analysis and Machine Intelligence*, vol. 35, no. 1, pp. 171–184, 2013.

[29] S. Yang, Z. Feng, Y. Ren, H. Liu, and L. Jiao, "Semisupervised classification via kernel low-rank representation graph," *Knowledge-Based Systems*, vol. 69, no. 1, pp. 150–158, 2014.

[30] V. N. Vapnik and V. Vapnik, *Statistical Learning Theory*, John Wiley & Sons, New York, NY, USA, 1998.

[31] H. Nguyen, W. Yang, F. Shen, and C. Sun, "Kernel Low-Rank Representation for face recognition," *Neurocomputing*, vol. 155, pp. 32–42, 2015.

7

The Café Wall Illusion: Local and Global Perception from Multiple Scales to Multiscale

Nasim Nematzadeh[1,2] and David M. W. Powers[1]

[1]College of Science and Engineering, Flinders University, Adelaide, SA, Australia
[2]Department of Science and Engineering, Faculty of Mechatronics, Karaj Branch, Islamic Azad University (KIAU), Karaj-Alborz, Iran

Correspondence should be addressed to Nasim Nematzadeh; nasim.nematzadeh@flinders.edu.au

Academic Editor: Mourad Zaied

Geometrical illusions are a subclass of optical illusions in which the geometrical characteristics of patterns in particular orientations and angles are distorted and misperceived as a result of low-to-high-level retinal/cortical processing. Modelling the detection of tilt in these illusions, and its strength, is a challenging task and leads to the development of techniques that explain important features of human perception. We present here a predictive and quantitative approach for modelling foveal and peripheral vision for the induced tilt in the Café Wall illusion, in which parallel mortar lines between shifted rows of black and white tiles appear to converge and diverge. Difference of Gaussians is used to define a bioderived filtering model for the responses of retinal simple cells to the stimulus, while an analytical processing pipeline is developed to quantify the angle of tilt in the model and develop confidence intervals around them. Several sampling sizes and aspect ratios are explored to model variant foveal views, and a variety of pattern configurations are tested to model variant Gestalt views. The analysis of our model across this range of test configurations presents a precisely quantified comparison contrasting local tilt detection in the foveal sample sets with pattern-wide Gestalt tilt.

1. Introduction

Visual processing starts within the retina from the photoreceptors passing the visual signal through bipolar cells to the Retinal Ganglion Cells (RGCs) whose axons carry the encoded signal to the cortex for further processing. The intervening layers incorporate several types of cell with large dendritic arbors, divided into horizontal cells that control for different illumination conditions and feedback to the receptor and bipolar cells and amacrine cells that feed into the center-surround organization of the Retinal Ganglion Cells. High-resolution receptors in the foveal area have a direct 1:1 pathways from photoreceptors, via bipolar cells to ganglion cells [1].

It is commonly believed that the center-surround organization in RGCs and their responses are the results of the lateral inhibitory effect in the outer and the inner retina [2] in which the activated cells inhibit the activation of nearby cells. At the first synaptic level, the lateral inhibition [2–4] enhances the synaptic signal of photoreceptors, which is specified as

a retinal point spread function (PSF) seen as a biological convolution with the edge enhancement property [3]. At the second synaptic level, the lateral inhibition mediates the more complex properties such as the responses of directional selective receptive fields (RFs) [2].

The complexity of interneural circuitries and activation and responses of the retinal cells have been investigated [5, 6] in a search for the specific encoding role of each individual cell in the retinal processing leading to new insights. This includes the existence of a diverse range of Retinal Ganglion Cells (RGCs) in which the size of each individual type varies in relation to the eccentricity of neurons and the distance from the fovea [5] supporting our biological understanding of the retinal multiscale encoding [7], completed in the cortex [5, 6, 8]. ON and OFF cells of each specific type are noted to have a variant size [5, 9] as well. It is also reported that there are different channels for passing the encoded information of ON-center and OFF-surround (and vice versa) activation of retinal RFs [6] to the cortex. Moreover, the possibility of simultaneous activation of a group of RGCs (as a combined activity) in the retina by the output of amacrine cells is noted in the literature [10–12]. Some retinal cells have been found with a directional selectivity property such as the cortical cells [5, 6]. It is noteworthy that, despite the complexity and variety of retinal cells circuitry and coding, there are a few constancy factors common to them, valid even for amacrine and horizontal cells. The constancy of integrated sensitivity is one of these factors mentioned in the literature [13–15] which is quite useful for quantitative models for visual system.

The perception of directional tilt in the Café Wall illusion might tend to direct explanations toward the cortical orientation detectors or complex cells [8, 16]. We have shown that the emergence of tilt in the Café Wall illusion specifically [17–21], and in tile illusions generally [17, 22], is a result of simple cells processing with circularly symmetric activation/inhibitions. Low-level filtering models [23, 24] commonly apply a filter similar to a Gaussian or Laplacian of a specific size on the Café Wall to show the appearance of slanted line segments referred to as Twisted Cord [25] elements in the convolved output. These local tilts are assumed then to be integrated into continuous contours of alternating converging and diverging mortar lines at a more global level [22–24]. A hybrid retinocortical explanation as a midlevel approach containing light spread, compressive nonlinearity, and center-surround transformation has been proposed by Westheimer [26]. Some other explanations rely on Irradiation Hypothesis [27] and Brightness Induction [28]. There are also high-level descriptive approaches such as "Border Locking" [29] and "Phenomenal Model" [30] for the illusion with little consideration to the underlying neurological mechanisms involved in the emergence of tilt in the Café Wall illusion.

Modelling the receptive field responses dates back to Kuffler's demonstration of roughly concentric excitatory center and inhibitory surround [31]. Then, Rodieck and Stone [32] and Enroth-Cugell and Robson [33] modelled the center and surround signals of the photoreceptors by two concentric Gaussians with different diameters. The computational modelling of early visual processing was followed by Marr and Ullman [34] who were inspired by Hubel and Wiesel's [8] discovery of cortical simple and complex cells. Laplacian of Gaussian (LoG) has been proposed by Marr and Hildreth [35] as an optimal operator for low-level retinal filtering and an approximation filter of Difference of Gaussians (DoG) instead of LoG, considering a ratio of ~1.6 for the Gaussians diameters.

The model here [17–22] is a most primitive implementation for the contrast sensitivity of RGCs based on classical circular center and surround organization of the retinal RFs [32, 33]. The output of the model is a simulated result for the responses of the retinal/cortical simple cells to stimuli/image. This image representation is referred to as an "edge map" utilizing Difference of Gaussians (DoG) at multiple scales to implement the center-surround activity as well as the multiscale property of the RGCs. Our explanation differs from the previous low-level models [23, 24, 27, 36] due to the concept of filtering at multiple scales in our model in which the scales are tuned to the resolutions of image features, not the resolutions of the individual retinal cells. We show also that our model is a quantitative approach capable of even

predicting the strength of the Café Wall illusion based on different characteristics of the pattern [21].

This work is a complete collection of our findings on the underlying mechanism involved in our foveal and peripheral vision for modelling the perception of the induced tilt in the Café Wall illusion. It draws together and extends our previous studies on the foveal/local investigations of tilt on Café Wall illusion [18, 19] and extends our investigations for the peripheral/global analysis of the perceived tilt not in just one specific sample (to overcome the shortcomings of our previous studies [18, 19]), but for variations of different configurations modelling the Gestalt perception of tilt in the illusion.

In Section 2, we describe the characteristics of a simple classical model for simulating the responses of simple cells based on Difference of Gaussians (DoG) and utilize the model for explaining the Café Wall illusion qualitatively (Section 2.2.1) and quantitatively (Section 2.2.2). Afterwards, in Section 3, the experimental results on variations of foveal sample sets are provided (Section 3.1), followed by the report of quantitative tilt results for variations of different configurations of the Café Wall illusion with the same characteristics of mortar lines and tiles but with different arrangements of a whole pattern (Section 3.2), which had then been completed by a thorough comparison of the local and global mean tilts of the pattern found by our simulations (Section 3.3). We conclude by highlighting the advantages and disadvantages of the model in predicting the local and global tilt in the Café Wall pattern and proceed to outline a roadmap of our future work (Section 4).

2. Materials and Methods

2.1. Formal Description and Parameters. Applying a Gaussian filter on an image generates a blurred version of the image. In our DoG model, the difference of two Gaussian convolutions of an image generates one scale of the *edge map* representation. For a 2D signal such as image I, the DoG output, modelling the retinal ganglion cell responses with the center-surround organization, is given by

$$
\begin{aligned}
&\text{DoG}_{\sigma, s\sigma}(x, y) \\
&= I \times \frac{1}{2\pi\sigma^2 \exp\left[-\left(x^2 + y^2\right) / \left(2\sigma^2\right)\right]} - I \\
&\quad \times \frac{1}{2\pi (s\sigma)^2 \exp\left[-\left(x^2 + y^2\right) / \left(2s^2\sigma^2\right)\right]},
\end{aligned}
\tag{1}
$$

where DoG is the convolved filter output, x and y are the horizontal and vertical distances from the origin, respectively, and σ is the scale of the center Gaussian ($\sigma = \sigma_c$). $s\sigma$ in (1) indicates the scale of the surround Gaussian ($\sigma_s = s\sigma_c$), and s is referred to as *Surround ratio* in our model as shown in

$$
s = \frac{\sigma_{\text{surround}}}{\sigma_{\text{center}}} = \frac{\sigma_s}{\sigma_c}.
\tag{2}
$$

Increasing the value of s results in a wider suppression effect from the surround region, although the height of the

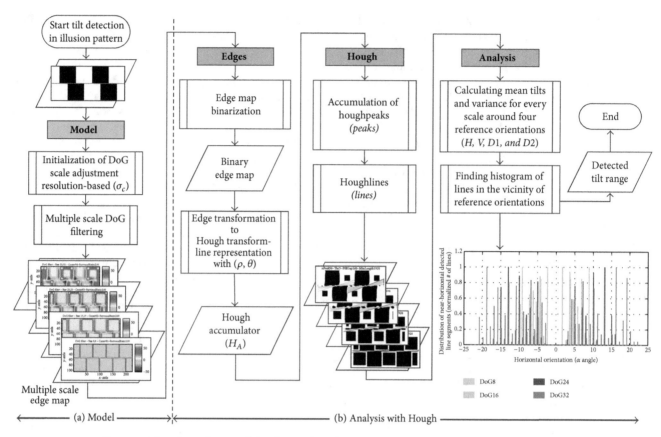

FIGURE 1: Flowchart of our model with Hough analytic processing pipeline (adapted from [19, 20]).

surround Gaussian declines (normalized Gaussians are used in our model). A broader range of *Surround ratios* from 1.4 to 8.0 have been tested with little difference to our results. We have considered another parameter in the model for the filter size referred to as *Window ratio* (*h*). To generate edge maps we have applied DoG filters within a window in which the values of both Gaussians are insignificant outside the window. The window size is determined based on the parameter *h* that determines how much of each Gaussian (center and surround) is included inside the DoG filter and the scale of the center Gaussian (σ_c) such that

$$\text{WindowSize} = h \times \sigma_c + 1. \qquad (3)$$

+1 as given in (3) guaranties a symmetric DoG filter. In the experimental results the *Window ratio* (*h*) has been set to 8 to capture more than 95% of the surround Gaussians in the DoG convolved outputs.

2.2. Model and Image Processing Pipeline.

An image processing pipeline has been used [18–21] here to extract edges and their angles of tilt (in the edge maps), as shown in Figure 1 for a crop section of a Café Wall pattern of size 2×4.5 tiles (the precise height is 2 tiles + mortar = $2T + M$). In this research, we concentrate on the analysis of the induced tilt in the Café Wall illusion, to include the details of the parameters used in the simulations in order to quantify the tilt angle in this stimulus by modelling our foveal and peripheral vision.

2.2.1. DoG Edge Map at Multiple Scales. The DoG representation at multiple scales is the output of the model, which is referred to as an *edge map* of an image. The DoG is highly sensitive to spots and moderately sensitive to lines that match the center diameter. We have used this representation for modelling the responses of visual simple cells especially on tile illusions in our investigations [18–20, 22]. An appropriate range for σ_c can be determined for any arbitrary pattern/image considering the pattern characteristics as well as the filter size matched with the image features (by applying (3)) in our model. The step sizes determine the accuracy of the multiple scale representation here and again are pattern specific for preserving the visual information with minimum redundancy but at multiple scales.

For Café Wall illusion, the DoG edge map indicates the emergence of divergence and convergence of the mortar lines in the pattern, similar to how it is perceived as shown in Figure 2. The edge map has been shown at six different scales in jetwhite color map [37] for a Café Wall of 3×8 tiles with 200×200 px tiles (*T*) and 8 px mortar (*M*). In order to extract the tilted line segments along the mortar lines referred to as Twisted Cord [25] elements, the DoG filter should be of the same size as the mortar size [18, 24, 36]. The edge map should contain both high frequency details as well as low frequency contents in the image. We start DoG filtering below the mortar size at scale 4 ($\sigma_c = 4$; as the finest scale) and extend the scales gradually until scale 28 for a large filter to capture the tiles fully, with incremental steps of 4 (in the figure we

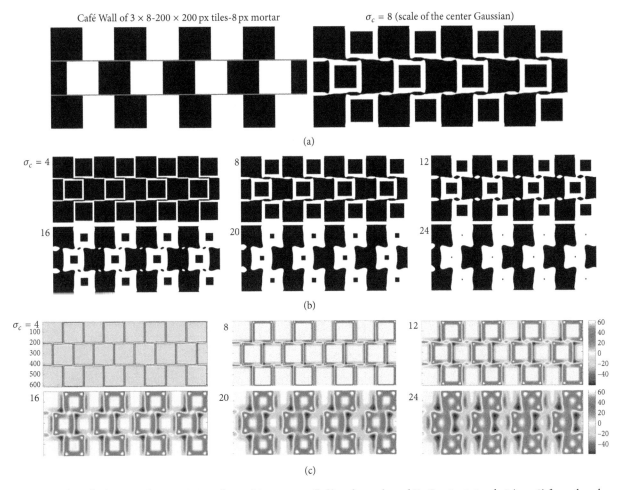

FIGURE 2: (a) Café Wall of 3×8 with 200×200 px tiles and 8 px mortar (left) and an enlarged DoG output at scale 8 ($\sigma_c = 8$) from the edge map of the pattern (right). (b) The binary edge map at six scales ($\sigma_c = 4$ to 24 with incremental steps of 4). (c) The same edge map but presented in the jetwhite color map [37]. The noncritical parameters of the DoG model are $s = 2$ and $h = 8$ (the *Surround* and *Window ratios*, resp.).

have shown this till $\sigma_c = 24$ due to shortage of space). Other noncritical parameters of the model are $s = 2$ and $h = 8$, representing the *Surround* and *Window ratios*, respectively.

The DoG outputs in Figure 2 show that the tilt cues appear at fine to medium scales and start to disappear as the scale of the center Gaussian increases in the model. At fine to medium scales, there are some corner effects that appear in the edge maps which highlight the emergence of tilted line segments and result in the appearance of square tiles that look similar to trapezoids. This may be referred to as wedges in the literature [29], inducing convergent and divergent mortar lines. So, at fine scales around the size of the mortar, we see the groupings of identically colored tiles with the Twisted Cord elements along the mortar lines. By increasing the scales gradually from the medium to coarse scales, when the mortar cues disappear completely in the edge map, other groupings of identically colored tiles are emerged in the edge map, connecting tiles in zigzag vertical orientation. What we see across multiple scales in the edge map of the pattern are two incompatible groupings of pattern elements: groupings of tiles in two consecutive rows by the mortar lines at fine scales with nearly horizontal orientation (as focal/local view) and then groupings of tiles in zigzag vertical direction at coarse

scales (as peripheral/global view). These two incompatible groupings occur simultaneously across multiple scales and exhibit systematic differences according to the size of the Gaussian and predicts the change in illusion effects with distance from the focal point in the pattern.

We have shown that, in the edge map at multiple scales, not only do we extract the information of edges/textures with the shades and shadows around the edges, but we are also able to show the emergence of other cues related to tilt and perceptual grouping as features for mid-to-high-level processing [17, 22]. Also we have shown in another article that even the prediction of the strength of tilt effect in different variations of Café Wall illusion is possible from the persistence of mortar cues across multiple scales [21] in the edge map. Highly persistent mortar cue in the edge map is an indication for a stronger induced tilt in the stimulus.

2.2.2. Second-Stage Processing. The Hough analysis is used for quantitative measurement of tilt in our model and consists of three stages of Edges, Hough, and Analysis as shown in Figure 1, explained below.

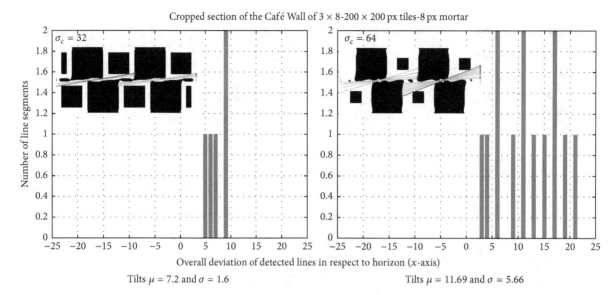

Cropped section of the Café Wall of 3 × 8-200 × 200 px tiles-8 px mortar

Tilts $\mu = 7.2$ and $\sigma = 1.6$ Tilts $\mu = 11.69$ and $\sigma = 5.66$

FIGURE 3: *Hough* stage output. Distribution of line segments detected near the horizontal orientation, presented for two scales of the DoG edge map at scales 32 and 64 ($\sigma_c = 32, 64$). Mean tilt and variance for each graph have been also provided.

Edges. We used here an analysis pipeline to characterize the tilted line segments presented in the edge map of the Café Wall pattern. First, the edge map is binarized and then the Standard Hough Transform (SHT) [38, 39] is applied to it to detect line segments inside the binary edge map at multiple scales. SHT uses a two-dimensional array called the accumulator (H_A) to store line information of edges based on the quantized values of ρ and θ in a pair (ρ, θ) using Hough function in MATLAB. ρ specifies the distance between the line passing through the edge point and θ is the counterclockwise angle between the normal vector (ρ) and the x-axis ranges from 0 to π, $[0, \pi)$. Therefore, every edge pixel (x, y) in the image space corresponds to a sinusoidal curve in Hough space such that $\rho = x \cdot \cos\theta + y \cdot \sin\theta$, with θ as free parameter corresponding to the angle of the lines passing through the point (x, y) in the image space. The output of *Edges* is the accumulator matrix (H_A) with all the edge pixel information.

Hough. The *Edges* stage provides all possible lines that could pass through every edge point of the edge map inside the H_A matrix. We are more interested in detecting the induced tilt lines inside the Café Wall image. Two MATLAB functions called *houghpeaks* and *houghlines* are employed for the further processing of the accumulator matrix (H_A). The *houghpeaks* function finds the peaks in the H_A matrix with three parameters of *NumPeaks* (maximum number of line segments to be detected), *Threshold* (threshold value for searching the peaks in the H_A), and *NHoodSize* (the size of the suppression neighbourhood that is set to zero after the peak is identified). The *houghlines* function extracts line segments associated with a particular bin in the accumulator matrix (H_A) with two parameters of *FillGap* (the distance between two line segments associated with the same Hough bin; line segments with shorter gaps are merged into a single line

segment) and *MinLength* (specifies keeping or discarding the merged lines; lines shorter than this value are discarded).

A sample output of *Hough* processing stage is given in Figure 1 with the detected houghlines displayed in green on the binary edge map at four different scales (the cropped section is selected from a Café Wall with 50 × 50 px tiles and 2 px mortar, with the DoG scales from 0.5M to 2M in the figure around the mortar size with the incremental steps of 0.5M). The results of *Hough* analysis stage for a different cropped section of a Café Wall pattern with higher resolution (cropped from a Café Wall with 800 × 800 px tiles and 32 px mortar) are shown in Figure 3 for two scales of the DoG edge map ($\sigma_c = 32, 64$-M and 2M; Blue lines indicate the longest line segments detected). The histograms of detected houghlines near the horizontal orientation have been provided for these scales. The absolute mean tilts and the standard deviation of tilts are calculated and presented in the figure below the graphs.

Analysis. The detected line segments and their angular positions are saved inside four orientation matrices considering the closest to any of the reference orientations of horizontal (H), vertical (V), positive diagonal (+45°, $D1$), and negative diagonal (−45°, $D2$) orientations. We consider an interval of $[-22.5°, 22.5°)$ around each reference orientation to cover the whole space. The statistical analysis of tilt angles of the detected lines around each reference orientation is the output of this stage and includes the mean tilts and the standard errors around the means for each scale of the DoG edge map.

Hough Parameters for Tilt Investigations of Café Wall Stimulus. Recall that *NumPeaks* indicates the maximum number of line segments to be detected and *FillGap* shows the distance between two line segments associated with the same Hough bin in which line segments with shorter gaps are merged

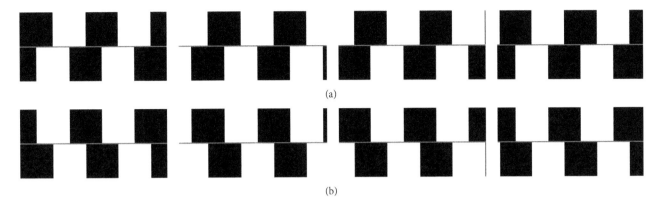

(a)

(b)

FIGURE 4: Examples of systematically cropped samples along Falling (a) and Rising mortar lines (b), selected from the Café Wall of 3 × 9 tiles with 400 × 400 px tiles (*T*) and 16 px mortar (*M*), Café Wall 3 × 9 *T*400-*M*16. In total, 50 samples are taken along each mortar line with an offset of 32 px between samples in each step. Cropped samples have a size of (2*T* + *M*) × 4.5*T* with the mortar line positioned in the middle.

into a single line segment. The other Hough parameter is *MinLength*, which specifies keeping or discarding of the line segments considering this minimum length and discarding the lines shorter than this value. To select an appropriate value for these parameters we should consider pattern features and the scales of the DoG edge map. In the Café Wall pattern, in order to detect the Twisted Cord elements at fine scales, the *MinLength* value should be in a reliable range. The Twisted Cord elements have a minimum length of 2.5*T* (*MinLength* ≈ 2.5*T*), and therefore, for a Café Wall with 200 × 200 px tiles, *MinLength* = 500 px. We set this parameter a bit smaller than this value equal to *MinLength* ≈ 2.25*T* = 450 px for our experiments in Section 3. The *FillGap* parameter is chosen equal to 1/5th of a tile size (1/5*T*) in our experiments (to merge the disconnected mortar cues of each Twisted Cord elements at fine to medium scales in the edge maps). *NumPeaks* is selected appropriately based on the size of the pattern, and, for small foveal sets (Section 3.1), this is set to 100 but has a higher range, 520 and 1000 for larger Café Wall stimulus for global investigation of tilt (Section 3.2).

3. Results and Discussions

3.1. Local Tilt Investigation

3.1.1. Falling and Rising Mortar Investigation. This work draws together and extends our previous studies on the foveal/local investigations of tilt on Café Wall illusion [18, 19], and the extension of our investigations for the peripheral/global analysis of the perceived tilt not in just one specific sample but for variations of different configurations. The quantitative mean tilts of similar shape samples but with variant resolutions have been investigated in our previous work [20]. We have shown that, for variations with different resolutions, the tilt prediction of the model stays nearly the same when the dependent parameters of the model to the spatial content of the pattern have been updated accordingly in each resolution (σ_c and Hough parameters).

We report here the evaluation results of our model's predictions for the *direction of detected tilts* for two types of

mortar lines in the Café Wall illusion [20]. Instead of referring to the mortar lines as either convergent or divergent, we rather talk about Falling or Rising mortar lines, in which, in the Falling mortar, the direction of induced tilt is downwards on its right side compared to the horizontal direction and for the Rising mortar the vice versa. For instance, in Figure 2(a)-(left) the top mortar line is Falling while the bottom one is Rising. In this experiment the cropped samples specifically selected in such a way to contain only one mortar line indicate the emergence of tilt in only one direction of either positive or negative in the DoG edge maps (Falling or Rising). The samples have a height of two tiles and the mortar line in between (2*T* + *M*) and the width of 4.5 tiles (4.5*T*; *T*: tile size, *M*: mortar size), with the same height above and below the mortar line. In Section 3.1.2, we show the results for samples of variant sizes and different cropping technique for a more general investigation of the foveal/local perception of the induced tilt in the pattern.

To fix parameters not being investigated, we restrict consideration initially to the Café Wall of 3 × 9 tiles with 400 × 400 px tiles and 16 px mortar. Here, in a systematic approach, 50 samples were selected from the Falling mortar and 50 samples from the Rising mortar with the dimensions described above from the Café Wall of 3 × 9 tiles. The sampling process starts from the leftmost side of the pattern and with a horizontal shift size/offset of 32 pixels between the samples for the cropping window. A few examples of the Falling and Rising samples have been provided in Figure 4. The cropped samples at the bottom of the figure are symmetrical crops from the Rising mortar lines selected from the stimulus (Café Wall of 3 × 8). In the DoG edge maps of these samples, the scale of the center Gaussian is in the range of 1/2*M* to 2*M* with the incremental steps of 1/2*M* = 8 px (σ_c = 8, 16, 24, and 32) to detect both mortar lines and the outlines of the tiles for detecting near-horizontal tilts in the edge maps.

For individual samples of the Falling and Rising mortar, the near-horizontal mean tilts and variance of the detected houghlines have been shown in Figure 5. As the scale of the center Gaussian (σ_c) in our model increases, the variance of tilt also increases. The mean tilt results of the Falling and

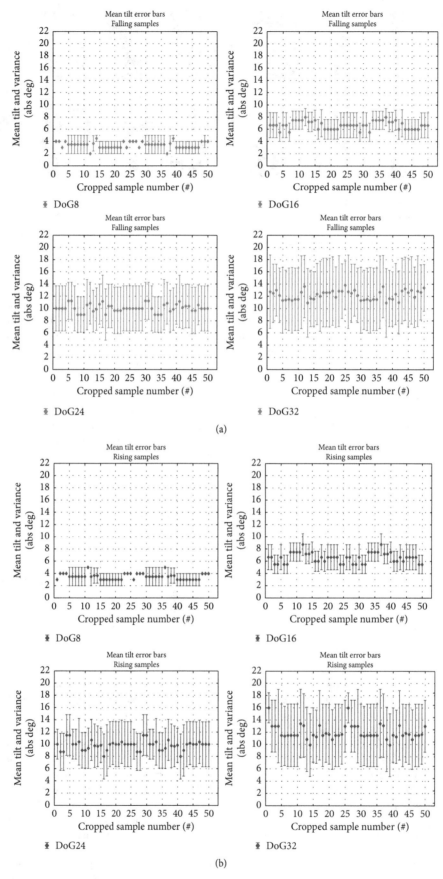

FIGURE 5: Mean tilts and variance error bars for individual samples of Falling (a) and Rising mortar lines (b) specified along horizontal axis (100 samples in total; DoG8 means $\sigma_c = 8$). As explained in Figure 4, the cropped samples are from the Café Wall of 3×9 tiles with 400×400 px tiles and 16 px mortar (DoG4: $\sigma_c = 4$).

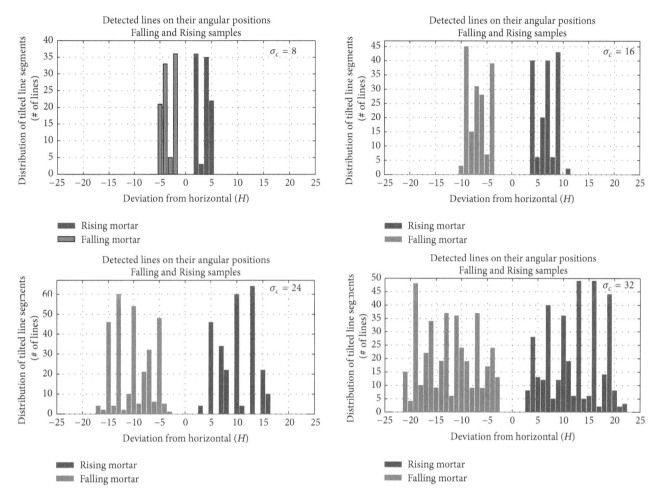

FIGURE 6: Distribution of line segments detected by deviation in degrees from the horizontal (*x*-axis), for the total 100 samples of Falling (Blue bars) and Rising mortar lines (Red bars), as explained in Figure 4. The scales of the edge maps (σ_c) range from 8 to 32 with step sizes of 8 (1/2*M* to 2*M* with incremental steps of 1/2*M* = 8 px). Other parameters of the model and Hough analysis are as follows: *s* = 2 and *h* = 8 (the *Surround* and *Window ratios*), with *NumPeaks* = 50, *Threshold* = 3, *FillGap* = 80, and *MinLength* = 960 as the Hough parameters (see [20] for the resolution analysis and its effect on the Hough parameters).

Rising mortar samples in Figure 5 indicate that both types of mortar lines follow nearly the same pattern.

The near-horizontal line segments detected in the DoG edge maps (houghlines) at four scales (σ_c = 8, 16, 24, and 32) are shown in Figure 6 for the Falling (Blue bars) and the Rising (Red bars) mortar samples. These graphs are summarized in Figure 7 in a single graph, indicating normalized distribution of line segments detected with their deviations in degrees from the horizontal (*x*-axis) orientation for the 100 samples. When the DoG scale increases, the detected tilt range covers a wider neighbourhood area around the horizontal axis as their details given in Figure 6. The deviations of the detected lines from the horizontal orientation in Figures 6 and 7 are very small at the finest scale (σ_c = 8). The range of tilt angles increases along the following scales of the edge maps reaching a wide range of variations at scale 32 (σ_c = 32 or DoG32) that is not reflected in our subjective experience of tilt in the pattern (it is overestimated at this scale). In the literature [18, 19, 22, 24, 36] it is noted that the size of DoG filter should be close to the size of the mortar

for the Twisted Cord elements to appear along the mortar lines, here DoG16 (σ_c = 16). We have demonstrated that this is not applicable for Café Wall patterns with very thick mortar lines [21]. In this case, the mortar cues are lost completely in the edge map even by applying DoG filters smaller than the mortar size. The strength of the illusion is highly dependent on the characteristics of the pattern such as the luminance of the mortar, the mortar size, the contrast of the tiles, the aspect ratio of the tile size to the mortar size, and other parameters of the stimulus. We noted that there exists a correlation between the strength of the illusion with the persistence of the mortar cues in the edge maps across multiple scales [21].

3.1.2. Variant Sampling Sizes: Two Methods of Sampling. As explained in Section 2.2.2, an analytical processing pipeline is used to quantify the tilt angles in the DoG edge maps. For modelling variant foveal views, several sampling sizes and aspect ratios have been investigated across multiple scales in order to find the confidence intervals around the predicted tilts reported in our previous work [18, 19]. These variations

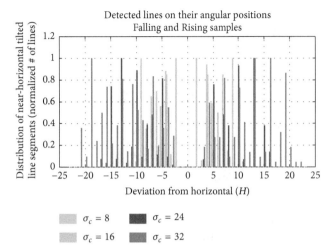

FIGURE 7: The normalized graph of lines detected from the DoG edge maps of the 100 cropped samples by deviation in degrees from the horizontal (H) orientation. Samples are from the Falling and Rising mortar lines from the Café Wall 3×9-$T400$-$M16$. The characteristics of the samples are provided in Figure 4, and the edge maps have four different scales ($\sigma_c = 8, 16, 24$, and 32, based on [20]).

are verified and quantified in simulations using two different sampling approaches. The contrast of local tilt detection with a global average across the whole Café Wall pattern will be discussed in Section 3.2.

The eyes process the visual scene at different scales at different times, due to the intentional and unintentional eye movements while we look at the scene (pattern). Notably overt saccades and gaze shifts result in a rapid scan of the field of view by the fovea for the pertinent high-resolution information. Our visual perception of tilt in the Café Wall is affected by our *fixation* on the pattern. The induced tilts weakened in a region around fixation point, but the peripheral tilts stay unaffected with stronger tilts. It seems that, in the Café Wall illusion, the final induced tilts get greater effect from the peripheral tilt recognition compared to the foveal/local tilt perception. The possible correlations that might exist between the tilt effect to our foveal/peripheral view of the pattern due to gaze shifts and saccades are further investigated here. The local "cropped" samples simulate foveal-sized locus only, but different scales of the DoG edge maps represent different degrees of eccentricity (the distance from the fovea) in the periphery.

In this section we are reporting the experimental results from [18, 19] and we restrict consideration initially to Café Wall of 9×14 tiles with 200×200 px tiles and 8 px mortar (Figure 8(a)), with three "foveal" crop sizes to be explored, Crop4 $\times$ 5 (Cropped section of a 4×5 tiles), Crop5 $\times$ 5, and Crop5 $\times$ 6 (Figure 8(b)). Although the size of foveal image can be estimated by factors such as specific image size, viewing distance, or human subject in mind (which usually are considered in psychophysical experiments), the sample sizes explored in our experiments for the simulation results are selected for convenience without considering those restrictive factors.

Two sampling methods have been applied: *Systematic* and *Random Cropping*. In the "*Systematic Cropping*" [18] for each specified crop window size, 50 samples are taken from the Café Wall of 9×14 tiles, in which the top left corner for the first sample is selected randomly from the pattern and, for the rest of the samples, the cropping window shifts horizontally to the right with an offset of 4 pixels in each step. The total shift is equal to a tile size (200 px) at the end, so there is no repeated versions of any samples. In the "*Random Cropping*" [19] approach, for each specified crop window size, 50 samples are taken from randomly selected locations with the only consideration of the crop borders to stay inside the pattern.

The range of DoG scales of these samples is from $0.5M$ to $3.5M$ with the incremental steps of $0.5M$, and coarser scales exceeding the tile size (T; using (3)), resulting in a very distorted edge pattern. We calculated [19] not only the near horizontal mean tilts but also the vertical and diagonal tilts at medium to coarse scales in this experiment. Unlike the previous experiment in Section 3.1.1, detecting only horizontal tilts, we extended the range of scales in the model from $2M$ in the previous experiment to $3.5M$ for these experiments. With DoG filters larger than the mortar size, ultimately reaching the coarsest size selected ($3.5M$, using (3)), then the tiles are fully captured at the coarsest scales of the edge maps. These are being used for the vertical and diagonal deviations and the groupings of tiles in zigzag vertical orientation in our investigations. The Hough parameters (of both houghpeaks and houghlines functions) should have a proper range to detect the near-horizontal slanted line segments in the edge maps at fine scales (refer to Section 2.2.2). For example, *FillGap* should assign a value to fill small gaps between the line segments that appeared in the edge map at fine scales to detect near-horizontal tilted lines, and *MinLength* should be larger than an individual tile size (T) to avoid the detection of the outlines of the tiles in the calculations. The values of Hough parameters depend on the pattern's attributes (features) and they are selected empirically for the tilt investigation in the experiments. To attain reliable and comparable tilt results, a constant set of these parameters have been used in this experiment and in Section 3.2 for the global tilt investigation, which is as follows: *NumPeaks* = 100, *Threshold* = 3, *FillGap* = 40, and *MinLength* = 450. Other values for *NumPeaks* have been also tested for the global tilt investigation in Section 3.2 (520 and 1000).

Figure 9 shows a binary DoG edge map at seven different scales (a), the edge map presented in the jetwhite color map (b), and the detected houghlines displayed in green on the edge map (c) for a sample of Crop4 $\times$ 5 tiles, selected from the Café Wall of 9×14 tiles (Figure 8).

The absolute mean tilts in box plot have been graphed for the detected lines in the DoG edge maps at seven different scales for each sample set and the two sampling methods and around the four reference orientations of horizontal (H), vertical (V), and diagonals ($D1$, $D2$) orientations in Figures 10(a) and 10(b). As the figure indicates, the "*Random Cropping*" approach produces more stable tilt results across variant foveal sample sizes compared to the "*Systematic*" sampling method. We noted [19] that the *Systematic* sampling

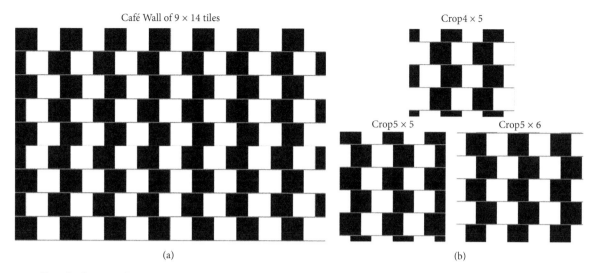

Café Wall of 9 × 14 tiles

Crop4 × 5

Crop5 × 5   Crop5 × 6

(a)   (b)

FIGURE 8: Café Wall of 9 × 14 tiles with 200 × 200 px tiles and 8 px mortar (a) and three "foveal" sample sizes explored (based on [18, 19]) (Crop $H \times W$ is $H \times W$ tiles).

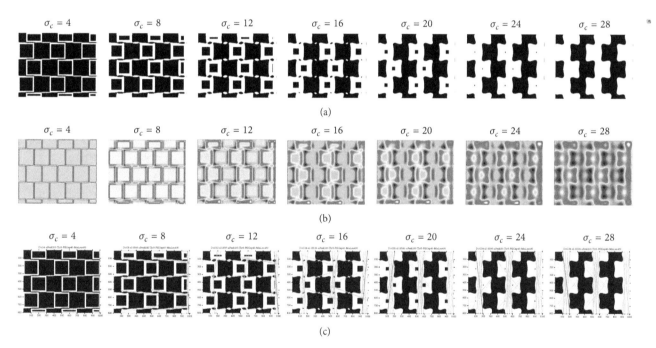

$\sigma_c = 4$ $\sigma_c = 8$ $\sigma_c = 12$ $\sigma_c = 16$ $\sigma_c = 20$ $\sigma_c = 24$ $\sigma_c = 28$

(a)

$\sigma_c = 4$ $\sigma_c = 8$ $\sigma_c = 12$ $\sigma_c = 16$ $\sigma_c = 20$ $\sigma_c = 24$ $\sigma_c = 28$

(b)

$\sigma_c = 4$ $\sigma_c = 8$ $\sigma_c = 12$ $\sigma_c = 16$ $\sigma_c = 20$ $\sigma_c = 24$ $\sigma_c = 28$

(c)

FIGURE 9: (a) A binary DoG edge map at seven scales (σ_c = 4, 8, 12, 16, 20, 24, and 28) of a cropped section of size 4 × 5 tiles from a Café Wall with 200 × 200 px tiles and 8 px mortar. (b) The DoG edge map displayed in the jetwhite color map [37]. (c) Detected houghlines from the edge map displayed in green, overlaid on the binary edge map with Hough parameters as: *NumPeaks* = 100, *Threshold* = 3, *FillGap* = 40, and *MinLength* = 450 (based on [19]).

approach is closer to the bias of our saccades and gaze shifts toward interest points, but the *Random* sampling is a more standard statistical approach. At fine to medium scales of both sampling methods, there are only horizontal and vertical lines detected. A few samples of Crop5 × 5 have D2 components at scale 16 due to the border effects (only 4 out of 50 samples). The results for near-horizontal mean tilts at scale 8 (σ_c = 8) show a nearly stable range around 7° in all samples (the DoG filter size apparently correlates with the mortar size). As the scale increases from 20 onwards,

there are no near-horizontal lines detected, but more vertical and diagonal lines are extracted from the edge maps. This is because the mortar cues in the edge maps at these scales start to fade, and also the enlargement of the outlines of the tiles results in more lines detected around the vertical and diagonal orientations at coarse scales of the DoGs. By increasing the scale, the horizontal mean tilt also increases and at scales 8 and 12 it is nearly 8°; however, at the finest scale (σ_c = 4) the horizontal mean tilt is quite small (~3.5°). When we fixate on the pattern, we encounter a weaker tilt

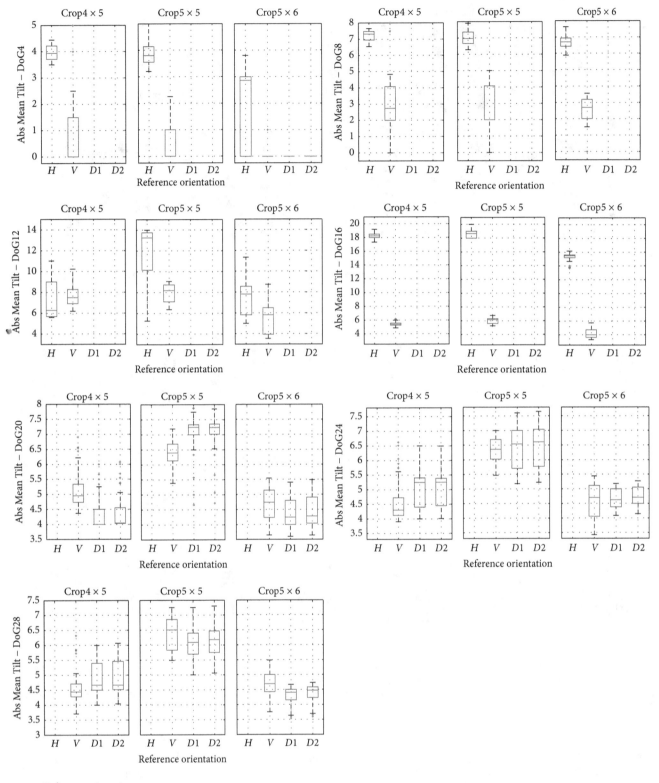

Reference orientations:
(*H*) Horizontal, (*V*) vertical
(*D*1) Positive diagonal (+45°)
(*D*2) Negative diagonal (−45°)
Crop4 × 5: cropped window of a 4 × 5 Tiles
DoG4: $\sigma_c = 4$

(a) Systematic Cropping

FIGURE 10: Continued.

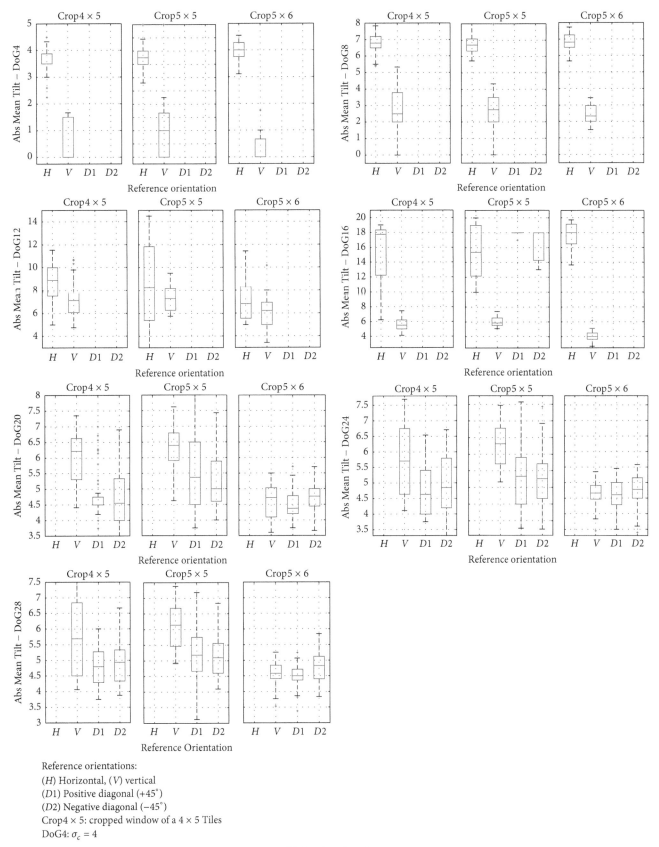

(b) Random Cropping

FIGURE 10: Mean tilts and standard errors around the four reference orientations (H, V, $D1$, and $D2$), for the three "foveal" sample sets (Figure 8) with the two sampling approaches of (a) Systematic and (b) Random methods. The parameters of the model and Hough processing are as follows: edge maps at seven DoG scales ($\sigma_c = 4, 8, 12, 16, 20, 24$, and 28), $s = 2$, and $h = 8$, with Hough parameters $NumPeaks = 100$, $Threshold = 3$, $FillGap = 40$, and $MinLength = 450$ (based on [19]).

effect, since similarly in the fovea the acuity is high because of high density of small size receptors. The vertical mean tilts are approximately 5-6° at medium to coarse scales. The diagonal mean tilts (around $D1$ and $D2$ axes) are around 4-5° which can be seen again at medium to coarse scales ($\sigma_c = 20$, 24, and 28).

The results of the detected mean tilts at a given scale show slight differences across foveal sample sets, and this is expected because of the Random sampling and the fixed Hough parameters that are not optimized for each scale and sampling size, and they are kept constant here for the consistency of the higher level analysis/model. The tilt detection results are sensible when compared to our angular tilt perception of the pattern, but more accuracy may be achieved by optimizing parameters based on the psychophysical experiments.

Figures 11(a) and 11(b) show the distribution of lines detected from the DoG edge maps at seven scales and around the four reference orientations (H, V, $D1$, $D2$) for the three foveal sample sets and the two sampling methods. The near-diagonal tilted lines (around $D1$ and $D2$ axes) have been graphed together for fairer representation. Figures 11(a) and 11(b) show that the houghlines detected in (b) are more normally distributed around the reference orientations compared to (a). All the graphs indicate the effect of the edge maps at multiple scales on the range of detected mean tilts and the distribution of the lines detected by their deviations in degrees from the reference orientations. The mean tilts cover a wider angular range when the DoG scale increases. We should be reminded that the number of detected lines is highly dependent on the sample size and the *NumPeaks* parameter. We explain the tilt results in Figure 11(b) but the same explanation can be used for part (a).

Figure 11(b) (left-column) shows the near-horizontal lines detected for the three foveal sets. At scale 4 ($\sigma_c = 4$), the detected tilt angles are very small, ranging between 2 and 5°, with the peak of 4°. Furthermore, at scale 16, the detection of a high range of variations of tilt angle is not reflected in our perception of the pattern. To detect horizontal tilt cues along the mortar lines, the scale of the center Gaussian in our model should be close to the mortar. At scale 8, the mean tilts are between 3 and 10° with the peak of 7° for most lines, and at scale 12 it is increased to ~14°. At scale 16 the results show a wider range of horizontal lines detected and a fairly broad range of vertical lines, and this fits as a transition stage between the "horizontal groupings" of identically colored tiles with the mortar lines at a focal view and the "zigzag vertical groupings" of the tiles [22] at a more peripheral/global view.

Figure 11(b) (center-column) shows the near-vertical lines detected. Similar to the indications of Figure 10, they start to be detected at fine scales due to some edge effects in a few samples, but as color code indicates, the majority of the near-vertical lines are detected at scales 20 and 24, with the mean tilts in the range of 2–15° and the peak close to the V axis. In Figure 11(b) (right-column) the detected lines with near-diagonal deviations indicate that the dominant scales for detection of the diagonal lines are mainly at coarse scales of 24

and 28 ($\sigma_c = 24$, 28) with approximately 5-6° deviation from the diagonal axes ($D1$, $D2$).

3.2. Global Tilt Investigation

3.2.1. Global Tilts in the Café Wall of 9×14 Tiles. The Café Wall illusion is characterized by the appearance of Twisted Cord elements along the mortar lines [23–25], making the tiles seem wedge-shaped [29]. These local tilt elements are believed to be integrated and produce slanted continuous contours along the whole mortar lines by the cortical cells [16, 27] resulting in alternating converging and diverging mortar lines at a global view.

Because the tilt effect in the Café Wall is highly directional, it raises the question of whether lateral inhibition and point spread function (PSF) of retinal cells can explain the tilt effect in the pattern or not. We demonstrated that a bioplausible model [17–22], with a circularly symmetric organization as a simplified model for the retinal ganglion cell responses [32, 33], is able to reveal the tilt cues in the Café Wall illusion across multiple scales of the edge map. To explain the emergence of tilt in the Café Wall, there is no need to utilize complex models of non-CRFs [40–44] implementing the retinal/cortical orientation selective cells.

In this experiment, the intention is to investigate the Gestalt pattern, simulating peripheral awareness across the entire image, and overcome the shortcomings of our previous investigations. We investigate here the global tilts in the Café Wall of 9×14 with 200×200 px tiles and 8 px mortar (Figure 8(a)) and on its DoG edge map at seven different scales to quantify the tilt angles around the four reference orientations. The DoG scales have a range from $0.5M$ to $3.5M$ with the incremental steps of $0.5M$ the same as the foveal samples in Section 3.1.2.

In our first attempt to examine the robustness of the model for global tilt investigation [18, 19], the analysis was done with the parameters appropriate for local features. We have tested *NumPeaks* = 100 in [18] and *NumPeaks* = 520 in [19], but we have not achieved convincing results. Increasing the value of *NumPeaks* from 100 to 520 did not show any significant change to the mean tilts although it substantially increased the variance. The results showed that the near-horizontal mean tilt was approximately 4° at scale 4 and around 7° at scale 8 nearly the same as the foveal sample sets (Figure 10). The near-vertical mean tilts at medium to coarse scales were around 2°, while they were around 6° in the foveal sets. The near-diagonal mean tilts were approximately 3° and they were in the range of 5-6° in the foveal sample sets. Please refer to [19, Figure 6] for more details. In this work, we perform a global analysis with larger numbers of line segments as appropriate to the large global pattern. *NumPeaks* is a size relevant parameter, and its value is critical for achieving reliable results. Increasing this value for Hough analysis on the foveal sets does not affect the detected houghlines there, but an appropriate value for large samples is essential to detect all the relevant houghlines available in the edge map with smooth variations reflecting our estimation of tilt that is comparable with the detected lines in the foveal sets in our simulations.

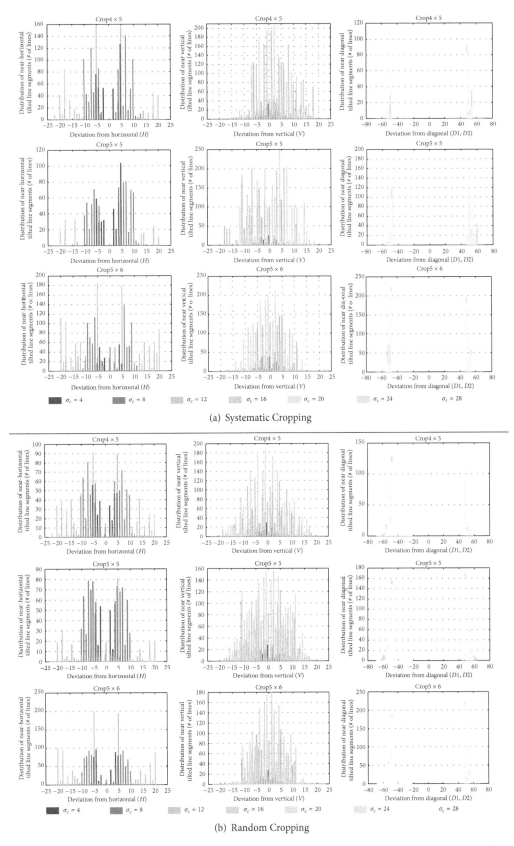

FIGURE 11: The distribution of the line segments detected from the edge maps of the foveal sets (Figure 8), having either horizontal (left-column), vertical (center-column), or diagonal (right-column) deviations, with the two sampling methods: (a) Systematic and (b) Random Cropping. The edge maps are at seven different scales (σ_c = 4, 8, 12, 16, 20, 24, and 28) and a fixed set of Hough parameters are used as *NumPeaks* = 100, *Threshold* = 3, *FillGap* = 40, and *MinLength* = 450 (based on [19]).

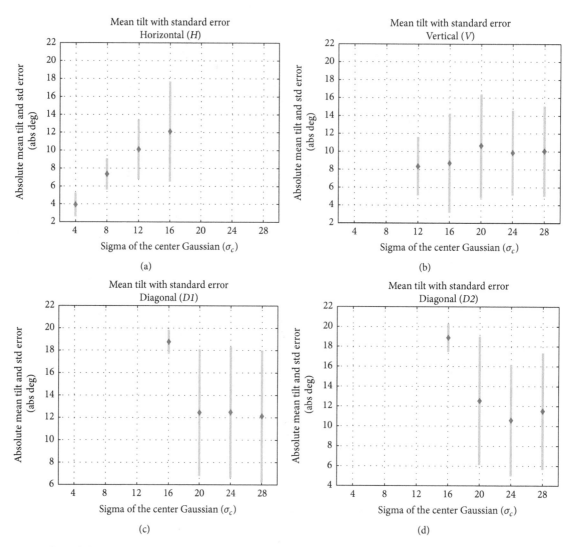

FIGURE 12: Mean tilts and the standard errors of detected tilt angles around the four reference orientations (H, V, $D1$, and $D2$) from the DoG edge map at seven different scales of the whole Café Wall of 9×14 with 200×200 px tiles and 8 px mortar. Green error bars correspond to Hough *NumPeaks* = 1000, with mean values shown in Red.

The new experimental results for mean tilts and standard errors of the detected tilt angles have been presented in Figure 12 for the Café Wall of 9×14 tiles with *NumPeaks* = 1000. The other parameters are kept the same as Figures 10 and 11 for the foveal sets. As indicated in Figure 12(a), the near-horizontal mean tilt is approximately $4°$ at scale 4 and $7.5°$ at scale 8 nearly the same as the foveal sample sets (Figure 10). In the horizontal graph, we see that, by increasing the DoG scale, the mean tilt also increases from $7.5°$ to ~$10°$ at scale 12 with higher variations compared to the foveal sample sets. The new results for the vertical and diagonal mean tilts at coarse scales have been improved dramatically from our previous reports (explained in previous paragraph) and show a variation of tilt angles for the detected houghlines. The near-vertical mean tilts at medium to coarse scales were around $2°$ that are quite negligible in the previous report; now they are around $10°$ while they were around $6°$ in the foveal sets. The near-diagonal mean tilts at medium to coarse

scales were approximately $3°$ in the previous reports; now the value is ~$10°$ and they were in the range of 5-$6°$ in the foveal sample sets. We have shown here that the new results with periphery appropriate parameterization are reliable and comparable with the previous results for foveal parameterization (Section 3.1.2). We will explain more on these results in Sections 3.2.2 and 3.3.

3.2.2. Variant Sized Café Wall Patterns with the Same Aspect Ratios of Tile Size to Mortar Size. We can assume that the tilt perception of the Café Wall illusion starts by a wholistic view to the pattern, which then extends to a local focusing view along the mortar lines in search for further cues of tilt in the pattern. Both of these local and global views to the Café Wall have their own effect on the strength of our perceptual understanding of tilt in this pattern. We started our investigations of the global tilt analysis in the Café Wall stimulus by first addressing the shortcomings of

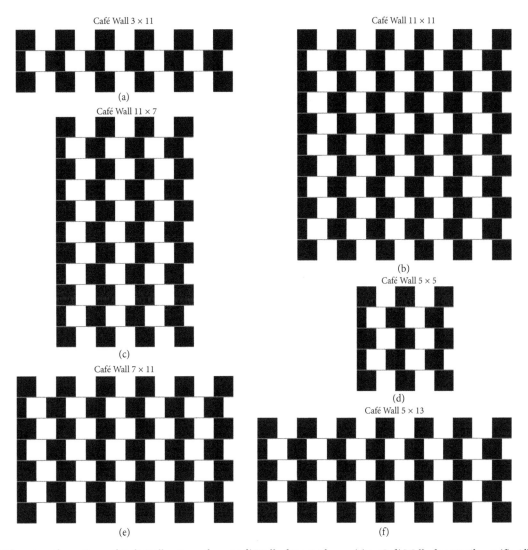

FIGURE 13: Different configurations of Café Wall pattern, from Café Wall of 3 × 11 tiles on (a) to Café Wall of 5 × 13 tiles at (f). All the patterns have the same tile size of 200 × 200 px and the mortar size of 8 px.

our previous reports [18, 19] as reflected in the previous section and presented reliable tilt results for a specific sample (Café Wall of 9 × 14 tiles) based on periphery appropriate parameterization. We show in this experiment our deep investigations of the global tilts on variations of Café Wall with the same characteristics of mortar lines and tiles but with different arrangements of a whole pattern. We have explored here the correlation between the tilt effect and the layout of the pattern in general (how the tiles are arranged to build the stimulus).

In this experiment, variations of Café Wall pattern have been investigated with the same aspect ratios of tile size (T) to mortar size (M) ($T/M = const.$) in order to check whether # rows and # columns in the overall arrangement of tiles in the Café Wall pattern have an effect on the detected tilts in our simulation results or not. In other words, we check the Gestalt perception of the Café Wall pattern and its relation to visual angle of the whole pattern (not just the visual angle of an individual tile and mortar line investigated so far [18, 19, 21]).

We show here that our model can predict slightly different tilt results for these variations, similar to our global perception of illusory tilt in the pattern in the same way as human is affected by the configurations of the pattern. This is being reported for the first time with the quantitative results.

The patterns explored here have the same size of tiles (200 × 200 px) and mortar lines (8 px) with these variations: Café Walls of 3 × 11, 5 × 5, 5 × 13, 7 × 11, 11 × 7, and 11 × 11 tiles, as shown in Figure 13. Looking at these variations, we see, for instance, a stronger tilt effect in the 5 × 13 tiles compared to the 5 × 5 tiles. Similarly, a stronger tilt effect is perceived in the variation of 7 × 11 tiles compared to weaker tilts in the 11 × 7 tiles.

To eliminate the effect of *NumPeaks* on detected hough-lines, in this experiment, we have selected *NumPeaks* = 1000 to attain more accurate tilt measurements when the overall sizes of the Café Wall samples are not the same (similar to Section 3.2.1). We have also tested values above 1000 up to 5000 for this parameter, but we found empirically that there is no significant difference in the mean tilt results above *NumPeaks* = 1000 for the samples tested and around four reference orientations. Increasing this value is computationally expensive and we need to keep a trade-off between the efficiency and the accuracy. The rest of the parameters are kept the same as Figures 10–12 for the local and global investigations of tilt in variations of the Café Wall pattern. The Hough parameters are as follows: *NumPeaks* = 1000, *FillGap* = 40, and *MinLength* = 450 for all scales of the DoG edge maps (σ_c = 4, 8, 12, 16, 20, 24, and 28). Summary tables in Figure 14 present the quantitative mean tilts for the global tilt investigations on these configurations of the pattern. These include the mean tilts and the standard errors of the detected tilt angles around the four reference orientations (H, V, $D1$, and $D2$).

The DoG outputs of these variations are the same across multiple scales, since the tiles and mortar lines have fixed sizes and the same set of parameters for the *Surround* and *Window ratios* (s, h, resp.) have been used in the DoG model. Utilizing the Hough analytical pipeline for quantifying the tilt angles, we have measured slightly different tilts across the multiple scales of the edge maps of these variations around the four reference orientations. This is because Hough analyses more dominant lines (longest lines) first by applying the houghpeaks function prior to detecting lines with the houghlines function (MATLAB functions).

When the pattern is wider in horizontal direction such as the 3 × 11, 5 × 13, or 7 × 11 it seems that we see a stronger tilt effect along the mortar lines compared to the other variations. The quantitative mean tilts near horizontal orientation occur at fine to medium scales (σ_c = 4, 8, and 12) of the edge maps. The near-horizontal lines can be captured until scale 16 (σ_c = 16), with this mortar width (considering the same aspect ratio of the tile size to the mortar size), as well as the midluminance of the mortar lines relative to the luminance of the tiles [21]. This can be seen also for the edge map of Café Wall of 3 × 8 tiles in Figure 2. There is a transient stage at scale 16 (σ_c = 16), connecting the detected near-horizontal lines to the zigzag vertical line segments due to the arrangement of grouping of tiles in the zigzag vertical orientation at medium to coarse scales in the edge maps. The highest tilt range is shown in Figure 14 for the 5 × 13 configuration which is 3–10.6° at fine to medium scale (σ_c = 4, 8, and 12), as expected. Then the variations of 7 × 11 (3.8–10.3°) and 11 × 11 (4–10.5°) come next, followed by the 3 × 11, 5 × 5, and 11 × 7 tiles. Considering the two square patterns (the 5 × 5 and 11 × 11 tiles), there are similar horizontal mean tilts, starting around 4.0° at the finest scale (σ_c = 4) and it is one degree wider in the 11 × 11 variation at scale 12 (σ_c = 12), ~10.5° compared to ~9.5° in the 5 × 5, but the differences are only significant for σ_c = 4.

The near-vertical mean tilts at medium to coarse scales (σ_c = 20, 24, and 28) show good results. The weakest vertical mean tilts correspond to the Café Wall of 3 × 11 tiles which ranges from 7.1° to 7.5°. For the patterns of medium size height such as the 5 × 13 and 7 × 11 tiles, it is ~9-10°. It is in the highest range around 10.5° when the pattern is spread along the vertical orientation such as the 11 × 7 and 11 × 11 variations. This is nearly the same for the 5 × 5 tiles having the ratio of height/width = 1 and with a maximum value for the 11 × 11

tiles (>10.6°). So the Café Wall of 5 × 13 tiles from the samples explored has the *strongest horizontal tilt* range while the 11 × 7 tiles show the *strongest vertical tilt* range. It seems that there is a trade-off in the mean tilts of the vertical and the horizontal orientation, and, for a stronger effect of vertical tilts, we encounter weaker horizontal tilts along the mortar lines. For the diagonal mean tilts the results show roughly similar deviations (in both positive and negative diagonals) at the coarse scales (σ_c = 24, 28) which is ~11-12° across the samples tested.

We note that the results reported here are based on our investigations on the number of lines detected at their angular positions and we have not considered any weights for the length of the lines in the mean tilts calculations. For the horizontal mean tilts this does not affect the results, since at fine to medium scales the local tilted line segments (Twisted Cord elements) are extracted for all of these variations nearly the same with roughly similar size. The detected houghlines at scale 12 (medium scale) for all variations tested have been provided in Figure 15, highlighting local tilts of the nearly horizontal Twisted Cords and small tilt deviations from the vertical orientation. However, if a Café Wall pattern is more spread along the vertical orientation compared to the horizontal, then longer lines are detected with less deviation along the vertical at coarse scales (the whole tiles are present in the edge maps with no mortar cues left at these scales). Figure 16 clarifies this more: the detected houghlines at scale 28 (the coarsest scale) have been presented for these variations, indicating the global tilts of the lines detected with zigzag vertical orientation. In fact, as we expect from the tilt estimation, deviations from the vertical orientation increase as the lines found get shorter.

3.3. Comparison of Local and Global Tilts in Café Wall Illusion. We have shown in the last two sections that the mean tilt results with periphery appropriate parameterization are reliable and comparable with the previous results for foveal parameterization. The results for near-horizontal global tilts in these variations are nearly the same as the local tilts detected in the foveal sample sets (Section 3.1.2) 4° at scale 4 and ~7° at scale 8. At scale 12, we have a higher tilt angle ~9.5–10.5° here compared to the local tilts around 8°. The results of the vertical and diagonal mean tilts are slightly larger than the predicted values for the foveal samples (7–10° for the vertical and 11-12° for the diagonal tilts here compared to ~6° for the vertical and 5-6° for the diagonal tilts in the foveal samples). The results here seem more realistic in our perception of zigzag vertical lines at coarse scales considering the phase shift of rows of tiles in the Café Wall pattern (the deviations from the diagonal axes are more than 5°, considering the geometry of the pattern).

The quantitative modelling presented for the perceived tilt in the Café Wall illusion considering the foveal/local aspects as well as the peripheral/global view to the pattern leads us to achieve reliable results in our investigations. However, we illustrate some improvements to the current evaluation for future studies on the topic. First, for near-horizontal mean tilts, although the tilt analysis pipeline in our model detects the local Twisted Cord elements as local tilt

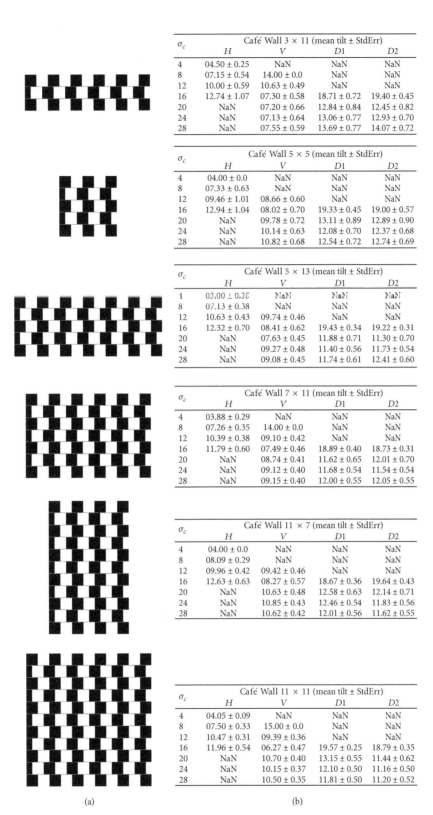

σ_c	Café Wall 3 × 11 (mean tilt ± StdErr)			
	H	V	D1	D2
4	04.50 ± 0.25	NaN	NaN	NaN
8	07.15 ± 0.54	14.00 ± 0.0	NaN	NaN
12	10.00 ± 0.59	10.63 ± 0.49	NaN	NaN
16	12.74 ± 1.07	07.30 ± 0.58	18.71 ± 0.72	19.40 ± 0.45
20	NaN	07.20 ± 0.66	12.84 ± 0.84	12.45 ± 0.82
24	NaN	07.13 ± 0.64	13.06 ± 0.77	12.93 ± 0.70
28	NaN	07.55 ± 0.59	13.69 ± 0.77	14.07 ± 0.72

σ_c	Café Wall 5 × 5 (mean tilt ± StdErr)			
	H	V	D1	D2
4	04.00 ± 0.0	NaN	NaN	NaN
8	07.33 ± 0.63	NaN	NaN	NaN
12	09.46 ± 1.01	08.66 ± 0.60	NaN	NaN
16	12.94 ± 1.04	08.02 ± 0.70	19.33 ± 0.45	19.00 ± 0.57
20	NaN	09.78 ± 0.72	13.11 ± 0.89	12.89 ± 0.90
24	NaN	10.14 ± 0.63	12.08 ± 0.70	12.37 ± 0.68
28	NaN	10.82 ± 0.68	12.54 ± 0.72	12.74 ± 0.69

σ_c	Café Wall 5 × 13 (mean tilt ± StdErr)			
	H	V	D1	D2
4	03.00 ± 0.36	NaN	NaN	NaN
8	07.13 ± 0.38	NaN	NaN	NaN
12	10.63 ± 0.43	09.74 ± 0.46	NaN	NaN
16	12.32 ± 0.70	08.41 ± 0.62	19.43 ± 0.34	19.22 ± 0.31
20	NaN	07.63 ± 0.45	11.88 ± 0.71	11.30 ± 0.70
24	NaN	09.27 ± 0.48	11.40 ± 0.56	11.73 ± 0.54
28	NaN	09.08 ± 0.45	11.74 ± 0.61	12.41 ± 0.60

σ_c	Café Wall 7 × 11 (mean tilt ± StdErr)			
	H	V	D1	D2
4	03.88 ± 0.29	NaN	NaN	NaN
8	07.26 ± 0.35	14.00 ± 0.0	NaN	NaN
12	10.39 ± 0.38	09.10 ± 0.42	NaN	NaN
16	11.79 ± 0.60	07.49 ± 0.46	18.89 ± 0.40	18.73 ± 0.31
20	NaN	08.74 ± 0.41	11.62 ± 0.65	12.01 ± 0.70
24	NaN	09.12 ± 0.40	11.68 ± 0.54	11.54 ± 0.54
28	NaN	09.15 ± 0.40	12.00 ± 0.55	12.05 ± 0.55

σ_c	Café Wall 11 × 7 (mean tilt ± StdErr)			
	H	V	D1	D2
4	04.00 ± 0.0	NaN	NaN	NaN
8	08.09 ± 0.29	NaN	NaN	NaN
12	09.96 ± 0.42	09.42 ± 0.46	NaN	NaN
16	12.63 ± 0.63	08.27 ± 0.57	18.67 ± 0.36	19.64 ± 0.43
20	NaN	10.63 ± 0.48	12.58 ± 0.63	12.14 ± 0.71
24	NaN	10.85 ± 0.43	12.46 ± 0.54	11.83 ± 0.56
28	NaN	10.62 ± 0.42	12.01 ± 0.56	11.62 ± 0.55

σ_c	Café Wall 11 × 11 (mean tilt ± StdErr)			
	H	V	D1	D2
4	04.05 ± 0.09	NaN	NaN	NaN
8	07.50 ± 0.33	15.00 ± 0.0	NaN	NaN
12	10.47 ± 0.31	09.39 ± 0.36	NaN	NaN
16	11.96 ± 0.54	06.27 ± 0.47	19.57 ± 0.25	18.79 ± 0.35
20	NaN	10.70 ± 0.40	13.15 ± 0.55	11.44 ± 0.62
24	NaN	10.15 ± 0.37	12.10 ± 0.50	11.16 ± 0.50
28	NaN	10.50 ± 0.35	11.81 ± 0.50	11.20 ± 0.52

(a)   (b)

FIGURE 14: (a) Different configurations of the Café Wall pattern tested (Figure 13) from Café Wall of 3 × 11 tiles on the top to Café Wall of 11 × 11 tiles at the bottom. (b) Mean tilts and the standard errors of tilt angles for each variation are summarized in the mean tilt tables for the four reference orientations of horizontal (H), vertical (V), and diagonals (D1, D2) orientations at seven scales of the edge maps (σ_c = 4, 8, 12, 16, 20, 24, and 28).

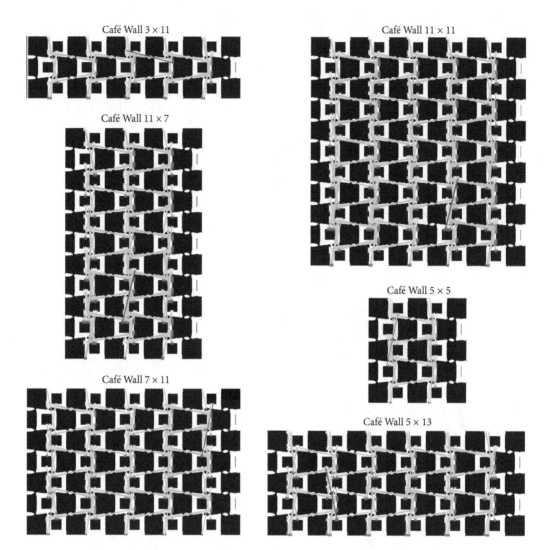

FIGURE 15: Detected houghlines displayed in green, overlaid on the binary edge maps at scale 12 ($\sigma_c = 12$) of different configurations of the Café Wall pattern in Figure 13. Hough parameters are as follows: *NumPeaks* = 1000, *Threshold* = 3, *FillGap* = 40, and *MinLength* = 450.

cues as shown in Figure 15 (for scale 12 for these variations), it seems that, in our perception of tilt, we intend to integrate these local tilt cues to construct a slanted continuous contour along the entire mortar as either diverging or converging [16, 27] tilt. Therefore, an edge integration technique is required for predicting a more precise value for the near-horizontal tilts as we perceive tilts in the Café Wall. Second, in the investigated tilts around the vertical orientation, we expect to see less deviations for the vertically spread configurations compared to the horizontally spread ones. However, the results showed the maximum vertical deviations for the Café Walls of 11×7 and 11×11 around $10.5°$ compared to $9°$ in others, except $7.5°$ for the Café Wall of 3×11. In the 3×11 tiles, we see more deviations around the diagonals compared to the rest of the configurations (as it is expected), where the range is ~12.5–$14°$ compared to 11–$12.5°$, and also less deviations from the vertical orientation due to the groupings of detected lines for the reference orientations. Our explanation of the results is getting clear by looking at the houghlines presented

in Figure 16. In the Hough analysis, we have applied the same weight for all the detected lines. Therefore for the patterns that are spread along the vertical orientation, although houghlines detect many longer lines with less deviations in the edge map, houghpeaks let more smaller line segments be detected (up to the maximum value of *NumPeaks*), with more deviations from the vertical orientation. For final validations of these results, psychophysical experiments are required as the priority of our future work. The results from psychophysical experiments lead us to assign weights to each scale and approximate tilt angles in our model based on the perceived tilt in real subjects.

4. Conclusion

A low-level filtering approach [17, 19, 22] has been explored here modelling the retinal/cortical simple cells in our early vision for revealing the tilt cues involved in the local and global perception of the Café Wall stimulus. The model has

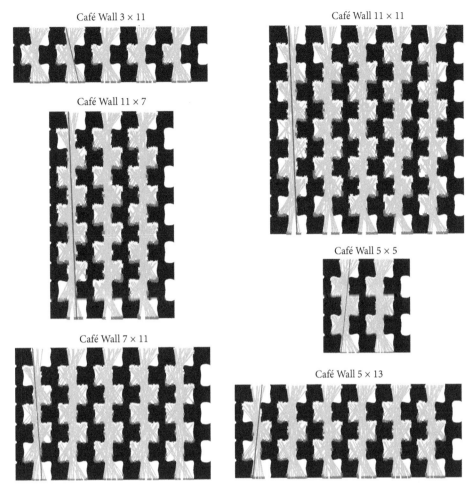

FIGURE 16: Detected houghlines displayed in green, overlaid on the binary edge maps at scale 28 ($\sigma_c = 28$) of different configurations of the Café Wall pattern in Figure 13. Hough parameters are as follows: *NumPeaks* = 1000, *Threshold* = 3, *FillGap* = 40, and *MinLength* = 450.

an embedded processing pipeline utilizing Hough transform to quantify the degrees of the induced tilts that appeared in the low-level representation for the stimulus in our model, referred to as the *edge map at multiple scales*.

The experiments reported have contributed new understanding of the relationship between the strength of tilt effect perceived in the Café Wall illusion as a function of eccentricity, that is, whether a cell or edge is foveated or perceived in the periphery.

Different size/shape cropped samples of the Café Wall pattern were used to model the role of the shape and size of the fovea and larger samples tended to induce a larger number of longer shallower lines, particularly in the vertical dimension. When we foveate a particular cell we tend to see that as having more horizontal mortar boundaries, while those outside the fovea are perceived as having larger tilts. This is consistent with the larger tilts perceived at lower resolutions, modelling the periphery, and the almost horizontal tilts seen in the foveal region, corresponding to the center of a larger pattern. This makes this a multiple scale model.

It is hypothesized that the multiple scale information from the retina is integrated later in the cortex into a true multiscale model and that the Gestalt illusions result from the angle misperceptions that are already encoded in the retina. The quantitative predictions are based on the analysis of Hough transform of the edge maps here with promising results reported. This tilt investigation can be replaced by any more bioderived techniques, modelling mid-to-high-level tilt integrations, capable of quantifying different degrees of tilt in variations of the Gestalt view of the pattern, as we perceive the tilt differently in those variations.

We regard the publication of the predictions before running experiments to validate them as essential to the integrity of science. A priority in our research is psychophysical experiments to validate the predictions of the model.

Conflicts of Interest

The authors declare that there are no conflicts of interest regarding the publication of this paper.

Acknowledgments

Nasim Nematzadeh was supported by an Australian Research Training Program (RTP) award for her Ph.D.

References

[1] L. Spillmann, "Receptive fields of visual neurons: The early years," *Perception*, vol. 43, no. 11, pp. 1145–1176, 2014.

[2] P. B. Cook and J. S. McReynolds, "Lateral inhibition in the inner retina is important for spatial tuning of ganglion cells," *Nature Neuroscience*, vol. 1, no. 8, pp. 714–719, 1998.

[3] J. Y. Huang and D. A. Protti, "The impact of inhibitory mechanisms in the inner retina on spatial tuning of RGCs," *Scientific Reports*, vol. 6, article 21966, 2016.

[4] F. Ratliff, B. W. Knight, and N. Graham, "On tuning and amplification by lateral inhibition.," *Proceedings of the National Acadamy of Sciences of the United States of America*, vol. 62, no. 3, pp. 733–740, 1969.

[5] G. D. Field and E. J. Chichilnisky, "Information processing in the primate retina: Circuitry and coding," *Annual Review of Neuroscience*, vol. 30, pp. 1–30, 2007.

[6] T. Gollisch and M. Meister, "Eye smarter than scientists believed: neural computations in circuits of the retina," *Neuron*, vol. 65, no. 2, pp. 150–164, 2010.

[7] T. Lindeberg and L. Florack, "Foveal scale-space and the linear increase of receptive field size as a function of eccentricity," KTH Royal Institute of Technology, 1994.

[8] D. H. Hubel and T. N. Wiesel, "Receptive fields, binocular interaction, and functional architecture in the cat's visual cortex," *The Journal of Physiology*, vol. 160, pp. 106–154, 1962.

[9] P. H. Schiller, "Parallel information processing channels created in the retina," *Proceedings of the National Acadamy of Sciences of the United States of America*, vol. 107, no. 40, pp. 17087–17094, 2010.

[10] H. B. Barlow, A. M. Derrington, L. R. Harris, and P. Lennie, "The effects of remote retinal stimulation on the responses of cat retinal ganglion cells.," *The Journal of Physiology*, vol. 269, no. 1, pp. 177–194, 1977.

[11] L. J. Frishman and R. A. Linsenmeier, "Effects of picrotoxin and strychnine on non-linear responses of Y-type cat retinal ganglion cells.," *The Journal of Physiology*, vol. 324, no. 1, pp. 347–363, 1982.

[12] B. Roska and F. Werblin, "Rapid global shifts in natural scenes block spiking in specific ganglion cell types," *Nature Neuroscience*, vol. 6, no. 6, pp. 600–608, 2003.

[13] L. J. Croner and E. Kaplan, "Receptive fields of P and M ganglion cells across the primate retina," *Vision Research*, vol. 35, no. 1, pp. 7–24, 1995.

[14] C. Enroth-Cugell and R. M. Shapley, "Adaptation and dynamics of cat retinal ganglion cells," *The Journal of Physiology*, vol. 233, no. 2, pp. 271–309, 1973.

[15] R. A. Linsenmeier, L. J. Frishman, H. G. Jakiela, and C. Enroth-Cugell, "Receptive field properties of X and Y cells in the cat retina derived from contrast sensitivity measurements," *Vision Research*, vol. 22, no. 9, pp. 1173–1183, 1982.

[16] S. Grossberg and E. Mingolla, "Neural dynamics of form perception. boundary completion, illusory figures, and neon color spreading," *Psychological Review*, vol. 92, no. 2, pp. 173–211, 1985.

[17] N. Nematzadeh, T. W. Lewis, and D. M. W. Powers, "Bioplausible multiscale filtering in retinal to cortical processing as a model of computer vision," in *Proceedings of the 7th International Conference on Agents and Artificial Intelligence, ICAART 2015*, pp. 305–316, January 2015.

[18] N. Nematzadeh and D. M. W. Powers, "A quantitative analysis of tilt in the Café Wall illusion: a bioplausible model for foveal and peripheral vision," in *Proceedings of the 2016 International Conference on Digital Image Computing: Techniques and Applications, DICTA 2016*, December 2016.

[19] N. Nematzadeh and D. M. W. Powers, "A bioplausible model for explaining Café Wall illusion: foveal vs peripheral resolution," in *Proceedings of the International Symposium on Visual Computing*, pp. 426–438, Springer International Publishing, 2016.

[20] N. Nematzadeh, D. M. W. Powers, and T. W. Lewis, "Quantitative analysis of a bioplausible model of misperception of slope in the Café Wall illusion," in *Proceedings of the Asian Conference on Computer Vision*, pp. 622–637, Springer, 2016.

[21] N. Nematzadeh and D. M. Powers, "A predictive account of Café Wall illusions using a quantitative model," submitted, https://arxiv.org/abs/1705.06846.

[22] N. Nematzadeh, D. M. Powers, and T. W. Lewis, "Bioplausible multiscale filtering in retino-cortical processing as a mechanism in perceptual grouping," *Brain Informatics*, pp. 1–23, 2017.

[23] D. C. Earle and S. J. Maskell, "Fraser cords and reversal of the café wall illusion.," *Perception*, vol. 22, no. 4, pp. 383–390, 1993.

[24] M. J. Morgan and B. Moulden, "The Münsterberg figure and twisted cords," *Vision Research*, vol. 26, no. 11, pp. 1793–1800, 1986.

[25] J. FRASER, "A new visual illusion of direction 1904–1920," *British Journal of Psychology*, vol. 2, no. 3, pp. 307–320, 1908.

[26] G. Westheimer, "Irradiation, border location, and the shifted-chessboard pattern," *Perception*, vol. 36, no. 4, pp. 483–494, 2007.

[27] B. Moulden and J. Renshaw, "The Munsterberg illusion and 'irradiation'," *Perception*, vol. 8, no. 3, pp. 275–301, 1979.

[28] M. E. McCourt, "Brightness induction and the Café Wall illusion.," *Perception*, vol. 12, no. 2, pp. 131–142, 1983.

[29] R. L. Gregory and P. Heard, "Border locking and the Cafe Wall illusion," *Perception*, vol. 8, no. 4, pp. 365–380, 1979.

[30] A. Kitaoka, B. Pinna, and G. Brelstaff, "Contrast polarities determine the direction of Café Wall Tilts," *Perception*, vol. 33, no. 1, pp. 11–20, 2004.

[31] S. W. Kuffler, "Neurons in the retina: organization, inhibition and excitation problems," *Cold Spring Harbor Symposium on Quantitative Biology*, vol. 17, no. 0, pp. 281–292, 1952.

[32] R. W. Rodieck and J. Stone, "Analysis of receptive fields of cat retinal ganlion cells," *Journal of Neurophysiology*, vol. 28, no. 5, pp. 833–849, 1964.

[33] C. Enroth-Cugell and J. G. Robson, "The contrast sensitivity of retinal ganglion cells of the cat," *The Journal of Physiology*, vol. 187, no. 3, pp. 517–552, 1966.

[34] D. Marr and S. Ullman, "Directional selectivity and its use in early visual processing," *Proceedings of the Royal Society B Biological Science*, vol. 211, no. 1183, pp. 151–180, 1981.

[35] D. Marr and E. Hildreth, "Theory of edge detection," *Proceedings of the Royal Society of London—Biological Sciences*, vol. 207, no. 1167, pp. 187–217, 1980.

[36] D. P. Lulich and K. A. Stevens, "Differential contributions of circular and elongated spatial filters to the Café Wall illusion," *Biological Cybernetics*, vol. 61, no. 6, pp. 427–435, 1989.

[37] D. M. W. Powers, "Jetwhite color map. Mathworks," 2016 https://au.mathworks.com/matlabcentral/fileexchange/48419-jetwhite-colours-996/content/jetwhite.m.

[38] P. V. Hough, "Method and means for recognizing complex patterns," (No. US 3069654), 1962.

[39] J. Illingworth and J. Kittler, "A survey of the hough transform," *Computer Vision Graphics and Image Processing*, vol. 44, no. 1, pp. 87–116, 1988.

[40] B. Blakeslee and M. E. McCourt, "A multiscale spatial filtering account of the White effect, simultaneous brightness contrast and grating induction," *Vision Research*, vol. 39, no. 26, pp. 4361–4377, 1999.

[41] M. Carandini, "Receptive fields and suppressive fields in the early visual system," in *Cognitive Neurosciences Iii*, vol. 3, pp. 313–326, 3rd edition, 2004.

[42] E. Craft, H. Schütze, E. Niebur, and R. Von Der Heydt, "A neural model of figure-ground organization," *Journal of Neurophysiology*, vol. 97, no. 6, pp. 4310–4326, 2007.

[43] C. L. Passaglia, C. Enroth-Cugell, and J. B. Troy, "Effects of remote stimulation on the mean firing rate of cat retinal ganglion cells," *The Journal of Neuroscience*, vol. 21, no. 15, pp. 5794–5803, 2001.

[44] H. Wei, Q. Zuo, and B. Lang, "Multi-scale image analysis based on non-classical receptive field mechanism," *Lecture Notes in Computer Science (including subseries Lecture Notes in Artificial Intelligence and Lecture Notes in Bioinformatics): Preface*, vol. 7064, no. 3, pp. 601–610, 2011.

8

A SVR Learning Based Sensor Placement Approach for Nonlinear Spatially Distributed Systems

Xian-xia Zhang,[1] Zhi-qiang Fu,[1] Wei-lu Shan,[1] Bing Wang,[1] and Tao Zou[2]

[1]*Shanghai Key Laboratory of Power Station Automation Technology, School of Mechatronics and Automation, Shanghai University, Shanghai 200072, China*
[2]*Shenyang Institute of Automation, Chinese Academy of Sciences, Shenyang 110016, China*

Correspondence should be addressed to Xian-xia Zhang; xianxia_zh@shu.edu.cn

Academic Editor: Wu Deng

Many industrial processes are inherently distributed in space and time and are called spatially distributed dynamical systems (SDDSs). Sensor placement affects capturing the spatial distribution and then becomes crucial issue to model or control an SDDS. In this study, a new data-driven based sensor placement method is developed. SVR algorithm is innovatively used to extract the characteristics of spatial distribution from a spatiotemporal data set. The support vectors learned by SVR represent the crucial spatial data structure in the spatiotemporal data set, which can be employed to determine optimal sensor location and sensor number. A systematic sensor placement design scheme in three steps (data collection, SVR learning, and sensor locating) is developed for an easy implementation. Finally, effectiveness of the proposed sensor placement scheme is validated on two spatiotemporal 3D fuzzy controlled spatially distributed systems.

1. Introduction

Many industrial processes are inherently distributed in space and time, such as fluid flow process, spray deposition process, heat exchange process, and snap curing process. These systems are usually called spatially distributed dynamical systems (SDDSs) or distributed parameter systems (DPSs) [1]. Traditionally, the spatially distributed nature is ignored, and then an SDDS is simplified into a lumped parameter system (LPS). However, its performance will deteriorate if the system dynamics significantly vary with space [2]. To satisfy tighter product quality requirements, the spatial nature should be considered in the modeling and control. Consequently, the spatiotemporal modeling and control for SDDSs have become the highlight in the modern modeling and control theory.

On the research of SDDS, since sensor placement affects capturing the spatial distribution, it becomes one of key issues to influence the performance of spatiotemporal modeling or control. Sensor placement is a difficult problem, particularly in nonlinear and multivariable case [3].

In the past several decades, sensor placement has been studied and can be classified into two categories, that is, model-based method and data-driven based method. For the first category, the sensor placement is dependent on an accurate mathematical model. Some methods aim at achieving better parameter estimation with different criteria, for example, scalar criteria of the covariance matrix [4] and scalar measure of performance defined on the Fisher information matrix [5]. Some methods intend to improve state estimation or state observer with possible criteria, such as observability measures [6], convergence properties of observer [7], and cost function related to Gramian observability matrix [8]. Some methods integrate optimal actuator and sensor placement with nonlinear output feedback control [9–11] and improve control performance, where the penalty on the response of the closed-loop system is used for cost function of actuator placement and the control action, and the estimation error in the closed-loop infinite-dimensional system is used for cost function of sensor placement.

For the second category, only data information is used for sensor placement. Wouwer et al. [12] proposed the determinant of Fisher information matrix formed by sensitivity functions for parameter estimation and the Gram determinant formed by sensor responses for observer estimation. Zamprogna et al. [13] selected the most suitable secondary process variable as soft sensor inputs for batch distillation by exploiting the properties of principal component analysis (PCA) on the sensitivity matrix. Tongpadungroda et al. [14] identified the optimal position of an applied load by GA under the criterion related to PCA. Zhang et al. [15] proposed a sensor placement method for spatiotemporal 3D fuzzy control system based on spatial constrained fuzzy c-means algorithm. Compared with the model-based method, the data-driven method is very promising in practical engineering applications since no mathematical model is used.

In this study, a new data-driven based sensor placement method is proposed. Support vector regression (SVR) algorithm is used to extract the main characteristics of spatial distribution from a spatiotemporal data set, which can be directly used for the sensor placement. The support vectors learned by SVR represent the crucial spatial data structure hidden in the spatiotemporal data set, which can be employed to determine the optimal sensor location and sensor number. A systematic sensor placement design scheme is developed for an easy implementation, which consists of data collection, SVR learning, and sensor locating. The effectiveness of the proposed sensor placement scheme is validated on two spatiotemporal 3D fuzzy controlled nonlinear spatially distributed systems.

This paper is organized as follows. Preliminaries about nonlinear spatially distributed systems and SVR algorithm are described in Section 2. In Section 3, the SVR learning based sensor placement method is presented in detail. Two illustrative examples are given in Section 4. Finally, Section 5 summarizes the conclusion.

2. Preliminaries

2.1. Nonlinear Spatially Distributed Dynamical Systems. Many industrial processes exhibit highly nonlinear behavior and strong spatial variations. They usually can be represented by nonlinear partial differential equations. Some processes have strong convection characteristics [16], some have strong diffusion phenomena [17], and some have both convection and diffusion characteristics [18]. These systems are usually installed with multiple spatially distributed actuators and multiple sensors and give rise to nonlinear control problems that involve the regulation of highly distributed control variables using these spatially distributed actuators and sensors.

In the following subsections, two examples of SDDSs are presented and illustrated.

2.1.1. A Catalytic Packed-Bed Reactor. The catalytic packed-bed reactor [17, 19] in Figure 1 is a typical spatiotemporal dynamic system. A reaction of the form $C \to D$ takes place on the catalyst. The reaction is endothermic and a jacket is used to heat the reactor. The dimensionless mathematical model

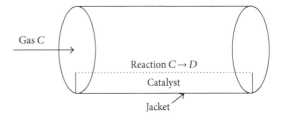

FIGURE 1: Sketch of a catalytic packed-bed reactor.

that describes this nonlinear tubular chemical reactor is given as follows:

$$\varepsilon_p \frac{\partial T_g(z,t)}{\partial t} = -\frac{\partial T_g(z,t)}{\partial z} + \alpha_c \left(T_s(z,t) - T_g(z,t) \right)$$
$$- \alpha_g \left(T_g(z,t) - u(t) \right),$$
$$\frac{\partial T_s(z,t)}{\partial t} = \frac{\partial^2 T_s(z,t)}{\partial z^2} + B_0 \exp \left(\frac{\gamma' T_s(z,t)}{1 + T_s(z,t)} \right) \quad (1)$$
$$- \beta_c \left(T_s(z,t) - T_g(z,t) \right)$$
$$- \beta_p \left(T_s(z,t) - b(z) u(t) \right)$$

subject to the following boundary conditions:

$$z = 0,$$
$$T_g(z,t) = 0,$$
$$\frac{\partial T_s(z,t)}{\partial z} = 0,$$
$$z = 1, \quad (2)$$
$$\frac{\partial T_s(z,t)}{\partial z} = 0,$$

where $T_g(z,t)$ and $T_s(z,t)$ denote the dimensionless temperature of gas and catalyst, respectively, which are spatially dependent on $z \in [0,1]$, $b(z)u(t)$ denotes the spatiotemporal heating source with the distribution $b(z)$ and the manipulated input $u(t)$, and $u(t)$ denotes the dimensionless temperature of jacket. The values of the process parameters are given as follows:

$$\varepsilon_p = 0.01,$$
$$\gamma = 21.14,$$
$$\beta_c = 1.0,$$
$$\beta_p = 15.62, \quad (3)$$
$$B_0 = -0.003,$$
$$\alpha_c = 0.5,$$
$$\alpha_g = 0.5.$$

In this application, the control target is to control the catalyst temperature $T_s(z,t)$ throughout the reactor in order

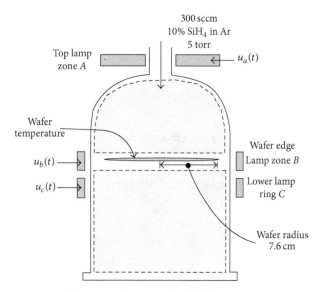

FIGURE 2: Structure of a RTCVD system.

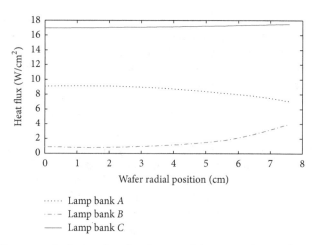

FIGURE 3: Radiation flux distribution of three-zone heating lamp banks.

to maintain a desired degree of reaction rate using the measurements of catalyst temperature from q sensing locations $z' = [z_1 \ z_2 \ \cdots \ z_q]$ and manipulating one spatially distributed heating source ($b(z) = 1 - \cos(\pi z)$). The spatial reference profile is given as $T_{sd}(z) = 0.42 - 0.2\cos(\pi z)$, $0 \leq z \leq 1$, and then the entire spatial catalyst temperature should follow this reference.

2.1.2. A Rapid Thermal Chemical Vapor Deposition System. Consider a rapid thermal chemical vapor deposition (RTCVD) reactor with three-zone heating banks (Adomaitis 1995; Theodoropoulou et al., 1998). The sketch of the RTCVD system is depicted in Figure 2, where the lamp bank A mainly heats the total area of the wafer, the lamp bank B mainly heats the wafer edge, and the lamp bank C is used to coarsely adjust the wafer temperature average. When a wafer is being heated, it is rotated for azimuthal temperature uniformity. 10% silane feed in inert gas is inputted into the reactor from the top, and the silane is decomposed into silicon and hydrogen. A 0.5 μm film of polysilicon is expected to deposit on the wafer when deposition temperature appears at near 800 K or higher. The temperature is controlled by operating the power to lamp banks A, B, and C. A dimensionless wafer thermal dynamics equation (Adomaitis 1995) over the wafer domain is given as follows:

$$\frac{\partial T_r'}{\partial t'} = \kappa_0 \left[\left(\frac{1}{r'}\right) \frac{\partial T_r'}{\partial r'} + \frac{\partial^2 T_r'}{\partial r'^2} \right] + \sigma_0 \left(1 - T_r'^4\right) \tag{4}$$

$$+ \omega_r q_a \left(r'\right) u_a + \omega_r q_b \left(r'\right) u_b + \omega_r q_c \left(r'\right) u_c$$

subject to the boundary condition

$$\frac{\partial T_r'}{\partial r'} = \sigma_{ed} \left(1 - T_r'^4\right) + q_{ed} u_b \quad \text{when } r' = 1$$

$$\frac{\partial T_r'}{\partial r'} = 0 \quad \text{when } r' = 0, \tag{5}$$

where $T_r' = T_r/T_{\text{amb}}$ denotes dimensionless wafer temperature, T_r denotes the actual wafer temperature, and $T_{\text{amb}} = 300$ K denotes ambient temperature; $r' = r/R_w$ denotes the dimensionless radial position of the wafer with r denoting the actual radial position of the wafer and R_w denoting the wafer radius ($R_w = 7.6$ cm); $t' = t/\tau$ denotes dimensionless time, t denotes the actual time, and $\tau = 2.9$ s denotes residence time of upper chamber; $q_a(r')$, $q_b(r')$, and $q_c(r')$ denote the radiant energy flux on the radial position r' from the lamp banks A, B, and C to the wafer, respectively (the distributions are shown in Figure 3); u_a, u_b, and u_c denote the percentage of the lamp power for the three-zone lamp banks. The values of the process parameters are given as follows:

$$\kappa_0 = 0.0021,$$

$$\sigma_0 = 0.0012,$$

$$\sigma_{ed} = 0.0037, \tag{6}$$

$$q_{ed} = 4.022,$$

$$\omega_r = 0.0256.$$

From (4) and (5), we can find that the wafer temperature is a variable varying with time and space. The concerned control problem is to control the wafer temperature throughout the wafer radius to arrive at the set temperature 1000 K quickly and uniformly using the measurements of wafer temperature from q sensing locations $z' = [z_1 \ z_2 \ \cdots \ z_q]$ and manipulating power percentage (u_a, u_b, and u_c) to three zones of lamp banks.

2.2. SVR Algorithm. Support vector regression (SVR) is a learning technique that originated from theoretical foundations of the statistical learning theory [20]. Over the past decade, SVR has become one of the most popular regression techniques and has been employed in a variety of applications. It performs a new inductive principle (structural risk minimization) for learning from finite training data sets and chooses a model of the right complexity from a large number of candidate models (learning machines) to describe training data pairs.

Suppose we have a training set $D = \{[x_i, y_i] \in R^s \times R, \ i = 1, \ldots, q\}$ consisting of q pairs $(x_1, y_1), (x_2, y_2), \ldots, (x_q, y_q)$, where the inputs are s-dimensional vectors and the labels are continuous values. SVR builds a function as follows:

$$f(x, w) : R^s \longrightarrow R$$
$$x \longmapsto \langle w, \psi(x) \rangle_\wp + b, \tag{7}$$

where b is a bias term and $\psi(\cdot) : R^s \to \wp$ is an application mapping the space of factors into a feature space $\wp$.

The regression problem can be formulated as a convex optimization problem as follows:

$$\min_{w,b} \frac{1}{2} \|w\|^2 + C \left(\sum_{i=1}^{l} [f(x_i, w) - y_i]_\varepsilon \right), \tag{8}$$

where C is a design parameter chosen by the user, which determines the trade-off between the complexity of $f(x, w)$

and the approximate error, and $[\cdot]_\varepsilon$ is the ε-insensitive loss function which is defined as follows:

$$[f(x, w) - y]_\varepsilon$$
$$= \begin{cases} 0 & \text{if } |f(x, w) - y| \le \varepsilon \\ |f(x, w) - y| - \varepsilon & \text{otherwise.} \end{cases} \tag{9}$$

In practice, $\wp$, $w \in \wp$ and $\psi(x) \in \wp$ are deduced from a kernel $K(\cdot, \cdot) : R^s \times R^s \to R$ involved in the computation of a scalar product:

$$w = \sum_i w_i K(x_i, \cdot),$$
$$\psi(x) = K(x_i, \cdot), \tag{10}$$
$$\langle w, \psi(x) \rangle_\wp = \sum_i w_i K(x_i, x).$$

The above optimization problem can be solved in a dual space. By introducing the Lagrange multipliers α_i (α_i^*), the primal optimization problem can be formulated in its dual form as follows:

$$\max_{\alpha_i, \alpha_i^*} \left\{ -\frac{1}{2} \sum_{i=1}^{q} \sum_{j=1}^{q} (\alpha_i^* - \alpha_i)(\alpha_j^* - \alpha_j) K(x_i, x_j) - \varepsilon \sum_{i=1}^{q} (\alpha_i^* + \alpha_i) + \sum_{i=1}^{q} (\alpha_i^* - \alpha_i) y_i \right\} \tag{11}$$

$$\text{subject to} \quad \sum_{j=1}^{q} \alpha_i^* = \sum_{i=1}^{q} \alpha_i \quad 0 \le \alpha_i^* \le C, \ 0 \le \alpha_i \le C, \ i = 1, \ldots, q.$$

Solving the dual quadratic programming problem, we can find an optimal weight vector w and an optimal bias b of the regression hypersurface given in

$$w = \sum_{i=1}^{q} (\alpha_i^* - \alpha_i) \psi(x_i)$$
$$b = \frac{1}{q} \left(\sum_{i=1}^{q} (y_i - \langle w \cdot \psi(x_i) \rangle) \right). \tag{12}$$

Then, the best regression hypersurface is given by

$$f(x, w) = \sum_{i=1}^{q} (\alpha_i^* - \alpha_i) K(x_i, x) + b$$
$$= \sum_{i \in SV} (\alpha_i^* - \alpha_i) K(x_i, x) + b. \tag{13}$$

The training pattern x_i with nonzero $(\alpha_i^* - \alpha_i)$ is called support vector (SV).

3. SVR Learning Based Sensor Placement Scheme

3.1. Design Methodology. Consider a nonlinear SDDS in Figure 4, $\mathbf{u}(t) \in R^{\underline{L}}$ is the temporal input, and $y(z, t) \in R$ is the spatiotemporal output, where t is the time variable, $z \in \overline{Z}$ is the spatial variable, and $\overline{Z}$ is the spatial domain. Here suppose the system is controlled by the $\underline{L}$ actuators with implemental temporal signal $\mathbf{u}(t) = [u_1(t) \ u_2(t) \ \cdots \ u_{\underline{L}}(t)]$ and certain spatial distribution. The output is measured at the p spatial locations $z_1, z_2, \ldots, z_p$ $(p \ge 1)$; therefore, let $\overline{Z} = [z_1, z_2, \ldots, z_p]$ and let $y(\overline{Z}, t) = [y(z_1, t), y(z_2, t), \ldots, y(z_p, t)]$ be spatial sensing output. Let $\mathbf{S} = [S_1 \ S_2 \ \cdots \ S_p]$ be a collected data set, where $S_j = [X_j, z_j]$, $X_j = [x_{j1}, \ldots, x_{jN}]$ is the collected measurement data from the jth $(1 \le j \le p)$ sensing location in the time interval $[t_0, t_1]$, and $x_{js} = y(z_j, s)$ is the output measurement at the sth sampling period, $1 \le s \le N$. The sensor placement problem is to learn optimal sensor locations from the spatiotemporal data set $\mathbf{S}$.

The design methodology can be depicted in Figure 4. $\mathbf{S}$ is taken as the training set. ε-SVR is used to find support vectors and produce a function so that all training patterns X have

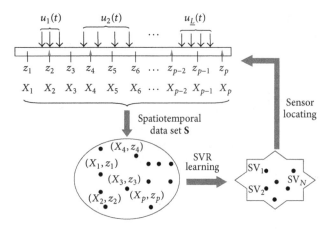

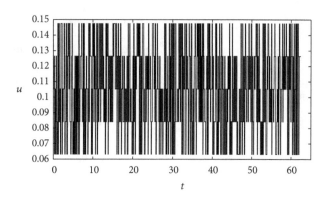

FIGURE 6: Perturbation signal generated by PRQS.

FIGURE 4: Methodology of SVR learning based sensor placement.

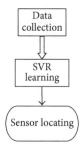

FIGURE 5: Systematic design for sensor placement.

a maximum deviation ε from the target values z_i and have a maximum margin. The support vectors, as crucial data points that represent principle spatial structures, are employed to determine the optimal sensor location and sensor number.

3.2. Systematic Design Scheme. The systematic sensor placement design scheme is composed of three steps shown in Figure 5, including data collection, SVR learning, and sensor locating. Firstly, a set of data is collected as the fundamental data for sensor locating. To acquire sufficiently rich information from the system, the system should be excited by adding persistently exciting perturbation signals. Secondly, SVR is used to extract crucial data points from the collected data set. Thirdly, the sensor location is determined in terms of the extracted crucial data.

(1) Data Collection. The idea data should contain sufficiently rich information of dynamic characteristics. To acquire the sufficiently rich data, one possible method is to add persistently exciting perturbation signals to the input $\mathbf{u}(t)$. In this study, we use white noise and the pseudorandom multilevel signals (PRMSs) with maximal length [21] as the input perturbation signals for two application examples, respectively. When input perturbation signals are sequentially added to the input $\mathbf{u}(t)$, the system output is collected. The collected data and its corresponding spatial location consist of fundamental data set $\mathbf{S}$ for the subsequent support vector learning.

(2) SVR Learning. Before the learning, Gaussian kernel function with its spread σ is selected and two learning parameters C and ε are required to be set. We use K-Fold Cross-Validation method to acquire C, ε, and σ. Root mean-squared error (RMSE) is employed as quantitative performance criteria for test, which is defined as follows:

$$\text{RMSE} = \sqrt{\sum_{k=1}^{p} \frac{\left(z_k^* - z_k\right)^2}{p}}, \qquad (14)$$

where z_k^* denotes the predicted spatial point after learning, z_k denotes the practical spatial point, and p denotes the number of sensors.

(3) Sensor Locating. After the second step, we can obtain some data points that represent the spatial structure implied in the data set. In this step, we can easily determine the sensor locations, namely, the spatial locations in these support vectors. The number of support vectors is equal to the number of sensors.

4. Case Studies

In this section, we take the two practical applications described in Section 2 as examples. The mathematical model (1) and (2) in the catalytic packed-bed reactor and the mathematical model (4) and (5) in the RTCVD system are only for the process simulation for evaluation of the sensor placement scheme. The method of lines [22] is used to simulate the two models.

4.1. The Catalytic Packed-Bed Reactor. The pseudorandom quinary signal (PRQS) with maximum length of 624 is used as the perturbation signal. The parameters of PRQS are chosen as follows: the lowest and uppermost values of input are 0.1474 and 0.0632, respectively, the number of the levels is 5, the sampling time is 0.1, the length of the period is 624, and the minimum switching time (clock period) is 0.1. The perturbation signal generated by PRQS is depicted in Figure 6.

The space domain of the system is discretized uniformly into 81 points; that is, $\overline{Z} = [z_1, z_2, \ldots, z_{81}]$, the sampling period is set as 0.1, and the time interval of simulation is

TABLE 1: Performance index comparisons (SVR learning based sensing locations versus evenly distributed locations).

Performance index	Sensor number with evenly distributed locations								SVR learning based sensor number (sensor location)
	2	3	4	5	6	7	8	9	8 {0.0625, 0.275, 0.475, 0.5375, 0.575, 0.7625, 0.8125, 1}
SSE ($\times 10^{-2}$)	3.332	1.73	1.74	1.74	1.74	1.74	1.75	1.74	1.70
IAE ($\times 10^{-1}$)	3.382	2.355	2.362	2.366	2.36	2.364	2.365	2.362	2.341
ITAE ($\times 10^{-1}$)	10.751	5.715	5.749	5.761	5.754	5.753	5.771	5.754	5.615

$[0, 62.3]$. We collect the catalytic temperature measurements from the system over the space domain and constitute the data set $\mathbf{S} = [S_1 \ S_2 \ \cdots \ S_{81}]$, where $S_j = [X_j, z_j]$, $X_j = [x_{j1}, \ldots, x_{j624}]$ $(1 \leq j \leq p)$, $x_{js} = y(z_j, s)$ is the catalytic temperature measurement at the sth sampling period from the jth sensing location, $1 \leq s \leq 624$.

Then, the SVR is used to learn support vectors from the data set $\mathbf{S}$. As for model selection problem of the SVR, we employ 5-Fold Cross-Validation method to select proper C from $[2^2, 2^{15}]$ with step-size set as 10, ε from $[2^{-10}, 2^2]$ with step-size set as 0.01, and σ from $\{\sigma_0/100, \sigma_0/95, \ldots, \sigma_0/(n+5), \sigma_0/n, \sigma_0/(n-5), \ldots, \sigma_0/10, \sigma_0/5, \sigma_0\}$, where σ_0 is set as 10% of the length of the input interval of $y(\overline{Z}, t)$ denoted by

$$\sigma_0 = \max_{1 \leq j \leq p} (\sigma_j) = \max_{1 \leq j \leq p} \left\{ \left(\frac{y^{\max}(z_j) - y^{\min}(z_j)}{10} \right) \right\}, \quad (15)$$

where $y^{\max}(z_j)$ and $y^{\min}(z_j)$ are the maximum and the minimum bound value of temperature measurements from the jth spatial input variable, respectively. In this application, $\sigma_0 = 0.03969$.

After 5-Fold Cross-Validation, we can find a group of best parameters; that is, $C = 4096$, $\varepsilon = 0.174$, and $\sigma = \sigma_0/19 = 0.00209$. The learned support vectors are $\mathbf{S} = \{S_6, S_{23}, S_{39}, S_{44}, S_{47}, S_{62}, S_{66}, S_{81}\}$. Therefore, the optimal sensor locations are $\{z_6, z_{23}, z_{39}, z_{44}, z_{47}, z_{62}, z_{66}, z_{81}\}$; that is, $\{0.0625, 0.275, 0.475, 0.5375, 0.575, 0.7625, 0.8125, 1\}$. At the same time, we can find the optimal sensor number is eight.

The effectiveness of the proposed sensor locating method is validated on the 3D fuzzy controlled catalytic packed-bed reactor. The design of 3D FLC is given in Appendices A and B. We carried out two different sensor placement schemes on the 3D fuzzy controlled catalytic packed-bed reactor. One is that two to nine sensors are evenly distributed in the space domain, respectively. The other is the proposed sensor locating scheme. The control performance comparison of the two schemes is given in Table 1, where SSE, IAE, and ITAE [23] stand for steady-state error, integral of the absolute error, and integral of time multiplied by absolute error for spatiotemporal dynamic systems, respectively. Graph comparison is given in Figure 7, where eight sensors in (a) are placed in the proposed optimal locations, while eight sensors in (b) are evenly placed. In terms of Table 1 and Figure 7, we can find that the proposed sensor placement scheme has improved the control performance.

4.2. The RTCVD System. To acquire sufficiently rich information from the system, white noise signals, whose values are less than 10% steady state, are added as perturbation signals to the manipulated variables u_a, u_b, and u_c. Therefore, the manipulated variables with perturbation signals are given as follows:

$$u_{a\_excite}(t) = 0.2028 + 0.1 * 0.2028 * \text{rand}()$$
$$* \text{sgn}(\text{rand}() - 0.5),$$
$$u_{b\_excite}(t) = 0.1008 + 0.1 * 0.1008 * \text{rand}()$$
$$* \text{sgn}(\text{rand}() - 0.5), \quad (16)$$
$$u_{c\_excite}(t) = 0.2245 + 0.1 * 0.2245 * \text{rand}()$$
$$* \text{sgn}(\text{rand}() - 0.5).$$

In this application, the sample interval is 0.5 s, and the simulation duration is 100 s. The evolution profiles of manipulated variables are shown in Figure 8, and the measured wafer temperature $y(z, t)$ is shown in Figure 9.

The space domain of the system is discretized uniformly into 61 points; that is, $\overline{Z} = [z_1, z_2, \ldots, z_{61}]$. We collect the wafer temperature measurements from the system over the wafer radius and constitute the data set $\mathbf{S} = [S_1 \ S_2 \ \cdots \ S_{61}]$, where $S_j = [X_j, z_j]$, $X_j = [x_{j1}, \ldots, x_{j200}]$ $(1 \leq j \leq p)$, and $x_{js} = y(z_j, s)$ is the wafer temperature measurement at the sth sampling period from the jth sensing location, $1 \leq s \leq 200$.

Then, the SVR is used to learn support vectors from the data set $\mathbf{S}$. As for model selection problem of the SVR, we employ 5-Fold Cross-Validation method to select proper C from $[2^2, 2^{15}]$ with step-size set as 10, ε from $[2^{-10}, 2^2]$ with step-size set as 0.01, and σ from $\{\sigma_0/130, \sigma_0/125, \ldots, \sigma_0/(n+5), \sigma_0/n, \sigma_0/(n-5), \ldots, \sigma_0/10, \sigma_0/5, \sigma_0\}$, where σ_0 is the initial set as in (15). In this application, $\sigma_0 = 1.2816$.

Using 5-Fold Cross-Validation, we can find a group of best parameters; that is, $C = 7000$, $\varepsilon = 0.146$, and $\sigma = \sigma_0/50 = 0.00256$. The learned support vectors are $\mathbf{S} = \{S_5, S_{13}, S_{27}, S_{39}, S_{49}, S_{61}\}$. Therefore, the optimal sensor locations are $\{z_5, z_{13}, z_{27}, z_{39}, z_{49}, z_{61}\}$; that is, $\{0.507, 1.52, 3.29, 4.81, 6.08, 7.60\}$. At the same time, we can find the optimal sensor number is six.

The effectiveness of the proposed sensor placement method is validated on the space decomposition and coordination based 3D fuzzy controlled RTCVD system. The design of space decomposition and coordination based 3D FLC is given in Appendix C. We carried out two different sensor placement schemes on the 3D fuzzy controlled RTCVD system. One is that three to eleven sensors are evenly distributed in the space domain, respectively. The other is the proposed sensor placement scheme. The control performance

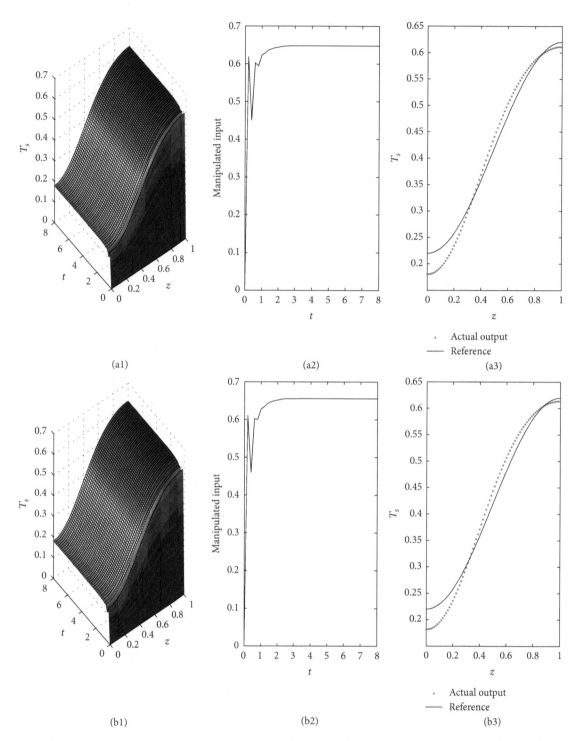

FIGURE 7: Control performance comparisons with different sensor placement schemes: (a1)–(a3) using proposed sensor locations (eight optimal locations); (b1)–(b3) using eight evenly distributed sensor locations. (∗1) denotes catalyst temperature evolution profile, (∗2) denotes manipulated input signal, and (∗3) denotes catalyst temperature under steady state, where ∗ may be (a) or (b).

comparison of the two schemes is given in Table 2. Graph comparison is given in Figure 10, where six sensors in (a) are placed in the proposed optimal locations, while nine sensors in (b) are evenly placed. In the case of six sensors located at the proposed optimal locations, that is, {0.507, 1.52, 3.29, 4.81, 6.08, 7.60}, the RTCVD system is decomposed into

three subsystems with one distributed control source, that is, u_a and sensing locations {0.507, 1.52, 3.29} for subsystem 1, u_b and sensing locations {3.29, 4.81, 6.08, 7.60} for subsystem 2, and u_c and sensing locations {4.81, 6.08, 7.60} for subsystem 3. In the case of nine sensors located at evenly placed locations, that is, {1/9, 2/9, 3/9, 4/9, 5/9, 6/9, 7/9, 8/9, 1}, the

TABLE 2: Performance index comparisons (SVR learning based sensing locations versus evenly distributed locations).

| Performance index | Sensor number with evenly distributed locations | | | | | | | | SVR learning based sensor number (sensor location) |
	3	4	5	6	7	8	9	10	6 {0.507, 1.52, 3.29, 4.81, 6.08, 7.60}
Max nonuniformity (K)	3.48	84.58	4.46	1.013	6.687	3.905	2.795	5.993	0.8620
SSE	8.352	56.34	5.49	4.37	18.42	7.77	6.038	10.16	4.2195
IAE ($\times 10^4$)	3.327	3.64	3.285	3.268	3.313	3.276	3.271	3.285	3.268
ITAE ($\times 10^5$)	1.764	4.00	1.51	1.473	1.737	1.505	1.485	1.593	1.469

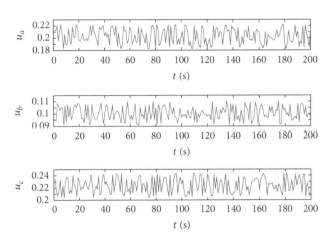

FIGURE 8: Evolution profiles of manipulated variables u_a, u_b, and u_c with perturbed signals.

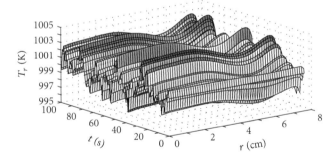

FIGURE 9: The measured wafer temperature with perturbed signals.

decomposed three subsystems are given as follows: u_a and sensing locations {1/9, 2/9, 3/9, 4/9} for subsystem 1, u_b and sensing locations {3/9, 4/9, 5/9, 6/9, 7/9} for subsystem 2, and u_c and sensing locations {5/9, 6/9, 7/9, 8/9, 1} for subsystem 3. In terms of Table 2 and Figure 10, we can find that the proposed sensor locating scheme has improved the control performance in the RTCVD system.

4.3. Discussions. According to the experiment results in the two examples, we can find that the proposed sensor placement scheme outperforms all evenly distributed sensor placement scheme. The results validate the effectiveness of the proposed sensor placement method in terms of the spatiotemporal 3D fuzzy control system.

5. Conclusion

The sensor placement for an unknown nonlinear SDDS is necessary for various applications (e.g., modeling and control design). In this paper, a data-based SVR learning based sensor placement method was proposed. The systematic design method is divided into three steps. Firstly, sufficiently rich data information is generated by adding persistently exciting perturbation signals and is collected as fundamental data for sensor placement. Secondly, SVR is used to extract the characteristics of spatial distribution that is expressed as support vectors. Thirdly, the learned support vectors are employed to determine optimal sensor location and sensor number. Simulations were presented to illustrate the effectiveness of this sensor placement method and its potential for a wide range of SDDSs.

Appendix

A. Introduction of 3D FLC

Three-dimensional fuzzy logic controller (3D FLC) [23, 24] is a novel rule-based fuzzy logic controller developed for SDDSs. It is based on a 3D fuzzy set (see Figure 11) for the spatial information and is based on a 3D inference engine to deal with spatial information. The central idea of the 3D FLC is to emulate the human operators' knowledge or expert experience to control a temperature field from the point of view of overall space domain. Similar to the traditional FLC, the 3D FLC still consists of fuzzification, rule inference, and defuzzification as shown in Figure 12. Due to its unique 3D nature, some detailed operations of the 3D FLC are different from the traditional one for spatial information expression, processing, and compression. The basic concept and basic components of the 3D FLC are introduced briefly as follows (refer to [23] for the detailed explanation).

(1) Spatial Input Variable and 3D Fuzzy Set. Spatial input variable, as an extension of the traditional input variable, is the function of the spatial coordinates and represents that the input information comes from the overall space domain. In actual application, finite point sensors can be used for measurement; therefore, the input information of spatial input variable comes from the sensors located in the space domain.

The 3D fuzzy set is an extension of the traditional fuzzy set by adding three coordinates for the spatial information. As shown in Figure 11, the 3D fuzzy set has three coordinates: one

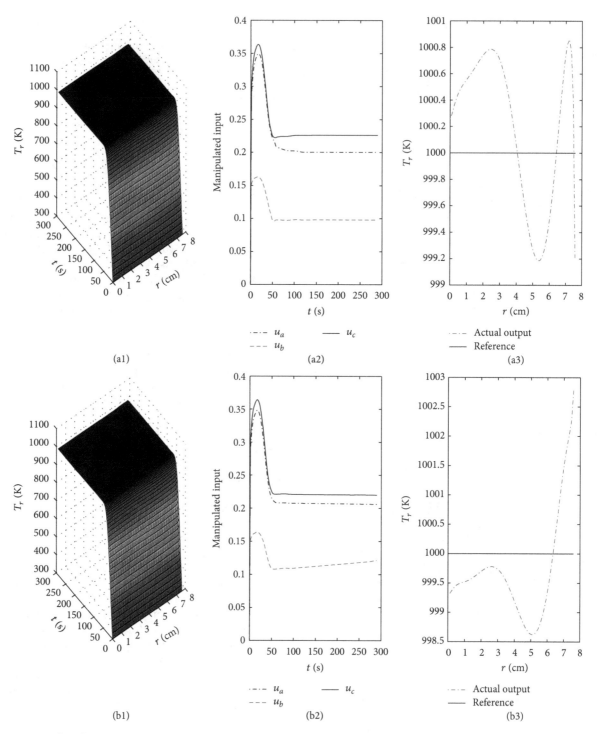

FIGURE 10: Control performance comparisons with different sensor placement schemes: (a1)–(a3) using proposed sensor locations (six optimal locations); (b1)–(b3) using nine evenly distributed sensor locations. (∗1) denotes wafer temperature evolution profile, (∗2) denotes three input signals, and (∗3) denotes wafer temperature under steady state, where ∗ may be (a) or (b).

is for the universe of discourse of the variable, another is for the spatial information, and the third is for the membership degree. If finite sensors are used, this 3D fuzzy set can be considered as the assembly of the traditional 2D fuzzy sets at each sensing location.

(2) Fuzzification. The fuzzification involving the spatial dimension will map crisp spatial inputs into 3D fuzzy inputs. There are two types of fuzzifiers: singleton fuzzifier and non-singleton fuzzifier, whose detailed definitions are given in [23]. If finite sensors are used, this 3D fuzzification can be

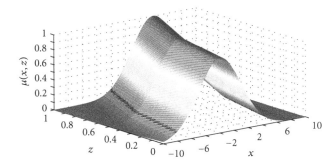

FIGURE 11: A three-dimensional fuzzy set.

considered as the assembly of the traditional 2D fuzzification at each sensing location.

(3) Rule Inference

(i) Rule Base. Rules represent control strategy and human experience. For a 3D FLC with two spatial input variables, the *l*th rule in the rule base can be expressed as follows:

$$\text{If } e(z) \text{ is } \overline{C}_1^l \text{ and } \Delta e(z) \text{ is } \overline{C}_2^l \text{ Then } \Delta u \text{ is } G^l, \quad \text{(A.1)}$$

where $e(z)$ and $\Delta e(z)$ denote scaled spatial input variables for error and error in change, respectively; $\overline{C}_1^l$ and $\overline{C}_2^l$ denote 3D fuzzy sets; Δu denotes the incremental control output; G^l denotes a traditional fuzzy set.

(ii) Inference Engine. As the kernel of 3D FLC, the inference engine is able to process spatial information and realizes two main functions: one is for overall behavior capture from spatial domain and the other is for traditional fuzzy inference. These two functions are realized in three following operations: spatial information fusion, dimension reduction, and traditional inference operation as shown in Figure 12. The spatial information fusion operation will fuse information at each spatial point and ultimately form a spatial membership distribution for each fired rule. The dimension reduction operation is to compress the 3D spatial distribution information into 2D information for each fired rule. Different method can be designed for this operation according to different control and design requirement. In this paper, a centroid approach will be employed to represent the overall behavior of the spatial domain.

(4) Defuzzification. After the 3D inference operation, a traditional fuzzy output is produced. Then, the traditional defuzzifier can be used to yield a crisp control action. Numerous candidates can be chosen for engineering applications, such as maximum, mean-of-maxima, centroid, center-of-sums, height, modified height, and center-of-sets.

Generally speaking, once fuzzy set and rule base are designed, the 3D FLC is determined. To reduce the complexity to tune the controller, scaling factors can be added to the inputs and output.

B. 3D FLC Design for the Catalytic Packed-Bed Reactor

The error of spatial catalyst temperature and its error change are taken as two spatial inputs for the 3D FLC; that is, $e^*(z) = \{e_1^*, \ldots, e_p^*\}$ and $\Delta e^*(z) = \{\Delta e_1^*, \ldots, \Delta e_p^*\}$, where $e_i^* = T_{sd}(z_i) - T_s(z_i, k)$ and $\Delta e_i^* = e_i^*(k) - e_i^*(k-1)$. Let $ke_z = \{ke_1, \ldots, ke_p\}$, $kr_z = \{kr_1, \ldots, kr_p\}$, and $k_{\Delta u}$ be the spatial scaling factors of $e^*(z)$, $\Delta e^*(z)$, and the incremental control action Δu, respectively. Then, the scaled error $e(z)$ and the change error $\Delta e(z)$ are the direct spatial inputs of 3D FLC, where $e(z) = \{e_1, \ldots, e_p\}$ with $e_i = ke_i e_i^*$ and $\Delta e(z) = \{\Delta e_1, \ldots, \Delta e_p\}$ with $\Delta e_i = kr_i \Delta e_i^*$.

(1) 3D Fuzzy Set. Since 3D fuzzy set can be regarded as the assembly of traditional 2D fuzzy set from each sensing input, the design of 3D fuzzy set is transformed to the design of 2D fuzzy set. The 2D fuzzy set for each sensing input can be chosen as triangular shape as shown in Figure 13, where each input is classified into seven linguistic labels as positive large (PL), positive middle (PM), positive small (PS), zero (O), negative small (NS), negative middle (NM), and negative large (NL).

(2) 3D Fuzzification. Since 3D fuzzification can be regarded as the assembly of the traditional 2D fuzzification at each sensing location, the design of 3D fuzzification is transformed to the design of traditional 2D fuzzification. In this study, singleton fuzzification is used.

(3) 3D Rule Base. The linear control rule base is used; for instance, one of the rules is expressed as "if $e(z)$ is $\overline{\text{PM}}$ and $\Delta e(z)$ is $\overline{\text{NB}}$ then Δu is NS," where $\overline{\text{PM}}$ and $\overline{\text{NB}}$ are 3D fuzzy sets, which are assembled by 2D fuzzy sets PM and NB at each sensing location; Δu is the incremental control action, whose fuzzy set is triangular in shape and classified into seven linguistic labels as shown in Figure 13; NS is the 2D fuzzy set. And the rule weight is defaulted as unity.

(4) 3D Rule Inference. The spatial *t*-norm in spatial information fusion operation is chosen as "minimum." The centroid approach is used for the dimension reduction operation. In traditional inference operation, "minimum" and "maximum" are used for the *t*-norm in the intersection operation and for the *t*-conorm in the union operation, respectively.

(5) Defuzzification. The center-of-sets type defuzzifier is used.

(6) Spatial Scaling Factors. Scaling factor for each e_i^* is set to be 1.5, the scaling factor for each Δe_i^* is set to be 0.5, and the scaling factor for Δu is 1.0.

C. The Design of Space Decomposition and Coordination Based 3D FLC for the RTCVD System

The RTCVD system is an SDDS with three control sources, where multiple control sources have the local influence feature on the space domain. Utilizing the concept of influence

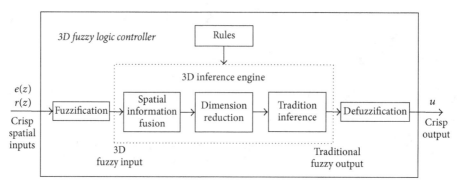

FIGURE 12: Basic structure of 3D FLC.

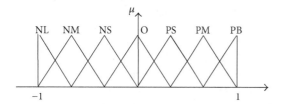

FIGURE 13: Fuzzy sets for e_i, Δe_i, and Δu.

degree [25], the space domain of the wafer along the radius can be partitioned into three subregions, and then the system is decomposed into three subsystems with one distributed control source.

For each subsystem, a 3D FLC as in Appendix B is designed based on expert experience; in order to relieve the stronger couplings among subsystems, local coordination was added to the three 3D FLCs. Scaling factors for 3D FLCs and local coordination factors among them were given as follows:

$$
\begin{aligned}
k_e^A &= 0.0006, \\
k_r^A &= 0.006, \\
k_u^A &= 0.13, \\
\lambda_{BA} &= -0.1, \\
k_e^B &= 0.0006, \\
k_r^B &= 0.006, \\
k_u^B &= 0.07, \\
\lambda_{AB} &= -0.2, \\
\lambda_{CB} &= -0.05, \\
k_e^C &= 0.0006, \\
k_r^C &= 0.006, \\
k_u^C &= 0.115, \\
\lambda_{BC} &= -0.1,
\end{aligned}
\tag{C.1}
$$

where k_e^i, k_r^i, and k_u^i ($i = A$, B, or C) denote the gains for spatial error, error in change, and output for the ith 3D FLC and λ_{jk} ($j, k = A$, B, or C) denotes the coordination factor from the kth subsystem to the jth subsystem.

For detailed introduction, one can refer to [26].

Competing Interests

The authors declare that there is no conflict of interests regarding the publication of this paper.

Acknowledgments

This work was supported by the project from the National Science Foundation of China under Grants no. 61273182 and no. 31570998.

References

[1] P. D. Christofides, *Nonlinear and Robust Control of Partial Differential Equation Systems: Methods and Applications to Transport-reaction Processes*, Birkhäuser, Boston, Mass, USA, 2001.

[2] C. K. Qi, H.-X. Li, S. Y. Li, X. Zhao, and F. Gao, "A fuzzy-based spatio-temporal multi-modeling for nonlinear distributed parameter processes," *Applied Soft Computing*, vol. 25, pp. 309–321, 2014.

[3] H.-X. Li and C. K. Qi, "Modeling of distributed parameter systems for applications—a synthesized review from time-space separation," *Journal of Process Control*, vol. 20, no. 8, pp. 891–901, 2010.

[4] A. Rensfelt, S. Mousavi, and M. Mossberg, "Optimal sensor locations for nonparametric identification of viscoelastic materials," *Automatica*, vol. 44, no. 1, pp. 28–38, 2008.

[5] D. Ucinski, "Optimal sensor location for parameter estimation of distributed processes," *International Journal of Control*, vol. 73, no. 13, pp. 1235–1248, 2000.

[6] A. Armaou and M. A. Demetriou, "Optimal actuator/sensor placement for linear parabolic PDEs using spatial H2 norm," *Chemical Engineering Science*, vol. 61, no. 22, pp. 7351–7367, 2006.

[7] A. A. Alonso, I. G. Kevrekidis, J. R. Banga, and C. E. Frouzakis, "Optimal sensor location and reduced order observer design for distributed process systems," *Computers and Chemical Engineering*, vol. 28, no. 1-2, pp. 27–35, 2004.

[8] I. Bruant, L. Gallimard, and S. Nikoukar, "Optimal piezoelectric actuator and sensor location for active vibration control, using genetic algorithm," *Journal of Sound and Vibration*, vol. 329, no. 10, pp. 1615–1635, 2010.

[9] C. Antoniades and P. D. Christofides, "Integrating nonlinear output feedback control and optimal actuator/sensor placement for transport-reaction processes," *Chemical Engineering Science*, vol. 56, no. 15, pp. 4517–4535, 2001.

[10] C. Antoniades and P. D. Christofides, "Integrated optimal actuator/sensor placement and robust control of uncertain transport-reaction processes," *Computers and Chemical Engineering*, vol. 26, no. 2, pp. 187–203, 2002.

[11] Y. Lou and P. D. Christofides, "Optimal actuator/sensor placement for nonlinear control of the kuramoto-sivashinsky equation," *IEEE Transactions on Control Systems Technology*, vol. 11, no. 5, pp. 737–745, 2003.

[12] V. A. Wouwer, N. Point, S. Porteman, and M. Remy, "Approach to the selection of optimal sensor locations in distributed parameter systems," *Journal of Process Control*, vol. 10, no. 4, pp. 291–300, 2000.

[13] E. Zamprogna, M. Barolo, and D. E. Seborg, "Optimal selection of soft sensor inputs for batch distillation columns using principal component analysis," *Journal of Process Control*, vol. 15, no. 1, pp. 39–52, 2005.

[14] P. Tongpadungroda, T. D. L. Rhysb, and P. N. Brettc, "An approach to optimise the critical sensor locations in one-dimensional novel distributive tactile surface to maximise performance," *Sensors and Actuators, A: Physical*, vol. 105, no. 1, pp. 47–54, 2003.

[15] X.-X. Zhang, H.-X. Li, and C.-K. Qi, "Spatially constrained fuzzy-clustering based sensor placement for spatio-temporal fuzzy-control system," *IEEE Transactions on Fuzzy Systems*, vol. 18, no. 5, pp. 946–957, 2010.

[16] R. N. Silva, J. M. Lemos, and L. M. Rato, "Variable sampling adaptive control of a distributed collector solar field," *IEEE Transactions on Control Systems Technology*, vol. 11, no. 5, pp. 765–772, 2003.

[17] P. D. Christofides, "Robust control of parabolic PDE systems," *Chemical Engineering Science*, vol. 53, no. 16, pp. 2949–2965, 1998.

[18] J. J. Winkin, D. Dochain, and P. Ligarius, "Dynamical analysis of distributed parameter tubular reactors," *Automatica*, vol. 36, no. 3, pp. 349–361, 2000.

[19] K. A. Hoo and D. Zheng, "Low-order control-relevant models for a class of distributed parameter systems," *Chemical Engineering Science*, vol. 56, no. 23, pp. 6683–6710, 2001.

[20] V. N. Vapnik, *Statistical Learning Theory*, John Wiley & Sons, New York, NY, USA, 1998.

[21] R. Haber and L. Keviczky, *Nonlinear System Identification—Input-Output Modeling Approach, Volume 1: Nonlinear System Parameter Identification*, Kluwer Academic Publishers, Dordrecht, The Netherlands, 1999.

[22] W. E. Schiesser, *The Numerical Methods of Lines Integration of Partial Differential Equations*, Academic Press, San Diego, Calif, USA, 1991.

[23] H.-X. Li, X.-X. Zhang, and S.-Y. Li, "A three-dimensional fuzzy control methodology for a class of distributed parameter systems," *IEEE Transactions on Fuzzy Systems*, vol. 15, no. 3, pp. 470–481, 2007.

[24] X.-X. Zhang, H.-X. Li, and S.-Y. Li, "Analytical study and stability design of a 3-D fuzzy logic controller for spatially distributed dynamic systems," *IEEE Transactions on Fuzzy Systems*, vol. 16, no. 6, pp. 1613–1625, 2008.

[25] C. B. Kellogg and F. Zhao, "Influence-based model decomposition for reasoning about spatially distributed physical systems," *Artificial Intelligence*, vol. 130, no. 2, pp. 125–166, 2001.

[26] X.-X. Zhang, S. Y. Li, and H.-X. Li, "Decomposition-coordination-based fuzzy logic control for spatially distributed systems," *Control and Decision*, vol. 23, no. 6, pp. 709–713, 2008.

9

The Performance of LBP and NSVC Combination Applied to Face Classification

Mohammed Ngadi, Aouatif Amine, Bouchra Nassih, Hanaa Hachimi, and Adnane El-Attar

Systems Engineering Laboratory, National School of Applied Sciences, Ibn Tofail University, Kenitra, Morocco

Correspondence should be addressed to Mohammed Ngadi; ngadi.mohammed@univ-ibntofail.ac.ma

Academic Editor: Lei Zhang

The growing demand in the field of security led to the development of interesting approaches in face classification. These works are interested since their beginning in extracting the invariant features of the face to build a single model easily identifiable by classification algorithms. Our goal in this article is to develop more efficient practical methods for face detection. We present a new fast and accurate approach based on local binary patterns (LBP) for the extraction of the features that is combined with the new classifier Neighboring Support Vector Classifier (NSVC) for classification. The experimental results on different natural images show that the proposed method can get very good results at a very short detection time. The best precision obtained by LBP-NSVC exceeds 99%.

1. Introduction

Researchers have shown that, to recognize a face, human uses different features such as geometry, texture, and colors of different parts of the face: eyes, mouth, nose, the front, and the cheeks. Based on this observation, several studies have been developed to verify whether it was possible to model this behavior in a computational way.

This article is devoted to the problem of computer based face classification [1], which became a popular and important research topic in recent years thanks to its many applications such as indexing and searching for image and video, security access control, video surveillance. Despite many efforts and progress that have been made during recent years, it remains an open problem and is still considered one of the most difficult problems in the community of computer vision, mainly due to the similarities between the classes and class variations such as occlusion, background clutter, perspective changes, poses scaling, and lighting. Nowadays popular detection approaches are based on descriptors and classifiers, which generally extract visual descriptors in the pictures and videos and then perform the classification using machine learning algorithms based on the extracted features.

Generally, the size of the data can be measured by two dimensions: the number of variables and the number of examples. These two dimensions can take very high values, which can be a problem with the exploration and analysis of these data. In this context, it is essential to implement some data processing tools that allow us to better understand the information contained in our dataset. Dimensionality reduction is one of the oldest approaches that answers this problem. Its objective is to select or retrieve an optimal subset of relevant characteristics according to a previously fixed criterion. This selection/extraction allows reducing the dimension of the space of the examples and making all the data more representative of the problem.

This reduction has a dual purpose, the first is to reduce redundancy, and the second allows facilitating subsequent treatments (feature extraction reduces required storage space and accordingly reduces the classification learning time and accelerates the pattern recognition process) and therefore the data interpretation.

The first step aims to select the best feature extraction [2, 3] method for the context of face classification. In this context, we found that the LBP descriptor gives the most optimal representation of the image. The principle of this descriptor is to compare each pixel (considered as central pixel in a window of radius R and containing P points) to its neighbors and generate a binary code based on this comparison [4]. For the validation of our choice, we make a comparison with other feature extractions descriptors such as Discrete Wavelet Transform (DWT) [5] and Histogram of Oriented Gradients (HOG) [6].

The second step concerns the selection of the classification function. We have chosen to use a method placed in the context of the semisupervised classifiers, the NSVC. It is based on the combination of two classifiers belonging to two different families (nonsupervised classification: Fuzzy C-Means and supervised one: SVM). The basic idea of the Neighboring Support Vector Classifier (NSVC) is to build new vicinal kernel functions, obtained by supervised clustering in feature space. These vicinal kernel functions are then used for learning.

Finally, our experiments show that LBP-NSVC outperforms all other feature selection and classification algorithms. The main criteria used for comparison are the accuracy of the classification and the execution time, without forgetting the ability of the classifier to effectively manage practical applications where the training data may come from different environments.

The rest of the paper is organized as follows. A brief description of LBP is given in Section 2. Section 3 introduces the NSVC based on supervised partitioning of features space. Experimental results are presented in Section 4, while Section 5 concludes the article.

2. Local Binary Patterns (LBP)

The LBP method can be regarded as a unifying statistical and structural approach to texture analysis. Instead of trying to explain the formation of the texture on the pixel level, local models are formed around each pixel. Each pixel is labeled with the code of the texture that is best at the local level in his neighborhood. Thus, each LBP code can be regarded as the code that best represents the local vicinity of the pixel. The LBP distribution therefore has both structural properties: primitives of textures and the rules for placement of these primitives. For these reasons, the LBP method can be used successfully to recognize a variety of textures, in which structural and statistical methods have been traditionally applied separately.

Local binary patterns were originally proposed by Ojala et al. in 1996 [7]. The concept of the LBP is simple; it proposes assigning a binary code to a pixel based on its neighborhood. This code describing the local texture of a region is calculated by thresholding of a neighborhood with the gray of the central pixel level. In order to generate a binary pattern, all the neighbors will then take a value "1" if their value is greater than or equal to the current pixel and "0" otherwise. This binary pattern's pixels are then multiplied by weights and summoned to obtain a current pixel LBP code. We thus obtain, for any image, pixels with intensity between 0 and 255 as in an ordinary 8-bit image. Rather than describing the image by the sequence of the LBP codes,

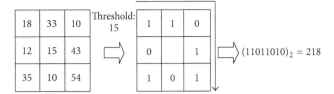

FIGURE 1: Example of LBP calculation.

one can choose as texture descriptor using a 255-dimension histogram (Figure 1).

The LBP was extended later by using different neighborhood sizes [8–10]. In this case, a circle of radius R around the central pixel is considered. Values of P points sampled on the edge of the circle are taken and compared with the value of the central pixel. To obtain the values for P points sampled in the vicinity for any radius R, an interpolation is necessary. The notation (P, R) is adopted to define the vicinity of P points of radius R of a pixel. LBPP, R is the LBP code for the radius R and the number of neighbors P. The main difference is that the pixels must be interpolated to obtain the values of the points on the circle. The important property of the LBP code is that this code is invariant to uniform illumination changes because the LBP for a pixel depends only on differences between its gray-level and that of its neighbors.

To calculate LBP code in a neighborhood of P pixels in RADIUS R, one simply counts the occurrences of pixels g_i superior or equal to the central value:

$$\text{LBP}_{m,R} = \sum_{i=0}^{m-1} u\left(g_i - g_c\right) \cdot 2^i, \tag{1}$$

where $u(\cdot)$ is the sign function and where g_i and g_c are, respectively, a nearby pixel and the central pixel grayscale

$$u(x) = \begin{cases} 1, & \text{si } x \geq 0, \\ 0, & \text{otherwise.} \end{cases} \tag{2}$$

The concept of the multiscale LBP is based on the choice of the vicinity in order to calculate LBP code to process textures at different scales [11, 12]. A neighborhood for a central pixel is distributed on a circle and built from two parameters: the number of neighbors "P" on the circle and radius "R" to define a distance between a central pixel and its neighbors (Figure 2). The texture T of an image I is categorized by the combined distribution of gray values of $n + 1$ pixels (where $n > 0$): $T = t(g_c, g_0, \ldots, g_{p-1})$, and g_c corresponds to the value of the central pixel and g_p, with $p = 0, \ldots, P - 1$, corresponds to the level of P pixels regularly spaced on a circle of radius R. If g_c coordinates are equal to $(0, 0)$, then g_p coordinates are given by the following equation:

$$\left(x_p, y_p\right) = \left(x_c + R\cos\left(\frac{2\Pi p}{P}\right), y_c - R\sin\left(\frac{2\Pi p}{P}\right)\right). \tag{3}$$

From the definition of neighborhood, the authors define, first, a local binary pattern that is invariant to any monotonic transformation of grayscale, LBPP, R. For each pixel

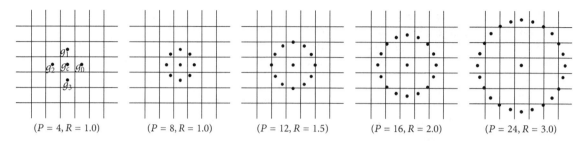

FIGURE 2: Multiscale LBP. Examples of neighborhoods obtained for various values of (P, R).

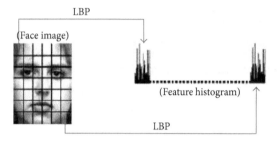

FIGURE 3: LBP-based facial representation.

(x, y) $(g_c = g(x, y))$, the central pixel is not used for the characterization of textures. Indeed, regardless of g_p vicinity, that pixel only describes a light intensity which is not necessarily useful [11]. Subsequently, g_c is used as a threshold in the following manner:

$$T = t\left(u\left(g_0 - g_c\right), \ldots, u\left(g_0 - g_{p-1}\right)\right). \quad (4)$$

Accordingly, the calculation of the LBP code can be obtained in the same way as the basic LBP (see (1)).

LBP-based face representation: each face image can be considered to be a composition of micropatterns which can be effectively detected by the LBP operator. Hadid et al. [13] introduced LBP-based face representation for facial recognition. To examine the face shape information, they divided the images of face to M small nonoverlapping areas $R0, R1, \ldots, RM$ (as shown in Figure 3).

The NSVC is a classifier adaptive to different datasets. It is based, on one hand, on a nonsupervised approach such as K-means or FCM and, on the other hand, on a supervised approach: SVM.

3. Neighboring Support Vector Classifier (NSVC)

Support Vector Machines, first introduced by Vapnik and colleagues for the problems of classification and regression, can be seen as a new training technique based on traditional polynomial and radial basis function (RBF). As discussed before, SVMs have attracted considerable attention because of their high generalization ability and higher classification performance relative to other pattern recognition algorithms.

However, the assumption that the training data are identically generated from unknown probability distributions may

limit the application of SVM to the problems of everyday life [14].

To relax the assumption of identical distribution, the NSVC [15–17] uses a set of vicinal cores functions built based on supervised clustering in the feature space induced by the kernel. The basic idea of the NSVC is to build new vicinal core functions obtained by supervised clustering in the feature space. These vicinal core functions are then used to SVM training.

This approach consists of two steps:

(i) Supervised clustering step based on SKDA algorithm (for supervised kernel-based deterministic annealing, used to partition the training data in different vicinal areas).

(ii) A training step where the SVM technique is used to minimize the vicinal risk function (VRM) under the constraints defined in clustering step based on SKDA.

Consider the following input output data together:

$$(x_i, y_i)_{i=1}^{l}, \quad x_i \in R^n, \ y_i \in \{-1, 1\}, \quad (5)$$

where l is the number of input data points and n is the dimension of the input space.

The vicinity functions $v(x_i)$ of x_i data points are built if test data points satisfy two assumptions:

(i) The unknown density function is smooth in the neighborhood of each point x_i.

(ii) The function minimizing the functional risk is also smooth and symmetric in the neighborhood of each point x_i.

The optimization problem based on the principle of VRM named vicinal linear SVM [18, 19] can then be formulated as

$$\text{minimize:} \quad \phi(w) = \frac{1}{2}w^T w + C\sum_{i=1}^{l}\xi_i$$

$$\text{subject to:} \quad y_i \int_{V(x_i)} \left([\langle x, w \rangle + b]\, p\left(x \mid V\left(x_i\right)\right)\right)dx \quad (6)$$

$$\geq 1 - \xi_i$$

$$\xi_i \geq 0, \ i = 1, \ldots, l,$$

where w is a weight, C is a punishment constant for ξ_i, b is the offset, $v(x_i)$ is the vicinity associated with the test point x_i, and

$p(x \mid V(x_i))$ is the conditional probability of the respective vicinity in the input space.

The following theorem for the vicinal SVM solution is true (see [18] for a proof):

$$f(x) = \sum_{i=1}^{l} y_i \beta_i L(x, x_i) + b, \qquad (7)$$

where to define the coefficients β_i one has to maximize

$$W(\beta) = \sum_{i=1}^{l} \beta_i - \frac{1}{2} \sum_{i,j=1}^{l} \beta_i \beta_j y_i y_j M(x_i, x_j)$$

$$\text{subject to} \quad \sum_{i=1}^{l} \beta_i y_i = 0 \qquad (8)$$

$$\beta_i \geq 0,$$

where $L(x, x_i)$ is called the monovicinal kernel and $M(x_i, x_j)$ is the bivicinal kernel of the vicinal SVM [18].

3.1. Supervised Kernel-Based Deterministic Annealing for NSVC.

The clustering of training data in the feature space is a well-documented subject [20, 21]. It consists of nonlinearly mapping the observed data of an input low-dimensional space to a high-dimensional feature space using a kernel function, which facilitates the separation of linear data, denoting a nonlinear transformation of the input space X to a high-dimensional space using a kernel function as

$$\Phi : \mathfrak{R}^n \longrightarrow F$$

$$x_i \longrightarrow \Phi(x_i), \qquad (9)$$

$$j = 1, \ldots, l,$$

where $\Phi(x_i)$ is the transformed point x_i.

All training data points are distributed in c vicinities/clusters in the feature space, where $\phi_k(z)$ is the center of mass of the kth vicinity residing in F. This is a similar representation to clustering based on the characteristic space of k-means:

$$\phi_k = \sum_{i=1}^{l} \alpha_{ki} z_i, \quad k = 1, 2, \ldots, c, \qquad (10)$$

where c is the number of clusters, α_{ki} are the parameters to be defined by the clustering technique (SKDA), and $z_i = y_i \phi(x_i)$ denotes the data points labeled in the feature space.

The classification problem is usually defined mathematically by a cost function to be minimized; for NSVC case, this function is the distortion function. Similar to the notation used in [22], we let $p(\phi_k \mid z_i)$ denote the probability of association of points z_i mapped to the cluster center ϕ_k. Using the square distance $D_k(z_i)$ [15] between the center ϕ_k and the training vector z_i, the distortion function in the function space becomes

$$J_\phi = \sum_{i=1}^{l} \sum_{k=1}^{c} p(z_i) p(\phi_k \mid z_i) D_k(z_i). \qquad (11)$$

Since no a priori knowledge of the distribution of data is assumed, over all possible distributions which give a given value of J_ϕ we choose the one that maximizes the conditional Shannon entropy in the characteristic space:

$$H_\phi = -\sum_{i=1}^{l} \sum_{k=1}^{c} p(z_i) p(\phi_k \mid z_i) \log p(\phi_k \mid z_i). \qquad (12)$$

The optimization problem can be reformulated as the minimization of the Lagrangian:

$$F_\phi = J_\phi - T H_\phi, \qquad (13)$$

where T is the Lagrange multiplier.

To determine α_{ki} parameter, we minimize the free energy function F with respect to the likelihood of association [22], which is related to the Gibbs distribution as

$$p(\phi_k \mid z_i) = \frac{p(\phi_k) e^{-(D_k(z_i)/T)}}{\sum_{m=1}^{c} p(\phi_m) e^{-(D_m(z_i)/T)}}, \qquad (14)$$

where $p(\phi_k)$ is the mass probability for kth cluster:

$$p(\phi_k) = \sum_{i=1}^{l} p(z_i) p(\phi_k \mid z_i). \qquad (15)$$

And so the energy function is

$$F_\phi^* = \min_{p(\phi_k \mid z_i)} \left(J_\phi - T H_\phi \right)$$

$$= -T \sum_{i=1}^{l} p(z_i) \log \sum_{k=1}^{c} p(\phi_k) e^{-(D_k(z_i)/T)}. \qquad (16)$$

The partial derivative of F with respect to ϕ_k is

$$\frac{\partial \left(F_\phi^* \right)}{\partial \left(\phi_k \right)} = 0. \qquad (17)$$

Accordingly

$$\sum_{i=1}^{l} p(z_i) p(\phi_k) e^{-(D_k(z_i)/T)} [z_i - \phi_k] = 0. \qquad (18)$$

By dividing by the normalization factor

$$Z_{z_i} = \sum_{m=1}^{c} p(\phi_m) e^{-(D_m(z_i)/T)}. \qquad (19)$$

And, so,

$$\sum_{i=1}^{l} \frac{p(z_i) p(\phi_k) e^{-(D_k(z_i)/T)}}{Z_{z_i}} z_i$$

$$= \sum_{i=1}^{l} \frac{p(z_i) p(\phi_k) e^{-(D_k(z_i)/T)}}{Z_{z_i}} \phi_k. \qquad (20)$$

Using (14) leads to

$$\sum_{i=1}^{l} p(z_i) p(\phi_k \mid z_i) z_i = \sum_{i=1}^{l} p(z_i) p(\phi_k \mid z_i) \phi_k, \qquad (21)$$

$$\phi_k = \sum_{i=1}^{l} \frac{p(z_i) p(\phi_k \mid z_i)}{\sum_{i=1}^{l} p(z_i) p(\phi_k \mid z_i)} z_i \qquad (22)$$

$$= \sum_{i=1}^{l} \alpha_{ki} z_i.$$

Finally, we obtain the expression of α_{ki} that will be used to construct the vicinal kernel for NSVC functions:

$$\alpha_{ki} = \frac{p(z_i) p(\phi_k \mid z_i)}{\sum_{j=1}^{l} p(z_j) p(\phi_k \mid z_j)}. \qquad (23)$$

3.2. NSVC with the Feature Space Partitioning. The optimization problem based on feature space partitioning is formulated as follows [18]:

$$\text{minimise:} \quad \phi(w) = \frac{1}{2} w^T w + C \sum_{k=1}^{K} \xi_k$$

$$\text{subject to:} \quad y_k \int_{V(\phi_k)} [\langle z, w \rangle + b] \, p(z \mid \phi_k) \, dz \qquad (24)$$

$$\geq 1 - \xi_k,$$

$$i = 1, \ldots, l$$

$$\xi_k \geq 0, \quad k = 1, \ldots, K,$$

where $v(\phi_k)$ represents the kth vicinity associated with the mass center ϕ_k in the feature space and $p(z \mid \phi_k)$ is the conditional probability of respective vicinity in the feature space. According to Bayes theorem, we have

$$p(z_i \mid \phi_k) = \frac{p(z_i) p(\phi_k \mid z_i)}{p(\phi_k)}$$

$$= \frac{p(z_i) p(\phi_k \mid z_i)}{\sum_{j=1}^{l} p(z_j) p(\phi_k \mid z_j)}. \qquad (25)$$

By comparing (22) and (25), we get

$$\phi_k = \sum_{i=1}^{l} p(z_i \mid \phi_k) z_i. \qquad (26)$$

And the optimization constraint becomes

$$y_k \int_{V(\phi_k)} [\langle z, w \rangle + b] \, p(z \mid \phi_k) \, dz$$

$$= y_k \left[\left\langle \int_{V(\phi_k)} p(z \mid \phi_k) z \, dz, w \right\rangle \right.$$

$$\left. + \int_{V(\phi_k)} b p(z \mid \phi_k) \, dz \right]$$

$$= y_k \left[\left\langle \sum_{i=1}^{l} p(z_i \mid \phi_k) z_i, w \right\rangle + \sum_{i=1}^{l} b p(z_i \mid \phi_k) \right]$$

$$= y_k \left[\langle \phi_k, w \rangle + b \right]. \qquad (27)$$

Let one define the mono- and bivicinal kernels as

$$L_k(x) = \sum_{i=1}^{l} y_i \alpha_{ki} K(x, x_i), \quad k = 1, 2, \ldots, K,$$

$$M_{km}(x) = \sum_{i=1}^{l} \sum_{j=1}^{l} y_i y_j \alpha_{ki} \alpha_{mj} K(x_i, x_j), \qquad (28)$$

$$k, m = 1, 2, \ldots, K,$$

where α_{ki} parameters are obtained from the SKDA clustering step. The decision boundary is

$$f(x) = \sum_{k=1}^{c} \beta_k y_k L_k(x) + b, \qquad (29)$$

where β_k is the coefficient that maximizes the dual function:

$$\text{maximize} \quad W(\beta)$$

$$= \sum_{k=1}^{c} \beta_k - \frac{1}{2} \sum_{k,m=1}^{c} \beta_k \beta_m y_k y_m M_{km}(x) \qquad (30)$$

$$\text{subject to} \quad \sum_{k=1}^{c} \beta_k y_k = 0,$$

$$\beta_k \geq 0.$$

In order to obtain a sparse solution at the cost of the extra clustering procedure, a good selection of the number of clusters is required.

4. Experimental Results

We will now carry out a deep evaluation of the classifiers mentioned in previous sections. We start by a detailed description of the dataset and then present the classification results of all classifiers.

4.1. Dataset. Among the factors that influence or affect the performance of face detection system are scale, pose, lighting conditions, facial expression, and occlusion. For this reason we established a robust database based on diverse illumination conditions and different color and texture variations and, then, under various emotional facial expressions such as neutral expression, anger, scream, sadness, sleepiness, being surprised, wink, frontal smile, frontal smile with teeth, open or closed eyes, and facial details (glasses/no glasses, hats/no hats, and caps/no caps). Then, to use our database in the context of face classification, the different facial images were

FIGURE 4: Typical people images of database in varied environment.

TABLE 1: Accuracy of the method of extraction of features with polynomial kernel of NSVC.

	SLBP	ULBP	HOG	DWT
Accuracy %	99.99	99.47	95.73	91.90
Parameter of kernel	2	3	6	3

ULBP: Uniform Local Binary Pattern. SLBP: Simple Local Binary Pattern.

TABLE 2: Accuracy of the method of extraction of features with polynomial kernel of NSVC.

	SLBP + DWT	SLBP + HOG	ULBP + DWT
Accuracy %	99.53	99.50	99.57
Parameter of kernel	2	3	2

taken at different lighting conditions to make the classification model invariant to illumination. The images were adopted under divers unconstrained environment (Figure 4).

We detect people's faces in our database using the cascade detected of Viola-Jones algorithm and normalized the detected faces with a fixed size of $30 * 30$ pixels. Figure 5 presents some typical face images of database.

4.2. Results of NSVC. The basic idea of Neighboring Support Vector Classifier (NSVC) is to build new neighboring kernel functions, obtained by supervised clustering in feature space.

These neighboring kernel functions are then used in SVM based learning.

When using polynomial and RBF kernels, we have used cross-validation in order to compute optimal learning parameters for both kernels.

We evaluate the accuracy of each feature extraction method with NSVC. The results obtained are shown in Tables 1 and 2.

To test the performance of the proposed approach, we compare the precision of the LBP-NSVC algorithm with other combinations such as HOG-NSVC and DWT-NSVC.

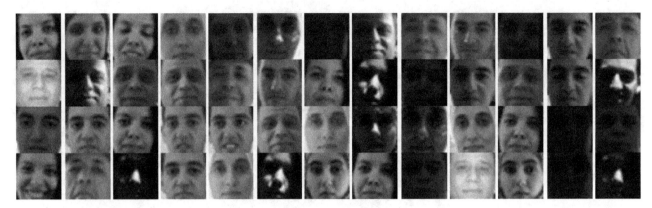

FIGURE 5: Typical face images of database.

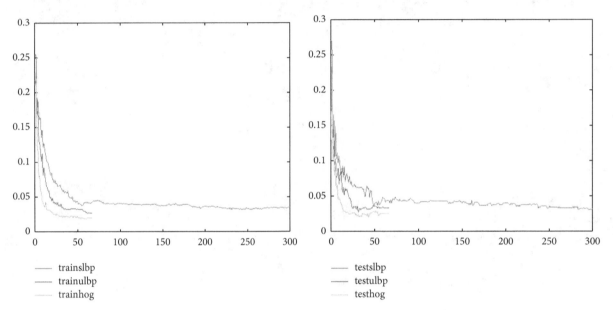

FIGURE 6: Classification error with respect to the number of weak classifiers.

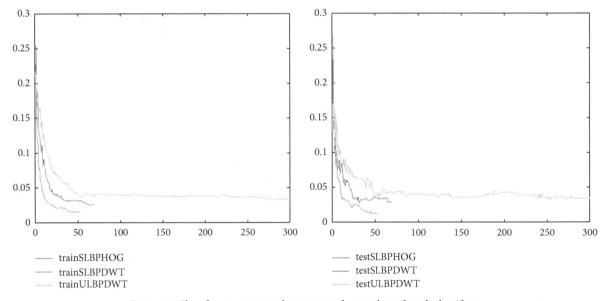

FIGURE 7: Classification error with respect to the number of weak classifiers.

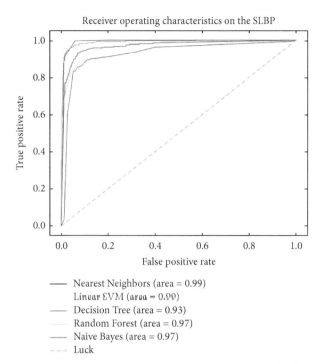

Receiver operating characteristics on the SLBP

— Nearest Neighbors (area = 0.99)
— Linear SVM (area = 0.99)
— Decision Tree (area = 0.93)
— Random Forest (area = 0.97)
— Naive Bayes (area = 0.97)
--- Luck

FIGURE 8: Comparison results of different classifiers methods on SLBP.

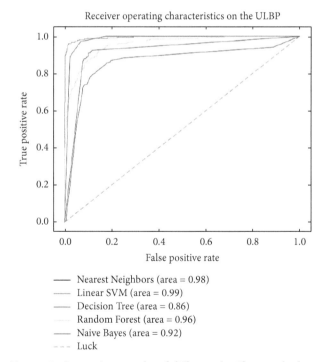

Receiver operating characteristics on the ULBP

— Nearest Neighbors (area = 0.98)
— Linear SVM (area = 0.99)
— Decision Tree (area = 0.86)
— Random Forest (area = 0.96)
— Naive Bayes (area = 0.92)
--- Luck

FIGURE 9: Comparison results of different classifiers methods on ULBP.

So, every time we use LBP-NSVC in our experiments, we must consider polynomial kernel to obtain more accurate results. The following sections show a comparison of the accuracies achieved with our experiences and other classifiers.

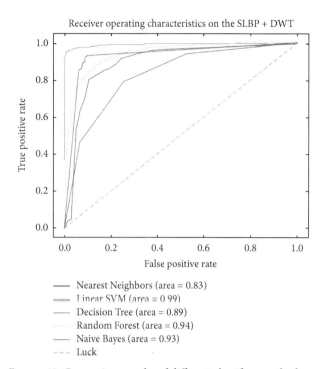

Receiver operating characteristics on the SLBP + DWT

— Nearest Neighbors (area = 0.83)
— Linear SVM (area = 0.99)
— Decision Tree (area = 0.89)
— Random Forest (area = 0.94)
— Naive Bayes (area = 0.93)
--- Luck

FIGURE 10: Comparison results of different classifiers methods on SLBP + DWT.

4.3. Results of Adaboost. After classifying our database using Adaboost, the method of boosting is particularly interesting because we can choose the number of classifiers in order to achieve the desired error rates on samples examples. Moreover, we observe that the error rate decreases exponentially with the number of used weak classifiers (Figures 6 and 7).

Figure 6 shows the classification error with respect to the number of weak classifiers for SLBP, ULBP and HOG with Adaboost, and SLBP + DWT, SLBP + HOG, and ULBP + DWT for Figure 7.

4.4. Classifiers Comparison. LBP-NSVC gave the best results for dataset. We seek to demonstrate the performance of this method in comparison with other classification methods.

Classifiers used for our comparison experiments are the following: Naive Bayes, Decision Tree, K Nearest Neighbors (KNN), linear Support Vector Machines (linear SVM), and Random Forest. We compare the classification results of these five algorithms together with our proposed NSVC on the SLBP (Figure 8), ULBP (Figure 9), SLBP + DWT (Figure 10), SLBP + HOG (Figure 11), and ULBP + DWT (Figure 12).

Figures 8–12 show the percentage of classification accuracy of different matching algorithms. It clearly shows that the classification accuracy is best for the majority of algorithms.

It is clear that the approach of the proposed LBP-NSVC produced the best or equal classification accuracy compared to other methods.

In addition to its high performance, the NSVC is a new theoretical method of classification which combines two methods of classification belonging to two different families (unsupervised method: Fuzzy C-Means and supervised method: SVM).

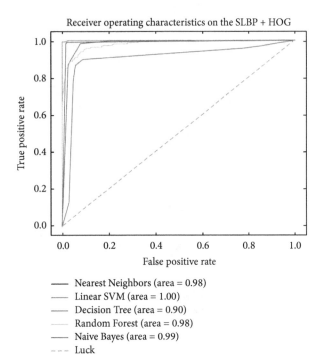

FIGURE 11: Comparison results of different classifiers methods on SLBP + HOG.

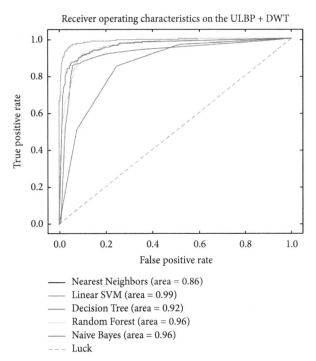

FIGURE 12: Comparison results of different classifiers methods on ULBP + DWT.

5. Conclusion

We have proposed an original method for face detection. Our system is based on the combination of two types of information: LBP descriptors and descriptors such as DWT and HOG. In order to manage these descriptors and combine

them in an optimized way, we propose using an advanced learning system the NSVC. It allows selecting the most important information through kernel weighting depending on their relevance.

The experimental results on different real images show that the proposed method can get very good results.

Our goal in the near future is to continue the study of LBP-NSVC to test it on different datasets from other research areas and try to find the best compromise between precision and execution time.

Competing Interests

The authors declare that they have no competing interests.

References

[1] S. Zafeiriou, C. Zhang, and Z. Zhang, "A survey on face detection in the wild: past, present and future," *Computer Vision and Image Understanding*, vol. 138, pp. 1–24, 2015.

[2] A. Amine, S. Ghouzali, M. Rziza, and D. Aboutajdine, "Investigation of feature dimension reduction based DCT/SVM for face recognition," in *Proceedings of the 13th IEEE Symposium on Computers and Communications (ISCC '08)*, pp. 188–203, July 2008.

[3] A. Majid, A. Khan, and A. M. Mirza, "Gender classification using discrete cosine transformation: a comparison of different classifiers," in *Proceedings of the 7th IEEE International Multi Topic Conference (INMIC '03)*, pp. 59–64, Islamabad, Pakistan, December 2003.

[4] X. Wang, T. X. Han, and S. Yan, "An HOG-LBP human detector with partial occlusion handling," in *Proceedings of the IEEE 12th International Conference on Computer Vision (ICCV '09)*, pp. 32–39, September 2009.

[5] O. Jemai, M. Zaied, C. Ben Amar, and M. A. Alimi, "Fast learning algorithm of wavelet network based on fast wavelet transform," *International Journal of Pattern Recognition and Artificial Intelligence*, vol. 25, no. 8, pp. 1297–1319, 2011.

[6] N. Dalal and B. Triggs, "Histograms of oriented gradients for human detection," in *Proceedings of the IEEE Computer Society Conference on Computer Vision and Pattern Recognition (CVPR '05)*, pp. 886–893, San Diego, Calif, USA, June 2005.

[7] T. Ojala, M. Pietikäinen, and D. Harwood, "A comparative study of texture measures with classification based on feature distributions," *Pattern Recognition*, vol. 29, no. 1, pp. 51–59, 1996.

[8] M. Pietikäinen, A. Hadid, G. Zhao, and T. Ahonen, *Computer Vision Using Local Binary Patterns*, vol. 40, Springer, 2011.

[9] T. Ahonen, A. Hadid, and M. Pietikaäinen, "Face recognition with local binary patterns," in *Computer Vision—ECCV 2004: 8th European Conference on Computer Vision, Prague, Czech Republic, May 11–14, 2004. Proceedings, Part I*, vol. 3021 of *Lecture Notes in Computer Science*, pp. 469–481, Springer, Berlin, Germany, 2004.

[10] A. Gunay and V. V. Nabiyev, "Automatic age classification with LBP," in *Proceedings of the 23rd International Symposium on Computer and Information Sciences (ISCIS '08)*, pp. 1–4, Istanbul, Turkey, October 2008.

[11] T. Ojala, M. Pietikäinen, and T. Mäenpää, "Multiresolution gray-scale and rotation invariant texture classification with local binary patterns," *IEEE Transactions on Pattern Analysis and Machine Intelligence*, vol. 24, no. 7, pp. 971–987, 2002.

[12] T. Ojala, M. Pietikäinen, and T. Mäenpää, "A generalized local binary pattern operator for multiresolution gray scale and rotation invariant texture classification," in *Advances in Pattern Recognition—ICAPR 2001: Second International Conference Rio de Janeiro, Brazil, March 11–14, 2001 Proceedings*, vol. 2013 of *Lecture Notes in Computer Science*, pp. 399–408, Springer, Berlin, Germany, 2001.

[13] A. Hadid, M. Pietikainen, and T. Ahonen, "A discriminative feature space for detecting and recognizing faces," in *Proceedings of the IEEE Computer Society Conference on Computer Vision and Pattern Recognition (CVPR '04)*, Washington, DC, USA, June 2004.

[14] K. R. Müller, S. Mika, G. Rätsch, K. Tsuda, and B. Schölkopf, "An introduction to kernel-based learning algorithms," *IEEE Transactions on Neural Networks*, vol. 12, no. 2, pp. 181–201, 2001.

[15] X. Yang, A. Cao, Q. Song, G. Schaefer, and Y. Su, "Vicinal support vector classifier using supervised kernel-based clustering," *Artificial Intelligence in Medicine*, vol. 60, no. 3, pp. 189–196, 2014.

[16] A. Cao, Q. Song, X. Yang, S. Liu, and C. Guo, "Mammographic mass detection by vicinal support vector machine," in *Proceedings of the IEEE International Joint Conference Neural Networks*, vol. 3, pp. 1953–1958, Budapest, Hungary, July 2004.

[17] M. Ngadi, A. Amine, H. Hachimi, and A. El-Attar, "A new optimal approach for Breast Cancer Diagnosis Classification," *International Journal of Imaging and Robotics*, vol. 16, no. 4, pp. 25–36, 2016.

[18] V. N. Vapnik, *The Nature of Statistical Learning Theory*, Springer, New York, NY, USA, 2nd edition, 2000.

[19] O. Chapelle, J. Weston, L. Bottou, and V. Vapnik, "Vicinal risk minimization," in *Proceedings of the 14th Annual Neural Information Processing Systems Conference (NIPS '00)*, MIT Press, December 2000.

[20] F. Camastra and A. Verri, "A novel Kernel method for clustering," *IEEE Transactions on Pattern Analysis and Machine Intelligence*, vol. 27, no. 5, pp. 801–805, 2005.

[21] J. M. Leski, "Fuzzy c-varieties/elliptotypes clustering in reproducing kernel Hilbert space," *Fuzzy Sets and Systems*, vol. 141, no. 2, pp. 259–280, 2004.

[22] K. Rose, "Deterministic annealing for clustering, compression, classification, regression, and related optimization problems," *Proceedings of the IEEE*, vol. 86, no. 11, pp. 2210–2239, 1998.

10

An Efficient Two-Objective Hybrid Local Search Algorithm for Solving the Fuel Consumption Vehicle Routing Problem

Weizhen Rao,[1] Feng Liu,[2] and Shengbin Wang[3]

[1]*College of Economics and Management, Shandong University of Science and Technology, Qingdao 266590, China*
[2]*School of Management Science and Engineering, Dongbei University of Finance and Economics, Dalian 116025, China*
[3]*Department of Marketing, Transportation and Supply Chain, School of Business and Economics,*
North Carolina A & T State University, Greensboro, NC 27411, USA

Correspondence should be addressed to Feng Liu; liufengapollo@163.com

Academic Editor: Sebastian Ventura

The classical model of vehicle routing problem (VRP) generally minimizes either the total vehicle travelling distance or the total number of dispatched vehicles. Due to the increased importance of environmental sustainability, one variant of VRPs that minimizes the total vehicle fuel consumption has gained much attention. The resulting fuel consumption VRP (FCVRP) becomes increasingly important yet difficult. We present a mixed integer programming model for the FCVRP, and fuel consumption is measured through the degree of road gradient. Complexity analysis of FCVRP is presented through analogy with the capacitated VRP. To tackle the FCVRP's computational intractability, we propose an efficient two-objective hybrid local search algorithm (TOHLS). TOHLS is based on a hybrid local search algorithm (HLS) that is also used to solve FCVRP. Based on the Golden CVRP benchmarks, 60 FCVRP instances are generated and tested. Finally, the computational results show that the proposed TOHLS significantly outperforms the HLS.

1. Introduction

In recent years, consequences from natural resource depletion and environmental degradation have made sustainability a more important objective than profitability for public and private transportation systems. As a result, sustainability has become one of the most popular topics studied by both practitioners and academic researchers in transportation area [1–7]. For instance, logistics service providers (LSPs) are paying increasing attention to the environmental externalities of the transportation operations [1], for example, fuel consumption and carbon dioxide equivalent (CO_2e) emissions. These emissions can cause a lot of serious problems such as respiratory diseases and global warming. As pointed out in Demir et al. [5, 6], most LSPs have been using heavy- and medium-duty vehicles such as trucks and vans to perform a large amount of freight transportation operations at the local and regional levels. Trucks, whose power mainly comes from diesel engines, are one of the major sources of CO_2e emissions (e.g., nitrogen oxides (N_2O), particulate matter (PM), and carbon dioxide (CO_2)). Thus, minimizing the CO_2e emissions from trucks as well as other types of vehicles while simultaneously completing the required transportation tasks has always been a key issue for these LSPs in the past two decades. This paper aims to provide an insight and a methodology to efficiently resolve this issue.

In the most recent literature, vehicle carbon emission problems have been addressed in the area of transportation research, for example, Bigazzi and Bertini [8], Eglese and Black [9], Demir et al. [10], Dekker et al. [11], Lin et al. [12], and Demir et al. [5, 6]. The models proposed in these papers are mainly variants of the well-known vehicle routing problem (VRP), which focuses on determining the optimal visiting routes for a fleet of vehicles in a transportation network to satisfy the transportation demands of a set of customers subject to given constraints. The classical VRP model typically minimizes either the total vehicle travelling distance/time or the total number of all vehicles dispatched in field [13–16]. Of all the extended VRPs, the fuel consumption VRP (FCVRP) has received most attentions over the years. The FCVRP is a variant of the capacitated VRP (CVRP); the latter imposes additional vehicle capacity constraint for a certain commodity on the regular VRP. One of the differences between the FCVRP and CVRP is that the objective function of FCVRP is to minimize total fuel consumption instead of the total traveling distance or cost. However, this difference makes FCVRP more difficult to solve using existing methodologies due to the following reasons. First, the solution space is huge as a result of additional factors (such as road gradient) considered that could affect the fuel consumption. For example, even for the same route, the fuel consumption for a vehicle traveling in one direction is different from that in the opposite direction because of the consideration of road gradient. Likewise, the complexities of basic improvement operations (*2-opt, or-opt, exchange,* and *swap*) can also increase. In this paper, we focus on the FCVRP and provide a mixed integer programming (MIP) model in which fuel consumption is measured by the degree of road gradient. We propose an efficient two-objective hybrid local search algorithm (TOHLS) to solve this problem. The TOHLS algorithm is an extension of a hybrid local search algorithm (HLS) that is also able to solve the FCVRP. In addition, we generate 60 FCVRP instances based on the Golden CVRP benchmarks. These testing instances are used to compare the performances of the TOHLS and HLS algorithms. The computational results demonstrate that the TOHLS is very effective and efficient in solving the FCVRP.

The remainder of this paper is organized as follows. In Section 2, we provide a detailed literature review of FCVRP and other related work. In Section 3, we formally formulate the problem as a MIP model and perform a complexity analysis through analogy with CVRP. After that, an efficient two-objective hybrid local search algorithm (TOHLS) is proposed to solve this model in Section 4. Section 5 performs computational studies of the proposed algorithm on 60 testing problem instances. Finally, Section 6 concludes the paper.

2. Literature Review

One of the most important issues in FCVRP research is how to accurately estimate the vehicle fuel consumption. There are a few studies that provide insightful estimation methodologies, for example, Bigazzi and Bertini [8], Eglese and Black [9], and Demir et al. [10]. Demir et al. [6] categorized the existing factors that can determine the fuel consumption into five classes: vehicle, environment, traffic, driver, and operations. Vehicle factors include vehicle curb weight, vehicle shape, engine size, and fuel type. Environment factors include road gradient, pavement type, and surface. Traffic factors include speed, acceleration or deceleration, and traffic congestion. Driver factors include driver aggressiveness, gear selection, and idle time. Finally, operations related factors include fleet size/mix, payload, and empty kilometers. According to Demir et al. [6], the vehicle, traffic, and environment factors are measurable and have received

more research interest, whereas the driver and operations factors can hardly be measured and are sometimes treated as externalities to affect fuel consumption. In this paper, we focus on the vehicle, traffic, and environment factors. In particular, we are interested in how the vehicle type, vehicle speed, and the degree of road gradient can affect fuel consumption. First, the manufacturing information for a certain type of vehicles somehow determines their fuel consumption levels. A heavy-duty truck essentially consumes more energy than a medium-duty one assuming they are required to complete the same tasks. Second, speed is more effective than traveling distance for emission estimates since speed can affect inertia, rolling resistance, and air resistance [6, 9]. Demir et al. [10] stated a rule of thumb for a medium-duty vehicle: if the speed is above 55 kilometers/hour, every kilometer/hour increase leads to a fuel consumption increase of 0.001 liters/kilometer approximately. An optimum driving speed at each point of a certain transportation network was obtained in Demir et al. [17] to minimize the emissions. Third, coupled with speed, road gradient is also considered to have an impact on the emissions. Intuitively, on an uphill slope, vehicles require more horsepower and fuel consumption due to gravity force than on a downhill road. According to Demier et al. [10], if a medium-duty vehicle is traveling on a 100-kilometer road segment with 1% road slope, its fuel consumption may take up to six liters more than on the flat road. Meanwhile, in most cases fuel consumption data derived under real driving conditions are significantly different from those provided by vehicle manufacturers [18]. In sum, by combining the vehicle type, speed, and the degree of road gradient information, the fuel consumption in our model can be measured accurately. Demier et al. [6] summarized three approaches of modeling fuel consumption (with increasing complexity): factor models, macroscopic models, and microscopic models. In this research, we adopt the microscopic fuel consumption model.

FCVRP has been extensively studied in the literature. Urquhart et al. [19] focused on vehicle routing problem with time windows and studied the trade-offs between carbon dioxide savings, traveling distance, and the number of vehicles using evolutionary algorithms. The authors found out that up to 10% savings could be achieved. Bandeira et al. [20] performed three distinctive case studies in the USA and Portugal to evaluate the impact of traffic peak hours on ecofriendly routes changes. A microscopic fuel consumption model was used in their paper. The empirical results indicated that the most ecofriendly routes during off-peak and peak hours are essentially the same. In a follow-up study, Bandeira et al. [21] examined how to make the emission information available to drivers to help them select their preferred vehicle routes. It was found that the selected route has a substantial impact on pollutant emission rate and that a considerable emission reduction could be obtained from a smoother driving style. Correia et al. [22] proposed fuel consumption model to analyze ecofriendly routes in France. They utilized geographical features for eco-routing search, and the results indicated that ecoroutes were able to provide fuel savings between 1% and 36% comparing with fastest routes. Minett et al. [23] incorporated different roadway types (e.g., motorway, local, and provincial routes) into their fuel consumption model. Their results from the field study showed that driving in provincial routes saved for the drivers an average of 10.41 minutes and 1.25 liters of fuel comparing to driving in local routes and motorway routes, respectively.

A few papers combine the total fuel consumption and the total cost together in the objective function. Bektaş and Laporte [24] extended the VRP with time windows to a vehicle pollution routing problem by considering both total fuel consumption and total cost as the objective function. The decisions to be made in their model included the vehicle routing to serve a set of customers and the vehicle speed on each segmented route. The computational studies indicated that up to 10% energy savings could be achieved. Similarly, Demir et al. [17] also constructed a fuel consumption model and proposed an algorithm that iteratively improved the solutions to the model between vehicle routing problem with time window and a speed optimization problem. In order to precisely estimate the fuel consumption, the authors randomly selected cities from the United Kingdom and used real geographical distances to generate benchmark instances. The computational results indicated that around 10% carbon dioxide emission reduction could be achieved. Since fuel consumption and cost are inherently contradicting each other, their trade-offs must be considered when they both appear as the objectives. Demir et al. [5] studied the trade-offs between the two factors and concluded that a fuel consumption reduction did not always come at a cost of long driving time. Ramos et al. [25] considered a multicommodity transportation network consisting of multiple depots. The authors applied a decomposition solution procedure to determine the optimal vehicle routing in order to minimize the carbon dioxide emission. The computational result of a case study indicated that up to 20% potential savings could be achieved if the company agreed to reshape the service areas and vehicle routes according to solutions. Franceschetti et al. [26] minimized the total fuel consumption, carbon dioxide emission, and driver costs under traffic congestion. They developed the optimal waiting conditions at certain locations for vehicles to avoid being stuck in traffic and to reduce the fuel consumption. Using the same instances generated in Demir et al. [17], the authors obtained a 20% reduction of total cost.

In comparison with the aforementioned studies, the main contribution of this research is a formulation of the sustainable FCVRP that incorporates road gradient into the fuel consumption model and a two-objective hybrid local search algorithm to efficiently solve the FCVRP. The complexity results are critical for connecting our problem with the numerous existing results in CVRP studies. Like most studies in VRP, the optimization techniques proposed here can also be applied to other transportation and routing problems in similar environments.

3. Problem Formulation

3.1. Problem Statement. The research problem we investigate is defined as follows. The transportation network consists of a distribution center (DC) denoted by 0 and a set of n customers: $V_0 = \{1, 2, \ldots, n\}$. Each customer demands a given number of goods that are distributed from the DC. The DC and customers are all located in a given three-dimensional space. The position of each customer is described using the spacial coordinates with meter as unit, (x_i, y_i, z_i) ($0 \le i \le n$), where x_i and y_i are horizontal coordinates and z_i is vertical coordinate. The DC holds a set of vehicles for delivery purposes, but the exact number of vehicles to be used is unknown and must be determined optimally. Each vehicle has a loading capacity of Q with kilogram (kg) as its unit, and the curb weight of the vehicle is given by $r \cdot Q$ ($r > 0$). The demand of each customer is given by q_i that must satisfy $0 \le q_i \le Q, 1 \le i \le n$. The Euclidean distance between any two customers in V_0 is calculated as $d_{ij} = \sqrt{(x_i - x_j)^2 + (y_i - y_j)^2 + (z_i - z_j)^2}$. For any two customers that have the same vertical coordinates, their plane distance is hence $c_{ij} = \sqrt{(x_i - x_j)^2 + (y_i - y_j)^2}$. Let v_{ij} denote the speed of the vehicle traveling from customer i to customer j and Q_{ij} denote the loading weight of the vehicle traversing the directed arc(i, j). In addition, we have the following assumptions.

(i) All vehicles are identical; that is, they have the same type of engine, fuel consumption rate, and loading capacity.

(ii) The road gradient between any two customers is approximated by the difference between their vertical coordinates. Each directed arc has a unique road gradient angle.

(iii) The traveling speed in the transportation network for all vehicles is the same for the same arc and different for different arcs. The details about the derivation of vehicle traveling speed are elaborated in Section 3.

(iv) The fuel consumption is determined by engine operations.

(v) Each vehicle must start and end at the DC.

(vi) The loading capacity constraint for each vehicle cannot be violated.

(vii) Each customer must be serviced once and only once and by a single vehicle.

(viii) Each vehicle has a given maximum traveling distance L.

We must determine an optimal number of vehicles and their optimal delivery routes such that the total fuel consumption for all vehicles is minimized. The resulting problem is called fuel consumption vehicle routing problem or FCVRP. The main difference between FCVRP and VRP model lies in the objective function where we consider minimizing total fuel consumption instead of total operations cost.

3.2. The FCVRP Model. In this subsection, we first analyze the factors that affect the fuel consumption rate (fuel consumption amount per time unit) and then formulate the problem as mixed integer programming model.

We begin with an existing fuel consumption rate model following Barth et al. [27]:

$$\text{FR} = \frac{\varphi\left(k \cdot N \cdot V_s + P/\eta\right)}{\mu}$$

$$P = \frac{P_{\text{tract}}}{\eta_{\text{tf}}} + P_{\text{acc}} \tag{1}$$

$$P_{\text{tract}}$$
$$= \frac{\left(M \cdot a + M \cdot g \sin\theta + 0.5 C_d \rho S \cdot v^2 + M \cdot g \cdot C_r \cos\theta\right) v}{1000},$$

where FR is the fuel consumption rate with gallon/second as the unit while all the other denotations are the factors that determine fuel consumption. These factors can be categorized into the following two groups.

The first group contains all factors that are irrelevant to vehicle routing decisions: φ: the air-fuel-ratio, N: the operating engine speed, μ: the fuel consumption coefficient, η_{tf}: the traditional efficiency, C_d: the aerodynamic drag coefficient, S: the vehicle's frontal area size, ρ: the air density, k: the engine fraction factor, V_s: the engine discharge rate, g: the gravity coefficient that is equal to 9.81 in this paper, P_{acc}: the other vehicle energy requirements, η: the engine efficiency parameter, and C_r: the roll damping coefficient. The second group contains all factors that are directly relevant to vehicle routing decisions: d: the vehicle traveling distance, M: the combined weight of the vehicle itself and the loaded goods, θ: the angle degree of road gradient, v: the vehicle traveling speed, and a: the vehicle acceleration rate that is equal to 0 in this paper.

Note that the values of d, M, θ, and v can change according to various distribution and routing results in reality. For example, v is determined by the vehicle's route and speed limit, M is determined by vehicle visiting sequences, and d is determined by the degrees of road gradients in a route. Consequently, we must incorporate a dynamic driving status in the model. The vehicle driving status between customers i and j can be described using the second-class factors d_{ij}, M_{ij}, θ_{ij}, and v_{ij} and is shown in Figure 1.

These two groups of factors play different roles in calculating the fuel consumption coefficient ω_{ij} of the directed arc(i, j). Group 1 factors are constants (C_1, C_2, and C_3 in the following formula), while group 2 factors are arc-specific parameters. The detailed formula for ω_{ij} is as follows:

$$\omega_{ij} = \text{FR} \cdot t = C_1 \frac{d_{ij}}{v_{ij}} + C_2 \left(M_{ij} g d_{ij} \sin\theta_{ij} + C_3 v_{ij}^2 d_{ij}\right.$$
$$\left. + M_{ij} g d_{ij} C_r \cos\theta_{ij}\right), \tag{2}$$

where $C_1 = \varphi k N V_s/\mu$, $C_2 = \varphi/(1000\eta\mu\eta_{\text{tf}})$, and $C_3 = 0.5 C_d \rho S$.

In formula (2), we can see that ω_{ij} is a function of M_{ij}, θ_{ij}, d_{ij}, and v_{ij}. The first three values are predetermined in the

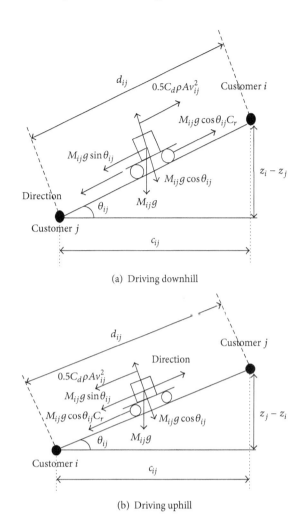

(a) Driving downhill

(b) Driving uphill

FIGURE 1: The vehicle driving status when going uphill and downhill.

problem, and v_{ij} is determined by the two distances from each customer to the city center:

$$v_{ij} = v_{\min} + \frac{ud_i + ud_j}{2ud} \cdot (v_{\max} - v_{\min}), \tag{3}$$

where $v_{\max}$ is the highest speed limit in the given urban area, $v_{\min}$ is the vehicle speed in the downtown area, ud is the maximum distance between the border of the downtown area and the border of the suburban area, and ud_i and ud_j are the distances from customers i and j to the city center, respectively, satisfying $\max\{ud_i \mid 1 \leq i \leq n\} \leq ud$. City center is considered as a traffic congestion factor that affects fuel consumption. Vehicle can travel at a higher speed when it is farther away from the city center. To summarize, the vehicle fuel consumption from customer i to customer j ($1 \leq i \neq j \leq n$) can be calculated as follows:

$$\omega_{ij} = f^{ij}\left(M_{ij}, d_{ij}, \theta_{ij}, v_{ij}\right) = \begin{cases} f_1^{ij} + f_2^{ij} & f_2^{ij} > 0 \\ f_1^{ij} & f_2^{ij} \leq 0 \end{cases}$$

$$f_1^{ij} = \frac{C_1 d_{ij}}{v_{ij}}$$

TABLE 1: Values of parameters affecting vehicle fuel consumption.

Parameters	φ	k	N	V_s	μ	g	η_{tf}	C_d	η	S	C_r	ρ
Values	1	0.2	16–48 r/s	2–8 L	44	9.81	0.45	0.4	0.6	2.1–5.6 m^2	0.01	1.20 kg/m^3

f_2^{ij}

$$= C_2\left(M_{ij}gd_{ij}\sin\theta_{ij} + C_3 v_{ij}^2 d_{ij} + M_{ij}gd_{ij}C_r\cos\theta_{ij}\right)$$

$$M_{ij} = rQ + Q_{ij}$$

$$\theta_{ij} = \arcsin\frac{z_j - z_i}{d_{ij}},$$

$$(4)$$

where f_1^{ij} is the fuel consumption caused by engine usage and f_2^{ij} is the fuel consumption caused by driving on an upward gradient road. Note that when vehicle is driving on a downward gradient road, large values of θ_{ij} can lead to negative values of f_2^{ij}. This situation makes no sense in practice, and therefore when this case occurs, we make $\omega_{ij} = f_1^{ij}$.

The constant parameters in formula (4) can be determined from formula (2) and the empirical results in Table 1 (see Barth and Boriboonsomsin [28]).

In this paper, we consider a medium-duty vehicle, a van manufactured by Chinese Jianghuai Shuailing, Inc., and the vehicle factors are $V_s = 4.5$ L, $S = 7$ m^2, and $N = 41.6$ r/s. Based on the values in Table 1, we have $C_1 = 0.851$, $C_2 = 6.313 \times 10^{-5}$, and $C_3 = 1.686$.

The relationship between vehicle velocity and fuel consumption has been widely explored in literature. One representative result can be attributed to Carslawa et al. [29]. In order to validate our model, we empirically examine the relationship between v_{ij} and ω_{ij} and compare the empirical result with that obtained in Carslawa et al. [29]. We fix $C_1 = 0.851$, $C_2 = 6.313 \times 10^{-5}$, $C_3 = 1.686$, $M_{ij} = 1500$ kg, $\theta_{ij} = 0$, and $d_{ij} = 1000$ m and increase v_{ij} from 1.0 to 30 (m/s) with 0.1 as the step length. The total number of values for v_{ij} would be 291. The relationship mapping between v_{ij} and ω_{ij} is drawn and compared with the mapping between vehicle speed and CO_2 emission in Carslawa et al. [29]. The results are summarized in Figure 2.

From Figure 2, we can observe that our fuel consumption model has a similar curve as illustrated in Carslawa et al. [29]. As the velocity increases, the fuel consumption decreases sharply. If the velocity exceeds a certain threshold, the fuel consumption will increase, but slowly. Thus, our fuel consumption function model is verified.

We have so far derived the fuel consumption model and determined the parameters used in the model. According to formula (4), we are able to calculate the entire fuel consumption of all vehicles. Let x_{ijk} be a binary variable. Consider $x_{ijk} = 1$ when a directed arc(i, j) is serviced by vehicle k and $x_{ijk} = 0$ otherwise. The mixed integer programming model for the FCVRP that minimizes the total fuel consumption for all vehicles is formulated as follows:

FCVRP:

$$\min \sum_{k=1}^{m}\sum_{i=0}^{n}\sum_{j=0}^{n} w_{ij}x_{ijk} \qquad (5)$$

subject to
$$\sum_{i=1}^{n}\sum_{j=1}^{n} q_i x_{ijk} \le Q \quad (1 \le k \le m) \qquad (6)$$

$$q_j x_{ijk} \le Q_{ij} \le (Q - q_i)x_{ijk}$$
$$(i, j) \in A \ (1 \le k \le m) \qquad (7)$$

$$\sum_{j=0}^{n}\left(Q_{ji} - Q_{ij}\right) = q_i \quad i \in V_0 \qquad (8)$$

$$\sum_{i=0}^{n}\sum_{j=0}^{n} d_{ij}x_{ijk} \le L \quad (1 \le k \le m) \qquad (9)$$

$$\sum_{j=1}^{n}\sum_{k=1}^{m} x_{ijk} = 1 \quad (1 \le i \le n) \qquad (10)$$

$$\sum_{i=1}^{n}\sum_{k=1}^{m} x_{ijk} = 1 \quad (1 \le j \le n) \qquad (11)$$

$$\sum_{j=1}^{n}\sum_{k=1}^{m} x_{0jk} = \sum_{i=1}^{n}\sum_{k=1}^{m} x_{i0k} = m \quad (1 \le i, j \le n) \qquad (12)$$

$$\sum_{i,j\in H\times H} x_{ijk} \le |H| - 1, \quad H \subset V_k, \ H \ne \varnothing, \qquad (13)$$

$$x_{ijk}$$
$$= \begin{cases} 1 & \text{the } k\text{th vehicle traverse arc }(i, j) \\ 0 & \text{otherwise} \end{cases} \qquad (14)$$

$$Q_{ij} \ge 0 \quad (i, j) \in A. \qquad (15)$$

The objective function (5) is the total fuel consumption for a feasible delivery schedule, and ω_{ij} is calculated according to formula (4). Constraint (6) are vehicle loading capacity constraints. Constraint (7) ensure that a vehicle is not overloaded on any arc it travels. Constraint (8) indicate the loading quantity is decreased by q_i after visiting customer i. Constraint (9) are the vehicle traveling distance constraints. Constraints (10) and (11) are routing constraints, meaning each customer is served by only one vehicle. Constraint (12)

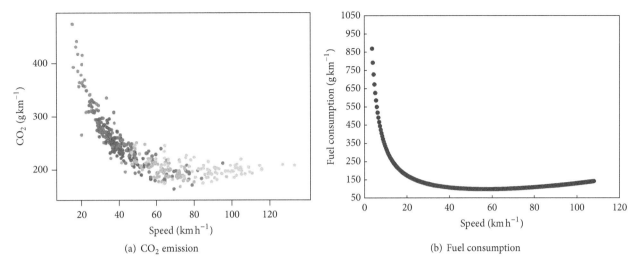

(a) CO_2 emission   (b) Fuel consumption

FIGURE 2: The relationships between driving speed and CO_2 emission and fuel consumption.

ensure all vehicles start and end at the DC. Constraint (13) ensures that each vehicle route is a simple cycle, where V_k is the set of customers serviced by vehicle k ($1 \leq k \leq m$). Finally constraints (14) and (15) are variable integrity and nonnegativity requirements.

3.3. Complexity Analysis of the FCVRP Model. The following theorem specifies the relationship between FCVRP and CVRP.

Theorem 1. *When it holds that $r \gg 1$, $v_{ij} = v$ for $(i, j) \in A$, $z_i = z$ for $i \in V$, the FCVRP can be reduced to CVRP.*

Proof. ω_{ij} in the objective function can be expressed as follows:

$$
\begin{aligned}
\omega_{ij} = {} & C_1 \frac{d_{ij}}{v_{ij}} + C_2 \left(M_{ij} g d_{ij} \sin \theta_{ij} + C_3 v_{ij}^2 d_{ij} \right. \\
& \left. + M_{ij} g d_{ij} C_r \cos \theta_{ij} \right) = C_1 \frac{d_{ij}}{v} + C_2 \left[C_3 v^2 d_{ij} \right. \\
& \left. + \left(rQ + Q_{ij} \right) g d_{ij} C_r \right] \approx C_1 \frac{d_{ij}}{v} + C_2 \left(C_3 v^2 d_{ij} \right. \\
& \left. + rQg d_{ij} C_r \right) = \left[\frac{C_1}{v} + C_2 \left(C_3 v^2 + rQgC_r \right) \right] c_{ij} \\
= {} & \beta c_{ij}.
\end{aligned}
\tag{16}
$$

Since β is a constant that is independent of vehicle route selection, the fuel consumption for traveling from customer i to customer j can be replaced by the length of arc(i, j), c_{ij}. To minimize the total fuel consumption is equivalent to minimizing the total lengths of all vehicle routes, given the constraints on the vehicle traveling distances. Therefore, Theorem 1 holds.

Since CVRP is a special case of FCVRP, the computational complexity of FCVRP is higher than CVRP. The following

argument elaborates the complexity analysis from two perspectives: the size of the solution space and the complexity of improvement operations in solutions.

First, let Ω_E and Ω_C denote the solution space for FCVRP and CVRP, respectively. Based on Theorem 1, we have $\Omega_C \subset \Omega_E$. One feasible solution to CVRP is also a feasible solution to FCVRP. We use the following notations to determine the exact relationship between the two sets.

(i) k is the number of vehicles.

(ii) n_i^s is the number of customers serviced by vehicle i.

(iii) u is the number of vehicles satisfying $n_i^s = 1$; we have $0 \leq u \leq n$.

(iv) $k_{\min}$ is the minimum number of vehicles required when there are u vehicles; each of these vehicles services only one customer in its route.

(v) K is the number of those vehicles that can serve at least 2 customers in its route ($n_i^s \geq 2$).

We have $k \in [k_{\min}, n]$, and

$$
k_{\min} = u + K_{\min}, \quad K_{\min} = \left\lceil \frac{\left(\sum_{i=1}^n q_i \right) - Q_u}{Q} \right\rceil
$$

$$
K = k - u \geq k_{\min} - u = K_{\min},
$$

$$
\begin{cases}
K \leq \dfrac{n}{2} & n \text{ is even} \\[2mm]
K \leq \dfrac{(n-1)}{2} & n \text{ is odd}
\end{cases}
\tag{17}
$$

$$
\sum_{i=1}^k n_i^s = \sum_{i=1}^u n_i^s + \sum_{i=u+1}^k n_i^s = u + \sum_{i=u+1}^k n_i^s = n
$$

$$
\left(1 \leq s \leq U_n^k \right),
$$

where Q_u is the total demand of u customers and U_n^k is the total number of ways to separate n customers into k groups that can be serviced by k vehicles. U_n^k is just the number of combinations (n, k). For example, there are two ways to separate four customers to two groups, 2-2 or 1-3. It means that we can use one of the vehicles to serve two customers and the other vehicle to serve the remaining two customers or we can use one vehicle to serve one customer and the other vehicle to serve the remaining three customers.

For CVRP, we have

$$\begin{aligned}|\Omega_C| &= \sum_{k=k_{\min}}^{n} \left\{ \sum_{s=1}^{U_n^k} \left[C^s \cdot \prod_{i=u+1}^{k} \frac{(n_i^s + 1 - 1)!}{2} \right] \right\} \\ &= \sum_{k=k_{\min}}^{n} \left\{ \sum_{s=1}^{U_n^k} \left(C^s \cdot \prod_{i=u+1}^{k} \frac{n_i^{s}!}{2} \right) \right\},\end{aligned} \tag{18}$$

where C^s is the number of different combination ways for a certain separating method s.

For FCVRP, we have

$$\begin{aligned}|\Omega_E| &= \sum_{k=k_{\min}}^{n} \left\{ \sum_{s=1}^{U_n^k} \left[C^s \cdot \prod_{i=u+1}^{k} (n_i^s + 1 - 1)! \right] \right\} \\ &= 2^K \sum_{k=k_{\min}}^{n} \left\{ \sum_{s=1}^{U_n^k} \left(C^s \cdot \prod_{i=u+1}^{k} \frac{n_i^{s}!}{2} \right) \right\}.\end{aligned} \tag{19}$$

Thus, we have $|\Omega_E| \geq 2^{K_{\min}} \cdot |\Omega_C|$. Due to $K_{\min} \geq 1$, we are able to obtain that the number of feasible solutions to FCVRP is at least twice that to CVRP.

Next, we evaluate the four common types of solution improvement operations for FCVRP: 2-opt, or-opt, exchange, and swap. The selection criterion for these operations is whether the total fuel consumption can be improved. From Figures 3 and 4, we can see that 2-opt and or-opt operations may only change the route of one vehicle, whereas exchange and swap operations may change the routes of two vehicles.   □

From formula (4), Q_{ij} is required to calculate the fuel consumption in FCVRP. In order to evaluate the fuel consumption increment, the changes of Q_{ij} caused by the four operations must be considered. On the contrary, in CVRP only the difference between the total length of newly added arcs and that of deleted arcs needs to be considered to evaluate objective increment. Because $k_{\min} \geq 2$, we obtain the following results on the complexity for one step of operation for the four operations:

$$\begin{aligned}\text{complexity}_E^{2\text{-}opt} &= O(j + 1 - i - 1) = O(i + p - i) \\ &= O(p) \leq O(n_k) \approx O\left(\frac{n}{k_{\min}}\right) \\ &\leq O(n)\end{aligned}$$

$$\begin{aligned}\text{complexity}_E^{or\text{-}opt} &= O(t - i) = O(p + 3) = O(p) \\ &\leq O(n_k) \approx O\left(\frac{n}{k_{\min}}\right) \leq O(n)\end{aligned}$$

$$\begin{aligned}\text{complexity}_E^{exchange} &= O(b) + O(d) \leq O(n_k + n_{k-1}) \\ &\approx O\left(\frac{2n}{k_{\min}}\right) \leq O(n)\end{aligned}$$

$$\begin{aligned}\text{complexity}_E^{swap} &= O(b) + O(d) \leq O(n_k + n_{k-1}) \\ &\approx O\left(\frac{2n}{k_{\min}}\right) \leq O(n).\end{aligned} \tag{20}$$

According to complexity theory, these four operations complexities are $O(n)$ for FCVRP. However, the results for CVRP are merely $O(1)$. Combining the results of $|\Omega_E| \geq 2^{K_{\min}} \cdot |\Omega_C|$ ($K_{\min} \geq 1$), we can conclude that FCVRP is more complicated and requires more time to solve than CVRP.

4. A Two-Objective Hybrid Local Search Algorithm for Solving FCVRP

In literature, capacitated vehicle routing problem is solved mainly through various heuristics. Since fuel consumption vehicle routing problem is more difficult than capacitated vehicle routing problem, these well-established heuristics for capacitated vehicle routing problem are not sufficient for our problem. In addition, it is usually required that a satisfactory solution is obtained within a reasonable computational time. Thus, in order to solve fuel consumption vehicle routing problem efficiently, we design a new algorithm that improves an existing hybrid local search approach used in both problems. This algorithm is based on the following analysis of the impact of the road gradient on the relationship between two problems.

4.1. The Impact of Road Gradient. Our proposed approach is primarily based on the analysis of the impact of the road gradient on capacitated and fuel consumption vehicle routing problems. This impact is illustrated in the following example (two scenarios) below.

A fuel consumption vehicle routing problem example consisting of one distribution center and 99 customers is generated from the benchmark instance kroa100 in TSP library. Assume that only one vehicle is required to service these 99 customers and that the location of the DC is given by coordinates $(1380, 939)$. The optimal total traveling distance for kroa100 is known to be 21282 m. The location of the city center is defined as the average coordinates of all customers and distribution center. The city radius ud is the maximum distance from all the customers or the distribution center to the city center. In the first scenario, we generate all vertical coordinates z_i for the distribution center and all customers randomly in order to add road gradient to the problem instance. These coordinates along with other parameters are summarized in Table 2.

From Table 2, the total demand of 99 customers equals 4970 kg, and the loading capacity of each vehicle is 5000 kg. Therefore, one vehicle is sufficient to service all customers in terms of the total loading weight. According to Theorem 1, the optimal solution to fuel consumption vehicle routing

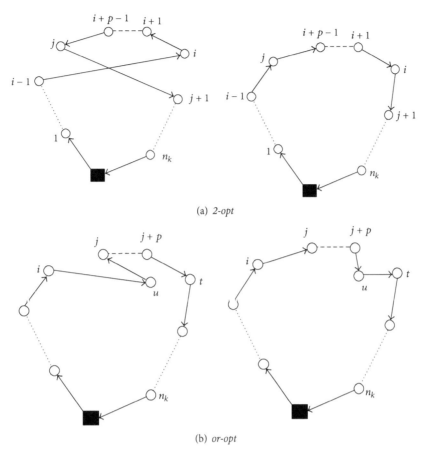

(a) *2-opt*

(b) *or-opt*

FIGURE 3: The *2-opt* and *or-opt* operations.

TABLE 2: The problem instance generated from kroa100.

DC and customers	z (km)	q (kg)	Value of parameters	
1	0	0	$l = 0.001$ km	$C_r = 0.01$
2–20	0.02	30	$r = 0.5$	$C_1 = 0.851$
21–40	0.03	40	$Q = 5000$ kg	$C_2 = 6.313 \times 10^{-5}$
41–60	0.04	50	$v_{max} = 25$ m/s	$C_3 = 1.686$
61–80	0.05	60	$v_{min} = 5$ m/s	
81–100	0.06	70	$g = 9.81$	

problem in this case is also the optimal solution to kroa100 (capacitated vehicle routing problem). The length of the total traveling distance is $21282 \times l = 21282 \times 0.0001$ km = 21.282 km. Associated with this optimal solution, two routing schedules with opposite directions can be generated, and their corresponding fuel consumption can also be calculated. The result is shown in Figure 5.

From Figure 5, the vehicle that travels the same distance of 21.282 km in opposite directions consumes different levels of fuel: 4749.513 g and 5054.377 g. The difference is a result of the existence of road gradient since vehicles consume more fuel when they travel uphill than downhill. This example demonstrates that when road gradient exists,

total fuel consumption of opposite vehicle routes for the same optimal sequence (thus same total distance) can have approximately 6% difference. Therefore, a simple application of existing capacitated vehicle routing problem algorithms to fuel consumption vehicle routing problem is not reliable. However, those algorithms can certainly guide solutions of fuel consumption vehicle routing problem. This is validated in the second scenario below.

In the second scenario, we further evaluate how road gradient affects the relationships between two problems. To do this, we fix all the z_i parameter values for the distribution center and the customers and let l take 101 consecutive values: $0.001, 0.00101, 0.00102, \ldots, 0.002$ (km). These l values are defined as the increment of the horizontal plane distance between two locations in the network. That is, the horizontal distance between any two customers in the entire network is increased by l. Through this way, we can alter the degree of road gradient by changing the ratio of vertical distance and horizontal distance. These l values are used to simulate 101 geographic environments with different road gradients. In addition, based on the solutions in Figure 5, we randomly generate an integer number n_1 that satisfies $1 < n_1 \leq 91$ and then randomly rearrange the visiting sequence of 10 customers from n_1 to $n_1 + 9$ to generate 1000 neighborhood solutions. The correlation between the total traveling distance and the total fuel consumption is evaluated through the 1000

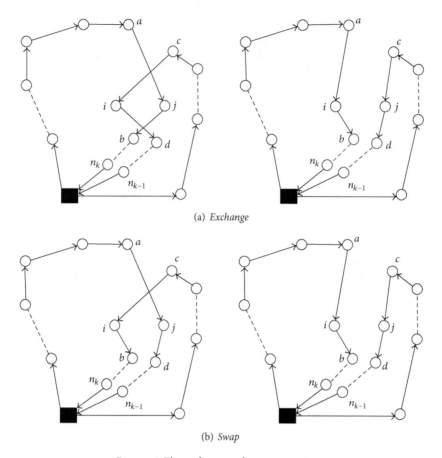

(a) *Exchange*

(b) *Swap*

FIGURE 4: The *exchange* and *swap* operations.

solutions. The correlation coefficient is defined as *Coef*. Besides, we also define an indicator *SlopeDegree* to measure the average road gradient. *SlopeDegree* is calculated as follows:

$$SlopeDegree = \begin{cases} \dfrac{\sum_{k=1}^{K} V_k}{n} \\ V_k = \displaystyle\sum_{i=1}^{n_k-1} sd_{S[i],S[i+1]} + sd_{S[n_k],S[1]} \\ sd_{ij} = \begin{cases} \dfrac{z_i - z_j}{d_{ij}} & z_i \geq z_j \\ \dfrac{z_j - z_i}{d_{ij}} & z_i < z_j, \end{cases} \end{cases} \quad (21)$$

where K stands for the number of vehicles in solution S and n_k stands for the number of customers served by vehicle k.

The mapping of *SlopeDegree* against *Coef* is shown in Figure 6. We can see that when *SlopeDegree* ≤ 9%, *Coef* > 0.9 and that as *SlopeDegree* increases, *Coef* decreases. When $l = 0.001$ in Figure 5, *SlopeDegree* = 12.63% and *Coef* = 0.81. The details regarding the 1000 pairs of total distances and total fuel consumption are described in Figure 7.

4.2. Solving Strategy Design. In China, the requirement on the degree of road gradient for inter- and intracity highways

is less than 12%. In many cities, the average degree of road gradient *SlopeDegree* is usually less than 7%. From Figure 6, when *SlopeDegree* = 7%, the correlation coefficient between fuel consumption and traveling distance satisfies *Coef* ≥ 0.95. According to the relationship, we can claim that the capacitated vehicle routing problem's optimal solutions are highly correlated with fuel consumption vehicle routing problem's optimal solutions in our case where road slope is reasonable. However, combining the first scenario, we find the difference between the two problems solutions is still significant. Thus, given a capacitated vehicle routing problem solution, we must adjust it through a way until it becomes a fuel consumption vehicle routing problem solution.

Based on the above observation, we design the two-objective hybrid local search (TOHLS) algorithm to solve the fuel consumption vehicle routing problem. The main idea behind our approach is to divide the solution procedure into two stages, and in each stage we solve an optimization problem towards a different objective function. In the first stage, an optimal solution to capacitated vehicle routing problem, in which we minimize the total traveling distance, is obtained using a hybrid of several existing local search heuristics in literature. The obtained solution can be used in two ways to calculate the total fuel consumption. One way is to directly calculate the total fuel consumption offline using the route sequence generated from this solution. We

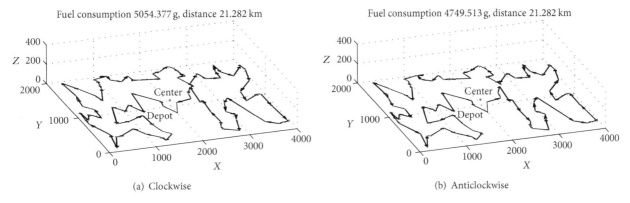

(a) Clockwise   (b) Anticlockwise

FIGURE 5: The comparison of fuel consumption of driving clockwise and anticlockwise.

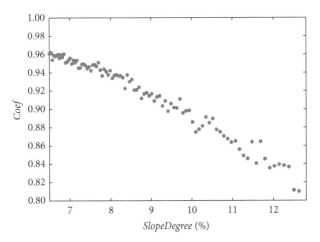

FIGURE 6: Relationship between *SlopeDegree* and *Coef*.

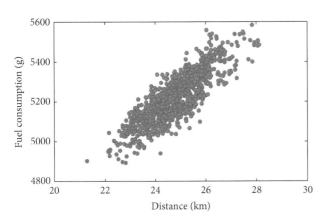

FIGURE 7: Relationship between distance and fuel consumption.

call this approach a hybrid local search (HLS) algorithm. The other way is to use it as an input for the second stage. In the second stage, the capacitated vehicle routing problem optimal solution in the first stage is improved by iteratively adjusting the traveling directions towards lower fuel consumption (new objective) until a satisfactory solution is obtained. This approach is our two-objective hybrid local search algorithm.

The details about the algorithm that incorporates *2-opt, or-opt, exchange*, and *swap* are shown in Algorithm 1.

A key issue in implementing the aforementioned approach is the allocation of limited computational resource. It is usually required in practice that the dynamic problem setting change should be completed in a given time period T. In order to efficiently utilize available computational resource, we allocate T into the two stages based on two factors. The first factor is the ratio of the operational complexity of fuel consumption vehicle routing problem to that of capacitated vehicle routing problem, n/k_{min}, and the second factor is the fuel-distance correlation coefficient, $Coef$. The specific allocation is as follows:

$$T = T_1 + T_2$$

$$T_1 = \alpha T$$

$$\alpha = \frac{k_{min} Coef}{n - (n - k_{min}) Coef}, \tag{22}$$

where T_1 is the running time for Stage 1 of the two-objective hybrid local search algorithm, T_2 is the running time for Stage 2, n is the number of customers, $Coef$ is the correlation coefficient, and k_{min} is the minimum number of vehicles required in the routing schedule. The values of $Coef$ for various *SlopeDegree* are shown in Table 3.

5. Computational Studies

5.1. Experiment Design Based on VRP Benchmark Instances. Since fuel consumption vehicle routing problem considering road gradient has rarely been studied in the VRP research community, it is difficult to directly compare our approach with the other cutting-edge algorithms by solving the same benchmark problems. Thus, we design 60 fuel consumption vehicle routing problem instances based on the 20 capacitated vehicle routing problem benchmark problems proposed in Golden et al. [30]. In the 20 problems, the number of customers ranges from 200 to 483. All customers and the DC are located on a horizontal plane where the position of the distribution center is $(0, 0)$ and all customers are within a circle that has a radius of R. The vertical coordinates

```
(1) Read ProblemInformation and ParameterInformation;
(2) Estimate SlopeDegree based on Landscape of distribution area;
(3) Input T;
(4) Determine T₁ and T₂;
(5) Solution = InitialSolution();
(6) BestSolution = Solution;
//** At first stage, the objective is minimizing the length of solution according to CVRP model**//
(7) StartTime = clock();
(8) While EndTime-StartTime < T₁ do
(9)     ImproveStrategy = RandChoose(2-opt, or-opt, exchange, swap);
(10)    NextSolution = ImproveStrategy(BestSolution);
(11)    If FunctionOf CVRP(NextSolution) < FunctionOf CVRP(BestSolution)
(12)        BestSolution = NextSolution;
(13)    else
(14)        EndTime = clock();
(15)        Continue do while;
(16)    EndIf
(17) EndWhile
//** At second stage, the objective is minimizing the energy consumption of solution according to FCVRP model**//
(18) StartTime = clock();
(19) While EndTime-StartTime < T₂ do
(20)    ImproveStrategy = RandChoose(2-opt, or-opt, exchange, swap);
(21)    NextSolution = ImproveStrategy(BestSolution);
(22)    If FunctionOf FCVRP(NextSolution) < FunctionOf FCVRP(BestSolution)
(23)        BestSolution = NextSolution;
(24)    else
(25)        EndTime = clock();
(26)        Continue do while;
(27)    EndIf
(28) EndWhile
(29) Return BestSolution;
```

ALGORITHM 1: Two-objective hybrid local search algorithm.

TABLE 3: The relationship between *SlopeDegree* and *Coef*.

SlopeDegree	0	(0, 1%]	(1%, 2%]	(2%, 3%]	(3%, 4%]	(4%, 5%]	(5%, 8%]	≥8%
Coef	0.99	0.98	0.97	0.96	0.95	0.94	0.90	0.80

$(z_i, 0 \leq i \leq n)$ and a city center are added to generate the fuel consumption vehicle routing problem instances.

   (i) The DC and the city center are both located at $(0, 0, 0)$.

   (ii) z_i's for the 483 customers and the DC are shown in Table 4.

   (iii) The loading capacity of each vehicle Q is set to be 5000 kg, and the demand of each customer is assigned accordingly.

   (iv) The arc length between any two customers is converted to three possible values, 5000, 3000 and 1000, according to the radius of location circle, R.

The 20 capacitated vehicle routing problem instances along with $3R$ values produce the 60 fuel consumption vehicle routing problem instances. In order to test the performance of two-objective hybrid local search algorithm, we use a hybrid of three local search heuristics, petal, nearest neighborhood, and insertion to generate optimal capacitated vehicle routing problem solutions in the first stage. In the second stage, we locally adjust the solutions from the first stage to improve them towards the direction of reducing fuel consumption, and to finally solve the 60 instances. Recall that we can also generate fuel consumption vehicle routing problem solutions from hybrid local search by using solutions obtained from the first stage. The maximum running time limit T takes 4 values: 2 minutes, 5 minutes, 10 minutes, and 30 minutes. The other parameters of fuel consumption vehicle routing problem model are shown in Tables 4 and 5. Our computational results show that two-objective hybrid local search algorithm significantly outperforms hybrid local search.

The results are shown in Tables 6–8. The problem instances are entitled as "Golden + n + (*num*)," where n is the number of customers and *num* is the *num*th instance. In Tables 6–8, the objective function values (i.e., the total fuel consumption) obtained by hybrid local search algorithm for the four different time limits are given. However, in order to make the comparison between two-objective hybrid local search algorithm and hybrid local search more clear, we present the results of two-objective hybrid local search

TABLE 4: The z_i values for DC and customers 1–483 of 20 instances.

DC and customers	z_i (m)	Customer	z_i (m)	Customer	z_i (m)	Customer	z_i (m)
0–25	100	126–150	75	251–275	50	376–400	25
26–50	95	151–175	70	276–300	45	401–425	20
51–75	90	176–200	65	301–325	40	426–450	15
76–100	85	201–225	60	326–350	35	451–475	10
101–125	80	226–250	55	351–375	30	476–483	5

TABLE 5: The parameter values in the model.

Parameter	Value
r	1
Q	2000 kg
v_{max}	25 m/s
v_{min}	5 m/s
g	9.81
ud	R
C_r	0.01
C_1	0.851
C_2	6.313×10^{-5}
C_3	1.686

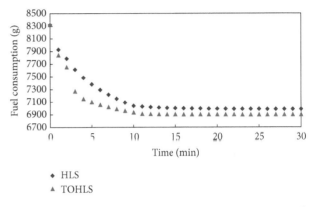

FIGURE 8: The optimization procedures of HLS and TOHLS for Golden200 when $T = 30$.

algorithm as the relative percentages of the results of hybrid local search.

5.2. Results and Analysis. From Table 6, when z_i take values in Table 4 and $R = 5000$ (m), the average slope *SlopeDegree* of the 20 Golden instances is 0.77% which is less than 1%. In this case, within given computational time two-objective hybrid local search algorithm can effectively improve the performance of hybrid local search. When $T = 2, 5, 10$ (minutes), the results of two-objective hybrid local search algorithm on 20 instances are all better than those of hybrid local search. The average solution percentages under these three time durations are 90.13%, 92.92%, and 95.23%, respectively. As the running time increases, the effectiveness of two-objective hybrid local search algorithm unfortunately decreases. When $T = 30$ (minutes), the results of two-objective hybrid local search algorithm for Golden240-2, Golden252, Golden255, Golden280, Golden399, Golden440, and Golden480-1 are slightly worse than those of hybrid local search. This is because fuel consumption vehicle routing problem is more complicated than capacitated vehicle routing problem. When the running time is sufficiently long, the performance of hybrid local search is close to that of two-objective hybrid local search algorithm. However, two-objective hybrid local search algorithm overall outperforms hybrid local search. Another observation that can be made from Table 6 is that the resulting difference between two-objective hybrid local search algorithm and hybrid local search increases as the problem size grows. This can be attributed to the fact that larger-size problems require longer running time for the algorithms to converge.

In Tables 7 and 8, R value is decreased to 3000 (m) and 1000 (m), while z_i still take values in Table 4. The average slope for the 20 problem instances is increased to 1.28% and 3.83%. Although the slope is changed, the effectiveness of two-objective hybrid local search algorithm with respect to n and T has similar trend in Tables 7 and 8 as in Table 6. We can also see that the superiority of two-objective hybrid local search algorithm over hybrid local search is more significant as the slope increases. This seems contradictive to the previous argument that larger slope should lead to smaller correlation between fuel consumption and distance. However, this can be explained from two aspects. First, the slope limit for practical roads is less than 12%, but we confine the average slope in problem instances to be less than 6%. Under this level of slope, the fuel consumption is still highly correlated with routing distance (as shown in Figure 2(a)). Second, with other parameters fixed, the increase in the degree of road gradient leads to a longer converging time for the algorithm.

We select one of the testing instances, Golden200 from Table 6 with $T = 30$ (minutes), and plot the solution converging processes of the two algorithms within 30 minutes in Figure 8. This figure is used to better demonstrate the superiority of two-objective hybrid local search algorithm to hybrid local search. In Figure 8, local optimal total fuel consumption obtained by hybrid local search and two-objective hybrid local search algorithm in every minute is recorded and plotted. For this problem case, we have *SlopeDegree* = 0.85% from Table 6 and *Coef* = 0.95 from Table 4. Based on the above information, we can obtain $T_1 = 579.66$ seconds and that e initial fuel consumption = 8324 (g). From Figure 8, the objective function values of two-objective hybrid local search algorithm decrease sharply in

TABLE 6: Comparison between HLS and TOHLS when $R = 5000$ (m).

Num	Instances	SlopeDegree (%)	HLS (fuel consumption g)				TOHLS (percentage of HLS)			
			$T = 2$	$T = 5$	$T = 10$	$T = 30$	$T = 2$	$T = 5$	$T = 10$	$T = 30$
1	Golden200	0.85	15362	14340	14004	13764	95.05	96.30	96.51	99.20
2	Golden240-1	0.46	23257	21787	21001	20532	94.52	95.66	97.95	99.84
3	Golden240-2	0.62	109506	102754	99391	96499	95.01	96.00	96.15	101.96
4	Golden252	0.62	112108	104938	100907	98835	94.58	95.71	95.32	101.21
5	Golden255	0.44	194771	180280	174719	173283	94.32	96.44	95.94	100.15
6	Golden280	0.55	20332	18756	18192	17650	93.22	94.40	96.66	101.68
7	Golden300	0.80	79789	73536	70472	69125	91.26	94.96	95.75	97.75
8	Golden320-1	0.61	25602	23703	22353	22237	90.58	93.99	95.95	96.14
9	Golden320-2	0.68	93881	87009	82038	81793	91.42	93.39	95.04	96.35
10	Golden323	0.56	152931	141203	134915	133108	90.84	93.42	94.68	98.60
11	Golden360-1	0.70	25209	22926	21707	21624	89.22	92.47	95.96	97.18
12	Golden360-2	1.01	58882	54023	51342	50186	89.37	91.46	95.85	96.66
13	Golden396	0.84	82670	75431	70798	69388	88.33	92.53	95.82	95.28
14	Golden399	0.84	125088	112599	106819	104470	88.31	91.73	95.78	101.08
15	Golden400	0.78	27921	25116	23953	23622	87.98	91.05	96.15	96.46
16	Golden420	1.25	49122	44707	41595	41042	85.99	90.30	94.03	98.54
17	Golden440	0.86	29214	26152	24487	24001	85.97	90.74	93.02	101.06
18	Golden480-1	0.95	27753	24649	23155	22552	84.85	89.12	94.48	100.61
19	Golden480-2	1.03	73902	66191	61692	60096	85.61	89.63	92.02	97.52
20	Golden483	0.85	103757	93077	85876	84082	86.27	89.15	91.53	95.74
	Average	0.77	—	—	—	—	90.14	92.92	95.23	98.65

TABLE 7: Comparison between HLS and TOHLS when $R = 3000$ (m).

Num	Instances	SlopeDegree (%)	HLS (fuel consumption g)				TOHLS (percentage of HLS)			
			$T = 2$	$T = 5$	$T = 10$	$T = 30$	$T = 2$	$T = 5$	$T = 10$	$T = 30$
1	Golden200	1.42	9983	9339	9129	9029	94.32	95.79	96.88	99.11
2	Golden240-1	0.77	15435	14540	13899	13810	93.74	94.86	95.48	99.29
3	Golden240-2	1.03	67896	63440	61547	60481	92.61	95.48	95.52	96.24
4	Golden252	1.03	69959	64928	62091	62468	92.22	94.34	94.86	95.58
5	Golden255	0.74	118322	109121	106592	105149	93.11	95.40	95.90	98.63
6	Golden280	0.91	13350	12445	11908	11803	91.82	94.07	94.31	97.20
7	Golden300	1.34	50545	46835	44908	44338	90.39	93.66	94.41	96.02
8	Golden320-1	1.02	17023	15794	14930	14553	90.48	92.43	94.86	100.15
9	Golden320-2	1.13	59402	54070	52388	51780	90.08	92.75	96.41	95.18
10	Golden323	0.93	93293	85550	81135	80035	89.97	92.84	94.43	95.61
11	Golden360-1	1.17	16717	15115	14527	14134	88.93	91.87	94.11	95.32
12	Golden360-2	1.69	39053	35573	33553	33521	86.99	91.22	93.09	98.01
13	Golden396	1.41	53097	47672	45872	44972	87.73	91.10	91.23	98.94
14	Golden399	1.41	76742	70105	65006	63782	86.67	89.76	92.27	96.44
15	Golden400	1.30	18574	16678	15825	15412	87.68	90.96	93.04	94.67
16	Golden420	2.08	34960	31362	29610	29080	84.86	89.15	91.19	93.99
17	Golden440	1.43	19582	17665	16584	16197	85.65	90.22	91.69	98.27
18	Golden480-1	1.59	18661	16569	15587	15049	83.66	87.86	92.20	95.61
19	Golden480-2	1.72	48506	43162	40209	39808	83.34	87.72	90.92	95.39
20	Golden483	1.41	63871	56936	53273	52020	83.88	88.47	92.92	96.05
	Average	1.28	—	—	—	—	88.91	92.00	93.79	96.79

TABLE 8: Comparison between HLS and TOHLS when $R = 1000$ (m).

Num	Instances	SlopeDegree (%)	HLS (fuel consumption g)				TOHLS (percentage of HLS)			
			$T = 2$	$T = 5$	$T = 10$	$T = 30$	$T = 2$	$T = 5$	$T = 10$	$T = 30$
1	Golden200	4.25	5031	4755	4540	4527	92.11	93.04	94.31	98.37
2	Golden240-1	2.30	7914	7443	7070	6980	92.54	95.00	95.05	94.72
3	Golden240-2	3.10	26936	25023	24356	23936	91.07	92.99	93.08	98.58
4	Golden252	3.08	28830	27057	25759	25705	91.39	93.54	93.24	99.22
5	Golden255	2.21	42113	39456	37685	37518	92.96	94.40	96.44	95.84
6	Golden280	2.74	7045	6508	6231	6202	91.74	93.70	96.71	95.79
7	Golden300	4.01	23740	22107	20943	20607	88.71	90.40	92.69	96.77
8	Golden320-1	3.06	8941	8138	7851	7771	89.85	92.41	93.49	92.93
9	Golden320-2	3.38	26673	24542	23180	23232	90.12	91.07	93.53	96.97
10	Golden323	2.80	33992	31158	29856	29131	90.31	91.61	95.54	93.69
11	Golden360-1	3.52	8805	8082	7652	7480	87.53	89.98	92.43	92.40
12	Golden360-2	5.07	22894	21090	19853	19529	86.09	88.43	89.98	94.14
13	Golden396	4.22	26017	23479	22470	21643	85.28	88.65	91.27	93.27
14	Golden399	4.22	28684	25974	24655	24092	86.14	87.81	92.28	93.48
15	Golden400	3.91	9716	8805	8250	8177	85.54	88.54	90.49	96.86
16	Golden420	6.24	22858	20569	19385	19022	81.61	85.18	89.50	90.21
17	Golden440	4.30	10397	9319	8831	8539	85.32	86.89	90.22	92.46
18	Golden480-1	4.75	10139	9093	8375	8296	83.44	86.36	91.15	91.12
19	Golden480-2	5.15	25464	22499	21190	20716	82.06	86.61	91.06	91.72
20	Golden483	4.23	24684	22102	20643	20038	84.01	86.84	91.92	92.35
	Average	3.83	—	—	—	—	87.89	90.17	92.72	94.54

the first stage, because the correlation coefficient is 0.95 (very significant) and minimizing the total traveling distance can minimize the total fuel consumption.

6. Conclusions

In this paper, we study the FCVRP in which road gradient is considered as one of the factors to measure fuel consumption. After constructing an MIP model, we present complexity analysis for this FCVRP based on comparison with CVRP. To solve this model, we propose an efficient algorithm called TOHLS. This algorithm is based on a hybrid local search algorithm (HLS) that is also used in this paper to solve FCVRP. Based on the existing CVRP testing problems, 60 FCVRP instances are generated and solved by both HLS and TOHLS. The computational results show that the proposed TOHLS has a better performance than the HLS algorithm in terms of solution qualities.

Some important concluding remarks can be summarized as follows. First, the size of solution space of FCVRP is $2^{K_{min}}$ times that of CVRP, and the complexities of common improvement operations including *2-opt, or-opt, exchange,* and *swap* are n times that in CVRP. Second, TOHLS algorithm can effectively improve the performance of HLS and reduce the total fuel consumption by 2%–13%. The improvement is more significant for problem instances with limited response time, large number of customers, and average road gradient. Third, it is indicated that the TOHLS is

particularly appropriate for FCVRP problems that have large sizes, consider road gradients, and require quick response. Fourthly, it is also worth pointing out that the idea behind the proposed TOHLS can be applied to improve algorithms other than HLS. Thus, one of the most promising future research directions is to apply the two-objective idea to various existing heuristics in CVRP to improve their algorithm performances.

There are also several limitations in our research. One of our assumptions is that the road gradient between any two customers is approximated by the difference between their vertical coordinates. This assumption may not be appropriate in the case where there are two city centers located at same geographic attitude but with a mountain somewhere in the middle. In this scenario, fuel consumption for vehicles traveling between the two city centers should be more than the one we proposed. Therefore, experimentally determining the more accurate fuel consumption in such case shall be one of the future research directions. In addition, our current modeling approach simplifies the speed factors and patterns by assuming that speeds are determined by the distance to the city center. However, in practice there are often more than one-road sections connecting customers with the city center, and these road sections often have different characteristics and traffic performance levels. In such case, it will be much more complicated to model the exact speeds between different locations. Thus, a thorough investigation on the speed patterns from a more practical point of view is needed for the future studies. Last but not least, in order to implement our approach, we can utilize the current available real-time traffic data sources, such as FCD, loop detectors, and GPS, to facilitate parameterizing our model. In particular, given the location and transportation situation of a city center, instead of simulation, it could easily adapt our model by generating real traffic data from these resources to be used for calculating the gradient, the speed, the fuel consumption, and the other related parameters. These data can be further used as inputs in our solution approach. And, finally, the optimal fuel consumption could be achieved by selecting the appropriate vehicle routes under the guidance of these advanced devices.

Conflict of Interests

The authors declare that there is no conflict of interests regarding the publication of this paper.

Acknowledgments

The authors thank the editor and two anonymous reviewers for their constructive comments, which helped them greatly improve the paper. They also gratefully acknowledge funding provided by the Promotion Research Fund for Excellent Young and Middle-Aged Scientists of Shandong Province (2014BSB01142), National Natural Science Foundation of China (71502026), and the Ministry of Education of Humanities and Social Science Project (15YJC630103).

References

[1] C. Schreyer, C. Schneider, M. Maibach, W. Rothengatter, C. Doll, and D. Schmedding, "External costs of transport: update study," Tech. Rep., INFRAS, 2004.

[2] M. Figliozzi, "Emissions minimization vehicle routing problem," in *Proceedings of the 89th Transportation Research Board Annual Meeting*, Washington, DC, USA, January 2010.

[3] D. Gulczynski, B. Golden, and E. Wasil, "The period vehicle routing problem: new heuristics and real-world variants," *Transportation Research E: Logistics and Transportation Review*, vol. 47, no. 5, pp. 648–668, 2011.

[4] E. Wygonik and A. Goodchild, "Using a GIS-based emissions minimization vehicle routing problem with time windows (EVRPTW) model to evaluate CO_2 emissions and cost trade offs in a case study of a an urban delivery system," in *Proceedings of the 90th Transportation Resarch Board Annual Meeting*, Washington, DC, USA, January 2011.

[5] E. Demir, T. Bektaş, and G. Laporte, "The bi-objective pollution-routing problem," *European Journal of Operational Research*, vol. 232, no. 3, pp. 464–478, 2014.

[6] E. Demir, T. Bektaş, and G. Laporte, "A review of recent research on green road freight transportation," *European Journal of Operational Research*, vol. 237, no. 3, pp. 775–793, 2014.

[7] Y. Huang, K. Wang, T. Zhang, and C. Pang, "Green supply chain coordination with greenhouse gases emissions management: a game-theoretic approach," *Journal of Cleaner Production*, vol. 112, Part 3, pp. 2004–2014, 2016.

[8] A. Y. Bigazzi and R. L. Bertini, "Adding green performance metrics to a transportation data archive," *Transportation Research Record*, vol. 2121, no. 1, pp. 30–40, 2009.

[9] R. W. Eglese and D. Black, "Optimizing the routing of vehicles," in *Green Logistics: Improving the Environmental Sustainability of Logistics*, A. McKinnon, S. Cullinane, M. Browne, and W. Whiteing, Eds., pp. 215–228, Kogan Page, London, UK, 2010.

[10] E. Demir, T. Bektaş, and G. Laporte, "A comparative analysis of several vehicle emission models for road freight transportation," *Transportation Research Part D: Transport and Environment*, vol. 16, no. 5, pp. 347–357, 2011.

[11] R. Dekker, J. Bloemhof, and I. Mallidis, "Operations Research for green logistics—an overview of aspects, issues, contributions and challenges," *European Journal of Operational Research*, vol. 219, no. 3, pp. 671–679, 2012.

[12] C. Lin, K. L. Choy, G. T. S. Ho, S. H. Chung, and H. Y. Lam, "Survey of green vehicle routing problem: past and future trends," *Expert Systems with Applications*, vol. 41, no. 4, pp. 1118–1138, 2013.

[13] K. C. Tan, L. H. Lee, and K. Ou, "Hybrid genetic algorithms in solving vehicle routing problems with time window constraints," *Asia-Pacific Journal of Operational Research*, vol. 18, no. 1, pp. 121–130, 2001.

[14] J. Zhang, J. Tang, and R. Y. K. Fung, "A scatter search for multi-depot vehicle routing problem with weight-related cost," *Asia-Pacific Journal of Operational Research*, vol. 28, no. 3, pp. 323–348, 2011.

[15] B. L. Hollis and P. J. Green, "Real-life vehicle routing with time windows for visual attractiveness and operational robustness," *Asia-Pacific Journal of Operational Research*, vol. 29, no. 4, Article ID 1250017, 2012.

[16] K. Wang, C. Ye, and A. Ning, "Achieving better solutions for vehicle routing problem involving split deliveries and pickups using a competitive decision algorithm," *Asia-Pacific Journal of Operational Research*, vol. 32, Article ID 1550022, 2015.

[17] E. Demir, T. Bektaş, and G. Laporte, "An adaptive large neighborhood search heuristic for the Pollution-Routing Problem," *European Journal of Operational Research*, vol. 223, no. 2, pp. 346–359, 2012.

[18] L. Pelkmans and P. Debal, "Comparison of on-road emissions with emissions measured on chassis dynamometer test cycles," *Transportation Research Part D: Transport and Environment*, vol. 11, no. 4, pp. 233–241, 2006.

[19] N. Urquhart, E. Hart, and C. Scott, "Building low CO_2 solutions to the vehicle routing problem with time windows using an evolutionary algorithm," in *Proceedings of the 6th IEEE Congress on Evolutionary Computation (CEC '10)*, pp. 1–6, Barcelona, Spain, July 2010.

[20] J. Bandeira, D. O. Carvalho, A. J. Khattak, N. M. Rouphail, and M. C. Coelho, "A comparative empirical analysis of eco-friendly routes during peak and off-peak hours," in *Proceedings of the Transportation Research Board 91st Annual Meeting*, Washington, DC, USA, 2012.

[21] J. Bandeira, T. G. Almeida, A. J. Khattak, N. M. Rouphail, and M. C. Coelho, "Generating emissions information for route selection: experimental monitoring and routes characterization," *Journal of Intelligent Transportation Systems*, vol. 17, no. 1, pp. 3–17, 2013.

[22] A. Correia, S. Amaya, S. Meyer, M. Kumagai, and M. Okude, "Eco routing for European market," in *Proceedings of the 17th World Congress and Exhibition on Intelligent Transport Systems and Services (ITS '10)*, Busan, South Korea, 2010.

[23] C. F. Minett, A. M. Salomons, W. Daamen, B. Van Arem, and S. Kuijpers, "Eco-routing: comparing the fuel consumption of different routes between an origin and destination using field test speed profiles and synthetic speed profiles," in *Proceedings of the IEEE Forum on Integrated and Sustainable Transportation Systems (FISTS '11)*, pp. 32–39, Vienna, Austria, July 2011.

[24] T. Bektaş and G. Laporte, "The pollution-routing problem," *Transportation Research Part B: Methodological*, vol. 45, no. 8, pp. 1232–1250, 2011.

[25] T. R. P. Ramos, M. I. Gomes, and A. P. Barbosa-Povoa, "Minimizing CO_2 emissions in a recyclable waste collection system with multiple depots," in *Proceedings of the EUROMA/POMS Joint Conference*, Amsterdam, The Netherlands, 2012.

[26] A. Franceschetti, D. Honhon, T. Van Woensel, T. Bektaş, and G. Laporte, "The time-dependent pollution-routing problem," *Transportation Research Part B: Methodological*, vol. 56, pp. 265–293, 2013.

[27] M. Barth, T. Younglove, and G. Scora, "Development of a heavy-duty diesel modal emissions and fuel consumption model," Tech. Rep., California Partners for Advanced Transit and Highways, San Francisco, Calif, USA, 2005.

[28] M. Barth and K. Boriboonsomsin, "Real-world CO_2 impacts of traffic congestion," *Transportation Research Record*, vol. 2058, no. 11, pp. 163–171, 2008.

[29] D. C. Carslaw, P. S. Goodman, F. C. H. Lai, and O. M. J. Carsten, "Comprehensive analysis of the carbon impacts of vehicle intelligent speed control," *Atmospheric Environment*, vol. 44, no. 23, pp. 2674–2680, 2010.

[30] B. Golden, J. Wasil, and I. M. Kelly, *Fleet Management and Logistics*, Kluwer Academic Publishers, Boston, Mass, USA, 1998.

11

A Regular k-Shrinkage Thresholding Operator for the Removal of Mixed Gaussian-Impulse Noise

Han Pan, Zhongliang Jing, Lingfeng Qiao, and Minzhe Li

School of Aeronautics and Astronautics, Shanghai Jiao Tong University, Shanghai, China

Correspondence should be addressed to Han Pan; hanpan@sjtu.edu.cn

Academic Editor: Ridha Ejbali

The removal of mixed Gaussian-impulse noise plays an important role in many areas, such as remote sensing. However, traditional methods may be unaware of promoting the degree of the sparsity adaptively after decomposing into low rank component and sparse component. In this paper, a new problem formulation with regular spectral k-support norm and regular k-support ℓ_1 norm is proposed. A unified framework is developed to capture the intrinsic sparsity structure of all two components. To address the resulting problem, an efficient minimization scheme within the framework of accelerated proximal gradient is proposed. This scheme is achieved by alternating regular k-shrinkage thresholding operator. Experimental comparison with the other state-of-the-art methods demonstrates the efficacy of the proposed method.

1. Introduction

Image restoration [1–4] attempts to recover a clear image from the observations of real scenes. As a fundamental procedure, it has been applied to various application areas, such as image fusion [5] and action recognition [6]. However, typically, the noise characteristics of imaging camera is completely or partially unknown. Among these, the removal of mixed noise has not been investigated because the noise model is not easy to establish accurately.

Recently, a patch based method [7] for video restoration has attracted much attention [8–10]. This method also is extended to video in-painting for archived films. However, the mechanisms of modeling the sparsity level of the grouping patches remain unclear.

To deal with the lack of adaptivity in sparsity level [7], a robust video restoration algorithm is proposed. The main idea of the proposed method is to model the sparsity levels of the low rank component by regular spectral k-support norm and sparse component by regular k-support ℓ_1 norm. Specially, a new problem formulation is presented, where the objective function is minimized under an upper bound constraint on the regularization term. However, it is not easy to solve the resulting problem. Some recent progress [11] in the theory of optimization on iterative shrinkage thresholding method

is considered. And, an efficient alternating minimization scheme is proposed to solve the new objective.

1.1. Related Works. Recently, the problem of denoising image corrupted by mixed Gaussian-impulse noise has been studied in many different contexts [8–10, 12, 13]. These methods fall into three categories: variational methods [9, 12], sparse representation [8, 10], and patch based method [7].

Variational methods are a new class of the solutions to promote edge-preservation, such as total variation [14]. These methods first utilized some spatial filters to detect and remove the corrupted pixels, for example, adaptive center-weighted median filter [15] (ACWMF) or rank order absolute differences [16] (ROAD) detector. In [12], Cai et al. employed Mumford-Shah regularization term to encourage sparsity in gradient domain. In [9], Rodríguez et al. presented a novel optimization method for the generalized total variation regularization method. It can be seen that the denoised performance of these methods relies on the detection for the damaged candidates. The adaptivity of sparsity level of the regularization terms has not been investigated carefully.

Sparse representation based methods have been extended to this problem. In the main idea of this scheme, it is assumed that the signal can be described by linear combination of a spare number of elements or atoms of an overcomplete dictionary. In [8], an efficient image reconstruction method by posing ℓ_1 norm on the error, and ℓ_0 norm on image patches in learned dictionary, was proposed. In [10], Filipovic and Jukic reformulated a new problem formulation by enforcing ℓ_0-ℓ_1 sparsity constraints. The resulting problem is solved by a mixed soft-hard thresholding method. However, it should be noted that these methods are time-consuming.

Patch based method is proven to be a state-of-the-art denoising scheme. In [7], Ji et al. approximated the patch stack by reformulating the problem as a low rank matrix completion problem. Despite its efficacy, one of the limitations of patch based method in [7] is that the degree of sparsity has not been considered carefully. When the underlying sparsity level is unknown, we may obtain a bias estimate, considerably. To alleviate these issues in a unified formulation, a new problem formulation is proposed

1.2. Contributions. The main idea of this paper is to deal with the weakness of the approach in [7]. Existing methods, such as ℓ_1 norm and trace norm, can not promote the sparsity level of all two components adaptively. The details or local fine content can not be represented and described well. To deal with these issues, a new problem formulation incorporating correlated and adaptive sparsity is proposed.

Our contributions can be summarized as follows.

(1) A new problem formulation to model the sparsity level of the patches is proposed. A new norm extended from k-support norm and ordered ℓ_1 norm is presented.

(2) An efficient minimization scheme with regular k-shrinkage thresholding operator is proposed, which is based on the optimization framework of accelerated proximal gradient (APG) method.

(3) Numerical experiments, compared to other state-of-the-art methods, demonstrate that the proposed method outperforms the related restoration methods.

1.3. Organization. The remainder of this paper is presented as follows. In Section 2, some basic notations are provided. In Section 3, a detailed description about the proposed objective function is given. In Section 4, an efficient minimization scheme within the framework of APG is proposed. Then, some experiments are conducted to validate the effectiveness of the proposed method in Section 5. Finally, we conclude the paper in Section 6.

2. Preliminaries

There are some notations presented for the simplicity of discussions. Frobenius norm and ℓ_1 norm of a matrix $X \in \mathbb{R}^{m \times n}$ are defined by $\|X\|_F$ and $\|X\|_1$, respectively. For a scalar τ, the shrinkage operator [17] $S_\tau(x)$ for ℓ_1 norm minimization problem is defined as follows:

$$S_\tau(x) = \mathrm{sgn}(x) \max(|x| - \tau, 0), \qquad (1)$$

where sgn is a signum function; $|\cdot|$ calculates the absolute value.

Assuming that X is of rank r, the singular value decomposition (SVD) of X with nonnegative singular values is defined by $X = U\Sigma V^T$, where Σ denotes a diagonal matrix with the singular values. Based on the SVD computation, the nuclear norm is defined in the following way:

$$\|X\|_* = \mathrm{tr}\left(\sqrt{X^t X}\right) = \mathrm{tr}\left(\sqrt{V\Sigma^2 V^T}\right) = \sum_{i=1}^{r} |\sigma_i|, \qquad (2)$$

where σ_i is the ith largest singular value of X. A solution with shrinkage operator to the nuclear norm is singular value shrinkage operator [18] $D_\tau(X)$, which can be expressed as follows:

$$D_\tau(X) = U\Sigma_\tau V^T, \qquad (3)$$

where $\Sigma_\tau : \mathbb{R} \to \mathbb{R}$ is defined as follows:

$$\Sigma_\tau = \mathrm{diag}\left(\mathrm{sgn}(\sigma_i) \max(|\sigma_i| - \tau, 0)\right). \qquad (4)$$

However, it should be noted that the shrinkage operator for ℓ_1 norm is different from singular value shrinkage operator for nuclear norm. There operators play an important role in joint sparse and low rank matrix approximation.

In this paper, ordered ℓ_1-norm [19] is provided as follows:

$$\ell_{O1} = \sum_{i=1}^{n} w |x|_i, \qquad (5)$$

where x is sorted in decreasing order. $|x|_i$ denotes the ith largest element of the magnitude vector $|x| = (|x_1|, \ldots, |x_n|)^T$. w is a trade-off vector in nonincreasing order. When w is a constant vector, (5) reduces to ℓ_1 norm. When $w_1 > 0$ and $w_{2 \le i \le n} = 0$, then (5) reduces to ℓ_∞-norm.

k-support norm [20] is defined as follows:

$$k_s(x) = \left\{x \in \mathbb{R}^n : \|x\|_0 \le S, \ \|x\|_2 \le 1\right\}, \qquad (6)$$

where S denotes the bound of the sparsity level of x, which is a positive integer. The details of k-support norm are introduced in [20, 21]. It has been extended to the case of matrix, which named by regular spectral k-support norm. Although this norm provides the number of elements of the sparsity level, it lacks of efficient mechanism to promote the sparsity adaptively.

After taking advantage of both ordered ℓ_1 norm and k-support norm, regular k-support ℓ_1 norm is defined as follows:

$$\lambda \|x\|_{1,k} = \sum_{i=1}^{k} \lambda_i |x|_i, \qquad (7)$$

where λ is a positive regularization vector in nonincreasing order. And $1 \le k \le n$, where n is the size of vector x.

For the case of matrix, regular spectral k-support norm is proposed, which can be expressed as follows:

$$\lambda \|X\|_k^* = \sum_{i=1}^{k} \lambda_i |\sigma_i|, \quad X \in \mathbb{R}^{m \times n}, \qquad (8)$$

where $1 \leq k \leq \min(m, n)$. It can be noted that the singular values are arranged in nonincreasing order.

3. Problem Setup

This section introduces the objective function in detail. For each reference patch p, similar patches in the spatial- and temporal-domain are obtained by utilizing the patch matching algorithm. The matched patches are denoted as $\{p_i\}_{i=1}^m$, where m stands for the size. It can be noted that each patch p_i is rearranged as a vector with size $\mathbb{R}^{n^2}$ through concatenating all columns into a column vector. At last, a matrix $O \in n^2 \times m$ is generated after considering all the m patches, which can be represented as follows:

$$O = (p_1, p_2, \ldots, p_m). \quad (9)$$

In this paper, we assumed that the observed patch matrix O can be decomposed into three components:

$$O = L + S + N, \quad (10)$$

where L stands for low rank component, S is sparse component, and N is additive noise. There are some regularization methods for (10), such as L with nuclear norm (also known as the trace norm) and S with ℓ_1 norm. The problem formulation in [7] can be expressed as follows:

$$\begin{aligned} \min_{L,S} \quad & \|L\|_* + \lambda \|S\|_1, \\ \text{s.t.} \quad & \|O - L - S\|_F \leq \epsilon, \end{aligned} \quad (11)$$

where $\|\cdot\|_*$ is nuclear norm, and $\|\cdot\|_1$ for ℓ_1 norm.

However, these norms may lead to a large estimation bias [19] but can not promote the sparsity level adaptively. For example, the limitations of ℓ_1 norm have been investigated in [22, 23]. Similarly, some alternative cases, such as the ℓ_p quasinorm, also have been discussed in [24–26]. Thus, a suitable solution is required to recover these components.

To alleviate these limitations, a new problem formulation is proposed to model the sparsity levels both on L and S. Moreover, a unified formulation to describe the correlated variables is considered. To estimate the underlying structures of L and S, we focus on the following minimization function:

$$\begin{aligned} \min_{L,S} \quad & \lambda_1 \|L\|_k^* + \lambda_2 \|S\|_{1,k}, \\ \text{s.t.} \quad & \|O - L - S\|_F \leq \epsilon, \end{aligned} \quad (12)$$

where λ_1 and λ_2 are two positive regularization vectors in a nondecreasing order. $\lambda_1 \|L\|_k^*$ stands for regular spectral k-support norm on L. $\lambda_2 \|S\|_{1,k}$ denotes regular k-support ℓ_1 norm on S. And ϵ is the standard deviation of noise N.

The above formulation amounts to the constraint $\|O - L - S\|_F \leq \epsilon$, which is considered more natural than usual formulation because it stands for the tolerance on the error.

After choosing a suitable ϵ, (12) can be reformulated as follows:

$$\min_{L,S} \quad \lambda_1 \|L\|_k^* + \lambda_2 \|S\|_{1,k} + \frac{1}{2\mu} \|O - L - S\|_F^2, \quad (13)$$

where μ is a suitable positive value. It can be seen that these are some challenges to solve (13). First, regular k-support ℓ_1-norm is posed on sparse component S. Second, the low rank component L is penalized by regular spectral k-support norm.

There are several properties of our problem formulation in (13). First, the proposed regular spectral k-support norm on L and regular k-support ℓ_1 norm on S aim to reconstruct the local structures clearly. It should be noted that these modeling strategies can adaptively promote the sparsity level with an upper bound. Second, to the best of our knowledge, this is the first time of combining the advantages of both ordered ℓ_1 norm and k-support norm to yield a robust subspaces estimation against noise. Third, although the optimization method in [27] is very similar to the proposed method, the proposed method can deal with more complex situations. Moreover, the proposed method can adopt the more challenging situations, such as the removal of mixed Gaussian, salt-and-pepper noise, and random value impulse noise. It should be noted that this noisy situation has not been explored in [7].

4. Proposed Method

4.1. Proposed Framework. In this section, an optimization framework using regular k-shrinkage thresholding operator is presented. First, accelerated proximal gradient method (APG) is applied to the resulting problem because of its simplicity and popularity in imaging applications [28, 29]. Second, the proposed regular k-shrinkage thresholding operator is applied to the two resulting subproblems. As showed in [22, 23], nonconvex regularization functions have been shown both theoretically and experimentally to provide better results than ℓ_1 norm. Then, some explicit proximal mappings are developed.

APG based scheme aims to solve an unconstrained minimization problem by

$$\min_X \quad g(X) + f(X), \quad (14)$$

where g is assumed to be a nonsmooth function and f for a smooth function. Here, L_f denotes the Lipschitz constant of the gradient of f.

Applying the framework of APG to problem (13), we have the following expressions:

$$\begin{aligned} X &= (S, L), \\ g(X) &= \mu\lambda_1 \|L\|_k^* + \mu\lambda_2 \|S\|_{1,k}, \\ f(X) &= \frac{1}{2} \|O - L - S\|_F^2. \end{aligned} \quad (15)$$

Require: $L_0 = L_{-1} = 0$; $S_0 = S_{-1} = 0$; $t_0 = t_{-1} = 1$;
$\mu_0 > \overline{\mu} > 0, \rho < 1$;
repeat

$$Y_k^L = L_k + \frac{t_{k-1} - 1}{t_k} (L_k - L_{k-1});$$

$$Y_k^S = S_k + \frac{t_{k-1} - 1}{t_k} (S_k - S_{k-1});$$

$$G_k^L = Y_k^L - \frac{1}{2} \left(Y_k^L + Y_k^S - O \right);$$

$$G_k^S = Y_k^S - \frac{1}{2} \left(Y_k^L + Y_k^S - O \right);$$

$$(U, \Sigma, V) = \mathrm{svd}\left(G_k^L \right);$$

$$L_{k+1} = U \mathrm{RK}_{k,\lambda_1 \mu/2} (\Sigma) V^T$$

$$S_{k+1} = \mathrm{RK}_{k,\lambda_2 \mu/2} \left(G_k^S \right);$$

$$t_{k+1} = \frac{1 + \sqrt{4t_k^2 + 1}}{2}; \quad \mu_{k+1} = \max\left(\rho, \mu_k, \overline{\mu} \right); \quad k \longleftarrow k + 1;$$

until converged

ALGORITHM 1: An efficient minimization scheme with regular k-shrinkage thresholding operator.

Setting $L_f = 1$, then we have the following objective function:

$$\min_{L,S} \quad \mu\lambda_1 \|L\|_k^* + \mu\lambda_2 \|S\|_{1,k} + \left\| L - G_k^L \right\|_F^2 \tag{16}$$
$$+ \left\| S - G_k^S \right\|_F^2,$$

where the proximal points G_k^L and G_k^S in the framework of APG are defined in Algorithm 1. It can be noted that both the variables L and S are separable. Thus, there are two subproblems, which can be represented as follows:

$$\min_{L} \quad \mu\lambda_1 \|L\|_k^* + \left\| L - G_k^L \right\|_F^2, \tag{17}$$

$$\min_{S} \quad \mu\lambda_2 \|S\|_{1,k} + \left\| S - G_k^S \right\|_F^2. \tag{18}$$

It can be seen that (17) is a minimization problem with regular spectral k-support norm and (18) with regular k-support ℓ_1-norm. To deal with these problems, regular k-shrinkage thresholding operator (RK) is defined as follows:

$$\mathrm{RK}_{k,\tau}(x) = \mathrm{sgn}(x) \max(|x| \ominus \tau, 0), \quad \|x\|_0 \le k, \tag{19}$$

where $\ominus$ denotes an operation of direct minus in nonincreasing order. k denotes the sparsity level of the input vector. τ also is a vector in a nonincreasing order.

Remark 1. There are some differences between regular k-shrinkage thresholding operator and shrinkage operator [17]. First, the proposed operator models the sparsity level by the procedure of regular shrinkage adaptively. Second, the introduction of k-support constraint can bound the degree of the sparsity. Third, the combination of regular shrinkage and k-support leads to the modeling of the correlated variables robustly.

When applying the proposed operator to G_k^L and G_k^S, we have

$$L_{k+1} = U \mathrm{RK}_{k,\lambda_1 \mu/2} (\Sigma) V^T,$$
$$S_{k+1} = \mathrm{RK}_{k,\lambda_2 \mu/2} \left(G_k^S \right), \tag{20}$$

where Σ denotes the eigenvalues of G_k^L. It should be noted that the solution to L_{k+1} can be viewed as a generalization of singular value shrinkage operator. Based on the framework of APG, an optimization framework for the objective function (16) is presented in Algorithm 1. The detailed procedures for the two subproblems are provided in Algorithm 1.

4.2. Some Implementation Details. In our implementation, the sampled image patches with overlapping regions are considered. Then, each frame of the restored video may be replaced by the recovered patches. For the synthesis process, the outcome of each selected pixel is accomplished by calculating the average of multiple estimates from the related patches. This procedure could deal with the artifacts along the boundaries of patches and restore fine details locally.

5. Experiments and Discussion

5.1. Experimental Settings. To demonstrate the effectiveness and efficacy of the proposed method, some experiments are conducted. We focus on the removal of mixed Gaussian-impulse noise. Two types of noisy situations, including mixed Gaussian and random value impulse noise (GRV) denoted by (σ, si) and mixed Gaussian, salt-and-pepper noise, and random value impulse noise (GSPRV) by (σ, sp, si), are tested. Some samples of three videos (http://trace.eas.asu.edu/yuv/) are displayed in Figure 1. The sizes of *coastguard*, *flower*, and *news* in our experiments are $176 \times 144 \times 100$, $352 \times 240 \times 150$, and $352 \times 288 \times 150$, respectively. The parameter k of the

(a)   (b)

FIGURE 1: Two samples used in the experiments ((a) sample for *flower*, (b) sample for *news*).

TABLE 1: Numerical results by the removal of MGRV, measured by PSNR and FSIM.

Noise level	Indexes	Methods	*Coastguard*	*Flower*	*News*
(10, 10%)	PSNR	VBM3D	28.75	19.62	30.36
		RPCA	30.75	22.11	33.49
		ℓ_1-ℓ_0	28.49	19.45	28.40
		Ours	**31.07**	**23.01**	**34.86**
(15, 20%)	PSNR	VBM3D	27.37	18.72	28.10
		RPCA	28.98	19.66	30.24
		ℓ_1-ℓ_0	26.15	18.12	25.56
		Ours	**29.58**	**21.41**	**31.32**
(20, 30%)	PSNR	VBM3D	25.56	17.97	25.64
		RPCA	25.69	18.23	26.34
		ℓ_1-ℓ_0	23.06	16.66	24.20
		Ours	**27.17**	**19.30**	**27.41**
(10, 10%)	FSIM (%)	VBM3D	87.71	81.64	95.52
		RPCA	90.01	87.57	**96.47**
		ℓ_1-ℓ_0	91.35	84.94	90.11
		Ours	**92.04**	**92.14**	96.35
(15, 20%)	FSIM (%)	VBM3D	82.24	75.90	92.74
		RPCA	89.32	79.93	93.47
		ℓ_1-ℓ_0	84.33	79.25	87.10
		Ours	**90.13**	**87.58**	**94.06**
(20, 30%)	FSIM (%)	VBM3D	77.19	70.42	89.18
		RPCA	86.69	74.30	88.35
		ℓ_1-ℓ_0	79.47	73.35	82.41
		Ours	**87.82**	**77.09**	**89.48**

proposed method for the *coastguard* is set to 1000. For the other videos, that is, *flower* and *news*, k is set to 2000. All experiments are performed in MATLAB R2014 running on a desktop with Intel Core i7 at 3.2 GHz.

Three related methods are compared with the proposed method, including VBM3D [30], RPCA based method [7], and ℓ_0-ℓ_1 based method [8]. VBM3D based method is not originally designed for the removal of mixed Gaussian-impulse noise. To remedy this problem, adaptive center-weighted median filter [15] (ACWMF) is used to detect

and remove the impulse noise firstly. Two indexes are taken for assessing the denoised performance of all competing methods, that is, peak-signal-to-noise ratio (PSNR) and feature-similarity (FSIM) index [31].

5.2. Mixed Gaussian and Random Value Impulse Noise. In this subsection, the denoising results for three different scenarios are presented, including $(\sigma, \text{si}) = (10, 10\%)$, $(15, 20\%)$, and $(20, 30\%)$. Numerical results on three videos are presented in Table 1. It can be observed that the proposed

FIGURE 2: Visual comparison of denoising results on flower by noise level $(\sigma, \text{si}) = (10, 10\%)$. (a) Original sample (*flower*), (b) noisy image, (c) VBM3D based method (PSNR = 19.62), (d) RPCA based method (PSNR = 22.11), (e) ℓ_1-ℓ_0 based method (PSNR = 19.45), and (f) the proposed method (PSNR = 23.01, $k = 2000$).

method outperforms all the competing methods with respect to FSIM and PSNR. Visual outcomes are demonstrated in Figure 2. The recovered result of proposed method is presented in Figure 2(f). To examine the recovered details, the selected parts in the visual results are enlarged. It can be noted that the proposed method can reconstruct more local details.

5.3. Mixed Gaussian, Salt-and-Pepper Noise, and Random Value Impulse Noise.
In this subsection, the experimental results by the removal of Gaussian, salt-and-pepper, and random value impulse noise are demonstrated. Two noisy levels are assessed. The numerical results are presented in Table 2. It can be noted that the proposed method outperforms other methods. A visual assessment of the reconstruction performance of both algorithms is shown in Figure 3. As shown in the enlarged parts, the proposed method

presented in Figure 3(f) recovers more local details than other methods.

5.4. Discussion.
In this paper, an efficient image restoration scheme for hybrid Gaussian-impulse noise is proposed. The denoising performance of our method is examined in various noisy scenarios. When the strength of noisy levels increased, our method performed more efficiently than other methods. The outcomes of all experiments verified the effectiveness of the proposed method. The difference may be related to the modeling method and optimization strategy we taken. Moreover, the intrinsic sparsity structure of each decomposition component is explored. It should be noted that some limitations may be observed, such as being oversmooth on the local region.

In this paper, an alternating minimization method with regular k-shrinkage thresholding operator is proposed.

FIGURE 3: Visual comparison of denoising results by noise level (15, 15%, 15%). (a) Original sample *(news)*, (b) noisy image, (c) VBM3D based method (PSNR = 26.23), (d) RPCA based method (PSNR = 24.60), (e) ℓ_1-ℓ_0 based method (PSNR = 24.87), and (f) the proposed method (PSNR = 28.01, k = 2000).

Specially, a universal modeling strategy by exploiting the adaptivity of sparsity structure leads to higher quality reconstructions. The proposed method may provide a new class of denoising methods to deal with mixed Gaussian-impulse noise. The numerical results from various experiments validated the effectiveness of the proposed method again.

6. Conclusion

In this paper, an efficient video restoration scheme is proposed for the removal of mixed Gaussian-impulse noise.

Unlike traditional ℓ_1 norm based methods, which treat all the values equally, the proposed method tries to explore the additional structure by regular spectral k-support norm on low rank component and regular k-support ℓ_1 norm on sparse component. Then, the special structure can be promoted on the sparsity level of the decomposition matrices adaptively. To overcome the nonconvex problem, a solution with alternating regular k-shrinkage thresholding operator is proposed. The proposed method has good practical performance with appropriate structures. The numerical results, compared to

TABLE 2: Numerical results by the removal of GSPRV, measured by PSNR and FSIM.

Noise level	Indexes	Methods	*Coastguard*	*Flower*	*News*
(10, 10%, 10%)	PSNR	VBM3D	24.54	18.13	27.22
		RPCA	24.72	18.98	28.40
		ℓ_1-ℓ_0	**26.27**	18.35	27.05
		Ours	25.27	**20.51**	**29.32**
(15, 15%, 15%)	PSNR	VBM3D	23.79	17.62	26.23
		RPCA	22.11	16.65	24.60
		ℓ_1-ℓ_0	24.21	17.37	24.87
		Ours	**24.26**	**18.67**	**28.01**
(10, 10%, 10%)	FSIM (%)	VBM3D	85.32	78.72	93.52
		RPCA	**89.50**	82.94	93.75
		ℓ_1-ℓ_0	88.62	79.44	90.66
		Ours	89.43	**87.64**	**94.13**
(15, 15%, 15%)	FSIM (%)	VBM3D	80.05	74.39	90.87
		RPCA	83.33	75.13	82.78
		ℓ_1-ℓ_0	83.57	75.16	84.61
		Ours	**87.72**	**79.92**	**91.83**

some state-of-the-art methods, demonstrate the advantages of the proposed method.

Conflicts of Interest

The authors declare that they have no conflicts of interest.

Acknowledgments

This work is jointly supported by National Natural Science Foundation of China (Grants nos. 61603249 and 61673262) and key project of Science and Technology Commission of Shanghai Municipality (Grant no. 16JC1401100).

References

[1] R. Das, S. Thepade, S. Bhattacharya, and S. Ghosh, "Retrieval architecture with classified query for content based image recognition," *Applied Computational Intelligence and Soft Computing*, vol. 2016, Article ID 1861247, 9 pages, 2016.

[2] H. Pan, Z. Jing, M. Lei, R. Liu, B. Jin, and C. Zhang, "A sparse proximal Newton splitting method for constrained image deblurring," *Neurocomputing*, vol. 122, pp. 245–257, 2013.

[3] M. Kumar, S. K. Mishra, and S. S. Sahu, "Cat swarm optimization based functional link artificial neural network filter for gaussian noise removal from computed tomography images," *Applied Computational Intelligence and Soft Computing*, vol. 2016, Article ID 6304915, 6 pages, 2016.

[4] G. Zhang, P. Jiang, K. Matsumoto, M. Yoshida, and K. Kita, "Reidentification of persons using clothing features in real-life video," *Applied Computational Intelligence and Soft Computing*, vol. 2017, Article ID 5834846, 9 pages, 2017.

[5] H. Pan, Z. Jing, R. Liu, and B. Jin, "Simultaneous spatial-temporal image fusion using Kalman filtered compressed sensing," *Optical Engineering*, vol. 51, no. 5, pp. 23–29, 2012.

[6] X. Li, Y. Zhang, and D. Liao, "Mining key skeleton poses with latent svm for action recognition," *Applied Computational Intelligence and Soft Computing*, vol. 2017, Article ID 5861435, 11 pages, 2017.

[7] H. Ji, S. Huang, Z. Shen, and Y. Xu, "Robust video restoration by joint sparse and low rank matrix approximation," *SIAM Journal on Imaging Sciences*, vol. 4, no. 4, pp. 1122–1142, 2011.

[8] Y. Xiao, T. Zeng, J. Yu, and M. K. Ng, "Restoration of images corrupted by mixed Gaussian-impulse noise via l1-l0 minimization," *Pattern Recognition*, vol. 44, no. 8, pp. 1708–1720, 2011.

[9] P. Rodríguez, R. Rojas, and B. Wohlberg, "MIxed Gaussian-impulse noise image restoration via total variation," in *Proceedings of the 2012 IEEE International Conference on Acoustics, Speech, and Signal Processing, ICASSP 2012*, pp. 1077–1080, March 2012.

[10] M. Filipovic and A. Jukic, "Restoration of images corrupted by mixed gaussian-impulse noise by iterative soft-hard thresholding," in *Proceedings of the 22nd European Signal Processing Conference (EUSIPCO)*, pp. 1637–1641, IEEE, 2014.

[11] J. Woodworth and R. Chartrand, "Compressed sensing recovery via nonconvex shrinkage penalties," *Mathematics*, vol. 2012, no. 7, article 075004, 2015.

[12] J.-F. Cai, R. H. Chan, and M. Nikolova, "Two-phase approach for deblurring images corrupted by impulse plus Gaussian noise," *Inverse Problems and Imaging*, vol. 2, no. 2, pp. 187–204, 2008.

[13] Y.-R. Li, L. Shen, D.-Q. Dai, and B. W. Suter, "Framelet algorithms for de-blurring images corrupted by impulse plus Gaussian noise," *IEEE Transactions on Image Processing*, vol. 20, no. 7, pp. 1822–1837, 2011.

[14] L. I. Rudin, S. Osher, and E. Fatemi, "Nonlinear total variation based noise removal algorithms," *Physica D. Nonlinear Phenomena*, vol. 60, no. 1-4, pp. 259–268, 1992.

[15] T. Chen and H. R. Wu, "Adaptive impulse detection using center-weighted median filters," *IEEE Signal Processing Letters*, vol. 8, no. 1, pp. 1–3, 2001.

[16] R. Garnett, T. Huegerich, C. Chui, and W. He, "A universal noise removal algorithm with an impulse detector," *IEEE Transactions on Image Processing*, vol. 14, no. 11, pp. 1747–1754, 2005.

[17] D. L. Donoho, "De-noising by soft-thresholding," *IEEE Transactions on Information Theory*, vol. 41, no. 3, pp. 613–627, 1995.

[18] J.-F. Cai, E. J. Candès, and Z. Shen, "A singular value thresholding algorithm for matrix completion," *SIAM Journal on Optimization*, vol. 20, no. 4, pp. 1956–1982, 2010.

[19] M. Bogdan, E. V. D. Berg, W. Su, and E. Candes, "Statistical estimation and testing via the sorted l1 norm," *Statistics*, 2013.

[20] A. Argyriou, R. Foygel, and N. Srebro, "Sparse prediction with the k-support norm," *Advances in Neural Information Processing Systems*, vol. 2, pp. 1466–1474, 2012.

[21] A. Eriksson, T. T. Pham, T.-J. Chin, and I. Reid, "The k-support norm and convex envelopes of cardinality and rank," in *Proceedings of the IEEE Conference on Computer Vision and Pattern Recognition, CVPR 2015*, pp. 3349–3357, June 2015.

[22] R. Gribonval and M. Nielsen, "Sparse representations in unions of bases," *IEEE Transactions on Information Theory*, vol. 49, no. 12, pp. 3320–3325, 2003.

[23] A. M. Bruckstein, D. L. Donoho, and M. Elad, "From sparse solutions of systems of equations to sparse modeling of signals and images," *SIAM Review*, vol. 51, no. 1, pp. 34–81, 2009.

[24] R. Saab, R. Chartrand, and Ö. Yilmaz, "Stable sparse approximations via nonconvex optimization," in *Proceedings of the IEEE International Conference on Acoustics, Speech and Signal Processing (ICASSP '08)*, pp. 3885–3888, April 2008.

[25] X. Chen, F. Xu, and Y. Ye, "Lower bound theory of nonzero entries in solutions of $ell_2\text{-}ell_p$ minimization," *SIAM Journal on Scientific Computing*, vol. 32, no. 5, pp. 2832–2852, 2010.

[26] M. J. Lai and L. Y. Liu, "A new estimate of restricted isometry constants for sparse solutions," *Applied and Computational Harmonic Analysis*, vol. 30, no. 3, pp. 402–406, 2011.

[27] H. Ji, C. Liu, Z. Shen, and Y. Xu, "Robust video denoising using Low rank matrix completion," in *Proceedings of the 2010 IEEE Computer Society Conference on Computer Vision and Pattern Recognition, CVPR 2010*, pp. 1791–1798, June 2010.

[28] A. Beck and M. Teboulle, "A fast iterative shrinkage-thresholding algorithm for linear inverse problems," *SIAM Journal on Imaging Sciences*, vol. 2, no. 1, pp. 183–202, 2009.

[29] Z. Shen, K.-C. Toh, and S. Yun, "An accelerated proximal gradient algorithm for frame-based image restoration via the balanced approach," *SIAM Journal on Imaging Sciences*, vol. 4, no. 2, pp. 573–596, 2011.

[30] K. Dabov, A. Foi, and K. Egiazarian, "Video denoising by sparse 3d transform-domain collaborative filtering," in *Proceedings of the 15th European Signal Processing Conference*, vol. 1, p. 7, 2007.

[31] L. Zhang, L. Zhang, X. Mou, and D. Zhang, "Fsim: a feature similarity index for image quality assessment," *IEEE Transactions on Image Processing*, vol. 20, no. 8, pp. 2378–2386, 2011.

12

Failure Effects Evaluation for ATC Automation System

Rui Li, Zili Zhou, Yansong Cheng, and Jianqiang Wang

The Second Research Institute of CAAC, Chengdu, China

Correspondence should be addressed to Rui Li; sharplr@atmb.net.cn

Academic Editor: Fengxiang Xu

ATC (air traffic control) automation system is a complex system, which helps maintain the air traffic order, guarantee the flight interval, and prevent aircraft collision. It is essential to ensure the safety of air traffic. Failure effects evaluation is an important part of ATC automation system reliability engineering. The failure effects evaluation of ATC automation system is aimed at the effects of modules or components which affect the performance and functionality of the system. By analyzing and evaluating the failure modes and their causes and effects, some reasonable improvement measures and preventive maintenance plans can be established. In this paper, the failure effects evaluation framework considering performance and functionality of the system is established on the basis of reliability theory. Some algorithms for the quantitative evaluation of failure effects on performance of ATC automation system are proposed. According to the algorithms, the quantitative evaluation of reliability, availability, maintainability, and other assessment indicators can be calculated.

1. Introduction

ATC (air traffic control) is a service provided by ground-based controllers who direct aircraft on the ground and through controlled airspace and provide advisory services to aircraft in noncontrolled airspace. The main objectives of air traffic control (ATC) are to ensure flights safety and an efficient organization of traffic flows [1, 2]. ATC automation system is a kind of complex electronic system combined with computer and information technology. It is usually used to maintain the air traffic order, guarantee the interval, and prevent aircraft collision [3]. It is essential for regional control and terminal airspace control. The reliability of ATC automation system has direct effects on air traffic safety.

In recent years, the air traffic control efficiency has been improved due to the employment of various types of ATC automation systems. But the majority of imported ATC automation systems have been used for many years. The hardware and software have declined gradually. And because the serve time of homemade systems is relatively short, there is obvious uncertainty in the evaluation of failure and risk. So the collection of failure records and evaluation of the failure effects are especially urgent. Lots of researches are aimed at reliability forecasting of ATC software. Wang and Liu collected the 36-month failure data of ATC automation system, and Markov chain is employed to predict its reliability [4]. Ternov and Akselsson proposed a new method for identifying hazards in a complex system based on DBE (disturbance, effect, and barrier) analysis and applied it to an air traffic control unit in Malmoe, Sweden [5]. Gómez et al. illustrated a recommender framework for assisting flight controllers, which combines argumentation theory and model checking in the evaluation of trade-offs and compromises to be made in the presence of incomplete and potentially inconsistent information [6]. Zhang et al. established the air traffic management system safety evaluating indicator system considering person-equipment-environment-management [7]. Woltjer et al. described the approach taken and results to develop guidance and to include resilience engineering principles in methodology for safety assessment of functional changes, in air traffic management [8]. Mayer developed an integrated aviation and ATC modeling platform for comparing and evaluating proposed aircraft flight operations and ATC procedures [9]. Flavio Vismari and Camargo Junior proposed a methodology for safety assessment of ATC system by combining "absolute" and

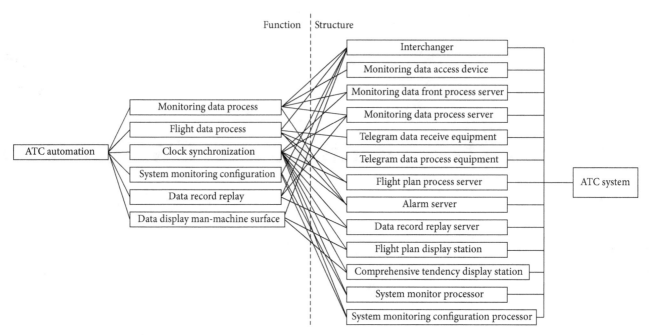

FIGURE 1: The structure and function corresponding diagram of ATC automation system.

"relative" safety assessment methods, using Fluid Stochastic Petri Nets (FSPN) as the modeling formalism [10]. Moon et al. had evaluated the relationship between air traffic volume and human error in air traffic control (ATC) on the basis of reviews of existing literature and interviews and surveys of ATC safety experts [11]. Vanderhaegen [12] also considered the effects of human errors on the ATC system.

The aim of this paper is to establish an available framework to evaluate the effects of failures of subsystems or components to the whole ATC system, so common reliability theory is utilized, such as reliability logic diagram and FMECA (Failure Mode, Effects, and Criticality Analysis), rather than the abstruse algorithms. A general structure of ATC automation system is used as the research object. The relationship between structure composition and functions is analyzed. An evaluation framework is established for failure effects appraisement according to performance effects and function effects. Section 2 gives the structure and function corresponding diagram of ATC automation system. In Section 3, evaluation framework of failure effects on performance is discussed and, in Section 4, evaluation framework of failure effects on function is proposed.

2. Basic Concept of ATC Automation System

An ATC automation system can deal with different types of radar data and form the flight path by information fusion. The autorelation of radar target and flight plan can be realized. The subsystems of a general ATC automation system include RFP (radar data front processing subsystem), RDP (radar processing subsystem), FDP (flight data processing subsystem), SDD (situation data display), FDD (flight data

processing terminal), DRP (data record play), and CMD (condition monitoring display). The structure and function corresponding diagram is shown in Figure 1.

Among the subsystems of ATC automation system, RFP, RDP, FDP, and DRP have two redundancies. When the main equipment fails, the spare one will be switched as main equipment. SDD and FDD are display terminals; the breakdown of a single SDD or FDD will not affect others. CMD is used to set up system parameters. Failures of each subsystem have effects on the function and performance of the whole ATC automation system.

3. Evaluation of Failure Effects on Performance of ATC Automation System

On the basis of the past records and history data, the reliability, availability, maintainability, system load, and system response time can be quantitatively evaluated using proper mathematical models. The diagram of performance evaluation is shown in Figure 2.

3.1. Evaluation of Failure Effects on Reliability. The redundant configuration of ATC automation has diversity in different manufactures, for example, single-redundancy, two-redundancy, or three-redundancy. The model for evaluating reliability should be established according to the actual redundant configuration. A general reliability based on diagram of ATC automation system is shown in Figure 3.

In Figure 3, the same redundant subsystems are parallel connection. The different redundant subsystems are serial connection. Supposing that there are n work points in the

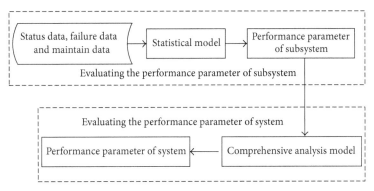

FIGURE 2: The diagram of performance evaluation.

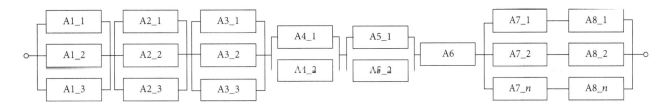

A1_1~A1_3: 3 RFPs; A2_1~A2_3: 3 RDPs;
A3_1~A3_3: 3 interchangers; A4_1~A4_2: 2 FDPs;
A5_1~A5_2: 2 DRPs; A6: CMD/DMS;
A7_1~A7_n: n SDDs; A8_1~A8_n: n FDDs;

FIGURE 3: General reliability based on diagram.

whole system, the system reliability can be calculated as follows:

$$R_s(t) = \left\{ \prod_{i=1}^{3} \left[1 - \prod_{j=1}^{3} \left(1 - R_{i\_j} \right) \right] \right\}$$

$$\cdot \left\{ \prod_{i=4}^{5} \left[1 - \prod_{j=1}^{2} \left(1 - R_{i\_j} \right) \right] \right\}$$

$$\cdot R_6$$

$$\cdot \left\{ 1 - \prod_{j=1}^{n} \left[\left(1 - R_{7\_j} \cdot R_{7\_j} \right) \right] \right\}, \tag{1}$$

where R_{i-j} is the reliability of the subsystem A_{i-j}.

3.2. Evaluation of Failure Effects on Availability. The indexes of availability of ATC automation system can be estimated on the basis of maintenance records and statistical models. For example, the stable availability of ATC automation can be calculated using

$$A = \frac{\text{MTBF}}{\text{MTBF} + \text{MTTR}}, \tag{2}$$

where MTBF is mean time between failures and MTTR is mean time to repair. MTBF can be calculated by

$$\text{MTBF} = \frac{\text{the sum of time between failures}}{\text{times of maintain}}. \tag{3}$$

3.3. Evaluation of Failure Effects on Maintainability. The indexes of maintainability of ATC automation system (e.g., repair rate, MTTR) can also be estimated on the basis of maintenance records and statistical models. The stable availability of ATC automation can be calculated using

$$\text{MTTR} = \frac{\text{the sum of time of maintain}}{\text{times of maintain}}. \tag{4}$$

The mean repair rate of ATC automation is

$$\mu = \frac{1}{\text{MTTR}}. \tag{5}$$

And the maintainability of ATC automation is

$$M(t) = 1 - \exp(-\mu t). \tag{6}$$

3.4. Evaluation of Failure Effects on System Load. When some redundant modules are broken down but at least a redundant

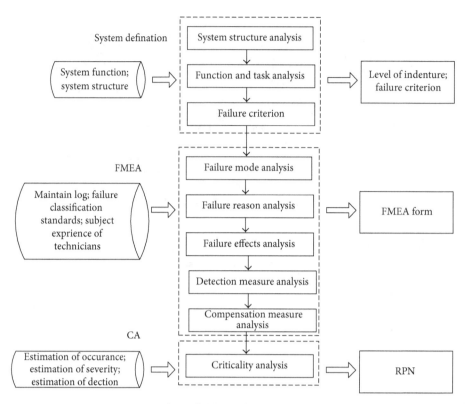

FIGURE 4: Procedure of FMECA for ATC automation system.

module is normal, the ATC system can work normally. But the loading of normal modules must be increased. For example, the occupancy rate of CPU, RAM, and hard disk of server may be increased and so is the network flow. According to historical data, the change of occupancy rate of each subsystem should be considered, and then the load-time curve can be plotted.

The equipment load in time t is the weighted sum of its single index Li(t) (e.g., RAM occupancy rate), as shown in

$$LE\left(t\right) = \sum_{i=1}^{n}\left[\alpha_i L_i\left(t\right)\right], \tag{7}$$

where LE(t) is the load of equipment in time t and α_i is the weight of the ith single index. The load of subsystem and the whole system are calculated as follows:

$$LS\left(t\right) = \sum_{i=1}^{n}\left[\beta_i LE_i\left(t\right)\right],$$
$$LSS\left(t\right) = \sum_{i=1}^{n}\left[\gamma_i LS_i\left(t\right)\right], \tag{8}$$

where LS(t) and LSS(t) are the load of subsystem and the whole system in time t, respectively. β_i is the weight of the ith equipment and γ_i is the weight of the ith subsystem.

3.5. Evaluation of Failure Effects on System Response Time. According to the operating data of ATC automation system,

response time of each typical operation is statistically calculated. And then the mean system response time is

$$\overline{y} = \frac{1}{N}\sum_{i=1}^{N}y_i, \tag{9}$$

where $\overline{y}$ is the mean response time of system. N is the number of typical operations. y_i is the response time of the ith typical operations.

4. Evaluation of Failure Effects on Function of ATC Automation System

The failure effects on function of ATC automation system are evaluated by using FMECA. FMECA (Failure Mode, Effects, and Criticality Analysis) is generally employed to analyze all the possible failure modes of components in a complex system in its whole lifetime [13]. The reasons of each mode and its effects to every layer are found out. And then improvement measures can be put forward. The procedure of FMECA for ATC automation system is shown in Figure 4.

4.1. Failure Modes Analysis. The purpose of failure mode analysis is to find out the possible failure modes of the ATC system from the requirement of the function and the failure criterion of the system definition.

Common failure modes are determined according to standard for failure classification of ATC equipment. The uncovered failures modes can be found out of maintain log or subjective experience of technicians.

TABLE 1: FMEA table of correlation between target trajectories and flight plans.

Number	Project	Function	Failure mode	Failure cause	Failure impact
1	Radar data	The basis of generating radar track	Radar track position is not accurate	Radar precision is insufficient	Radar track position causes the deviation
				Air complex environment causes interference	
			SSR code error	Radar signal interference that can lead to inaccurate SSR code	Wrong correlation
			The repeated SSR code	Double SSR code appears to be caused by mountain reflection, radar fault, false target, fusion algorithm, and so on	Unable to correlate with each other
			The radar flight number error of ADS or S model	ADS data or S mode's radar data transmission and processing is wrong	Wrong correlation
2	Flight telegraph	The basis of the flight plan	Poor timeliness of flight telegraph	Manually send flight telegraph delay	ATC system did not receive the message within prescribed time. Time deviation is too large, autorelated error, or wrong correlation
				Network communication link quality is poor	
			The sequential variation of flight telegraph	Network communication link quality is poor	The receiving and dispatched flight telegraph do not match the time order
			The format and content of flight telegraph are not accurate	Human error	The format and content of flight telegraph are wrong. Unable to get the correct route and calculate the flight status. Unable to automatically correlate with each other
				Network communication link quality is poor	
			Lost the flight telegraph	Network communication link quality is poor	Unable to get flight telegraph. Unable to get accurate route and calculate the flight status. Unable to automatically correlate with each other
3	Basic data	Provide the information of airport, airlines, aircraft, beacon, and punctuation	Basic data is not accurate	Basic database did not update the information of routes and beacon adjusted	Unable to establish accurate flight route. Unable to calculate accurate 4D track. Autorelated error or wrong correlation
			Basic data is not complete	Not existing	
				Code duplication	
4	4D track prediction	Establish the precise 4D track model of whole flight process	The calculated time deviation that through each way point is too large	4D track prediction algorithm is not accurate	State of the flight plan is not correct. The deviation between the planned track position and real target position is large. Unable to automatically correlate with each other or wrong correlation
			The calculated planned flight direction is far away from the actual direction	4D track prediction algorithm is not accurate	Unable to automatically correlate with each other or wrong correlation

TABLE 2: The Classification failure incidence.

Classification	Classification basis	Examples
A	Control unit cannot provide air control service	(1) Backbone of communication networks of control unit failure. (2) Internal phone communication system (very high frequency system) failure. (3) Main and backup functional automation device overall paralysis
B	Failures decline the control capability of air control service and greatly reduce the flight capacity	(1) The whole or part of the automation system cannot be recovered in a short time. (2) Failure of automatic transfer system. (3) Partial control seats at the same time failure or other equipment failure which leads to air to ground communication failure.
C	Failures cause the degradation of service quality on monitoring communication and navigation and reduce the control efficiency	(1) Short time main device or automatic transfer system performance degradation leading to failure of flight plan processing function. (2) Control coordination/transfer of telephone failure due to various causes.
D	Failures have no effects on flight and traffic control	(1) Single machine or single network of redundant system fault. (2) Transient control over telephone or other equipment performance degradation and rapid recovery does not affect the control operation.

4.2. Failure Reason Analysis. The failure reason is divided into direct causes and indirect reasons. The direct cause is the physical and chemical process of the ATC system itself, which leads to the failure or potential failure of the system, while the indirect failure is caused by the failure of other products, environmental factors, human factors, and so forth.

Failure reason analysis helps to identify the factors of the design, manufacture, usage, and maintenance that cause the failure. And then improvement measures and compensation measures can be taken into account to prevent or reduce the possibility of failure.

Before analysis, firstly the features of the ATC automatic system should be classified, and the relevant description should be determined. Analysts must be able to accurately describe each function and its related modules and failure mode.

The FMEA form of ATC automation system correlation between target trajectories and flight plans is shown in Table 1. Table 1 is established on the basis of the analysis of the anomalies of the track [14] and the causes of wrong correlation between target trajectories and flight plans [15], from the perspective of flight plan track related technology principle [16], radar system, and multiradar data processing system.

4.3. Failure Effect Analysis. Failure effect refers to the effects of each failure mode of the ATC system on its usage, function, and status.

When the failure mode of a module is affected by the failure of the other modules of the system, it is usually carried out according to the predefined system level structure. The structure and function corresponding diagram of ATC

TABLE 3: Scoring method of occurrence degree.

Score	The possibility of failure		Reference value of failure probability
1	Rare	Low possibility of failure mode	1/106
2	Low	Possibility of failure mode is relatively low	1/20000
3			1/4000
4	Middle	Middle possibility of failure mode	1/1000
5			1/400
6			1/80
7	High	High possibility of failure mode	1/40
8			1/20
9	Extremely high	Extremely high possibility of failure mode	1/2
10			1/8

TABLE 4: Scoring method of severity degree.

Score	The influence degree of the failure	
1	Slight	No impact on the performance of the system.
2	Low	A slight effect on system performance.
3		
4	Middle	General failure: the system performance is affected; it can be settled through the implementation of the corresponding treatment.
5		
6		
7	High	Serious failure: the system performance is seriously affected.
8		
9	Extremely high	Critical failure: system failure.
10		

automation system is shown in Figure 1. According to the hierarchical structure of ATC automatic system, it can be divided into inverted tree type structure. Through the hierarchical structure diagram and the structure and function corresponding diagram, the modules failure effects on ATC automation system capability can be analyzed.

The effects of failure are clarified into four levels based on different incidence of single equipment to control unit, as shown in Table 2.

4.4. Criticality Analysis. A failure assessment follows the failure analysis, and RPN (Risk Priority Number) number is generally used. RPN is the product of O, S, and D. With the RPN, a ranking of the identified failure causes and their failure connection to the failure effect can be done.

O, which indicates occurrence, estimates how probable the occurrence of the failure cause is. According to Table 3, the scoring criteria for the occurrence probability grade are given. The value of failure probability is corresponding to the rating of expected number of failures in the product life cycle.

S, which indicates severity, describes the severity of a failure effect. It used in the evaluation of the eventual impact on the failure mode of the analysis. Usually, the description of failure mode to the users should be visible. According to Table 4, the scoring methods of the severity are given.

D, which indicates detection, determines how successful the detection of the failure cause is.

According to Table 5, P_D is the probability of the failure mode and cause.

After completing the above steps, the number of RPN could be calculated. For the high harmful failure mode, we should put forward improvement measures.

5. Conclusion

In order to evaluate the effects of subsystem failures to ATC automation system, a framework considering effects on performance and function is established. On the basis of the framework, failure effects on system performance are calculated considering reliability, maintainability, availability, system load, and response time. The mathematical models for each index are given according to the reliability theory. The failure effects on function of ATC automation system are evaluated using FMECA. The procedure of FMECA of ATC

TABLE 5: Scoring method of detection degree.

Score		The difficulty of fault is detected
1	$P_D \approx 1$	Can completely find failure mode and causes
2	$3.3 \times 10^{-1} < P_D$	May find failure mode and causes
3	$5 \times 10^{-2} < P_D \leq 3.3 \times 10^{-1}$	May find failure mode and causes
4	$2 \times 10^{-2} < P_D \leq 5 \times 10^{-2}$	May find failure mode and causes
5	$1 \times 10^{-2} < P_D \leq 2 \times 10^{-2}$	May find failure mode and causes
6	$2 \times 10^{-3} < P_D \leq 1 \times 10^{-2}$	May find failure mode and causes
7	$2 \times 10^{-4} < P_D \leq 2 \times 10^{-3}$	May find failure mode and causes
8	$2 \times 10^{-6} < P_D \leq 2 \times 10^{-4}$	May find failure mode and causes
9	$P_D \approx 2 \times 10^{-6}$	May find failure mode and causes
10	$P_D < 2 \times 10^{-6}$	May find failure mode and causes or may be unable to detect them

automation system is proposed. The framework can be used to guide the reliability analysis procedures of ATC.

Conflicts of Interest

The authors declare that there are no conflicts of interest regarding the publication of this paper.

References

[1] T. Kistan, A. Gardi, R. Sabatini, S. Ramasamy, and E. Batuwangala, "An evolutionary outlook of air traffic flow management techniques," *Progress in Aerospace Sciences*, vol. 88, pp. 15–42, 2017.

[2] T. Jiang, J. Geller, D. Ni, and J. Collura, "Unmanned Aircraft System traffic management: concept of operation and system architecture," *International Journal of Transportation Science and Technology*, vol. 5, no. 3, pp. 123–135, 2016.

[3] T. Lehouillier, F. Soumis, J. Omer, and C. Allignol, "Measuring the interactions between air traffic control and flow management using a simulation-based framework," *Computers and Industrial Engineering*, vol. 99, no. 9, pp. 269–279, 2016.

[4] X. L. Wang and W. X. Liu, "research on air traffic control automatic system software reliability based on markov chain," *Physics Procedia*, vol. 24, pp. 1601–1606, 2012.

[5] S. Ternov and R. Akselsson, "A method, DEB analysis, for proactive risk analysis applied to air traffic control," *Safety Science*, vol. 42, no. 7, pp. 657–673, 2004.

[6] S. A. Gómez, A. Goron, A. Groza, and I. A. Letia, "Assuring safety in air traffic control systems with argumentation and model checking," *Expert Systems with Applications*, vol. 44, pp. 367–385, 2016.

[7] Z. N. Zhang, N. Meng, and P. Zhou, "Based on the fuzzy set-valued statistics and the fuzzy mathematics theory in air traffic control system safety appraisal application," *Physics Procedia*, vol. 33, pp. 511–521, 2012.

[8] R. Woltjer, E. Pinska-Chauvin, T. Laursen, and B. Josefsson, "Towards understanding work-as-done in air traffic management safety assessment and design," *Reliability Engineering and System Safety*, vol. 141, pp. 115–130, 2015.

[9] R. H. Mayer, "Estimating operational benefits of aircraft navigation and air traffic control procedures using an integrated aviation modeling and evaluation platform," in *Proceedings of the Winter Simulation Conference (WSC '06)*, vol. 8, pp. 1569–1577, IEEE, December 2006.

[10] L. Flavio Vismari and J. B. Camargo Junior, "A safety assessment methodology applied to CNS/ATM-based air traffic control system," *Reliability Engineering and System Safety*, vol. 96, no. 7, pp. 727–738, 2011.

[11] W. C. Moon, K. E. Yoo, and Y. C. Choi, "Air traffic volume and air traffic control human errors," *Journal of Transportation Technologies*, vol. 1, no. 3, pp. 47–53, 2011.

[12] F. Vanderhaegen, "mirror effect based learning systems to predict human errors—application to the air traffic control," *IFAC-Papers on Line*, vol. 49, no. 19, pp. 295–300, 2016.

[13] B. Bertsche, A. Schauz, and K. Pickard, *Reliability in Automotive and Mechanical Engineering*, Springer, Berlin, Germany, 2008.

[14] X. J. Jiang, "The abnormal phenomenon analysis about the tack of ATC automation system," *Information Security and Technology*, vol. 4, no. 9, pp. 86–87, 2013.

[15] G. Y. Tian and C. H. Shi, "Analysis of reasons for no correlation between target trajectories and flight plans," *Air Traffic Management*, no. 4, pp. 17–21, 2011.

[16] W. Guo, "Research on problems of correlation between target trajectories and flight plans," *Silicon Valley*, no. 3, pp. 8–25, 2015.

13

Representation for Action Recognition Using Trajectory-Based Low-Level Local Feature and Mid-Level Motion Feature

Xiaoqiang Li, Dan Wang, and Yin Zhang

School of Computer Engineering and Sciences, Shanghai University, Shanghai 200444, China

Correspondence should be addressed to Xiaoqiang Li; xqli@i.shu.edu.cn

Academic Editor: Francesco Carlo Morabito

The dense trajectories and low-level local features are widely used in action recognition recently. However, most of these methods ignore the motion part of action which is the key factor to distinguish the different human action. This paper proposes a new two-layer model of representation for action recognition by describing the video with low-level features and mid-level motion part model. Firstly, we encode the compensated flow (w-flow) trajectory-based local features with Fisher Vector (FV) to retain the low-level characteristic of motion. Then, the motion parts are extracted by clustering the similar trajectories with spatiotemporal distance between trajectories. Finally the representation for action video is the concatenation of low-level descriptors encoding vector and motion part encoding vector. It is used as input to the LibSVM for action recognition. The experiment results demonstrate the improvements on J-HMDB and YouTube datasets, which obtain 67.4% and 87.6%, respectively.

1. Introduction

Human action recognition has become a hot topic in the field of computer vision. It has developed a practical system which will be applied to video surveillance, interactive gaming, and video annotation. Despite remarkable research efforts and many encouraging advances in recent years [1–3], action recognition is still far from being satisfactory and practical. There are large factors affecting accurate rate of the recognition such as cluttered background, illumination, and occlusion.

Most action recognition focuses on two important issues: extracting features within a spatiotemporal volume and modeling the action patterns. Many existing researches on human action recognition tend to extract features from whole 3D videos using spatiotemporal interest points (STIP) [4]. In recent years, optical flow is applied to extract the trajectory-based motion features, which have been widely used in local spatiotemporal features. Local trajectory-based features are pooled and normalized to a vector as the video global representation in action recognition. Meanwhile, a lot of work has focused on developing discriminative dictionary for image object recognition or video action recognition. The Bag of Feature (BOF) model generates simple video model by clustering spatiotemporal features of all the training samples and is trained using χ^2-*kernel* Support Vector Machine (SVM). And the state of the art method is popular Fisher Vector (FV) [5] encoding model based on spatiotemporal local features. However, all these methods are not perfect, because they are only concerned about the low-level spatiotemporal features based on interest point and ignored the higher level features of motion part. For most actions, only a small subset of local motion features of the entire video is relevant to the action label. When a person is waving, only the movement around the arm or hand is responsible for the action clapping hand. Action Bank [6] and motionlets [7] adopt unsupervised learning to discover action parts. Many methods [8] cluster the trajectories and seek to understand spatiotemporal properties of movement to construct the mid-level action video representation. The Vector of Locally Aggregated Descriptors (VLAD) [9] is a descriptor encoding technique that aggregates the descriptors based on a locality criterion in the feature space. To keep more spatiotemporal characteristics of the processed motion part, VLAD encoding gets better results than BOF by [10]. Inspired by low-level local feature encoding and mid-level motion part model are key factors to distinguish the different human actions; we propose a new representation (depicted in Figure 2) for action

(a) iDT vectors   (b) w-flow DT vectors

FIGURE 1: A comparison of the iDT trajectories and w-flow dense trajectories. The red dot is the end point of the green optical flow vector in the current frame. (a) The optical flow vectors are tracked by the improve dense trajectories using SURF descriptors matching [12]. (b) Most of flow vectors due to camera motion are removed by w-flow method.

recognition based on local features and motion part in this paper. To reduce the background clutter noise, we extract the local trajectory-based features through a better compensated flow (w-flow) [11] dense trajectories method. Then we cluster the trajectories through the graph clustering algorithm and encode the group features to describe the different motion part. Finally, we represent the video through combining the low-level trajectory-based features encoding model with mid-level motion part model.

This paper is organized as follows. In Section 2, the local descriptors based on the w-flow dense trajectories and low-level video encoding with FV are introduced. Then we show clustering the motion part and introduce the representation for video in Section 3. We describe the evaluation of our approach and discuss the results in Section 4. Finally, the conclusion and future works are discussed in Section 5.

2. First Layer with FV

Trajectories are efficient in capturing object motions in videos. We extract spatiotemporal features along the w-flow dense trajectories to express low-level descriptors. In this section we introduce the w-flow dense trajectories and low-level descriptors with FV.

2.1. w-Flow Dense Trajectory. The idea of dense trajectory is based on tracking the interest points. The interest points are sampled on a grid spaced by $W = 5$ pixels and tracked in each frame. Points of subsequent frames are concatenated to form a trajectory: $(p_t, \ldots, p_{t+L})$. $p_t = (x_t, y_t)$ is the position of interest points at frame t. The length of a trajectory is $L = 15$ frames [1]. A recent work by Jain et al. [11] proposed the compensated flow (w-flow) dense trajectories which reduce the impact of the background trajectories. The w-flow dense trajectory is obtained by removing the affine flow vector from the original optical flow vector. The interest point of this method is tracked by w-flow [11] for compensating dominant motion (camera motion). It is beneficial for most of the existing descriptors used for action recognition. This method uses the 2D polynomial affine motion model for compensating camera motion. The affine flow $w_{\text{aff}}(p_t)$ is the main movement of the two consecutive images which is

usually caused by the movement of the camera. We compute the affine flow with the publicly available Motion2D software (http://www.irisa.fr/vista/Motion2D/) which implements a real-time robust multiresolution incremental estimation framework. The final flow vector $w(p_t)$ at point $p_t = (x_t, y_t)$ is obtained by removing the affine flow vector $w_{\text{aff}}(p_t) = (u(p_t), v(p_t))$ from the original optical flow vector as follows.

$$w(p_t) = w(p_t) - w_{\text{aff}}(p_t). \qquad (1)$$

Figure 1 shows the dense trajectories extracted by the iDT [12] method and the w-flow dense trajectories.

The shape of a trajectory encodes local motion patterns. The shape of a trajectory is described by concatenating a set of displacement vectors $\Delta P_t = (p_{t+1} - p_t) = (x_{t+1} - x_t, y_{t+1} - y_t)$. Meanwhile, to leverage the motion information in dense trajectories, we compute descriptors within a spatiotemporal volume around the trajectory. The size of a volume is 32×32. And the volume is divided into a $2 \times 2 \times 3$ spatiotemporal grid. The Histograms of Optical Flow (HOF and w-HOF) [1] descriptor captures the local motion information which is computed using the orientations and magnitudes of the flow field. Motion boundary histogram (MBH) [1] descriptor encodes the relative motion between pixels which is along both x and y image axis and describes the discriminatory features for the action recognition in background cluttering. The trajectory-based w-HOF features is computed on the compensated flow. For each trajectory, the descriptors combine motion information HOF, w-HOF, and MBH. The single trajectory feature is in the form of

$$F = \left(w\text{-HOF}, \text{HOF}, \text{MBH}_x, \text{MBH}_y, S\right). \qquad (2)$$

The trajectory shape $S = (\Delta P_t, \ldots, \Delta P_{t+L-1})/\sum_{j=t}^{t+L-1} \|\Delta P_j\|$ is normalized by the sum of the magnitudes of the displacement vectors and L is the length of trajectories.

2.2. Low-Level Video Encoding. The representation of video is a vital problem in action recognition. We first encode the low-level w-flow trajectory-based descriptors using the Fisher Vector (FV) encoding method which was proposed for image

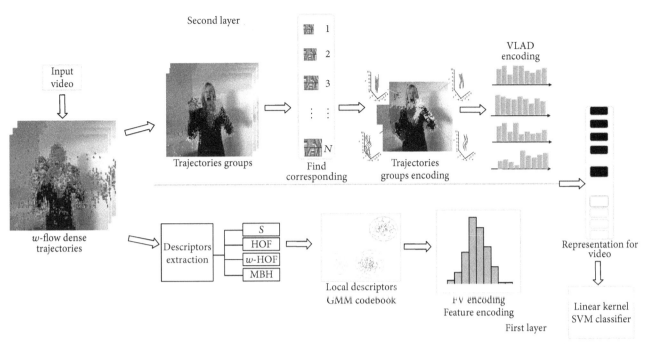

FIGURE 2: The recognition framework of the two-layer model. The first layer encodes the low-level w-flow trajectory-based descriptors using the Fisher Vector (FV). The second layer describes motion part with trajectories groups.

categorization [13]. FV is derived from Fisher kernel which encodes the statistics between video descriptors and Gaussian Mixture Model (GMM). We reduce the low-level features (w-HOF, HOF, and MBH) dimensionality by PCA keeping the 90% energy. The local descriptors X can be modeled by a probability density function $p(X, \theta)$ with parameters θ, which is usually modeled by GMM.

$$G_\theta^X = \frac{1}{N} \nabla_\theta \log p(X; \theta),$$

$$\theta = w_1, \mu_1, \delta_1, \ldots, w_k, \mu_k, \delta_k, \tag{3}$$

where w, μ, δ are the model parameters denoting the weights, means, and diagonal covariances of GMM. N is the number of local descriptors. k is the number of mixture components and we set k to 256 [5]. We can compute the gradient of the log likelihood with respect to the parameters of the model to represent a video. FV requires a GMM of the encoded feature distribution. The Fisher Vector is the concatenation of these partial derivatives and describes in which direction the parameters of the model should be modified to best fit the data [14]. To keep the low-level feature, we encode each video with the FV encoding feature.

3. Representation for Video

Motion part encoding has already been identified as a successful method to represent the video for action recognition. In this section, we use a graph clustering method to cluster the similarity trajectories into groups. Then representation for action video is concatenation of low-level local descriptors encoding and high-level motion part encoding.

3.1. Trajectories Group. To better describe the motion, we cluster the similarity trajectories into groups, because critical

regions of the video are relevant to a specific action. In the method of [22], they compute a hierarchical clustering on trajectories to yield trajectories group of action parts. Then we apply that efficient greedy agglomerative hierarchical clustering procedure to group the trajectories. There are a large number of trajectories in a video; that is, there are a large number of nodes in graph. By removing trajectories distance which is not spatially close will get a sparse trajectories graph. Greedy agglomerative hierarchical clustering is a fast, scalable algorithm, with almost linear complexity in the number of nodes for relatively sparse trajectories' graph. To group the trajectories we set $N \times N$ trajectories distance matrix for a video containing N trajectories. We use a distance metric between trajectories taking into consideration their spatial and temporal relations to cluster. Given two trajectories $P_a(t)_{t=t_a}^{T_a}$ and $P_b(t)_{t=t_b}^{T_b}$,

$$d(a, b) = \max d_s(t) \cdot \frac{1}{T_2 - T_1} \sum_{t=T_1}^{T_2} d_{\text{vel}}(t),$$

$$t \in [T_1, T_2], \tag{4}$$

$$d_s(t) = |P_a(t) - P_b(t)|_2,$$

$$d_{\text{vel}} = |\Delta P_a(t) - \Delta P_b(t)|_2,$$

where d_s and d_{vel} are the $L2$ distances of the trajectory points at corresponding time instances. We just calculate the distance between the trajectories P_a and P_b simultaneously existing in $[T_1, T_2]$. To ensure the spatial compactness of the estimated groups, we enforce the above affinity to be zero for trajectory pairs that are not spatially close $d_s \geq 30$. The number of clusters in a video is set as the number used in [22] and the number of trajectories in a cluster is below the 100 based on empirical value.

3.2. Second Layer with VLAD. The trajectory group describing the motion part in the same action categories will have similarities. To capture the coarser spatiotemporal characteristics of the descriptors in the group k, we compute the mean of group descriptors (w-HOF, HOF, and MBH) and trajectory shapes. Then, we concatenate all the group descriptors (w-HOF, HOF, and MBH) as G_r and group shape as the group descriptors G_g. So the group is described as $G = \{G_r, G_g\}$; VLAD [9] is a descriptor encoding technique that aggregates the descriptors based on a locality criterion in the feature space. As we know, the classic BOF uses the clustering centers statistics to represent the sample which will result in the loss of the lots of information. In group encoding, we denote the code words in the group codebook as $c_1, c_2, \ldots, c_k$. The group descriptors $G_i^k = \{G_r, G_g\}$ are all the group descriptors that belong to the kth word. The video will be encoded as a vector:

$$v = \left(\sum_{i=1}^{n_1} \left(G_i^1 - c_1 \right), \ldots, \sum_{i=1}^{n_k} \left(G_i^k - c_k \right) \right), \quad (5)$$

where k is the size of codebook learned by the k-means clustering. So the VLAD keeps more information than the BOF.

3.3. Video Encoding. We encode each video from the group descriptors of motion part using VLAD model. The codebook for each kind of group descriptors (w-HOF, HOF, MBH, and S) was separately constructed by using K-means cluster. According to the average number of groups in every video, we set the number of visual words to 50. In order to find the nearest center quickly we construct a KD-tree when each group descriptors are mapped to the codebook. We describe video encoding vector with the group model for different descriptors. Then, motion part model is encoded by the concatenation of different descriptors of the group VLAD model. Finally, the representation for action recognition is encoded by the concatenation of low-level local descriptors encoding and mid-level motion part encoding. Figure 2 shows an overview of our pipeline for action recognition.

4. Experiments

In this section, we implement some experiments to evaluate the performance of representation for action. We validate our model on several action recognition benchmarks and compare our results with different methods.

4.1. Datasets. We validate our model on three standard datasets for human action: KTH, J-HMDB, and YouTube dataset. The KTH dataset views actions in front of a uniform background, whereas the J-HMDB dataset [10] and YouTube dataset [16] are collected from a variety of sources ranging from digitized movies to YouTube. They cover different scales and difficulty levels for action recognition. We summarize them and the experimental protocols as follows.

The KTH dataset [23] contains 6 action categories: walking, handclapping, hand waving, jogging, running, and walking. The background is homogeneous and static in most sequences. We follow the experimental setting [23] dividing the dataset into the train set and test set. We train a multiclass

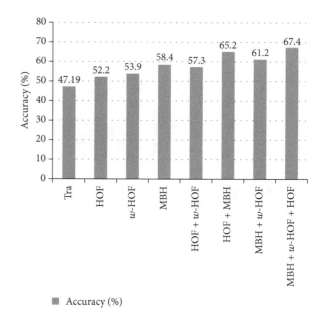

FIGURE 3: Illustration on the effect of our descriptors with FV encoding. Each bar corresponds to one of the feature descriptors or feature combinations.

classifier and report average accuracy over all classes as performance measure.

The J-HMDB [10] contains 21 action categories: brush hair, catch, clap, climb stairs, golf, jump, kick ball, pick, pour, pull-up, push, run, shoot ball, shoot bow, shoot gun, sit, stand, swing baseball, throw, walk, and wave. J-HMDB is a subset of the HMDB51 which is collected from the movies or Internet. This dataset excludes categories from HMDB51 that contain facial expressions like smiling and interactions with others such as shaking hands and focuses on single body action. We evaluate the J-HMDB which contains 11 categories involving one single body action. For multiclass classification, we use the one-vs-rest approach.

The YouTube Action dataset [16] contains 11 action categories: basketball, biking, diving, golf swinging, horse riding, soccer juggling, swinging, tennis swinging, trampoline jumping, volleyball spiking, and walking with a dog. Because of the large variations in camera motion, appearance, and pose, it is a challenging dataset. Following [16], we use leave-one-group-out cross-validation and report the average accuracy over all classes.

4.2. Experiment Result. The proposed method extract one-scale w-flow trajectory-based local features through tracking dense sampling interest points and, then, cluster the trajectories into groups to encode motion part.

In order to choose a discriminative combination of features to represent the low-level local descriptors, we evaluate the low-level local descriptors based on w-flow dense trajectories with Fisher Vector encoding in the first baseline experiment. GMM with 256 components is learned from a subset of 256,000 randomly selected trajectory-based local descriptors. Linear SVM with $c = 100$ is used as classifier. We compare different feature descriptors in Figure 3 where

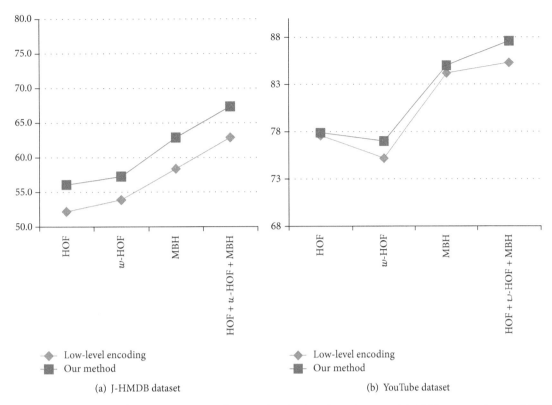

FIGURE 4: The accuracy of different features comparisons between low-level and two-layer model. (a) The comparison on J-HMDB dataset. (b) The comparison on YouTube dataset.

TABLE 1: The accuracy comparisons of representation for action recognition on J-HMDB dataset and YouTube dataset.

Datasets	Features	Low-level encoding	Two-layer model
JHMDB	HOF	52.2%	56.1%
	w-HOF	53.9%	57.3%
	MBH	58.4%	62.9%
	HOF + w-HOF + MBH	62.9%	67.4%
YouTube	HOF	77.6%	77.9%
	w-HOF	75.2%	77.0%
	MBH	84.2%	85.0%
	HOF + w-HOF + MBH	85.3%	87.6%

the average accuracy on J-HMDB dataset is reported. It can be seen that MBH descriptors, encoding the relative motion between pixels, work better than other descriptors. Figure 3 also shows that the combination of HOF, w-HOF, and MBH descriptors achieves 67.4%, which is the highest precision among all kinds of the low-level local descriptors. So, we use this combination in the second experiment.

In the second baseline experiment, the proposed two-layer model of the representation for action is the concatenation of low-level local descriptors and motion part descriptors encoding. Table 1 and Figure 4 compare the two-layer method with the low-level method for J-HMDB and YouTube datasets. It can be seen that the two-layer model

had better performance than the low-level encoding using different descriptors. In addition, we compare the proposed method with a few classic methods on KTH, J-HMDB, and YouTube datasets, such as DT + BoVW [1], mid-level parts [21], traditional FV [17], stacked FV [17], DT + BOW [10], and IDT + FV [17]. As shown in Table 2, the two-layer model obtains 67.4% and 87.6% accuracy on J-HMDB and YouTube datasets, respectively. And the recognition accuracy is improved by 4.6% on J-HMDB dataset and 2.2% on YouTube dataset compared with other state of the art methods. However, the performance on KTH dataset of the proposed method is not the same better as on the J-HMDB and YouTube datasets, because the KTH dataset is collected by the fixed camera with homogeneous background and the advantage of the w-flow trajectories is not shown in this case.

5. Conclusions

This paper proposed a two-layer model of representation for action recognition based on local descriptors and motion part descriptors, which achieved an improvement compared to the low-level local descriptors. Not only did it consider making use of low-level local information to encoding the video, but also it combined the motion part to represent the video. It also presented a discriminative and compact representation for action recognition. However, there is still room for improvement. First, the proposed method cannot determine the number of groups in different datasets while the number of groups affects the performance of mid-level encoding a

TABLE 2: Accuracy comparisons of different methods on KTH, YouTube and J-HMDB datasets.

KTH		YouTube		J-HMDB	
ISA [15]	86.5%	Liu et al. [16]	71.2%	Traditional FV [17]	62.83%
Yeffet and Wolf [18]	90.1%	Ikizler-Cinbis and Sclaroff [19]	75.21%	Stacked FV [17]	59.27%
Cheng et al. [20]	89.7%	DT + BoVW [1]	85.4%	DT + BOW [10]	56.6%
Le et al. [15]	93.9%	Mid-level parts [21]	84.5%	IDT + FV [17]	62.8%
Two-layer model	92.6%	Two-layer model	87.6%	Two-layer model	67.4%

lot. Second, many groups in video do not represent the action part; it is needed to develop a method to learn the discriminately groups for better representation of the video. In the future, we will do research on new group clustering method which can find the more discriminative groups of action part.

Conflicts of Interest

The authors declare that there are no conflicts of interest regarding the publication of this paper.

References

[1] H. Wang, A. Klaser, C. Schmid, and C.-L. Liu, "Dense trajectories and motion boundary descriptors for action recognition," *International Journal of Computer Vision*, vol. 103, no. 1, pp. 60–79, 2013.

[2] Y. Wang, B. Wang, Y. Yu, Q. Dai, and Z. Tu, "Action-Gons: Action recognition with a discriminative dictionary of structured elements with varying granularity," *Lecture Notes in Computer Science (including subseries Lecture Notes in Artificial Intelligence and Lecture Notes in Bioinformatics): Preface*, vol. 9007, pp. 259–274, 2015.

[3] I. Laptev, M. Marszałek, C. Schmid, and B. Rozenfeld, "Learning realistic human actions from movies," in *Proceedings of the 26th IEEE Conference on Computer Vision and Pattern Recognition (CVPR '08)*, June 2008.

[4] I. Laptev, "On space-time interest points," *International Journal of Computer Vision*, vol. 64, no. 2-3, pp. 107–123, 2005.

[5] J. Wu, Y. Zhang, and W. Lin, "Towards good practices for action video encoding," in *Proceedings of the 27th IEEE Conference on Computer Vision and Pattern Recognition, CVPR 2014*, pp. 2577–2584, Columbus, OH, USA, June 2014.

[6] S. Sadanand and J. J. Corso, "Action bank: a high-level representation of activity in video," in *Proceedings of the IEEE Conference on Computer Vision and Pattern Recognition (CVPR '12)*, pp. 1234–1241, June 2012.

[7] L. M. Wang, Y. Qiao, and X. Tang, "Motionlets: Mid-level 3D parts for human motion recognition," in *Proceedings of the 26th IEEE Conference on Computer Vision and Pattern Recognition (CVPR '13)*, pp. 2674–2681, June 2013.

[8] W. Chen and J. J. Corso, "Action detection by implicit intentional motion clustering," in *Proceedings of the 15th IEEE International Conference on Computer Vision, ICCV 2015*, pp. 3298–3306, chl, December 2015.

[9] H. Jégou, F. Perronnin, M. Douze, J. Sánchez, P. Pérez, and C. Schmid, "Aggregating local image descriptors into compact codes," *IEEE Transactions on Pattern Analysis and Machine Intelligence*, vol. 34, no. 9, pp. 1704–1716, 2012.

[10] H. Jhuang, J. Gall, S. Zuffi, C. Schmid, and M. J. Black, "Towards understanding action recognition," in *Proceedings of the 2013 14th IEEE International Conference on Computer Vision, ICCV 2013*, pp. 3192–3199, aus, December 2013.

[11] M. Jain, H. Jegou, and P. Bouthemy, "Better exploiting motion for better action recognition," in *Proceedings of the 26th IEEE Conference on Computer Vision and Pattern Recognition, CVPR 2013*, pp. 2555–2562, Portland, OR, USA, June 2013.

[12] H. Wang and C. Schmid, "Action recognition with improved trajectories," in *Proceedings of the 14th IEEE International Conference on Computer Vision (ICCV '13)*, pp. 3551–3558, Sydney, Australia, December 2013.

[13] F. Perronnin, J. Sánchez, and T. Mensink, "Improving the fisher kernel for large-scale image classification," in *Proceedings of the 11th European Conference on Computer Vision (ECCV '10)*, vol. 6314 of *Lecture Notes in Computer Science*, pp. 143–156, Crete, Greece, 2010.

[14] G. Csurka and F. Perronnin, "Fisher vectors: Beyond bag-of-visual-words image representations," *Communications in Computer and Information Science*, vol. 229, pp. 28–42, 2011.

[15] Q. V. Le, W. Y. Zou, S. Y. Yeung, and A. Y. Ng, "Learning hierarchical invariant spatio-temporal features for action recognition with independent subspace analysis," in *Proceedings of the IEEE Conference on Computer Vision and Pattern Recognition (CVPR '11)*, pp. 3361–3368, June 2011.

[16] J. Liu, J. Luo, and M. Shah, "Recognizing realistic actions from videos in the wild," in *Proceedings of the IEEE Computer Society Conference on Computer Vision and Pattern Recognition (CVPR '09)*, pp. 1996–2003, IEEE, Miami, Fla, USA, June 2009.

[17] X. Peng, C. Zou, Y. Qiao, and Q. Peng, "Action recognition with stacked fisher vectors," in *Computer Vision—ECCV 2014: 13th European Conference, Zurich, Switzerland, September 6–12, 2014, Proceedings, Part V*, vol. 8693 of *Lecture Notes in Computer Science*, pp. 581–595, Springer, Berlin, Germany, 2014.

[18] L. Yeffet and L. Wolf, "Local trinary patterns for human action recognition," in *Proceedings of the 12th International Conference on Computer Vision (ICCV '09)*, pp. 492–497, Kyoto, Japan, October 2009.

[19] N. Ikizler-Cinbis and S. Sclaroff, "Object, scene and actions: Combining multiple features for human action recognition," *Lecture Notes in Computer Science (including subseries Lecture Notes in Artificial Intelligence and Lecture Notes in Bioinformatics): Preface*, vol. 6311, no. 1, pp. 494–507, 2010.

[20] G. Cheng, Y. Wan, W. Santiteerakul, S. Tang, and B. P. Buckles, "Action recognition with temporal relationships," in *Proceedings of the 2013 IEEE Conference on Computer Vision and Pattern Recognition Workshops, CVPRW 2013*, pp. 671–675, Portland, OR, USA, June 2013.

[21] M. Sapienza, F. Cuzzolin, and P. H. S. Torr, "Learning discriminative space-time action parts from weakly labelled videos," *International Journal of Computer Vision*, vol. 110, no. 1, pp. 30–47, 2014.

[22] M. Raptis, I. Kokkinos, and S. Soatto, "Discovering discriminative action parts from mid-level video representations," in *Proceedings of the IEEE Conference on Computer Vision and Pattern Recognition (CVPR '12)*, June 2012.

[23] C. Schüldt, I. Laptev, and B. Caputo, "Recognizing human actions: a local SVM approach," in *Proceedings of the 17th International Conference on Pattern Recognition (ICPR '04)*, pp. 32–36, August 2004.

14

Sliding Window Based Machine Learning System for the Left Ventricle Localization in MR Cardiac Images

Abdulkader Helwan and Dilber Uzun Ozsahin

Department of Biomedical Engineering, Near East University, Near East Boulevard, 99138 Nicosia, Northern Cyprus, Mersin 10, Turkey

Correspondence should be addressed to Abdulkader Helwan; abdulkader.helwan90@gmail.com

Academic Editor: Mourad Zaied

The most commonly encountered problem in vision systems includes its capability to suffice for different scenes containing the object of interest to be detected. Generally, the different backgrounds in which the objects of interest are contained significantly dwindle the performance of vision systems. In this work, we design a sliding windows machine learning system for the recognition and detection of left ventricles in MR cardiac images. We leverage on the capability of artificial neural networks to cope with some of the inevitable scene constraints encountered in medical objects detection tasks. We train a backpropagation neural network on samples of left and nonleft ventricles. We reformulate the left ventricles detection task as a machine learning problem and employ an intelligent system (backpropagation neural network) to achieve the detection task. We treat the left ventricle detection problem as binary classification tasks by assigning collected left ventricle samples as one class, and random (nonleft ventricles) objects are the other class. The trained backpropagation neural network is validated to possess a good generalization power by simulating it with a test set. A recognition rate of 100% and 88% is achieved on the training and test set, respectively. The trained backpropagation neural network is used to determine if the sampled region in a target image contains a left ventricle or not. Lastly, we show the effectiveness of the proposed system by comparing the manual detection of left ventricles drawn by medical experts and the automatic detection by the trained network.

1. Introduction

Machine learning (ML) is a form of artificial intelligence (AI) which gives computers the skills to learn without being specifically programmed. It focuses on building computer programs which are subject to change when exposed to new data. Machine learning can be classified as either supervised or unsupervised. Supervised algorithms can apply past knowledge to new data whereas unsupervised algorithms make conclusions from datasets [1–5].

The field of medical imaging has witnessed a delay in embracing the novel ML techniques as compared to other fields. Despite machine learning being virtually new, its concept has been applied to medical imaging for years, particularly in areas of computer-aided diagnosis (CAD) and functional brain mapping [6]. Components of medical imaging (image analysis and reconstruction) tend to benefit from the merger of machine learning with medical

imaging. From this perspective, new methods for image reconstruction and exceptional performance in both clinical and preclinical applications will be achieved [6]. A study [7] sees machine learning as a major tool for current computer-aided analysis (CAD). Previous knowledge acquired from examples provided by medical experts has helped in areas like image registration, image fusion, segmentation, and other analyses steps towards describing accurately the initial data and CAD goals. Other applications of machine learning in medical imaging include but are not limited to tumour classification, tumour diagnosis, image segmentation, image reconstruction, and prediction [3, 6, 7].

In this research we focus on detection tasks employing artificial systems (machines). Such systems are required to "look" at an image and determine if a particular object of interest is contained anywhere in the image, in addition to detecting it. Medical object detection is a task that traditionally belongs to the class of computer vision problems.

It is noteworthy that while humans are very effective and efficient in detecting various complex objects irrespective of scene constraints such as varying background, object scale, object positional translation, object orientation, and object illumination; machines strive to achieve near human performance on object detection. Furthermore, it is stressed that object detection is quite more challenging for machines as compared to object recognition. In object detection, the object of interest to be detected can be positioned in any region of an image, while, in object recognition, the objects of interest to be recognized is usually already segmented, hence, making the recognition less challenging. In order to succeed in a task such as object detection, developed vision models or systems should be capable of coping with the aforementioned scene constraints. More important is that, in robotic systems, medical objects detection tasks are very delicate, requiring utmost accuracy. Since robotic systems are usually interacting with its environments in a somewhat real-time fashion, the consequence of wrongly detecting objects of interest can be very grave or serious.

In this paper, we design a sliding window based machine learning system for the detection of left ventricles in MRI slices. It is important to note that while any other object could have been used to demonstrate the effectiveness of the designed system, we found the detection of left ventricles in highly varying and unconstrained images sufficient. Furthermore, it will be seen later on in this work that the approach implemented for the detection of left ventricles in images can be easily extended and modified to realize the detection of other objects in images.

2. Sliding Window Machine Learning Approach

In the sliding window approach, a window of suitable size, say $m \times n$, is chosen to perform a search over the target image [8, 9]. First, a classifier is trained on a collection of training samples spanning the object of interest for detection as one class and random objects as the other class. Formally, samples belonging to the object of interest for detection are referred to as positive examples, while random object samples of no interest are referred to as negative examples. For a single object detection task, the idea is to train a binary classifier, which determines if the presented object is "positive" or "negative." The trained classifier can then be used to "inspect" a target image by sampling it, starting from the top-left corner. It is noteworthy that the input dimension of the trained classifier is generally a fraction of the size or dimension of the target image; hence, sampling of target images can be achieved.

Some of the classifiers that have found applications within the context of object detection include deep neural network (DNN), convolutional neural network (CNN), and decision trees (DT) [2, 10, 11]. Considering the aforementioned considerations for selecting a suitable classifier for object detection, the support vector machine (SVM), which is a maximum margin classifier, would be an obvious choice, but for the long training time as compared to backpropagation neural network and decision trees. In view of required training time, decision trees (DTs) usually have the least training

time as compared to the support vector machine (SVM) and backpropagation neural network (BPNN); however, decision trees tend to quickly overfit or "memorize" the training data. The consequence is such that the performance of decision trees on the test set (unseen examples) is not competitive. The backpropagation neural network (BPNN) seems to be the modest trade-off between training time and generalization power, since the BPNN has a training time that is in between that of the support vector machine and decision tree and a generalization performance that is better than that of decision trees and competitive with that of the support vector machine [12, 13]. Hence, in this project work, the backpropagation neural network has been used as the classifier for the object detection task.

3. The Proposed Automatic Left Ventricle Detection System

The aim of this work is to develop an artificial vision system that can perform the task of detecting left ventricle in images. In this work, considering challenges such as object illumination, scale, translation, and rotation, which make the detection a complex problem for such an open detection problem, we resolve to implementing an intelligent system which can somewhat graciously cope with the aforementioned detection constraints. Neural network, namely, the backpropagation neural network (BPNN), has been used in this work as the 'brain' behind the detection.

This research is achieved in two phases. First is the left ventricle recognition phase by training a backpropagation neural network (BPNN). The second phase is the detection of left ventricle objects in MRI slices using the backpropagation neural network. The flowchart for the system is shown in Figure 1 and both phases are briefly described below.

3.1. Phase 1: Left Ventricle Object Recognition. In this phase, a backpropagation neural network is trained to recognize left ventricle objects and nonleft ventricle objects. In order to achieve this binary classification task, training data is collected to span both left ventricle images and nonleft ventricle images. The data used for training and testing data are obtained from Sunnybrook Cardiac Data (SCD) [14]. The dataset contains 45 cine-MRI slices collected from a mix of patients and different pathologies such as healthy, hypertrophy, heart failure with infarction, and heart failure without infarction. A subset of 100 images was used for the proposed system training and testing purposes for both phases. Since the actual interest is to develop a system that recognizes left ventricle objects, MRI slices were cropped to have only the left ventricle and are referred to as positive examples or samples. Conversely, images containing random nonleft ventricle images are referred to as negative examples or samples. Note that, for earlier training phases, there was no constraint on the contents of the negative examples except that they do not contain left ventricle objects. However, it was discovered that the negative images can be collected by cropping the other parts of the whole MRI cardiac slice by excluding the left ventricle. This seems to improve the robustness of the system in distinguishing left ventricle and

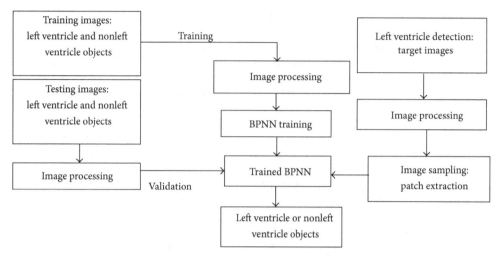

FIGURE 1: Flowchart for developed system.

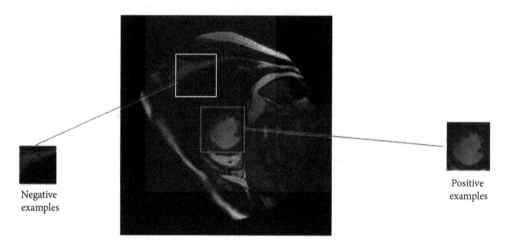

FIGURE 2: Positive and negative examples extraction from the MR images.

nonleft ventricle images. Cropping ventricle and nonventricle images from cardiac MR image is shown in Figure 2.

3.1.1. Image Processing. Since the positive and negative examples are cropped manually, they are of different sizes. Thus, in order to make the images consistent, they are all resized to 40×40 pixels (1600 pixels). Samples of positive and negative examples are shown in Figure 3.

3.1.2. Backpropagation Neural Network (BPNN) Design, Training, and Testing. A backpropagation neural network is trained on the collected samples spanning both positive and negative examples. For the positive examples (left ventricles), 100 samples cropped from different cardiac MRI slices are used, while, for the negative examples (nonleft ventricles), 200 samples are used. The negative images are more because one MR image can provide many negative images where the left ventricle is not included. The positive and negative samples form the training and testing data for the designed backpropagation neural network (BPNN). All images are first rescaled to 40×40 pixels (1600 pixels). The whole dataset is then divided into training and testing data. The testing data

allows the observation of performance of the trained BPNN on unseen or new data. It is very desirable that trained ANNs can perform well on unseen data, that is, generalization. 75 left ventricles and 275 nonleft ventricles are used for training, while 25 left ventricles and 25 nonleft ventricles are used for testing the trained BPNN. Hence, there are a total of 250 training images and 50 testing images.

(a) Input Data and Neurons. Considering that the training images are now 40×40 pixels, the designed BPNN has 1600 input neurons, where each input attribute or pixel is fed into one of the input neurons. Also, note that the input neurons are nonprocessing. That is, they basically receive input pixels and supply them to the hidden layer neurons which are processing neurons.

(b) Hidden Layer Neurons. The hidden layer is where the extraction of input data features that allows the mapping of input data to corresponding target classes is achieved. Unlike the input layer neurons, the hidden layer neurons are processing. Also, each hidden layer neuron receives inputs from all the input layer neurons. In this work, several

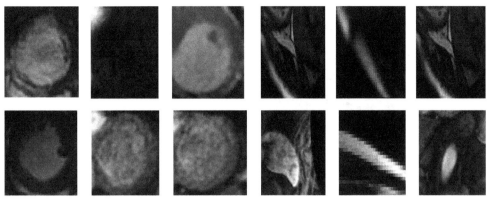

(a) Positive examples (left ventricles)   (b) Negative examples (nonleft ventricles)

FIGURE 3: Samples for (a) left ventricles (positive examples) and (b) nonleft ventricles (negative examples).

TABLE 1: Final training parameters for BPNN.

Network parameters	Values
Number of training samples	250
Number of input neurons	1600
Number of hidden neurons	80
Activation function at hidden and output layers	Log-Sigmoid
Learning rate (η)	0.11
Momentum rate (α)	0.80
Required error (MSE)	0.01
Epochs	1,215
Training time	40 secs

TABLE 2: Recognition rates for BPNN.

Parameter	Training	Testing
Number of samples	250	50
Number of samples correctly classified	255	44
Recognition rates	100%	88%

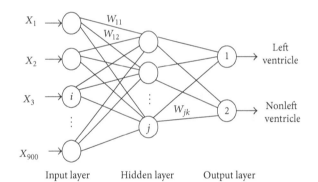

FIGURE 4: Designed backpropagation neural network (BPNN).

experiments are carried out to determine the suitable number of hidden layer neurons. Finally, the number of suitable hidden neurons was obtained as 80 during network training.

(c) Output Layer Coding. Considering that we aim to classify all images as left ventricle object or nonleft ventricle object, the BPNN has two output neurons. The output of the BPNN is coded such that output neurons activations are as shown in the following:

   (i) $\begin{bmatrix} 1 & 0 \end{bmatrix} \rightarrow$ a left ventricle object

   (ii) $\begin{bmatrix} 0 & 1 \end{bmatrix} \rightarrow$ a nonleft ventricle object.

Figure 4 shows the designed BPNN. The BPNN is trained on the processed images described in Figure 3. The final training parameters are shown in Table 1.

The Log-Sigmoid activation function allows neuron's output to be in the range of 0 to 1. From Table 1, it is seen that the BPNN achieve the required error of value 0.01 in 40 secs, with 1,215 epochs. The learning curve for the BPNN is shown in Figure 5.

The trained BPNN is then tested using the training and testing data. Table 2 shows the recognition rates of the BPNN on the training andtesting data.

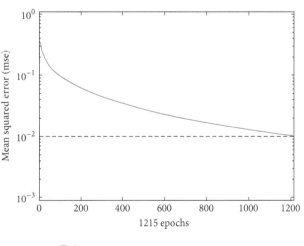

FIGURE 5: Error versus epochs curve for BPNN.

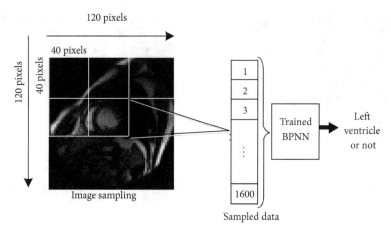

FIGURE 6: Sampling of image for left ventricle detection using trained BPNN.

It is seen in Table 2 that the BPNN achieved a recognition rate of 100% and 88% on the training and testing data, respectively. Note that a testing recognition rate of 88% is enough to show that the BPNN can generalize well on unseen data (images), that is, classifying new images as left ventricle or nonleft ventricle.

3.2. Phase 2: Left Ventricle Detection from Images. In this phase, the trained BPNN is used to detect left ventricles in images containing various objects, background, illumination, scale, and so on. In order to detect left ventricles in new images, the new images are sampled in a nonoverlapping fashion using a sliding window or mask. Firstly, all images in which left ventricles are to be detected are rescaled to 120 × 120 pixels; this significantly reduces the required number of samplings and therefore computations. Note that the new size of images containing left ventricle for detection is selected such that input field (40 × 40 pixels) of the earlier trained BPNN can fit in without falling off image edges.

It therefore follows that if the new images containing left ventricle for detection is rescaled to 120 × 120 pixels, and a sliding window of size 40 × 40 pixels is used for nonoverlapping sampling, 3 samplings are obtained in the *x*-pixel coordinate, and 3 samplings are obtained in the *y*-pixel coordinate; this makes a total of 9 samplings for an image. Figure 6 shows the analogy of the sampling technique.

The sampling outcomes using a sliding window of size 40 × 40 pixels (1600 pixels) is supplied as the input of the trained BPNN as shown in Figure 6. It is expected that, for windows containing a left ventricle, the BPNN gives an output of $[1 \ 0]$, as coded during the BPNN training. Also, it is expected that, for windows not containing left ventricles, the trained BPNN gives an output of $[0 \ 1]$. From the sampling approach described above, it will be observed that 9 samplings (patches) and therefore predictions are made for any target image. The BPNN output with the closest match with the desired output for left ventricle output, $[1 \ 0]$, is selected as containing a left ventricle, that is, with maximum activation value for neuron 1 in Figure 4. It is seen that to achieve the complete detection of left ventricles in images, both phases 1 and 2 are sandwiched together as one module.

4. Performance Evaluation

An example of left ventricle detection for the image shown in Figure 6 is shown in Figure 7 using the developed system. More examples of the left ventricle localizations of different types of MR images are shown in Figures 8 and 9.

The detected left ventricle is highlighted in a rectangular bounding box.

Also, samples of other target images for left ventricle detection using the developed system within this work are shown in Figures 8, 9, and 10. The detected left ventricle objects are highlighted as a rectangular bounding box.

Also, some instances where the developed failed to achieve the correct detection of left ventricle in images are shown in Figure 10.

Generally, most of the approaches provided in the state of the art of left ventricle detection can be considered as some variation of the active contour and segmentation models [15–19]. These models are meant to segment the endocardium and epicardium areas of the left ventricle. In contrast, our proposed model is a general squared detection or localization of the left ventricle in an MRI slice. This model is mainly a machine learning approach that aims to evaluate the effectiveness and capability of a simple backpropagation neural network in sampling an MRI slice for the purpose of finding and detecting a left ventricle object based on a sliding window's approach. The approach here is not to accurately segment the edges of the left ventricle; however, it is to find and localize the left ventricle as an object in the image. Therefore, in some images, a small part of the left ventricle can be undetected, and still this can be considered as a correct detection due to the application type which is to find or localize the left ventricle even though a small part of it is missing. Hence, our results cannot be compared to other research findings since the approach and the techniques used are totally different.

In order to show the effectiveness of the developed system, some left ventricles were manually detected by medical experts to validate our system capability in detecting the left ventricle in MRI slices. The idea is to compare both detections, that is, the network detection and the medical

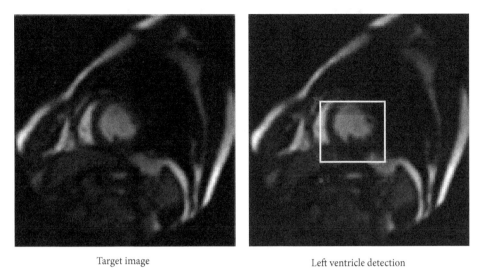

Target image   Left ventricle detection

FIGURE 7: Detection outcome using the developed system (gradient echo sequence, short axis image).

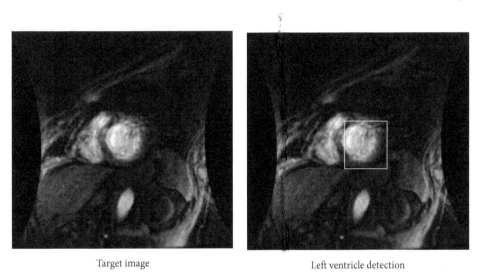

Target image   Left ventricle detection

FIGURE 8: Detection outcome using the developed system (short axis image).

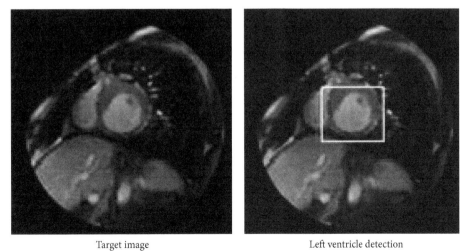

Target image   Left ventricle detection

FIGURE 9: Detection outcome using the developed system (short axis image).

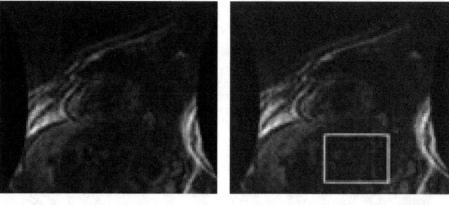

Target image   Incorrect left ventricle detection

FIGURE 10: Wrong detection outcome using the developed system (fast spin echo sequence, FSE).

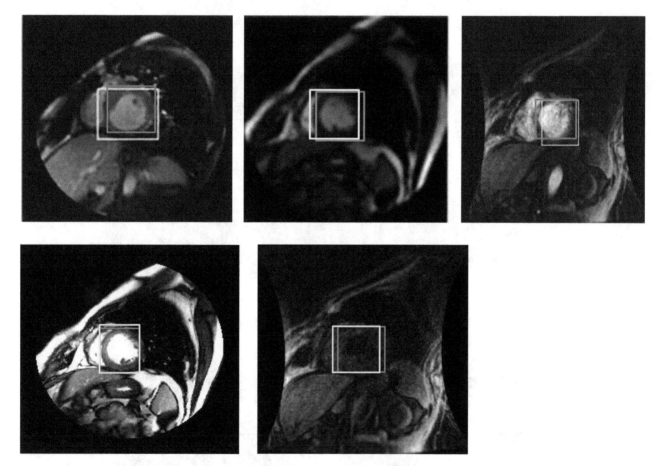

FIGURE 11: Manual and network detection results. Yellow color: network's detection; blue color: expert's manual detection.

expert manual detection of the left ventricles to check if the left ventricles were fit into the detected 40 ∗ 40 square in target images. In other words, it is to check how accurately the system was capable to detect the left ventricle by comparing the detected area to the left ventricle highlighted by the medical expert. Figure 11 illustrates some images where the manual and network's detection of the left ventricle are shown.

5. Results Discussion

Since artificial neural network weights are usually randomly initialized at the start of training, it therefore follows that trained BPNN is not always guaranteed to converge to the global minimum or good local minima. Consequently, the learning of left ventricles and nonleft ventricles can be negatively affected; this therefore affects the detection phase, where the trained BPNN may wrongly predict a sampling window or patch as containing a left ventricle. In order, to solve this problem, the MATLAB program written contains instructions to retrain the BPNN till a testing recognition (relating to BPNN generalization capability) of greater than 80% is obtained. This greatly reduces the BPNN's probability of wrongly predicting a sampling window (patch) as containing a left ventricle. In this project, we have allowed for a maximum of 30 retraining schedules of the BPNN. Therefore, when the MATLAB script for the developed whole detection system is run, it is possible that the BPNN may be automatically retrained a couple of times before the detection task is then executed.

Moreover, another challenge encountered is that even after the BPNN achieves a testing recognition rate of greater than 88%, it is still possible that sampling windows are wrongly classified, though the probability of this happening is quite small. In this project, it is found that when the BPNN achieves a testing recognition of greater than 88%, a maximum of 3 retraining schedules is required to correctly detect a left ventricle in the target image.

This work describes a highly challenging task in computer vision, medical object detection. We show that backpropagation neural network (BPNN) can be employed to learn the robust recognition/classification of left ventricles and nonleft ventricles as positive and negative training examples, respectively. The trained BPNN is then used in a nonoverlapping sampling fashion to "inspect" target images containing left ventricles for detection. The developed system is tested and found to be very effective in the detection of left ventricles in images containing other objects. Also it is important that the developed system is intelligent such that image scene constraints such as translation and scale only slightly affect the overall efficiency of the system.

6. Conclusion

In this research, an artificial vision system for left ventricle detection has been developed. It is important to note that the work in itself is broader than the detection of only left ventricles, since the same insight and approach presented within this work can be used to realize the detection of other objects. Also, considering the broadness of the scenes and environments in which the developed system will be deployed, we opt to reformulating the detection task as that of a machine learning problem. This allows some robustness to the aforementioned scene constraints which may render the developed system quite erroneous on the detection task. A backpropagation neural network (BPNN) has been used as the learning system in this research. The BPNN is trained on samples of left ventricles and nonleft ventricles (random) collected from the same samples. For the detection of left ventricles in target images, a window size (40 × 40 pixels) corresponding to the size of the input to the BPNN is used to sample the target image in a nonoverlapping fashion. The developed system tested some randomly collected target images containing left ventricles without any scene constraints such as the scale, translation, illumination, and orientation of left ventricles contained in the target images. The developed system is seen to perform quite well in detecting cub objects, including scenarios, where left ventricles are even partially occluded. Furthermore, to show the effectiveness and robustness of the developed system, the left ventricles were contoured or detected by medical experts beside the system detection to show the effectiveness and accuracy of the proposed system of performing the left ventricles detection.

Conflicts of Interest

The authors declare that there are no conflicts of interest regarding the publication of this paper.

Acknowledgments

The authors would like to thank Dr. Hadi Sasani for comments on earlier versions of this paper.

References

[1] H. Lee, R. Grosse, R. Ranganath, and A. Y. Ng, "Convolutional deep belief networks for scalable unsupervised learning of hierarchical representations," in *Proceedings of the 26th Annual International Conference (ICML '09)*, pp. 609–616, ACM, Montreal, Canada, June 2009.

[2] O. K. Oyedotun, E. O. Olaniyi, A. Helwan, and A. Khashman, "Hybrid auto encoder network for iris nevus diagnosis considering potential malignancy," in *Proceedings of the International Conference on Advances in Biomedical Engineering (ICABME '15)*, pp. 274–277, September 2015.

[3] A. Helwan and R. H. Abiyev, "ISIBC: an intelligent system for identification of breast cancer," in *Proceedings of International Conference on Advances in Biomedical Engineering (ICABME '15)*, pp. 17–20, September 2015.

[4] A. Helwan and D. P. Tantua, "IKRAI: intelligent knee rheumatoid arthritis identification," *International Journal of Intelligent Systems and Applications*, vol. 8, no. 1, article 18, 2016.

[5] A. Helwan, A. Khashman, E. O. Olaniyi, O. K. Oyedotun, and O. A. Oyedotun, "Seminal quality evaluation with RBF neural network," *Bulletin of the Transilvania University of Brasov, Series III: Mathematics, Informatics, Physics*, vol. 9, no. 2, 2016.

[6] M. Argyrou, D. Maintas, C. Tsoumpas, and E. Stiliaris, "Tomographic image reconstruction based on artificial neural network (ANN) techniques," in *Proceedings of the IEEE Nuclear Science Symposium and Medical Imaging Conference Record (NSS/MIC '12)*, pp. 3324–3327, November 2012.

[7] G. Wang, "A perspective on deep imaging," *IEEE Access*, vol. 4, pp. 8914–8924, 2016.

[8] A. Giusti, D. C. Ciresan, J. Masci, L. M. Gambardella, and J. Schmidhuber, "Fast image scanning with deep max-pooling convolutional neural networks," in *Proceedings of the 20th International Conference on Processing (ICIP '13)*, pp. 4034–4038, September 2013.

[9] H. G. Gouk and A. M. Blake, "Fast sliding window classification with convolutional neural networks," in *Proceedings of the 29th International Conference on Image and Vision Computing*, pp. 114–118, Hamilton, New Zealand, November 2014.

[10] D. Xie, L. Zhang, and L. Bai, "Deep learning in visual computing and signal processing," *Applied Computational Intelligence and Soft Computing*, vol. 2017, Article ID 1320780, pp. 1–13, 2017.

[11] M. Ranzato, Y.-L. Boureau, and Y. Le Cun, "Sparse feature learning for deep belief networks," in *Advances in Neural Information Processing Systems*, pp. 1185–1192, 2008.

[12] P. Kumar, D. K. Gupta, V. N. Mishra, and R. Prasad, "Comparison of support vector machine, artificial neural network, and spectral angle mapper algorithms for crop classification using LISS IV data," *International Journal of Remote Sensing*, vol. 36, no. 6, pp. 1604–1617, 2015.

[13] K. Dimililer, "Backpropagation neural network implementation for medical image compression," *Journal of Applied Mathematics*, vol. 2013, Article ID 453098, 8 pages, 2013.

[14] P. Radau, Y. Lu, K. Connelly, G. Paul, A. J. Dick, and G. A. Wright, "Evaluation framework for algorithms segmenting short axis cardiac MRI," *The MIDAS Journal—Cardiac MR Left Ventricle Segmentation Challenge*, 2009, http://www.midasjournal.org/browse/publication/658.

[15] C. Constantinides, E. Roullot, M. Lefort, and F. Frouin, "Fully automated segmentation of the left ventricle applied to cine MR images: description and results on a database of 45 Subjects," in *Proceedings of the Annual International Conference of the IEEE Engineering in Medicine and Biology Society (EMBC '12)*, pp. 3207–3210, San Diego, Calif, USA, September 2012.

[16] S. Huang, J. Liu, L. Lee et al., "Segmentation of the left ventricle from cine MR images using a comprehensive approach," in *Proceedings of the MICCAI 2009 Workshop on Cardiac MR Left Ventricle Segmentation Challenge. MIDAS Journal*, London, UK, September 2009.

[17] S. Huang, J. Liu, L. C. Lee et al., "An image-based comprehensive approach for automatic segmentation of left ventricle from cardiac short axis cine MR images," *Journal of Digital Imaging*, vol. 24, no. 4, pp. 598–608, 2011.

[18] M. Jolly, "Fully automatic left ventricle segmentation in cardiac cine MR images using registration and minimum surfaces," *The MIDAS Journal—Cardiac MR Left Ventricle Segmentation Challenge*, 2009, http://www.midasjournal.org/browse/publication/684.

[19] L. Marak, J. Cousty, L. Najman, and H. Talbot, "4D Morphological segmentation and the MICCAI LV-segmentation grand challenge," in *Proceedings of the MICCAI 2009 Workshop on Cardiac MR Left Ventricle Segmentation Challenge. MIDAS Journal*, pp. 1–8, MIDAS, France, November 2009, http://www.midasjournal.org/browse/publication/677.

15

Mining Key Skeleton Poses with Latent SVM for Action Recognition

Xiaoqiang Li,[1] **Yi Zhang,**[1] **and Dong Liao**[2]

[1]*School of Computer Engineering and Science, Shanghai University, Shanghai, China*
[2]*School of Mathematic and Statistics, Nanyang Normal University, Nanyang, China*

Correspondence should be addressed to Xiaoqiang Li; xqli@i.shu.edu.cn and Dong Liao; liaodong@nynu.edu.cn

Academic Editor: Lei Zhang

Human action recognition based on 3D skeleton has become an active research field in recent years with the recently developed commodity depth sensors. Most published methods analyze an entire 3D depth data, construct mid-level part representations, or use trajectory descriptor of spatial-temporal interest point for recognizing human activities. Unlike previous work, a novel and simple action representation is proposed in this paper which models the action as a sequence of inconsecutive and discriminative skeleton poses, named as key skeleton poses. The pairwise relative positions of skeleton joints are used as feature of the skeleton poses which are mined with the aid of the latent support vector machine (latent SVM). The advantage of our method is resisting against intraclass variation such as noise and large nonlinear temporal deformation of human action. We evaluate the proposed approach on three benchmark action datasets captured by Kinect devices: MSR Action 3D dataset, UTKinect Action dataset, and Florence 3D Action dataset. The detailed experimental results demonstrate that the proposed approach achieves superior performance to the state-of-the-art skeleton-based action recognition methods.

1. Introduction

The task of automatic human action recognition has been studied over the last few decades as an important area of computer vision research. It has many applications including video surveillance, human computer interfaces, sports video analysis, and video retrieval. Despite remarkable research efforts and many encouraging advances in the past decade, accurate recognition of the human actions is still a quite challenging task [1].

In traditional RGB videos, human action recognition mainly focuses on analyzing spatiotemporal volumes and representation of spatiotemporal volumes. According to the variety of visual spatiotemporal descriptors, human action recognition work can be classified into three categories. The first category is local spatiotemporal descriptors. An action recognition method first detects interesting points (e.g., STIPs [2] or trajectories [3]) and then computes descriptors (e.g., HOG/HOF [2] and HOG3D [4]) based on the detected local motion volumes. These local features are then combined (e.g., bag-of-words) to represent actions. The second

category is global spatiotemporal templates that represent the entire action. A variety of image measurements have been proposed to populate such templates, including optical flow and spatiotemporal orientations [5, 6] descriptors. Except the local and holistic representational method, the third category is mid-level part representations which model moderate portions of the action. Here, parts have been proposed which capture a neighborhood of spacetime [7, 8] or a spatial key frame [9]. These representations attempt to balance the trade-off between generality exhibited by small patches, for example, visual words, and the specificity by large ones, for example, holistic templates. In addition, with the advent of inexpensive RGB-depth sensors such as Microsoft Kinect [10], a lot of efforts have been made to extract features for action recognition in depth data and skeletons. Reference [11] represents each depth frame as a bag of 3D points along the human silhouette and utilizes HMM to model the temporal dynamics. Reference [12] learns semilocal features automatically from the data with an efficient random sampling approach. Reference [13] selects most informative joints based on the

FIGURE 1: Two athletes perform the same action (diving water) in different way.

discriminative measures of each joint. Inspired by [14], Sei-denari et al. model the movements of the human body using kinematic chains and perform action recognition by Nearest-Neighbor classifier [15]. In [16], skeleton sequences are represented as trajectories in an n-dimensional space; then these trajectories are then interpreted in a Riemannian manifold (shape space). Recognition is finally performed using kNN classification on this manifold. Reference [17] extracts a sparse set of active joint coordinates and maps these coordinates to lower-dimensional linear manifold before training an SVM classifier. The methods above generally extract the spatial-temporal representation of the skeleton sequences with well-designed handcrafted features. Recently, with the developing of deep learning, several Recurrent Neural Networks (RNN) models have been proposed for action recognition. In order to recognize actions according to the relative motion between limbs and the trunk, [18] uses an end-to-end hierarchical RNN for skeleton-based action recognition. Reference [19] uses skeleton sequences to regularize the learning of Long Short Term Memory (LSTM), which is grounded via deep Convolutional Neural Network (DCNN) onto the video for action recognition.

Most of the above methods relied on entire video sequences (RGB or RGBD) to perform action recognition, in which spatiotemporal volumes were always selected as representative feature of action. These methods will suffer from sensitivity to intraclass variation such as temporal scale or partial occlusions. For example, Figure 1 shows that two athletes perform some different poses when diving water, which makes the spatiotemporal volumes different. Motivated by this case, the question we seek to answer in this paper is whether a few inconsecutive key skeleton poses are enough to perform action recognition. As far as we know, this is an unresolved issue, which has not yet been systematically investigated. In our early work [20], it has been proven that some human actions could be recognized with only a few inconsecutive and discriminative frames for RGB video sequences. Related to our work, very short snippets [9] and discriminative action-specific patches [21] are proposed as representation of specific action. However, in contrast to our method, these two methods focused on consecutive frame.

In this paper, a novel framework is proposed for action recognition in which key skeleton poses are selected as representation of action in RGBD video sequences. In order to make our method more robust to translation, rotation, and scaling, Procrustes analysis [22] is conducted on 3D skeleton joint data. Then, the pairwise relative positions of the 3D skeleton joints are computed as discriminative features to represent the human movement. Finally, key skeleton poses, defined as the most representative skeleton model of the action, are mined from the 3D skeleton videos with the help of latent support vector machine (latent SVM) [23]. In early exploration experiments, we noticed that the number of the inconsecutive key skeleton poses is no smaller than 4. During testing, the temporal position and similarity of each of the key poses are compared with the model of the action. The proposed approach has been evaluated on three benchmark datasets: MSR Action 3D [24] dataset, UTKinect Action dataset [25], and Florence 3D Action dataset [26]; all are captured with Kinect devices. Experimental results demonstrate that the proposed approach achieves better recognition accuracy than a few existing methods. The remainder of this paper is organized as follows. The proposed approach is elaborated in Section 2 including the feature extracting, key poses mining, and action recognizing. Experimental results are shown and analyzed in Section 3. Finally, we conclude this paper in Section 4.

2. Proposed Approach

Due to the large performance variation of an action, the appearance, temporal structure, and motion cues exhibit large intraclass variability. So selecting the inconsecutive and discriminative key poses is a promising method to represent the action. In this section, we answer the question of what are and how to find the discriminative key poses.

2.1. Definition of the Key Poses and Model Structure. The structure of the proposed approach is shown in Figure 2. Each action model is composed of a few key poses, and each key pose in the model will be represented by three parts: (1) a linear classifier $g_i(x)$ which can discriminate the key

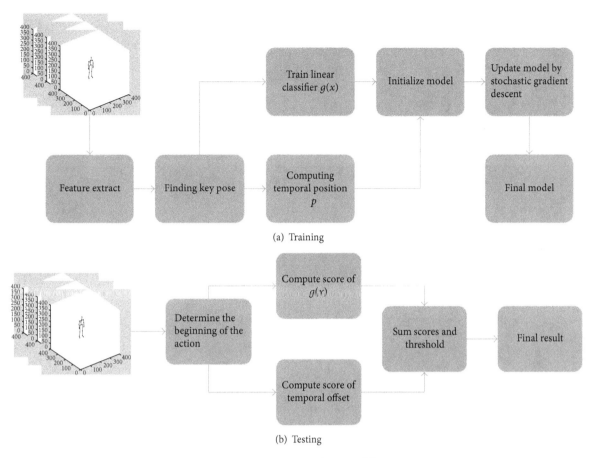

(a) Training

(b) Testing

FIGURE 2: Structure of our model.

pose from the others, (2) the temporal position p_i and offset o_i, where the key poses i are most likely to appear in the neighborhood of p_i with radius o_i, and (3) the weight of linear classifier w_{g_i} and weight of the temporal information w_{p_i}.

Given is a video that contains m frames $X = \{x_1, \ldots, x_m\}$, where x_i is the i-th frame of the video. The score will be computed as follows:

$$f\left(X_{T^n}\right) = \max_{t \in T^n} \sum_{i=1}^{n} \left(w_{g_i} \times g\left(x_{t_i}\right) + w_{p_i} \times \Delta t_i\right), \quad (1)$$

in which X_{T^n} is the set of key poses of video X, $T^n = \{t \mid t = (t_1, \ldots, t_n), \ 1 \le t_i \le m\}$, and $x_{t_i} \in X_{T^n}$. For example, T^n is $\{1, 9, 10, 28\}$ in Figure 3(a). n is the total number of key poses in the action model; in our following experiment, n is ranging from 1 to 20. t_i is the serial number of the key pose in the sequence of frames of video. And Δt_i is defined as follows:

$$\Delta t_i = \frac{1}{2\pi o_i} \exp\left(\frac{-\left(t_i - t_0 - p_i\right)^2}{2 o_i^2}\right), \quad (2)$$

in which t_0 is the frame at which action begins. Δt is a Gaussian function and reaches peak when $t_i - t_0 = p_i$. t_0 has been manually labeled on the training set. The method of finding t_0 in a testing will be discussed in Section 2.4.

2.2. Feature Extracting and Linear Classifier. With the help of real-time skeleton estimation algorithm, the 3D joint positions are employed to characterize the motion of the human body. Following the methods [1], we also represent the human movement as the pairwise relative positions of the joints.

For a human skeleton, joint positions are tracked by the skeleton estimation algorithm and each joint j has 3 coordinates at each frame. The coordinates are normalized based on Procrustes analysis [22], so that the motion is invariant to the initial body orientation and the body size. For a given frame $x = \{j_{1_x}, j_{1_y}, j_{1_z}, \ldots, j_{n_x}, j_{n_y}, j_{n_z}\}$, n is the number of joints. The feature of this frame $\varphi(x)$ is

$$\varphi(x) = \left\{j_{a,b} \mid j_{a,b} = j_a - j_b, \ 1 \le a < b \le n\right\}$$

$$+ \left\{j_{1_x}, j_{1_y}, j_{1_z}, \ldots, j_{n_x}, j_{n_y}, j_{n_z}\right\} \quad (3)$$

$$j_a - j_b = \left\{j_{a_x} - j_{b_x}, j_{a_y} - j_{b_y}, j_{a_z} - j_{b_z}\right\}.$$

And the feature is a 630-dimension (570 pairwise relative positions of the joint and 60 joint position coordinates) vector for MSR Action 3D and UTKinect Action dataset. AS for Florence 3D Action dataset, it is a 360-dimension vector. (The

(a) Key poses of drink are 1, 9, 10, and 28 (subject 1, action drink, video 4, total 32 frames)

(b) Key poses of stand up are 1, 3, 10, and 11 (subject 1, action stand up, video 21, total 29 frames)

(c) Key poses of wave are 4, 7, 8, and 12 (subject 2, action wave, video 1, total 13 frames)

(d) Key poses of drink are 5, 7, 9, and 11 (subject 2, action drink, video 3, total 14 frames)

FIGURE 3: Key poses for different action in Florence 3D Actions dataset.

selection of alternative feature representations will be discussed in Experiment Result.) Then, we train a linear classifier for each key pose according to the following equation:

$$g(x) = w \cdot \varphi(x). \tag{4}$$

The question of which frame should be used for training $g(x)$ will be discussed in Section 2.3.

2.3. Latent Key Poses Mining. It is not easy to decide which frames contain the key poses, because key poses' space T^n is too large to enumerate all the possible poses. Enlightened by [23], since the key pose positions are not observable in the training data, we formulate the learning problem as a latent structural SVM, regarding the key pose positions as the latent variable.

Rewrite (1) as follows:

$$f(X) = \max_{t \in T^n} W \cdot \Phi(X, t)$$

$$W = \left(w_{g_1}, w_{p_1}, \ldots, w_{g_n}, w_{p_n} \right) \tag{5}$$

$$\Phi(X, t) = \left(g\left(x_{t_1}\right), \Delta t_1, \ldots, g\left(x_{t_n}\right), \Delta t_n \right),$$

in which $t = (t_1, \ldots, t_n)$ is treated as the latent variable. Given a labeled set $D = \{\langle X_1, Y_1 \rangle, \ldots, \langle X_i, Y_i \rangle, \ldots\}$, where $X_i = \{x_1, \ldots, x_m\}$ and $Y_i \in \{-1, +1\}$, the objective is to minimize the objective function:

$$L_D(W) = \frac{1}{2} \|W\|^2 + C \sum_{i=1}^{n} \max\left(0, 1 - Y_i f\left(X_i\right)\right), \tag{6}$$

Require:

$D_p, D_n, N;$

$pos = 1, neg\_pose = \{x_i \mid i = random(), x_i \in X, X \in D_n\};$

for $i = 1 \dots N$ **do**

    $o_i = 5$

    $\varphi^{exp} = \varphi(x_{pos})$

    where x_{pos} is the pos-th frame of the first video in D_p

    for $X \in D_p$ **do**

        $pos\_pose = \left\{ pos\_pose, \arg\min_{x_j} \left(Euclidean\left(\varphi^{exp}, \varphi\left(x_j\right) \right) \right) \right\}$

        where $pos - o_i < j < pos + o_i$, $x_j \in X$

    end for

    Train $g_i(x)$ with pos_pose and neg_pose

    $p_i = average \{j \mid x_j \in pos\_pose\}$

    for $X \in D_p$ **do**

        For each frame $x_j \in X$, $s[j] = s[j] + g_i(x_j)$

    end for

    $pos = \arg\min_j(s[j])$

end for

Training w_{g_i} and w_{p_i} with linear SVM

ALGORITHM 1

in which C is the penalty parameter. Following [23], the model is first initialized: D_p and D_n are the positive and negative subsets of D, and the model is initialized with N key frames as shown in Algorithm 1. In Algorithm 1, pos_pose and neg_pose are the positive frame set and the negative frame set, respectively. They are used to train the linear classifier $g(x)$. In order to initialize our model, we firstly compute $\varphi(x_{pos})$, the feature of the pos-th frame which belongs to the first video sample in D_p. Then the Euclidean distance between $\varphi(x_{pos})$ and the feature of the frames in other samples in the neighborhood of temporal position pos with radius o_i in D_p is computed. The frame which has the minimum Euclidean distance from $\varphi(x_{pos})$ in each sample is added in pos_pose. Then pos_pose is used to train the linear classifier $g_i(x)$ and choose p_i as the average of frame number in pos_pose. To select the next key pose, pos chose j with the minimum score based on $g_i(x)$ for next loop; in other words, the j-th frame which is most different from previous key pose is selected in the next loop. Finally, all w_{g_i} and w_{p_i} are trained with the linear SVM when Algorithm 1 is completed.

Once the initialization is finished, the model will be iteratively trained as follows. First, to find the optimal value t subjected to $t^{opt} \in T^n$ where $t^{opt} = \arg\max_t(W \cdot \Phi(X, t))$ for each positive video example and update p with the average value of all t^{opt}, the new linear classifier $g(x)$ is trained with modified p for each key pose. Second, (6) is optimized over W, where $f(x) = W \cdot \Phi(X, t^{opt})$ with stochastic gradient descent. Thus, the models are modified to better capture skeleton characteristics for each action.

2.4. Action Recognition with Key Poses. The key technical issue in action recognition in real-world video is that we do not know where the action starts, and searching start position

in all possible places takes a lot of time. Fortunately, the score of each possible start position can be computed, respectively. So a parallel tool such as OpenMP or CUDA might be helpful.

Given a test video X with m frames, first, the skeleton feature score $g(x)$ of each frame has been computed in advance so we could reuse them later. Then for each possible action start position t_0, we compute the score of each key pose x_{t_i} according to the following equation:

$$score = \max_{t_i \geq t_0} \left(w_{g_i} \times g\left(x_{t_i}\right) + w_{p_i} \times \Delta t_i \right). \quad (7)$$

These scores are summed together as the final score of t_0. If the final score is bigger than the threshold, then an action beginning at t_0 has been detected and recognized. Figure 3 shows key poses for different actions in Florence 3D Action dataset.

3. Experiment Result

This section presents all experimental results. First, trying to eliminate the noise generated by translation, scale, and rotation changes of skeleton poses, we preprocess the dataset with Procrustes analysis [22]. And we conduct the experiment for action recognition with or without Procrustes analysis on UTKinect dataset to demonstrate effectiveness of Procrustes analysis. Second, the appropriate feature extraction was selected from four existing feature extraction methods according to experimental result on Florence 3D Action dataset. Third, quantitative experiment is conducted to select the number of inconsecutive key poses. Last, we evaluate our model and compare it with some state-of-the-art method on three benchmark datasets: MSR Action 3D dataset, UTKinect Action dataset, and Florence 3D Action dataset.

3.1. Datasets

(1) Florence 3D Action Dataset. Florence 3D Action dataset [26] was collected at the University of Florence during 2012 and captured using a Kinect camera. It includes 9 activities; 10 subjects were asked to perform the above actions for two or three times. This resulted in a total of 215 activity samples. And each frame contains 15 skeleton joints.

(2) MSR Action 3D Dataset. MSR Action 3D dataset [11] consists of the skeleton data obtained by depth sensor similar to the Microsoft Kinect. The data was captured at a frame rate of 15 frames per second. Each action was performed by 10 subjects in an unconstrained way for two or three times. The set of actions included *high arm wave, horizontal arm wave, hammer, hand catch, forward punch, high throw, draw x, draw tick, draw circle, hand clap, two-hand wave, side boxing, forward kick, side kick, jogging, tennis swing,* and *tennis serve.*

(3) UTKinect Action Dataset. UTKinect Action dataset [24] was captured using a single stationary Kinect and contains 10 actions. Each action is performed twice by 10 subjects in indoor setting. Three synchronized channels (RGB, depth, and skeleton) are recorded with a frame rate of 30 frames per second. The 10 actions are *walk, sit down, stand up, pick up, carry, throw, push, pull, wave hands,* and *clap hands.* It is a challenging dataset due to the huge variations in view point and high intraclass variations. So, this dataset is used to validate the effectiveness of Procrustes analysis [22].

3.2. Data Preprocessing with Procrustes Analysis.
Skeleton data in each frame of a given video usually consists of a fixed number of predefined joints. The position of joint is determined by three coordinates (x, y, z). Figure 4 shows the skeleton definition in MSR Action 3D dataset. It contains 20 joints which could be represented by their coordinates. Regarding raw human skeleton in the video as the features is not a good choice in consideration of the nature of skeleton—rotation, scaling, and translation. So, before the experiment, we should normalize the datasets by Procrustes analysis.

In statistics, Procrustes analysis is a form of statistical shape analysis used to analyze the distribution of a set of shapes and is widely applied to the field of computer vision such as face detection. In this paper, it is used to align the skeleton joints and eliminate the noise owed to rotation, scaling, or translation. Details of Procrustes analysis will be depicted next.

Given a skeleton data with k joints $((x_1, y_1, z_1), (x_2, y_2, z_2), \ldots, (x_k, y_k, z_k))$, the first step is to process the joints with translation transformation. We compute the mean coordinates $(\overline{x}, \overline{y}, \overline{z})$ of all joints and put them on the origin of coordinates. The translation is completed after each joint coordinate subtracting the mean coordinate, denoted as equation $(x_i, y_i, z_i) = (x_i - \overline{x}, y_i - \overline{y}, z_i - \overline{z})$. The purpose of scaling is making mean square root of all joint coordinates equivalent to 1. For the skeleton joints, we compute s according to the following equation:

$$ s = \sqrt{\frac{x_1^2 + y_1^2 + z_1^2 + \cdots + x_k^2 + y_k^2 + z_k^2}{k}}. \tag{8} $$

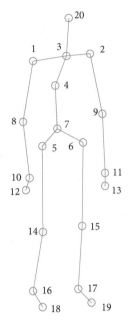

FIGURE 4: Skeleton of MSR Action 3D.

And the scaling result is calculated as follows: $(x_i, y_i, z_i) = (x_i/s, y_i/s, z_i/s)$. The rotation of skeleton is the last step of Procrustes analysis. Removing the rotation is more complex, as standard reference orientation is not always available. Given is a group of standard skeleton joint points $A = ((u_1, v_1, w_1), (u_2, v_2, w_2), \ldots, (u_k, v_k, w_k))$, which represent an action *stand* facing positive direction of x-coordinate axis. The mean coordinate of A is put on the origin of coordinate and the mean square root of coordinate is 1. Then we compute the rotation matrix R for skeleton $B = ((x_1, y_1, z_1), (x_2, y_2, z_2), \ldots, (x_k, y_k, z_k))$ which has been scaled and transformed as aforementioned method by (9), in which M is $3 * 3$ matrix. $U\Sigma V^T$ is the singular value decomposition with orthogonal U and V and diagonal Σ. And the rotation matrix R is equal to matrix V multiplied by the matrix transform of U. At last, skeleton joint points B can be aligned with A through computing R multiplied by B.

$$ M = B^T A $$
$$ M = U\Sigma V^T \tag{9} $$
$$ R = VU^T. $$

We followed the cross-subject test setting of [30] on UTKinect dataset to test the validity of Procrustes analysis. Result is shown in Table 1. It is easy to see that the recognition rate of almost all actions is improved after preprocessing skeleton joint point with Procrustes analysis. In particular, the recognition rate of action *walk* is improved by 10%. It turned out that the translation, scaling, and rotation of human action skeleton in the video affect the recognition accuracy and Procrustes analysis is an effective method to eliminate the influence of geometry transformation.

TABLE 1: Results of action recognition with or without Procrustes analysis.

	Walk	Sit down	Stand up	Pick up	Carry	Throw	Push	Pull	Wave	Clap
with PA	**93%**	**86%**	**91%**	**97%**	**92%**	**88%**	87%	**91%**	**99%**	**91%**
without PA	83%	84%	85%	92%	89%	83%	87%	82%	93%	87%

3.3. Feature Extraction Method Selection. With the deep research on action recognition based on skeleton, there are many efficient feature representations. We select four of them (Pairwise [1], the most informative sequences of joint angles (MIJA) [31], histograms of 3D joints (HOJ3D) [24], and sequence of the most informative joints (SMIJ) [13]) as alternative feature representations.

Given is a skeleton $x = \{j_1, j_2, \ldots, j_n\}$, in which $j_i = (j_{x_i}, j_{y_i}, j_{z_i})$. The Pairwise representation is computed as follows: for each joint a, we extract the pairwise relative position features by taking the difference between the position of joint a and the position of another joint b: $j_{ab} = j_a - j_b$, so the feature of x is $\varphi(x) = \{j_{ab} \mid j_{ab} = j_a - j_b, 1 \le a < b \le n\}$. Due to the informativeness of the original joints, we made an improvement on this representation by concatenating $\varphi(x)$ and x. Then the new feature is $\varphi(x) = \{j_{a,b} \mid j_{a,b} = j_a - j_b, 1 \le a < b \le n\} + \{j_1, j_2, \ldots, j_n\}$.

The most informative sequences of joint angles (MIJA) representation regards joint angle as features. The shape of trajectories of joints encodes local motion patterns for each action. It chooses to use 11 out of the 20 joints capturing information for an action and center the skeleton, using the hip center joint as the origin $(0, 0, 0)$ of the coordinate system. From this origin, vectors to the 3D position of each joint are calculated. For each vector, it computes the angle θ_1 of its projection onto the x-z plane with the positive x-axis and the angle θ_2 between the vector and y-axis. The feature consists of the 2 angles of each joint.

Histograms of 3D joints (HOJ3D) representation chooses 12 discriminative joints of 20 skeletal joints. It takes the hip center as the center of the reference coordinate system and defines x-direction according to left and right hip. The remaining 8 joints are used to compute the 3D spatial histogram. The Spherical Coordinates space is partitioned to 84 bins. And for each joint location, a Gaussian weight function is used for the 3D bins. Counting the votes in each bin and concatenating them, we can get an 84-dimension feature vector.

Sequence of the most informative joints (SMIJ) representation also takes the joint angle as feature but it is different from MIJA. It partitions the joint angle time series of an action sequence into a number of congruent temporal segments and computes the variance of the joint angle time series of each joint over each temporal segment. The top 6 most variable joints in each temporal segment are selected to extract features with mapping function Φ. Here $\Phi(a)$: $\mathbb{R}^{|a|} \to \mathbb{R}$ is a function that maps a time series of scalar values to a single scalar value.

In order to find the optimal feature, we conduct an experiment on Florence 3D Action dataset, in which each video is short. And we estimate other 5 joints coordinates from original 15 joints of each frame in Florence dataset to

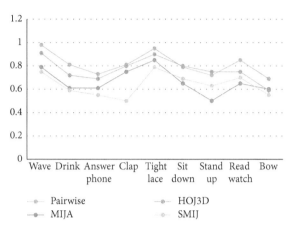

FIGURE 5: Features selection.

make the same joints number of each frame as MSR Action 3D or UTKinect dataset. The experiment takes cross-subject test settings; one half of the dataset is used to train the key pose model and the other is used for testing. The model has 4 key poses and Procrustes analysis has been done before the feature extracting. Results are shown in Figure 5. The overall accuracy of Pairwise feature across 10 actions is better than SMIJ and MIJA. And it is observed that, for all actions except sit down and stand up, the Pairwise representation shows promising results. So, in following experiment, we select Pairwise feature to conduct action recognition experiment. The estimated joints coordinates generate more noise, so the accuracy is lower than the results on original Florence 3D Action dataset (shown in Table 6).

3.4. Selection of Key Pose Numbers. In this section, we implement some experiments to determine how many key poses are necessary for action recognition. The experimental results are shown in Figure 6; the horizontal axis denotes the number of key poses, and the vertical axis denotes recognition accuracy of the proposed approach. The number of key poses ranges from 1 to 20. We can see that the accuracy increases with the number of key poses when the number is less than 4. The accuracy almost achieves maximum values when the number of key poses equals 4, and the accuracy does not increase when the number of key poses is more than 4. To consider the accuracy and computation time, 4 is selected as the number of key poses for recognition action in our following experiment.

Table 2 only enumerates recognition accuracy for each action in UTKinect Action dataset when the number of key poses ranges from 4 to 8. It can be seen that the recognition accuracy varies with different key poses number for one action. However, the average recognition accuracy is nearly

TABLE 2: Recognition accuracy on different number of key poses.

Number	Carry	Clap	Pick	Pull	Push	Sit	Stand	Throw	Walk	Wave	Average
4	0.960	0.870	0.900	0.980	0.930	0.850	0.890	0.890	0.970	0.920	0.915
5	0.910	0.860	0.910	0.970	0.920	0.840	0.900	0.910	0.980	0.930	0.913
6	0.910	0.890	0.920	0.970	0.920	0.910	0.880	0.890	0.980	0.960	0.923
7	0.920	0.870	0.890	0.970	0.940	0.900	0.910	0.890	0.980	0.940	0.921
8	0.900	0.860	0.900	0.990	0.920	0.900	0.920	0.900	0.980	0.940	0.921

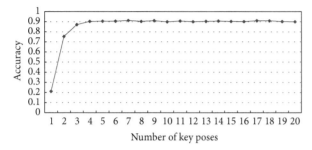

FIGURE 6: How many key poses does the model need?

TABLE 3: The three subsets of actions used in the experiments.

AS1	AS2	AS3
Bend	Draw circle	Forward kick
Forward punch	Draw tick	Golf swing
Hammer	Draw X	High throw
Hand clap	Forward kick	Jogging
High throw	Hand catch	Pick & throw
Horizontal arm wave	High arm wave	Side kick
Pickup & throw	Side boxing	Tennis serve
Tennis serve	Two-hand wave	Tennis swing

TABLE 4: Comparison of our method with the others on AS1, AS2, and AS3.

Action subset	Li et al. [11]	Xia et al. [24]	Yang and Tian [25]	Ours
AS1	72.9%	**89.8%**	80.5%	89.1%
AS2	71.9%	85.5%	73.9%	**88.7%**
AS3	79.2%	63.5%	**95.5%**	94.9%
Average	74.7%	79.6%	83.3%	**90.9%**

TABLE 5: Comparison of our method with the others on MSR Action 3D.

MSR Action 3D	
Histogram of 3D joints [24]	78.97%
EigenJoints [25]	82.30%
Angle similarities [27]	83.53%
Actionlet [1]	88.20%
Spatial and temporal part-sets [28]	90.22%
Covariance descriptors [29]	90.53%
Our approach	**90.94%**

Table 5 shows the results on MSR Action 3D dataset. The average accuracy of the proposed method achieves 90.94%. It is easy to see that our method performs better than the other six methods.

the same with different key poses number, so 4 is the high cost-effective choice.

3.5. Results on MSR Action 3D Dataset. According to the standard protocol provided by Li et al. [11], the dataset was divided into three subsets, shown in Table 3. AS1 and AS2 were intended to group actions with similar movement, while AS3 was intended to group complex actions together. For example, action *hammer* is likely to be confused with *forwardpunch* in AS1 and action *pickup & throw* in AS3 is a composition of *bend* and *high throw* in AS1.

We evaluate our method using a cross-subject test setting: videos of 5 subjects were used to train our model and videos of other 5 subjects were used for test procedure. Table 4 illustrates results for AS1, AS2, and AS3. We compare our performance with Li et al. [11], Xia et al. [24], and Yang and Tian [25]. We can see that our algorithm achieves considerably higher recognition rate than Li et al. [11] in all the testing setups on AS1, AS2, and AS3. For AS2, the accuracy rate of the proposed method is the highest. For AS1 or AS3, our recognition rate is only slightly lower than Xia et al. [24] or Yang and Tian [25], respectively. However, the average accuracy of our method on all three subsets is higher than the other methods.

3.6. Results on UTKinect Action Dataset. On UTKinect dataset, we followed the cross-subject test setting of [30], in which one half of the subjects is used for training our model and the other is used to evaluate the model. And we compare our model with Xia et al. [24] and Gan and Chen [30]. Figure 7 summarizes the results of our model along with competing approaches on UTKinect dataset. We can see that our method achieves the best performance on three actions such as pull, push, and throw. And the most important thing is that the average accuracy of our method achieves 91.5% and is better than the other two methods (90.9% and 91.1% for Xia et al. [24] and Gan and Chen [30], resp.). The accuracy of actions such as *clap hands* and *wave hands* is not so good; the reason may be the fact that the skeleton joint movement ranges of these actions are not large enough and the skeleton data contain more noise. So, it hinders our method from finding the optimal key poses and degrades the accuracy.

3.7. Result on Florence 3D Actions Dataset. We follow the leave-one-actor-out protocol which is suggested by dataset

TABLE 6: Results on Florence 3D Actions dataset.

Subject	1	2	3	4	5	6	7	8	9	10	Average
Wave	0.79	0.83	0.81	0.95	0.95	0.78	0.95	0.83	0.90	0.87	0.87
Drink	0.66	0.83	0.48	0.84	0.70	0.68	0.68	0.87	0.85	0.82	0.74
Answer	0.79	1.00	0.68	0.89	0.65	0.86	0.94	0.96	0.80	0.78	0.84
Clap	1.00	1.00	0.95	0.84	1.00	0.91	1.00	0.92	1.00	0.78	0.94
Tight	0.97	0.94	0.95	1.00	0.95	0.86	0.95	0.92	1.00	0.95	0.95
Sit down	0.72	0.89	0.90	0.90	0.76	0.86	0.79	1.00	0.80	0.91	0.85
Stand up	1.00	0.83	1.00	0.90	0.90	0.90	0.84	0.88	0.95	0.96	0.92
Read watch	0.59	0.89	0.90	0.84	0.75	0.82	0.68	0.75	0.85	0.73	0.78
Bow	0.86	0.89	0.86	1.00	0.85	1.00	1.00	0.96	0.90	0.74	0.91
Average	0.82	0.90	0.84	0.91	0.83	0.85	0.87	0.90	0.89	0.84	0.87

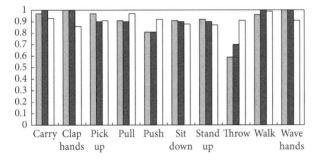

Xia et al. [24]
Gan and Chen [30]
Ours

FIGURE 7: Results on UTKinect Action dataset.

TABLE 7: Comparing of our method with the others on Florence 3D Actions dataset.

Florence 3D Actions		
Seidenari et al. [15]	Devanne et al. [16]	Our approach
82%	87%	87%

4. Conclusion

In this paper, we presented an approach for action recognition based on skeleton by mining the key skeleton poses with latent SVM. Experimental results demonstrated that human actions can be recognized by only a few frames with key skeleton pose; in other words, a few inconsecutive and representative skeleton poses can describe the video action. Starting from feature extraction using the pairwise relative positions of the joints, the positions of key poses are found with the help of latent SVM. Then the model is iteratively trained with positive and negative video examples. In test procedure, a simple method is given by computing the score of each start position to recognize the action.

We validated our model on three benchmark datasets: MSR Action 3D dataset, UTKinect Action dataset, and Florence 3D Action dataset. Experimental results demonstrated that our method outperforms all other methods. Because our method relies on extracting descriptors of simple relative positions of the joints, its performance degrades when the actions are little varied and uninformative, for instance, those actions that were performed only by forearm gestures such as *clap hands* in UTKinect Action dataset. In the future, we will explore the other local features reflecting minor motion for better understanding human action.

Competing Interests

The authors declare that there are no competing interests regarding the publication of this paper.

collector on original Florence 3D Action dataset. All the sequences from 9 out of 10 subjects are used for training, while the remaining one is used for testing. For each subject, we repeat the procedure and average the 10 classification accuracy values at last. For comparison with other methods, average action recognition accuracy is also computed. The experimental results are shown in Table 6. In each column, the data represent each action's recognition accuracy, while the corresponding subject is used for testing. The challenges of this dataset are the human-object interaction and the different ways of performing the same action. By analyzing the experiment result of our method, we can notice that the proposed approach obtains high accuracies for most of the actions. Our method overcomes the difficulty of intraclass variation such as bow and clap. The proposed approach gets lower accuracies for the actions such as answer the phone and read watch; this can be explained by the fact that these actions are human-object interaction with small range of motion and the Pairwise feature could not well reflect the motion. Furthermore, results compared with other methods are listed in Table 7. It is clear that our average accuracy is better than Seidenari et al. [15] and is the same as Devanne et al. [16].

References

[1] J. Wang, Z. Liu, Y. Wu, and J. Yuan, "Learning actionlet ensemble for 3D human action recognition," *IEEE Transactions on Pattern Analysis and Machine Intelligence*, vol. 36, no. 5, pp. 914–927, 2014.

[2] I. Laptev, M. Marszałek, C. Schmid, and B. Rozenfeld, "Learning realistic human actions from movies," in *Proceedings of the 26th IEEE Conference on Computer Vision and Pattern Recognition (CVPR '08)*, pp. 1–8, June 2008.

[3] H. Wang, A. Kläser, C. Schmid, and C.-L. Liu, "Dense trajectories and motion boundary descriptors for action recognition," *International Journal of Computer Vision*, vol. 103, no. 1, pp. 60–79, 2013.

[4] A. Klaser, M. Marszalek, and C. Schmid, "A spatio-temporal descriptor based on 3d-gradients," in *Proceedings of the 19th British Machine Vision Conference (BMVC '08)*, p. 275, British Machine Vision Association, 2008.

[5] K. G. Derpanis, M. Sizintsev, K. J. Cannons, and R. P. Wildes, "Action spotting and recognition based on a spatiotemporal orientation analysis," *IEEE Transactions on Pattern Analysis and Machine Intelligence*, vol. 35, no. 3, pp. 527–540, 2013.

[6] S. Sadanand and J. J. Corso, "Action bank: a high-level representation of activity in video," in *Proceedings of the IEEE Conference on Computer Vision and Pattern Recognition (CVPR '12)*, pp. 1234–1241, IEEE, Providence, RI, USA, June 2012.

[7] A. Fathi and G. Mori, "Action recognition by learning mid-level motion features," in *Proceedings of the 26th IEEE Conference on Computer Vision and Pattern Recognition (CVPR '08)*, pp. 1–8, IEEE, June 2008.

[8] M. Raptis, I. Kokkinos, and S. Soatto, "Discovering discriminative action parts from mid-level video representations," in *Proceedings of the IEEE Conference on Computer Vision and Pattern Recognition (CVPR '12)*, June 2012.

[9] K. Schindler and L. Van Gool, "Action snippets: how many frames does human action recognition require?" in *Proceedings of the 26th IEEE Conference on Computer Vision and Pattern Recognition (CVPR '08)*, pp. 1–8, June 2008.

[10] "kinect—australia," http://www.xbox.com/en-AU/Kinect.

[11] W. Li, Z. Zhang, and Z. Liu, "Action recognition based on a bag of 3D points," in *Proceedings of the IEEE Computer Society Conference on Computer Vision and Pattern Recognition Workshops (CVPRW '10)*, pp. 9–14, IEEE, San Francisco, Calif, USA, June 2010.

[12] J. Wang, Z. Liu, J. Chorowski, Z. Chen, and Y. Wu, "Robust 3D action recognition with random occupancy patterns," in *Computer Vision—ECCV 2012: 12th European Conference on Computer Vision, Florence, Italy, October 7–13, 2012, Proceedings, Part II*, pp. 872–885, Springer, Berlin, Germany, 2012.

[13] F. Ofli, R. Chaudhry, G. Kurillo, R. Vidal, and R. Bajcsy, "Sequence of the most informative joints (SMIJ): a new representation for human skeletal action recognition," *Journal of Visual Communication and Image Representation*, vol. 25, no. 1, pp. 24–38, 2014.

[14] M. Müller and T. Röder, "Motion templates for automatic classification and retrieval of motion capture data," in *Proceedings of the ACM SIGGRAPH/Eurographics Symposium on Computer Animation (SCA '06)*, pp. 137–146, Vienna, Austria, September 2006.

[15] L. Seidenari, V. Varano, S. Berretti, A. Del Bimbo, and P. Pala, "Recognizing actions from depth cameras as weakly aligned multi-part bag-of-poses," in *Proceedings of the IEEE Conference on Computer Vision and Pattern Recognition Workshops (CVPRW '13)*, pp. 479–485, Portland, Ore, USA, June 2013.

[16] M. Devanne, H. Wannous, S. Berretti, P. Pala, M. Daoudi, and A. Del Bimbo, "3-D human action recognition by shape analysis of motion trajectories on riemannian manifold," *IEEE Transactions on Cybernetics*, vol. 45, no. 7, pp. 1340–1352, 2015.

[17] T. Batabyal, T. Chattopadhyay, and D. P. Mukherjee, "Action recognition using joint coordinates of 3D skeleton data," in *Proceedings of the IEEE International Conference on Image Processing (ICIP '15)*, pp. 4107–4111, IEEE, Québec, Canada, September 2015.

[18] Y. Du, Y. Fu, and L. Wang, "Representation learning of temporal dynamics for skeleton-based action recognition," *IEEE Transactions on Image Processing*, vol. 25, no. 7, pp. 3010–3022, 2016.

[19] B. Mahasseni and S. Todorovic, "Regularizing long short term memory with 3D human-skeleton sequences for action recognition," in *Proceedings of the IEEE Conference on Computer Vision and Pattern Recognition (CVPR '16)*, pp. 3054–3062, Las Vegas, NV, USA, June 2016.

[20] X. Li and Q. Yao, "Action detection based on latent key frame," in *Biometric Recognition*, pp. 659–668, Springer, Berlin, Germany, 2015.

[21] W. Zhang, M. Zhu, and K. G. Derpanis, "From actemes to action: a strongly-supervised representation for detailed action understanding," in *Proceedings of the 14th IEEE International Conference on Computer Vision (ICCV '13)*, Sydney, Australia, December 2013.

[22] J. C. Gower, "Generalized procrustes analysis," *Psychometrika*, vol. 40, no. 1, pp. 33–51, 1975.

[23] P. F. Felzenszwalb, R. B. Girshick, D. McAllester, and D. Ramanan, "Object detection with discriminatively trained part-based models," *IEEE Transactions on Pattern Analysis and Machine Intelligence*, vol. 32, no. 9, pp. 1627–1645, 2010.

[24] L. Xia, C.-C. Chen, and J. K. Aggarwal, "View invariant human action recognition using histograms of 3D joints," in *Proceedings of the IEEE Computer Society Conference on Computer Vision and Pattern Recognition Workshops (CVPRW '12)*, pp. 20–27, June 2012.

[25] X. Yang and Y. Tian, "Effective 3D action recognition using EigenJoints," *Journal of Visual Communication and Image Representation*, vol. 25, no. 1, pp. 2–11, 2014.

[26] "Florence 3d actions dataset," http://www.micc.unifi.it/vim/datasets/3dactions/.

[27] C. Wang, Y. Wang, and A. L. Yuille, "An approach to pose-based action recognition," in *Proceedings of the 26th IEEE Conference on Computer Vision and Pattern Recognition (CVPR '13)*, pp. 915–922, IEEE, Portland, Ore, USA, June 2013.

[28] C. Wang, Y. Wang, and A. L. Yuille, "An approach to pose-based action recognition," in *Proceedings of the 26th IEEE Conference on Computer Vision and Pattern Recognition (CVPR '13)*, pp. 915–922, Portland, Ore, USA, June 2013.

[29] M. E. Hussein, M. Torki, M. A. Gowayyed, and M. El-Saban, "Human action recognition using a temporal hierarchy of covariance descriptors on 3d joint locations," in *Proceedings of the 23rd International Joint Conference on Artificial Intelligence (IJCAI '13)*, pp. 2466–2472, Beijing, China, August 2013.

[30] L. Gan and F. Chen, "Human action recognition using APJ3D and random forests," *Journal of Software*, vol. 8, no. 9, pp. 2238–2245, 2013.

[31] H. Pazhoumand-Dar, C.-P. Lam, and M. Masek, "Joint movement similarities for robust 3D action recognition using skeletal data," *Journal of Visual Communication and Image Representation*, vol. 30, article no. 1493, pp. 10–21, 2015.

16

Local Community Detection Algorithm Based on Minimal Cluster

Yong Zhou, Guibin Sun, Yan Xing, Ranran Zhou, and Zhixiao Wang

School of Computer Science and Technology, China University of Mining and Technology, Xuzhou 221008, China

Correspondence should be addressed to Yan Xing; xingyan_cumt@163.com

Academic Editor: Wu Deng

In order to discover the structure of local community more effectively, this paper puts forward a new local community detection algorithm based on minimal cluster. Most of the local community detection algorithms begin from one node. The agglomeration ability of a single node must be less than multiple nodes, so the beginning of the community extension of the algorithm in this paper is no longer from the initial node only but from a node cluster containing this initial node and nodes in the cluster are relatively densely connected with each other. The algorithm mainly includes two phases. First it detects the minimal cluster and then finds the local community extended from the minimal cluster. Experimental results show that the quality of the local community detected by our algorithm is much better than other algorithms no matter in real networks or in simulated networks.

1. Introduction

Community detection on complex networks has been a hot research field. Recently, a large number of algorithms for studying the global structure of the network are proposed, such as the modularity optimization algorithms [1, 2], the spectral clustering algorithms [3–6], the hierarchical clustering algorithms [7–10], and the label propagation algorithms [11–14]. However, with the continuous expansion of complex networks, it is easy to collect large network dataset with millions of nodes. How to store such a large-scale dataset in computer memory to analyze is a huge challenge for scholars. The calculation for studying the overall structure of this kind of large-scale networks is unimaginable. So local community detection becomes an appealing problem and has drawn more and more attention [15–18]. The main task of local community detection is to find a community using the local information of the network. Local community detection has good extensibility. If the local community detection algorithm is iteratively executed, more local communities can be found and the whole community structure of the network can be obtained. The time complexity of this kind of global community detection algorithm is dependent on the efficiency and accuracy of local community detection algorithms, so the research of local community detection

algorithm still has a long way to go. There are several problems that need to be solved in the research of local community detection. First, we should determine the initial state and find the initial node for local community detection, so as to determine the needed local information; then, we need to select an objective function, and through continuous iterative optimization of the objective function we find the community structure with high quality; after that we need to find a suitable node expansion method, so that the algorithm can extract the local community from the initial state step by step; finally, in order to terminate the algorithm, a suitable termination condition is needed to determine the boundary of the community.

Most of local community detection algorithms are based on the above-mentioned process. The definition of local community detection is to find the local community structure from one or more nodes, but most of the existing local community detection algorithms, including Clauset [15], LWP [16], and LS [17], are starting from only one initial node. They greedily select the optimal nodes from the candidate nodes and add them into the local community. LMD [18] algorithm extends not from the initial node but from its closest and next closest local degree central nodes. It discovers a local community from each of these nodes, respectively. It still starts from single node and discovers

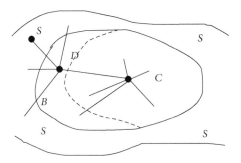

FIGURE 1: Definition of local community.

many local communities for the initial node. In general, the aggregation ability of a single node is lower than that of multiple nodes. So we do not just rely on the initial node as the beginning of local community expansion. Our primary goal is to find a minimal cluster closely connected to the initial node and then detect local community based on the minimal cluster. This can avoid instability because of the excessive dependence on the initial node. In this paper, we introduce a local community detection algorithm based on the minimal cluster—NewLCD. In this new algorithm, the beginning of community expansion is no longer from the initial node only, but a cluster of nodes relatively closely connected to the initial node. The algorithm mainly consists of two parts: one is the detection of the minimal cluster, and the other is the detection of the local community based on the minimal cluster. At the same time, the algorithm can be applied to the global community detection. After finding one local community using this algorithm, we can repeat the process to obtain the global community structure of the whole network.

2. Related Works of Local Community Detection

2.1. Definition of Local Community. The problem of local community detection is proposed by Clauset [15]. Usually we define the local community problem in the following way: there is a nondirected graph $G = (V, E)$, V represents the set of nodes, and E represents the edges in the graph. The connecting information of partial nodes in the graph is known or can be obtained. The local community is defined as D. The set of nodes connected with D is defined as S and the set of nodes in D connected with nodes in S is defined as the boundary node set B. That is to say, any node in B is connected to one node in S, and the rest of D is the core node set C, as shown in Figure 1.

Local community detection problem is to start from a preselected source node. It adds the node meeting the conditions in S into D and removes the node which does not meet the conditions from D gradually.

2.2. Related Algorithms. At present, many local community detection algorithms have been proposed. We introduce two representative local community detection algorithms.

(1) Clauset Algorithm. In order to solve the problem of local community detection, Clauset [15] put forward the local

community modularity R and gave a fast convergence greedy algorithm to find the local community with the greatest modularity.

The definition of local community modularity is as follows:

$$R = \frac{\sum_{ij} A_{ij}\delta\,(i,j)}{\sum_{ij} A_{ij}}, \tag{1}$$

where i and j represent two nodes in the graph. If nodes i and j are connected, the value of A_{ij} is 1; otherwise, it is 0; if nodes i and j are both in D, the value of $\delta(i, j)$ is 1; otherwise, it is 0.

The local community detection process of Clauset algorithm is similar to that of web crawler algorithm. First, Clauset algorithm starts from an initial node v. Node v is added to the subgraph D, and all its neighbor nodes are added to S. Then the algorithm adds the node in S which can bring the maximum increment of R into the local community iteratively, until the scale of the local community reaches the preset size. That is to say, the algorithm needs to set up a parameter to decide the size of the community, and the result is greatly influenced by the initial node.

(2) LWP Algorithm. LWP [16] algorithm is an improved algorithm and it has a clear end condition compared with Clauset algorithm. The algorithm defines another local community modularity M, which is expressed as

$$M = \frac{(1/2) \sum_{ij} A_{ij}\delta\,(i,j)}{\sum_{ij} \lambda\,(i,j)}, \tag{2}$$

where i and j represent two nodes in the graph. If nodes i and j are connected to each other, the value of A_{ij} is 1; otherwise, it is 0; if nodes i and j are both in D, the value of $\delta(i, j)$ is 1; otherwise, it is 0; if only one of the nodes i and j is in D, the value of $\lambda(i, j)$ is 1; otherwise, it is 0.

Given an undirected and unweighted graph $G(V, E)$, LWP algorithm starts from an initial node to find a subgraph with maximum value of M. If the subgraph is a community (i.e., $M > 1$), then it returns the subgraph as a community. Otherwise, it is considered that there is no community that can be found starting from this initial node. For an initial node, LWP algorithm finds a subgraph with the maximum value of local modularity M by two steps. First, the algorithm is initialized by constructing a subgraph with only an initial node v and all the neighbor nodes of node v are added to the set S. Then the algorithm performs incremental step and pruning step.

In the incremental step, the node selected from S which can make the local modularity of D increase with the highest value is added to D iteratively. The greedy algorithm will iteratively add nodes in S to D, until no node in S can be added. In the pruning step, if the local modularity of D becomes larger when removing a node from D, then really remove it from D. In the process of pruning, the algorithm must ensure that the connectivity of S is not destroyed until no node can be removed. Then update the set S and repeat the two steps until there is no change in the process. The algorithm has a high Recall, but its accuracy is low.

The complexity of these two algorithms is $O(K^2 d)$, where K is the number of nodes to be explored in the local community and d is the average degree of the nodes to be explored in the local community.

3. Description of the Proposed Algorithm

3.1. Discovery of Minimal Cluster. Generally, a network can be described by a graph $G = (V, E)$, where V is the set of nodes and E is the set of edges. It contains n nodes and m edges. C represents a node set of a local community in the network and $|C|$ is the number of nodes in C. We introduce two definitions related to the algorithm proposed in this paper.

Definition 1 (neighbor node set). It is a set of nodes connected directly to a single node or a community.

For node i, its neighbor node set can be expressed as $N(i) = \{j \mid (i, j) \in E\}$.

For community C containing n nodes, its neighbor node set can be expressed as follows:

$$N(C) = \bigcup_{i=1}^{n} N(i) - \bigcup_{i=1}^{n} i. \tag{3}$$

Definition 2 (number of shared neighbors). The number of shared neighbors for nodes i and j can be calculated as

$$W(i, j) = |N(i) \cap N(j)|. \tag{4}$$

The minimal cluster detection is the key of the algorithm. The minimal cluster is the set of nodes that connect to the initial node most closely. We introduce a method proposed in [22] to find the nodes that are closely connected with the initial nodes. It uses the density function Ψ [23] which is widely used and can be calculated as

$$\Psi(C) = \frac{|C^{in}|}{\binom{|C|}{2}},$$
$$\binom{|C|}{2} = \frac{|C|(|C| - 1)}{2}, \tag{5}$$

where $|C^{in}|$ represents the number of edges in community C and $|C|$ represents the number of nodes in community C. The larger $\Psi(C)$ is, the more densely the nodes in C are connected. It is necessary to set a threshold $\tau(C)$ for $\Psi(C)$ to decide which nodes are selected to form the initial minimal cluster. Reference [22] gave the definition of this threshold function as shown in

$$\tau(C) = \frac{\sigma(C)}{\binom{|C|}{2}}, \quad \text{where } \sigma(C) = \binom{|C|}{2}^{1 - 1/\binom{|C|}{2}}. \tag{6}$$

$\tau(C)$ and $\sigma(C)$ are the thresholds to select the nodes that constitute the minimal cluster C. If $\Psi(C) \geq \tau(C)$ or $|C^{in}| \geq \sigma(C)$, these nodes are considered to form a minimal cluster. Compared with other methods, the threshold value does not depend on the artificial setting, but it is totally dependent

```
Input: G = (V, E), v
Output: Minimal Cluster C
(1) C = Φ;
(2) for u ∈ N(v) do
(3)     if W(μ, v) is the largest
(4)         Let C = N(μ) ∩ N(v) ∪ {μ, v};
(5)     end if
(6) end for
(7) return C
```

ALGORITHM 1: Locating minimal cluster.

on the nodes in C, so the uncertainty of the algorithm is reduced. Through this process, all nodes in the network can be assigned to several densely connected clusters. In the process, the constraint conditions of the minimal clusters are relatively strict. Then the global community structure of the network is found by combining these minimal clusters. This is a process from local to global by finding all minimal clusters to obtain the global structure of the network. Our local community detection algorithm only needs to find one community in the global network. Inspired by this idea, we improve this algorithm as shown in Algorithm 1.

In the network G, we want to find the minimal cluster containing node v. First we need to traverse all the neighbors of node v and to find the node u which shares the most neighbors with node v (step 3). Then take nodes u, v and their shared neighbor nodes as the initial minimal cluster (step 4). Generally speaking, node v and its neighbor nodes are most likely to belong to the same community. We find the node u most closely connected with v according to the number of their shared neighbors. The more the number of their shared neighbors is, the more closely the two nodes are connected. That is to say, the nodes connected with both nodes u and v are more likely to belong to the same community. We put them together as the initial minimal cluster of local community expansion, which is effective and reliable verified by experiences.

The process of finding the minimal cluster is illustrated by an example shown in Figure 2. Suppose that we want to find the minimal cluster containing node 1. We need to traverse its neighbor nodes 2, 3, 4, and 6, where $W(1, 2) = 2$, $W(1, 3) = 3$, $W(1, 4) = 1$, and $W(1, 6) = 2$. We can see that node 3 is the most closely connected one to node 1, so the minimal cluster is $C = N(1) \cap N(3) \cup \{1, 3\} = \{1, 2, 3, 4, 6\}$. C is the starting node set of local community extension.

3.2. Detection of Local Community. First of all, we use Algorithm 1 to find the node which is most closely connected to the initial node. We take node u and node v as well as their shared neighbor nodes as the initial minimal cluster. The second part of the algorithm is based on the minimal cluster to carry out the expansion of nodes and finally find the local community. The specific process is shown in Algorithm 2.

In the algorithm, we still use M function used in the LWP algorithm as the criteria of local community expansion. Algorithm 1 can find the initial minimal cluster C. After that,

```
Input: G = (V, E), C
Output: Local Community LC
(01) Let LC = C
(02) Calculate N(LC), M
(03) While N(LC) ≠ Φ do
(04)     foreach u ∈ N(LC)
(05)         if ΔM is the largest
(06)             Let LC = LC ∪ {u}
(07)         End if
(08)     End for
(09)     Update N(LC), M
(10) Until no node can be added into LC
(11) Return LC
```

ALGORITHM 2: Local community detection.

TABLE 1: LFR benchmark network information.

Network ID	N	k	$\max k$	$\min c$	$\max c$	mu
B1	1000	20	50	10	50	0.1~0.9
B2	1000	20	50	20	100	0.1~0.9
B3	5000	20	50	10	50	0.1~0.9
B4	5000	20	50	20	100	0.1~0.9

TABLE 2: Real network information.

Network ID	Name	Number of nodes	Number of edges	Reference
R1	Karate	34	78	[19, 20]
R2	Football	115	613	[19, 21]
R3	Polbooks	105	441	[19]

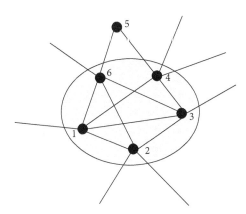

FIGURE 2: The discovery of minimal cluster.

Algorithm 2 finds the neighbor node set $N(LC)$ of LC and calculates the initial value of M (step 02). Then it traverses all the nodes in $N(LC)$ (steps 03-04) to find a node which can make ΔM maximum and add it into the local community LC (steps 05–08); update $N(LC)$ and M (step 09) until no new node is added to LC (step 10).

The complexity of the NewLCD algorithm is almost the same as the Clauset algorithm. The NewLCD algorithm uses extra time of finding minimal cluster which is linear to the degree of the initial node v.

4. Experimental Results and Analysis

In this section, the NewLCD algorithm is compared with several representative local community detection algorithms, namely, LWP, LS, and Clauset, to verify its performance. The experimental environment is the following: Intel (R) Core (TM) i5-2400 CPU @ 3.10 GHz; memory 2 G; operating system: Windows 7; programming language: C#.Net.

4.1. Experimental Data. The dataset of LFR benchmark networks and three real network datasets are used in the experiments.

(1) LFR benchmark networks [24] are currently the most commonly used synthetic networks in community detection.

It includes the following parameters: N is the number of nodes; $\min c$ is the number of nodes that the minimum community contains; $\max c$ is the number of nodes that the biggest community contains; k is the average degree of nodes in the network; $\max k$ is the maximum degree of node; mu is a mixed parameter, which is the probability of nodes connected with nodes of external community. The greater mu is, the more difficult it is to detect the community structure. We generate four groups of LFR benchmark networks. Two groups of networks, B1 and B2, share the common parameters of N = 1000, k = 20, and $\max k$ = 50. The other two groups of networks, B3 and B4, share the common parameters of N = 5000, k = 20, and $\max k$ = 50. The community size $\{\min c, \max c\}$ of B1 and B3 is $\{10, 50\}$ and the community size $\{\min c, \max c\}$ of B2 and B4 is $\{20, 100\}$, implying small community networks and large community networks, respectively; each group contains nine networks with mu ranging from 0.1 to 0.9 representing from low to high hybrid network. The details are shown in Table 1.

(2) We choose three real networks including Zachary's Karate club network (Karate), American college Football network (Football), and American political books network (Polbooks). The detailed information is shown in Table 2.

4.2. Experiments on Artificial Networks. Because of the large size of the synthetic networks, 50 representative nodes are randomly selected from each group as the initial node and all the experimental results are averaged as the final result. Figures 3–6 are the comparison chart of the experimental results of each algorithm on the four groups of LFR benchmark networks (B1–B4). The ordinate represents the three evaluation criteria for local community detection, respectively, and the abscissa is the value of mu (0.1–0.9). The following conclusions can be obtained by observation.

(1) LS and LWP algorithms have higher Precision compared with Clauset algorithm. But their Recall value is lower than Clauset algorithm. LS and LWP algorithms cannot have both high accuracy and Recall. Their comprehensive effect may be not higher than the benchmark algorithm Clauset.

(2) All these three indicators of NewLCD algorithm are significantly higher than Clauset algorithm, which shows that the initial state indeed affects the results of local community

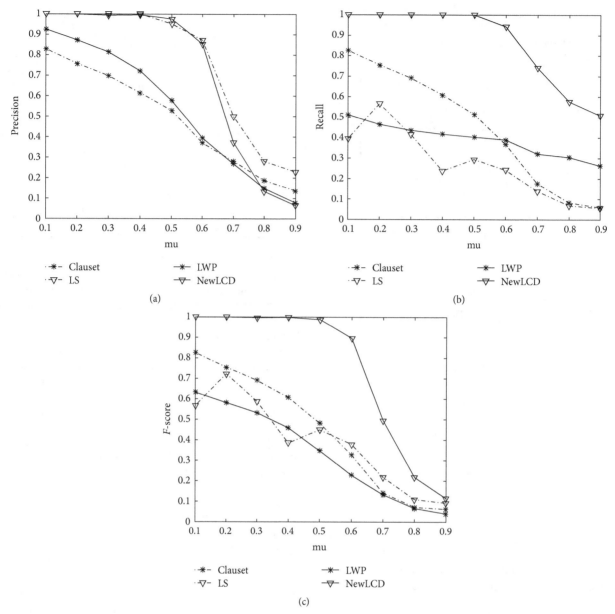

FIGURE 3: Comparison of B1.

detection algorithm, and starting from the minimal cluster is better than a single node.

(3) Overall, NewLCD algorithm is the best. On the four groups of networks, when the parameter mu is less than 0.5, NewLCD algorithm can find almost all the local communities where each node is located. In high hybrid networks, when the value of mu is greater than 0.8, the local community detection effect of NewLCD algorithm is not good, just like other algorithms. The main reason is that the community structure of the network is not obvious.

In summary, NewLCD algorithm can detect better local communities on the artificial networks than the other three local community detection algorithms.

4.3. Experiments on Real Networks. In order to further verify the effectiveness of NewLCD algorithm, we compare

it with three other algorithms on three real networks (Karate, Football, and Polbooks). These three networks are often used to verify the effectiveness of algorithms on complex networks. The experimental results are shown in Table 3 and the maximum values of each indicator are presented in boldface. The maximum value of Precision on Karate is 0.989 obtained by LS algorithm. But its Recall value is just 0.329 which is the minimum value among these four algorithms. So the result of LS algorithm is the worst. On Karate networks, Clauset algorithm and LWP algorithm have the same problem as LS, which means that their Recall value is low. While the Recall and *F*-score values of NewLCD algorithm are the largest, NewLCD algorithm is optimal. On the Football network, the comprehensive effect of NewLCD algorithm is also the best. On the Polbooks network, the advantages of NewLCD algorithm are more obvious, and the three indicators of its

TABLE 3: The comparison of algorithms on the real networks.

Dataset	Evaluation criteria	Clauset	LS	LWP	NewLCD
Karate	Precision	0.927	**0.989**	0.884	0.934
	Recall	0.526	0.329	0.529	**0.809**
	F-score	0.671	0.494	0.662	**0.867**
Football	Precision	0.803	**0.943**	0.680	0.880
	Recall	0.878	0.732	0.712	**0.940**
	F-score	0.839	0.824	0.696	**0.909**
Polbooks	Precision	0.741	0.879	0.770	**0.914**
	Recall	0.442	0.182	0.477	**0.757**
	F-score	0.554	0.301	0.589	**0.828**

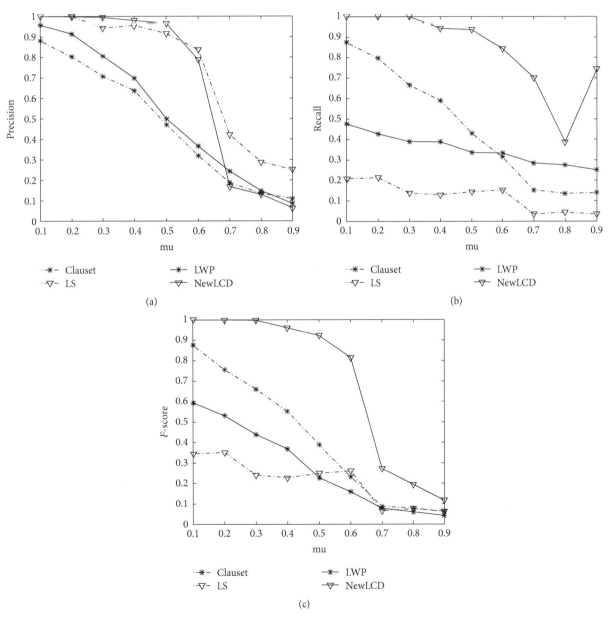

FIGURE 4: Comparison of B2.

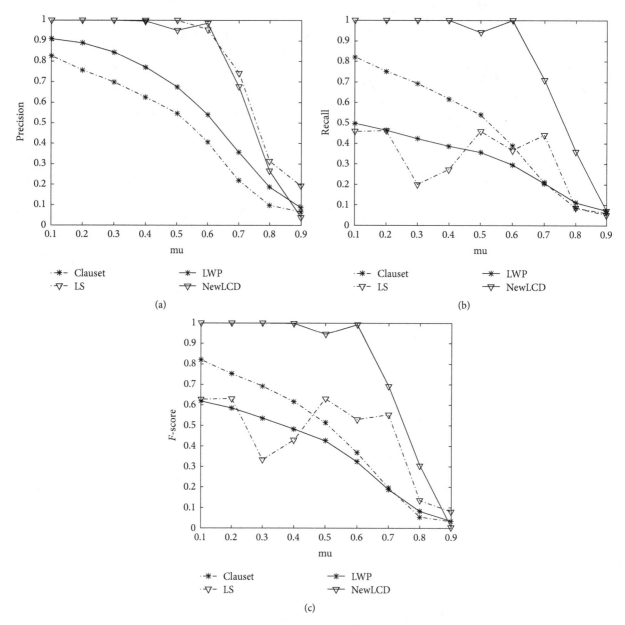

FIGURE 5: Comparison of B3.

results are all the best. In summary, not only can NewLCD algorithm be effectively applied on the artificial network, but it can also be very effective on the real networks.

Karate network is a classic interpersonal relationship network of sociology. It reflects the relationship between managers and trainees in the club. The network is from a Karate club in an American university. The club's administrator and instructor have different opinions on whether to raise the club fee. As a result, the club splits into two independent small clubs. Since the structure of Karate network is simple and it reflects the real world, many community detection algorithms use it as the standard experimental dataset to verify the quality of the community. In order to further verify the effectiveness of the algorithm,

we do a further experiment on Karate. Figure 7 is the real community structure of Karate. If we select node 8 as the initial node, Figures 8 and 9 are, respectively, the local community structure detected by NewLCD and Clauset. {9, 14, 15, 18, 20, 22, 28, 27, 24, 25, 32, 23, 26, 29, 8, 30, 33, 31} is the real local community containing node 8 and {14, 15, 18, 20, 22, 26, 29, 9, 8, 30, 32, 33, 23, 27, 2, 28} is the result of Clauset. We can see that node 2 is assigned to the local community, while nodes 23, 24, 25, and 31 are left out. The community containing node 8 detected by NewLCD is {9, 1415, 18, 20, 22, 28, 27, 24, 25, 32, 23, 26, 29, 8, 2, 30, 33, 31}. Only node 2 is wrongly assigned to the community and there is no omission of any node. The local community detected by NewLCD is more similar to the real one. While a node cannot represent

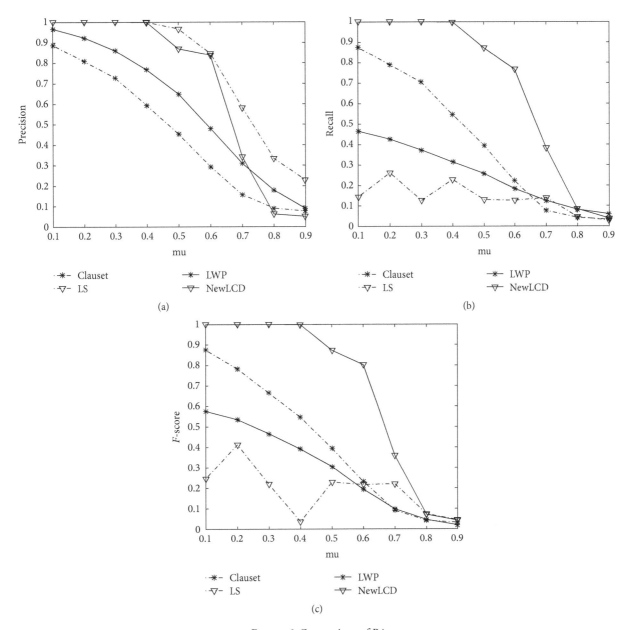

FIGURE 6: Comparison of B4.

all situation, we do more experiments expanding from each node of Karate and compare the corresponding Precision, Recall, and F-score, as shown in Figure 10. The abscissa represents the 34 nodes, from 0 to 33, and the ordinate is F-score, Recall, and Precision, respectively. Although the Precision values of Clauset are slightly higher than the results of NewLCD expanding from nodes {4, 5, 6, 10, 23, 26, 27, 29}, the Recall values of Clauset are far lower than the results of NewLCD. So NewLCD algorithm is much better than Clauset algorithm.

5. Conclusion

This paper proposes a new local community detection algorithm based on minimal cluster—NewLCD. This algorithm

mainly consists of two parts. The first part is to find the initial minimal cluster for local community expansion. The second part is to add nodes from the neighbor node set which meet the local community condition into the local community. We compare the improved algorithm with other three local community detection algorithms on the real and artificial networks. The experimental results show that the proposed algorithm can find the local community structure more effectively than other algorithms.

Competing Interests

The authors declare that there is no conflict of interests regarding the publication of this paper. They declare that they do not have any commercial or associative interest that

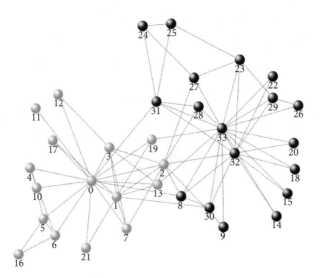

FIGURE 7: The real community structure of Karate.

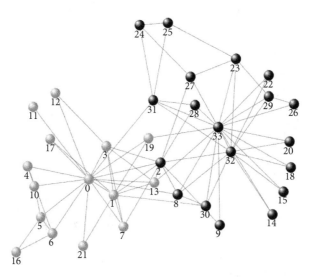

FIGURE 8: The result of NewLCD algorithm on Karate.

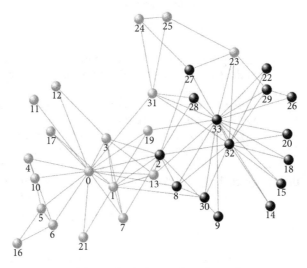

FIGURE 9: The result of Clauset algorithm on Karate.

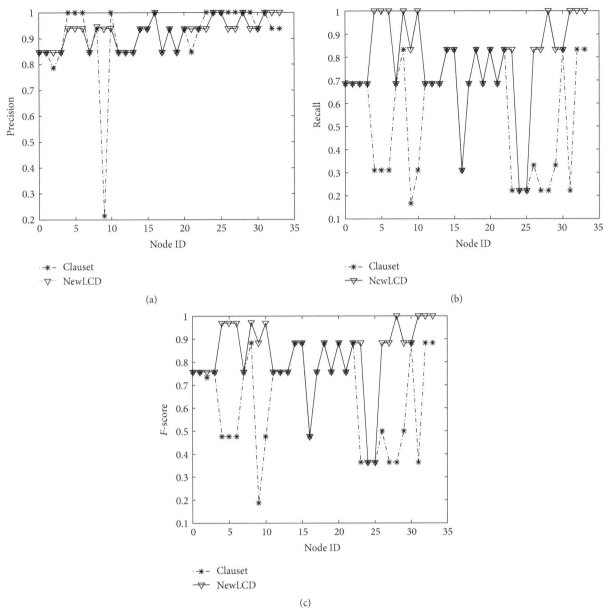

FIGURE 10: The contrast results of each node in Karate.

represents a conflict of interests in connection with the work submitted.

Acknowledgments

This work was supported by the National Natural Science Foundation of China (no. 61572505, no. 51404258, and no. 61402482), the National High Technology Research and Development Program of China (no. 2012AA011004), China Postdoctoral Science Foundation (no. 2015T80555), and Jiangsu Planned Projects for Postdoctoral Research Funds (no. 1501012A).

References

[1] M. E. J. Newman and M. Girvan, "Finding and evaluating community structure in networks," *Physical Review E-Statistical, Nonlinear, and Soft Matter Physics*, vol. 69, no. 2, pp. 292–313, 2004.

[2] J. Lee, S. P. Gross, and J. Lee, "Modularity optimization by conformational space annealing," *Physical Review E*, vol. 85, no. 5, Article ID 056702, pp. 499–508, 2012.

[3] H.-W. Shen and X.-Q. Cheng, "Spectral methods for the detection of network community structure: a comparative analysis," *Journal of Statistical Mechanics: Theory and Experiment*, vol. 2010, no. 10, Article ID P10020, 2010.

[4] J. Wu, Z.-M. Cui, Y.-J. Shi, S.-L. Sheng, and S.-R. Gong, "Local density-based similarity matrix construction for spectral clustering," *Journal on Communications*, vol. 34, no. 3, pp. 14–22, 2013.

[5] S. Mehrkanoon, C. Alzate, R. Mall, R. Langone, and J. A. K. Suykens, "Multiclass semisupervised learning based upon kernel spectral clustering," *IEEE Transactions on Neural Networks and Learning Systems*, vol. 26, no. 4, pp. 720–733, 2015.

[6] K. Taşdemir, B. Yalçin, and I. Yildirim, "Approximate spectral clustering with utilized similarity information using geodesic based hybrid distance measures," *Pattern Recognition*, vol. 48, no. 4, pp. 1461–1473, 2015.

[7] V. D. Blondel, J. Guillaume, R. Lambiotte et al., "Fast unfolding of communities in large networks," *Journal of Statistical Mechanics: Theory and Experiment*, vol. 30, no. 2, pp. 155–168, 2008.

[8] K. M. Tan, D. Witten, and A. Shojaie, "The cluster graphical lasso for improved estimation of Gaussian graphical models," *Computational Statistics and Data Analysis*, vol. 85, pp. 23–36, 2015.

[9] F. De Morsier, D. Tuia, M. Borgeaud, V. Gass, and J.-P. Thiran, "Cluster validity measure and merging system for hierarchical clustering considering outliers," *Pattern Recognition*, vol. 48, no. 4, pp. 1478–1489, 2015.

[10] A. Bouguettaya, Q. Yu, X. Liu, X. Zhou, and A. Song, "Efficient agglomerative hierarchical clustering," *Expert Systems with Applications*, vol. 42, no. 5, pp. 2785–2797, 2015.

[11] L. Subelj and M. Bajec, "Unfolding communities in large complex networks: combining defensive and offensive label propagation for core extraction," *Physical Review E. Statistical, Nonlinear, and Soft Matter Physics*, vol. 83, no. 3, pp. 885–896, 2011.

[12] S. Li, H. Lou, W. Jiang, and J. Tang, "Detecting community structure via synchronous label propagation," *Neurocomputing*, vol. 151, no. 3, pp. 1063–1075, 2015.

[13] Y. Yi, Y. Shi, H. Zhang, J. Wang, and J. Kong, "Label propagation based semi-supervised non-negative matrix factorization for feature extraction," *Neurocomputing*, vol. 149, pp. 1021–1037, 2015.

[14] D. Zikic, B. Glocker, and A. Criminisi, "Encoding atlases by randomized classification forests for efficient multi-atlas label propagation," *Medical Image Analysis*, vol. 18, no. 8, pp. 1262–1273, 2014.

[15] A. Clauset, "Finding local community structure in networks," *Physical Review E—Statistical, Nonlinear, and Soft Matter Physics*, vol. 72, no. 2, pp. 254–271, 2005.

[16] F. Luo, J. Z. Wang, and E. Promislow, "Exploring local community structures in large networks," *Web Intelligence and Agent Systems*, vol. 6, no. 4, pp. 387–400, 2008.

[17] Y. J. Wu, H. Huang, Z. F. Hao, and F. Chen, "Local community detection using link similarity," *Journal of Computer Science and Technology*, vol. 27, no. 6, pp. 1261–1268, 2012.

[18] Q. Chen, T.-T. Wu, and M. Fang, "Detecting local community structures in complex networks based on local degree central nodes," *Physica A: Statistical Mechanics and Its Applications*, vol. 392, no. 3, pp. 529–537, 2013.

[19] http://www-personal.umich.edu/~mejn/netdata/.

[20] W. W. Zachary, "An information flow model for conflict and fission in small groups," *Journal of Anthropological Research*, vol. 33, no. 4, pp. 452–473, 1977.

[21] M. Girvan and M. E. J. Newman, "Community structure in social and biological networks," *Proceedings of the National Academy of Sciences of the United States of America*, vol. 99, no. 12, pp. 7821–7826, 2002.

[22] N. P. Nguyen, T. N. Dinh, S. Tokala, and M. T. Thai, "Overlapping communities in dynamic networks: their detection and mobile applications," in *Proceedings of the 17th Annual International Conference on Mobile Computing and Networking (MobiCom '11)*, pp. 85–95, Las Vegas, Nev, USA, September 2011.

[23] S. Fortunato and C. Castellano, "Community structure in graphs," in *Computational Complexity*, pp. 490–512, Springer, 2012.

[24] A. Lancichinetti, S. Fortunato, and F. Radicchi, "Benchmark graphs for testing community detection algorithms," *Physical Review E*, vol. 78, no. 4, Article ID 046110, pp. 561–570, 2008.

17

CNN-Based Pupil Center Detection for Wearable Gaze Estimation System

Warapon Chinsatit and Takeshi Saitoh

Graduate School of Computer Science and Systems Engineering, Kyushu Institute of Technology, 680–4 Kawazu, Iizuka-shi, Fukuoka 820-8502, Japan

Correspondence should be addressed to Warapon Chinsatit; warapon@slab.ces.kyutech.ac.jp

Academic Editor: Fouad Slimane

This paper presents a convolutional neural network- (CNN-) based pupil center detection method for a wearable gaze estimation system using infrared eye images. Potentially, the pupil center position of a user's eye can be used in various applications, such as human-computer interaction, medical diagnosis, and psychological studies. However, users tend to blink frequently; thus, estimating gaze direction is difficult. The proposed method uses two CNN models. The first CNN model is used to classify the eye state and the second is used to estimate the pupil center position. The classification model filters images with closed eyes and terminates the gaze estimation process when the input image shows a closed eye. In addition, this paper presents a process to create an eye image dataset using a wearable camera. This dataset, which was used to evaluate the proposed method, has approximately 20,000 images and a wide variation of eye states. We evaluated the proposed method from various perspectives. The result shows that the proposed method obtained good accuracy and has the potential for application in wearable device-based gaze estimation.

1. Introduction

People obtain various information through the human vision system. By observing eyes, we can observe changes in pupil size, eye direction, and changes in eye state, for example, opening, closing, blinking, and crying. This information can be used to estimate emotions, traits, or interests. To analyze the eye, eye image processing is an important task, and the development and availability of wearable cameras and recording devices have made eye image processing, including gaze estimation, increasingly popular.

A gaze estimation system (GES) involves multiple cameras, and such systems can estimate gaze direction and what a user is looking at. Thus, GESs can estimate objects of interest. One type of GES uses an inside-out camera [1, 2], which is comprised of an eye camera and a scene camera. The eye camera captures images of the user's eyes. Such a GES detects the pupil center and maps it to a point in the scene image. Recently, GESs have been used in various applications, such as video summarization [3], daily activity

recognition [4], reading [5], human-machine interfaces [6], and communication support [7].

It is difficult to detect the pupil center because the eye is a nonrigid object, users blink frequently, and eyelid or eyelashes can occlude the pupil. Furthermore, the iris has various colors, such as blue, brown, and black. However, when an infrared camera is used to capture eye images, the iris fades out, which makes the pupil clearer. This approach makes the eye image easy to work with. However, blinking remains problematic because it is difficult to detect the pupil center point when a user blinks. Consequently, gaze direction errors can occur.

This research focuses on pupil center detection using infrared eye images captured by a wearable inside-out camera and proposes an accurate detection method that uses a convolutional neural network (CNN). The proposed method is composed of two CNN models. The first determines whether it is possible to detect a pupil in an input image. The second CNN model detects the pupil center in an input eye image. This model outputs the pupil center X- and Y-coordinates.

We evaluated the proposed method using a dataset of infrared eye images captured by our inside-out camera. The results demonstrate that the proposed method demonstrates higher accuracy than other methods.

Typically, CNNs are trained using supervised learning; thus, they require a large training dataset. There are some public datasets of eye images [8, 9]; however, such datasets do not typically include images of eyes in the blink state. We describe a process to capture a sufficiently large image dataset with good distribution and variety of pupil position and eye state.

2. Related Research

Several studies have focused on feature point detection based on eye images [10–13]. Li et al. proposed a hybrid eye-tracking method that integrates feature-based and model-based approaches [10]. They captured eye images using an inexpensive head-mounted camera. Their method detects pupil edge points and uses ellipse fitting to estimate the pupil center. Zheng et al. proposed an algorithm to detect eye feature points, including pupil center and radius, eye corners, and eyelid contours [11]. Moriyama et al. developed a generative eye region model that can meticulously represent the detailed appearance of the eye region for eye motion tracking [12]. Chinsatit and Saitoh proposed a fast and precise eye detection method using gradient value [13]. However, if the eye image contains unexpected objects with a high gradient or intensity, such as an eyelash with mascara or a specular point, it is difficult for such methods to detect the pupil.

CNNs outperform traditional algorithms in various research fields, such as artificial intelligence, image classification, and audio processing. Zhang et al. proposed a CNN-based gaze estimation method in an unconstrained daily life setting [8]. In that method, the input data are an eye image and the 2D head angle, and the output is a 2D gaze angle vector that consists of two gaze angles, that is, yaw and pitch. Fuhl et al. proposed a dual CNN pipeline for image-based pupil detection [14]. Here, the input is an eye image, and the output is an estimated pupil center position. In the first pipeline stage, an input image is downscaled and divided into overlapping subregions. A coarse pupil position is estimated by the first shallow CNN. In the second stage, subregions surrounding the initial estimation are evaluated using a second CNN, and the final pupil center position is detected. Choi et al. proposed a CNN model to categorize driver gaze zones [15]. Here the input image is an eye image, and the outputs are the probabilities of nine gaze zones. As mentioned previously, most related studies that employ CNNs attempt to detect only the center point of a pupil.

The objective of this study is to apply the proposed method to a GES. The proposed method is designed for daily life; thus, it must be robust because it is not always possible to detect the pupil center position, for example, when the eyelid overlays the pupil due to blinking. The proposed method is composed of two CNN models. The first model classifies the input image, as shown in Figure 1. The second model operates in a regression mode [16, 17]. Collectively, this CNN model outputs the X- and Y-coordinates of the pupil center point.

3. Proposed Method

A CNN is composed of a convolutional layer and a fully connected layer. Typically, the fully connected layer is a feed-forward neural network. The effective layer between the input data and the fully connected layer is the convolutional layer, which is used to detect the significant feature point in the input data prior to sending it to the fully connected layer. If the convolutional layer cannot detect the target feature point, it inputs zeros to the fully connected layer. Under this condition, the fully connected layer outputs only the bias effect of each layer. In other words, a CNN outputs a value regardless of the quality of the input data. We employ a CNN model to classify the input data prior to sending it to the detection model.

We describe the classification and detection models in the following subsections.

3.1. Classification Model. There are various CNN classification models, and each model has specific characteristics. AlexNet [18] is a well-known model for classification tasks. We selected this model to classify the eye state. We defined three states in eye images; that is, (1) the image shows the pupil as a full circle (open state), (2) an eyelid overlays the pupil (medium state), and (3) no pupil is observable in the image (closed state).

Some studies have used a separate CNN model to perform specific tasks. For example, Sun et al. created multiple models to detect each feature point [16]. We also propose using two methods, which we refer to as methods A and B. For method A, we create a CNN model to classify the input image as open, medium, or closed eye states, as shown in Figure 1(a). For medium and open eye images, we create two CNN regression models to detect the feature points from each image type. The details of method A's classification and regression models are listed in Table 1 (row 1). If the input image is an open eye image, it will be sent to a CNN model trained using only open eye images. Similarly, if the input image is a medium eye image, it is sent to a CNN model trained using only medium eye images.

The proposed CNN models can potentially solve multiple problems. Note that most previous studies employed an end-to-end CNN model to solve multiple problems. We use method B (Table 1, row 2) to classify input images as closed or nonclosed eye (i.e., open eye and medium eye images, respectively). This classification model selects only nonclosed eye images and sends those images to the CNN trained using nonclosed eye images, as shown in Figure 1(b). Note that we compare the performance of both methods.

A cost function must be defined prior to training the CNN. The training process attempts to minimize this cost function. In the proposed CNN classification model, we use the mean of the sum of squared errors as the cost function, which is expressed as follows:

$$\text{cost} = \frac{\sum_{i=1}^{N_o} (o_i - d_i)^2}{N_o}, \tag{1}$$

where o_i is an estimation output at i, d_i is a label at i, and N_o is the number of output classification results.

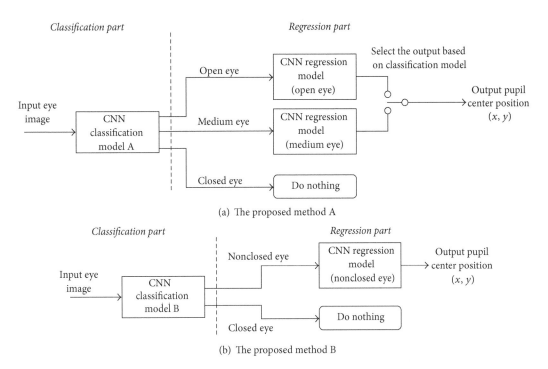

(a) The proposed method A

(b) The proposed method B

Figure 1: Proposed two-part CNN model.

Table 1: Proposed CNN architectures.

Name	Item	Conv1	Conv2	Conv3	Conv4	Conv5	Full1	Full2	Out
Classification model A	Channel	48	128	192	192	128	1024	1024	3 classes
	Filter size	11×11	5×5	3×3	3×3	3×3	—	—	—
	Pooling size	2×2	2×2	2×2	2×2	3×3	—	—	—
	Normalization	yes	—	—	—	—	Yes	Yes	—
	Dropout	—	—	—	—	—	Yes	Yes	—
Classification model B	Channel	48	128	192	192	128	1024	1024	2 classes
	Filter size	11×11	5×5	3×3	3×3	3×3	—	—	—
	Pooling size	2×2	2×2	2×2	2×2	3×3	—	—	—
	Normalization	yes	—	—	—	—	Yes	Yes	—
	Dropout	—	—	—	—	—	Yes	Yes	—
Regression model	Channel	96	256	512	512	512	4096	4096	2 reg.
	Filter size	7×7	5×5	3×3	3×3	3×3	—	—	—
	Pooling size	3×3	2×2	—	—	3×3	—	—	—
	Normalization	yes				—	Yes	Yes	—
	Dropout	—	—	—	—	—	Yes	Yes	—

3.2. Regression Model. The proposed CNN regression model (Table 1, row 3) is based on the pose regression ConvNet [17], which consists of five convolutional layers and three fully connected layers. The collection of convolutional layers is followed by pooling and local response normalization layers, and the fully connected layers are regularized using dropout. All hidden weight layers use a rectification activation (i.e., ReLU) function. Most CNN architectures for object localization use five convolutional layers [17, 19–21]. A difference between pose regression ConvNet and the proposed regression model is the normalization layer. ConvNet has a normalization layer after the last convolutional layer (Conv5).

However, in a preliminary experiment, we found that training using the eye image dataset does not converge when the normalization layer is applied after the final convolutional layer. Thus, we do not employ this architecture. This difference also applies to the fully connected layers. In our architecture, we use local response normalization [18] for Conv1 and use $L2$ normalization for fully connected layers. $L2$ normalization is defined as follows:

$$x'_k = \frac{x_k}{\sqrt{\sum_{i=1}^{N_i} x_i^2}}, \tag{2}$$

FIGURE 2: Collection experiment scene.

where k is the index of input nodes, x_k is the input data at node k, x_k^l is the output from the normalization process at node k, and N_i is the number of data elements in the layer. This normalization process is required for training to converge.

We remove the activation function to make the output value linear. The input to the proposed CNN is an eye image (120×80 pixels). The error function e of the CNN regression model is defined as follows:

$$e = \sqrt{\left(P_x - D_x\right)^2 + \left(P_y - D_y\right)^2}. \qquad (3)$$

This function is the distance between ground truth D and estimated point P.

4. Experiment

4.1. Dataset. A CNN is a supervised learning method that requires a large dataset to train a model. Moreover, a variety of ground truths are required to make the model more accurate. MPIIGaze [8] is a well-known eye image dataset composed of medial canthus, lateral canthus, and pupil points. However, the pupil points are not center points. For a GES, pupil center points are required to calculate gaze direction. In this study, we developed a system to capture a dataset with appropriate variation and reliability using an inside-out camera [2].

We required a dataset that contains blinking eye images to test the performance of the proposed CNN method. Thus, we had to design a system to capture multiple eye images under appropriate conditions. Note that the center of the pupil's position depends on gaze direction. To create the dataset, subjects wore an inside-out camera and observed a marker displayed on a monitor. Next, the system captures an image from the eye camera. We designed an additional process to ensure that the subject focused on the marker position. This capture system selects an arrow (up, right, down, and left) at random and displays it at the center of the marker. The subjects were tasked with pressing a corresponding arrow key. We asked the subjects to blink approximately five times before pressing the key. If the subject pressed the correct key, the capture system saved the eye images to the dataset. This process improved the variation of eye images in the dataset. The image collection environment is shown in Figure 2. Details about the data collection process are described in the following:

(i) We used a 24-inch widescreen display for this experiment, and the distance between the subject and the display was 60 cm. We captured the images for the dataset in a room with sufficient light from both natural and fluorescent light sources.

(ii) We divided the display area into 49 (7×7) sections and show the marker in that section, respectively. First, we shuffle the order of the marker position, in order to make the unpredictable position. The subject has to gaze at the marker without moving the head.

(iii) Then, the user was asked to blink approximately five times. Next, the subject pressed the direction key corresponding to the arrow shown in the center of the marker. The capture program stored 20 eye images captured approximately one second prior to the subject pressing the key. After the eye images were saved, the marker was moved to the next position automatically. This process was repeated 49 times to collect $49 \times 40 = 1960$ eye images.

After collecting all eye images, we manually annotated the pupil center position by one person for avoiding wrong categorization by multiple persons. We categorized the eye images into three classes: open, medium, and closed eyes. Each class is described as follows:

(i) An open eye image clearly shows the edge of the pupil, which makes it easy to estimate the pupil center position.

(ii) A medium eye image shows the eyelid overlaid on some part of the pupil, which makes it difficult to estimate the pupil position.

(iii) A closed eye image shows no pupil, which makes it impossible to estimate the pupil position.

Figure 3 shows sample eye images. Ten subjects (seven males (a)–(g); three females (h)–(j)) participated, and a total of 19,600 eye images were collected. All subjects were normally sighted and did not wear glasses. This dataset has 6,526 open eye images, 6,234 medium eye images, and 6,840 closed eye images.

The distribution of the pupil center position in our dataset is shown in Figure 4. The distributions of open, medium, and closed eye images are shown in Figures 4(b), 4(c), and 4(d), respectively. These distributions show that the number of image types is approximately equal for each section. Note that the pupil center positions were annotated manually. For medium and closed eye images, the exact pupil center position is unknown. We assume the pupil does not move during blinking; thus, we use the same annotation point from a previous open eye image frame, as shown in Figure 5, where the red dot shows the manually annotated ground truth. At frames one and two, the eye is open and easy to annotate. However, in frames three to five, the eye is in the medium or closed states; therefore, for such images, we used the ground truth from frame two.

4.2. Classification Evaluation. We evaluated the classification problem using leave-one-out cross-validation. We used a

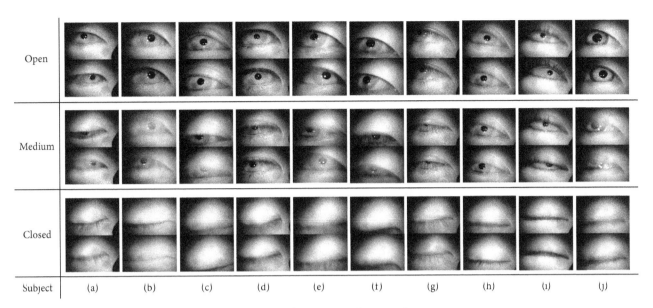

FIGURE 3: Sample eye images from our dataset.

Horizontal section

Vertical section	1	2	3	4	5	6	7	8	9	10	11	12	Total
1	0	0	0	1	0	0	0	0	0	0	0	0	1
2	0	0	0	0	11	0	0	0	0	0	0	0	11
3	0	0	39	813	1016	933	750	296	19	0	0	0	3866
4	0	0	34	1419	2314	2985	1383	504	36	0	0	0	8675
5	0	0	22	706	1186	1546	1367	351	0	0	0	0	5178
6	0	0	32	554	324	446	427	82	0	0	0	2	1867
7	0	0	0	0	0	0	0	0	0	0	0	0	0
8	0	0	0	0	0	0	0	0	0	0	0	2	2
total	0	0	127	3493	4851	5910	3927	1233	55	0	0	4	

(a) All images

Horizontal section

Vertical section	1	2	3	4	5	6	7	8	9	10	11	12	Total
1	0	0	0	0	0	0	0	0	0	0	0	0	0
2	0	0	0	0	6	0	0	0	0	0	0	0	6
3	0	0	0	211	331	278	325	138	11	0	0	0	1294
4	0	0	12	311	707	982	515	208	16	0	0	0	2751
5	0	0	6	254	446	583	537	134	0	0	0	0	1960
6	0	0	21	161	102	100	114	17	0	0	0	0	515
7	0	0	0	0	0	0	0	0	0	0	0	0	0
8	0	0	0	0	0	0	0	0	0	0	0	0	0
total	0	0	39	937	1592	1943	1491	497	27	0	0	0	

(b) Open eye image

Horizontal section

Vertical section	1	2	3	4	5	6	7	8	9	10	11	12	Total
1	0	0	0	0	0	0	0	0	0	0	0	0	0
2	0	0	0	0	2	0	0	0	0	0	0	0	2
3	0	0	19	257	300	289	161	75	5	0	0	0	1106
4	0	0	13	417	752	1034	406	158	7	0	0	0	2787
5	0	0	10	234	332	496	395	124	1	0	0	0	1592
6	0	0	1	212	116	195	184	39	0	0	0	0	747
7	0	0	0	0	0	0	0	0	0	0	0	0	0
8	0	0	0	0	0	0	0	0	0	0	0	0	0
total	0	0	43	1120	1502	2014	1146	396	13	0	0	0	

(c) Medium eye image

Horizontal section

Vertical section	1	2	3	4	5	6	7	8	9	10	11	12	Total
1	0	0	0	1	0	0	0	0	0	0	0	0	1
2	0	0	0	0	3	0	0	0	0	0	0	0	3
3	0	0	20	345	385	366	264	83	3	0	0	0	1466
4	0	0	9	691	855	969	462	138	12	0	0	0	3136
5	0	0	6	218	408	467	435	93	0	0	0	0	1627
6	0	0	10	181	106	151	129	26	0	0	0	2	605
7	0	0	0	0	0	0	0	0	0	0	0	0	0
8	0	0	0	0	0	0	0	0	0	0	0	2	2
total	0	0	45	1436	1757	1953	1290	340	15	0	0	4	

(d) Closed eye image

FIGURE 4: Distributions of our dataset.

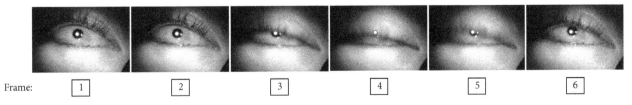

Frame: 1 2 3 4 5 6

FIGURE 5: Annotation of medium and closed eye image.

Table 2: Confusion matrices of CNN classification model.

(a) Classification result of method A

	Predict			
	Open	Medium	Closed	Accuracy
Actual				
Open	5465	1013	48	83.64%
Medium	784	4595	855	73.67%
Closed	0	707	6133	89.66%

(b) Classification result of method B

	Predict		
	Nonclosed	Closed	Accuracy
Actual			
Nonclosed	6596	244	96.43%
Closed	776	6064	88.65%

pretraining model trained using the ImageNet dataset [22] in order to avoid overfitting. The result from the pretraining model are better than without a pretraining model. The classification results of model A are shown in Table 2(a). The accuracy of this model was 82.58%. This result indicates that the accuracy of closed eye images is greater than that of the other classes. Some images for which classification failed are shown in Figure 6. The accuracy of the medium eye case (73.67%) is less than that of other classes because some of the medium eye images were difficult to classify, as shown in Figures 6(c) and 6(d). However, this level of accuracy is reasonable.

Next, we created a model to classify two classes for method B, which we refer to as classification model B. This model was designed to classify closed and nonclosed eye images. To train model B, we randomly selected nonclosed eye images from medium and open eye images to ensure that the number of nonclosed eye images was the same as closed eye images. The classification results of this model are shown in Table 2(b). The overall accuracy of this model was 92.54%, and the accuracy of nonclosed and closed eye images was 96.43% and 88.65%, respectively. This indicates that the classification accuracy of model B is better than that of model A. Classifying closed and nonclosed eye images is easier than doing so for the three classes of eye images because classification model B only classifies two classes, which improves accuracy compared to classification model A. However, all proposed classification models were designed to identify input images for which it is impossible to detect the pupil center position. Thus, both classification models can potentially identify closed eye images effectively.

4.3. Regression Model Evaluation.
We employed leave-one-out cross-validation to evaluate the regression model. As with the classification model, we used models pretrained using the ImageNet dataset [22] before training with our eye dataset. As discussed in Section 3, the input to the regression model is an eye image selected by the classification model. For the regression model, we had to train and evaluate the model using manually annotated eye images; we called the methods A^* and B^*. The regression model was trained using methods

Table 3: Confusion matrix of CNN classification model.

Method	Average error [pixel]			
	A	B	A^*	B^*
Open eye	0.79	—	0.80	—
Medium eye	2.19	—	1.21	—
Total	1.49	1.43	1.00	0.97

A^* and B^* before the regression model was integrated into the CNN classification model. Next, we evaluated the estimated point using an image from the classification model (methods A and B). Methods A and A^* have two CNN regression models to estimate the pupil center position in the specific input image (open and medium eye images). The average errors are shown in Table 3.

Methods A^* and B^* are the situation of classification model having a 100% accuracy. However, when we attempted to detect the pupil position in an image classified by the CNN classification model (methods A and B), the average error was somewhat high. Next, we compared the proposed method to a CNN with no classification model, which we refer to as the simple CNN. This model architecture is the same as the regression model of methods A and B. We trained this model using all eye images in the dataset. Figure 7 shows that the average errors of methods A and B are better than those of the regression model with no classification model. Moreover, we compared the proposed method to other well-known CNNs used in feature point detection research (Sun et al. [16]; Zhang et al. [23]). Sun et al. presented multiple CNN models to detect facial feature points. Zhang et al. presented Coarse-to-Fine Auto-Encoder Networks, which are used to detect multiple facial feature points. We trained the compared models under the same conditions as the simple CNN. The results show that the proposed simple CNN model obtained good accuracy compared to the other models.

Figures 8 and 9 show sample results for the estimated point obtained by method A. Here, the green point is the estimated pupil point, and the blue point is the ground truth

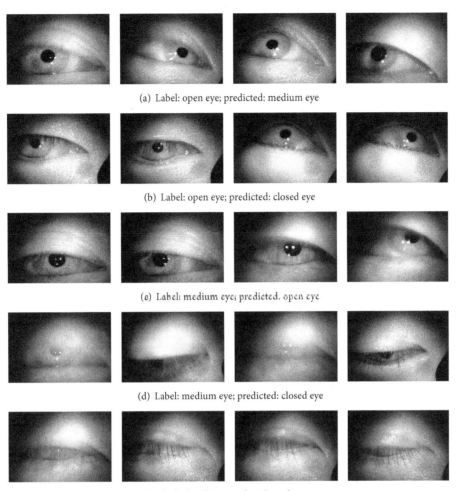

(a) Label: open eye; predicted: medium eye

(b) Label: open eye; predicted: closed eye

(c) Label: medium eye; predicted: open eye

(d) Label: medium eye; predicted: closed eye

(e) Label: closed eye; predicted: medium eye

FIGURE 6: Sample images from the failed classification model.

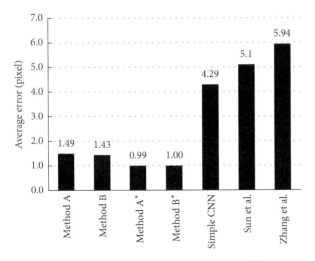

FIGURE 7: Average error of each CNN model.

from our dataset. As can be seen, these points are very accurate, and the estimated point nearly overlays the ground truth. However, for some difficult images in which the pupil is shown in the small part, the CNN generates more errors, as shown in Figure 10.

5. Discussion

We compared the proposed method to the simple CNN model. We also compared the different effects between method A and method B. Methods A^* and B^* represent methods A and B when the classification model achieves 100% accuracy. The results shown in Figure 7 indicate that the success rate of method A^* is better than that of method B^*. This result proves that when we allow the CNN model to learn a specific problem, the model can obtain better results than the single model. However, when we use an input image from the CNN classification, the success rate of method A is slightly less than that of method B because the classification accuracy of method B is better than that of method A. When we consider the difficulty of the classification problem, classifying nonclosed and closed eye images is easier than classifying eye states with three classes (i.e., open, medium, and closed). The single regression model (method B) was trained using both types of image (open and medium). Method B has robustness relative to classification error compared with method A.

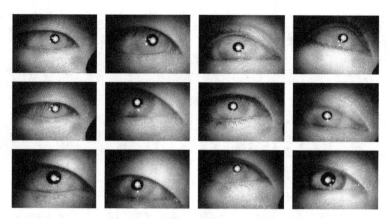

FIGURE 8: Success samples of open eye image.

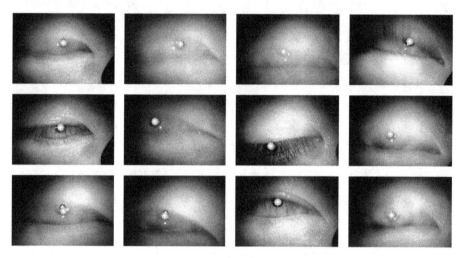

FIGURE 9: Success samples of medium eye image.

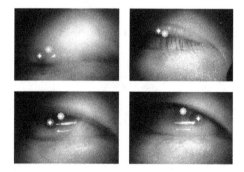

FIGURE 10: Failure samples.

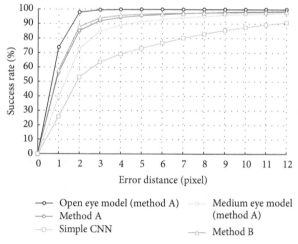

FIGURE 11: Performance curves.

However, the success rate of both models is better than that of the CNN model with no classification model (i.e., the simple CNN) and the compared models. Figure 11 shows the success rate of the proposed method. These results are the ratio of successful images compared to failed images when the distance between the ground truth and estimated point is less than the error distance. When the error distance is greater than four pixels, the success rate of methods A and B is greater than 90%. This shows that the proposed method has the potential for application in gaze estimation tasks.

6. Conclusion

This paper has presented methods to detect the pupil center position using a CNN model. We have focused on a wearable camera-based GES. When using a GES in daily life, it is sometimes impossible to detect the pupil center position from an eye image; thus, this paper has considered avoiding this situation, for example, when blinking obscures the pupil. For supervised learning of the CNN, the dataset required specific features, that is, effective variety, appropriate distributions of image types, and sufficient amounts of data, to make the training process successful. Thus, we created a capture system to construct an original dataset. This original dataset provided closed, open, and medium eye images with good distribution. Using pretrained models, the dataset contained approximately 20,000 images, which is sufficient to train the CNN model effectively.

The proposed CNN method has two parts. The first is the CNN model, which is used to classify the eye state, and the other is the CNN regression model, which detects the pupil center position. The results show that the proposed CNN model has the potential to classify the eye state. Moreover, the accuracy of the pupil detection is better than that of the simple CNN model.

Conflicts of Interest

The authors declare that there are no conflicts of interest regarding the publication of this paper.

References

[1] H. Fujiyoshi, Y. Goto, and M. Kimura, "Inside-out camera for acquiring 3D gaze points," in *Proceedings of the in Proceedings of the Workshop on Egocentric (First-Person) Vision in conjunction with CVPR*, 2012.

[2] J. Iwagami and T. Saitoh, "Easy calibration for gaze estimation using inside-out camera," in *Proceedings of the in Proceedings of the 20th Korea-Japan Joint Workshop on Frontiers of Computer Vision (FCV2014)*, pp. 292–297, 2014.

[3] J. Xu, L. Mukherjee, Y. Li, J. Warner, J. M. Rehg, and V. Singh, "Gaze-enabled egocentric video summarization via constrained submodular maximization," in *Proceedings of the IEEE Conference on Computer Vision and Pattern Recognition, CVPR 2015*, pp. 2235–2244, USA, June 2015.

[4] H. Pirsiavash and D. Ramanan, "Detecting activities of daily living in first-person camera views," in *Proceedings of the 2012 IEEE Conference on Computer Vision and Pattern Recognition, CVPR 2012*, pp. 2847–2854, USA, June 2012.

[5] A. Mazzei, S. Eivazi, Y. Marko, F. Kaplan, and P. Dillenbourg, "3D model-based gaze estimation in natural reading: A systematic error correction procedure based on annotated texts," in *Proceedings of the 8th Symposium on Eye Tracking Research and Applications, ETRA 2014*, pp. 87–90, USA, March 2014.

[6] A. Kiyohiko, N. Yasuhiro, O. Shoichi, and O. Minoru, "A support system for mouse operations using eye-gaze input," *IEEJ Transactions on Electronics, Information and Systems*, vol. 129, no. 9, pp. 11–1713, 2009.

[7] W. Chinsatit, M. Shibuya, K. Kawada, and T. Saitoh, "Character input system using gaze estimation," in *Proceedings of the in Proceedings of the International Conference on Communication Systems and Computing Application Science (CSCAS2016)*, 2016.

[8] X. Zhang, Y. Sugano, M. Fritz, and A. Bulling, "Appearance-based gaze estimation in the wild," in *Proceedings of the IEEE Conference on Computer Vision and Pattern Recognition (CVPR '15)*, pp. 4511–4520, Boston, Mass, USA, June 2015.

[9] Y. Sugano, Y. Matsushita, and Y. Sato, "Learning-by-synthesis for appearance-based 3D gaze estimation," in *Proceedings of the 27th IEEE Conference on Computer Vision and Pattern Recognition (CVPR '14)*, pp. 1821–1828, IEEE, Columbus, Ohio, USA, June 2014.

[10] D. Li, D. Winfield, and D. Parkhurst, "Starburst: A hybrid algorithm for video-based eye tracking combining feature-based and model-based approaches," in *Proceedings of the 2005 IEEE Computer Society Conference on Computer Vision and Pattern Recognition (CVPR'05) - Workshops*, pp. 79-79, San Diego, Calif, USA.

[11] Z. Zheng, J. Yang, and L. Yang, "A robust method for eye features extraction on color image," *Pattern Recognition Letters*, vol. 26, no. 14, pp. 2252–2261, 2005.

[12] T. Moriyama, T. Kanade, J. Xiao, and J. F. Cohn, "Meticulously detailed eye region model and its application to analysis of facial images," *IEEE Transactions on Pattern Analysis and Machine Intelligence*, vol. 28, no. 5, pp. 738–752, 2006.

[13] W. Chinsatit and T. Saitoh, "Eye detection by using gradient value for performance improvement of wearable gaze estimation system," IEICE Technical Report 115, no. 456, 2016, pp. 149-154.

[14] W. Fuhl, T. Santini, G. Kasneci, and E. Kasneci, "Pupilnet: Convolutional neural networks for robust pupil detection," *Computing Research Repository (CoRR)*, 2016, https://arxiv.org/abs/1601.04902.

[15] I.-H. Choi, S. K. Hong, and Y.-G. Kim, "Real-time categorization of driver's gaze zone using the deep learning techniques," in *Proceedings of the International Conference on Big Data and Smart Computing, BigComp 2016*, pp. 143–148, China, January 2016.

[16] Y. Sun, X. Wang, and X. Tang, "Deep convolutional network cascade for facial point detection," in *Proceedings of the 26th IEEE Conference on Computer Vision and Pattern Recognition (CVPR '13)*, pp. 3476–3483, IEEE, Portland, Ore, USA, June 2013.

[17] T. Pfister, K. Simonyan, J. Charles, and A. Zisserman, "Deep convolutional neural networks for efficient pose estimation in gesture videos," *Lecture Notes in Computer Science (including subseries Lecture Notes in Artificial Intelligence and Lecture Notes in Bioinformatics): Preface*, vol. 9003, pp. 538–552, 2015.

[18] A. Krizhevsky, I. Sutskever, and G. E. Hinton, "Imagenet classification with deep convolutional neural networks," in *Proceedings of the 26th Annual Conference on Neural Information Processing Systems (NIPS '12)*, pp. 1097-1105, Lake Tahoe, Nev, USA, December 2012.

[19] P. Sermanet, D. Eigen, X. Zhang, M. Mathieu, R. Fergus, and Y. LeCun, "Overfeat: Integrated recognition, localization and detection using convolutional networks," in *Proceedings of the in Proceedings of the International Conference on Learning Representations (ICLR2014)*, 2014.

[20] M. Oquab, L. Bottou, I. Laptev, and J. Sivic, "Learning and transferring mid-level image representations using convolutional neural networks," in *Proceedings of the 27th IEEE Conference on Computer Vision and Pattern Recognition (CVPR '14)*, pp. 1717–1724, IEEE, Columbus, Ohio, USA, June 2014.

[21] M. Oquab, L. Bottou, I. Laptev, and J. Sivic, "Is object localization for free? - Weakly-supervised learning with convolutional neural networks," in *Proceedings of the IEEE Conference on Computer Vision and Pattern Recognition, CVPR 2015*, pp. 685–694, June 2015.

[22] O. Russakovsky, J. Deng, H. Su et al., "ImageNet large scale visual recognition challenge," *International Journal of Computer Vision*, vol. 115, no. 3, pp. 211–252, 2015.

[23] J. Zhang, S. Shan, M. Kan, and X. Chen, "Coarse-to-Fine Auto-encoder Networks (CFAN) for real-time face alignment," *Lecture Notes in Computer Science (including subseries Lecture Notes in Artificial Intelligence and Lecture Notes in Bioinformatics): Preface*, vol. 8690, no. 2, pp. 1–16, 2014.

18

Modeling Punching Shear Capacity of Fiber-Reinforced Polymer Concrete Slabs: A Comparative Study of Instance-Based and Neural Network Learning

Nhat-Duc Hoang,[1] **Duy-Thang Vu,**[2] **Xuan-Linh Tran,**[1] **and Van-Duc Tran**[3]

[1]*Institute of Research and Development, Faculty of Civil Engineering, Duy Tan University, K7/25 Quang Trung, Danang, Vietnam*
[2]*Faculty of Architecture, Duy Tan University, K7/25 Quang Trung, Danang, Vietnam*
[3]*International School, Duy Tan University, 254 Nguyen Van Linh, Danang 550000, Vietnam*

Correspondence should be addressed to Nhat-Duc Hoang; hoangnhatduc@dtu.edu.vn

Academic Editor: Lukasz Sadowski

This study investigates an adaptive-weighted instanced-based learning, for the prediction of the ultimate punching shear capacity (UPSC) of fiber-reinforced polymer- (FRP-) reinforced slabs. The concept of the new method is to employ the Differential Evolution to construct an adaptive instance-based regression model. The performance of the proposed model is compared to those of Artificial Neural Network (ANN) and traditional formula-based methods. A dataset which contains the testing results of FRP-reinforced concrete slabs has been collected to establish and verify new approach. This study shows that the investigated instance-based regression model is capable of delivering the prediction result which is far more accurate than traditional formulas and very competitive with the black-box approach of ANN. Furthermore, the proposed adaptive-weighted instanced-based learning provides a means for quantifying the relevancy of each factor used for the prediction of UPSC of FRP-reinforced slabs.

1. Introduction

In civil engineering, fiber-reinforced polymer (FRP) composites have been increasingly employed due to their strength and stiffness, good thermomechanical properties, capacity for resisting corrosion, low weight, and outstanding durability [1–4]. It is proper to note that corrosion of steel reinforcement is the major factor which influences the deterioration and shortens the service life of reinforced concrete structures [5–7]. Thus, the utilizations of FRP composites have created the condition for enhancing the productivity of construction process, meliorating the performance of concrete structures, reduction of maintenance budgets spent for infrastructure, and possible elongation of structure service lives [8, 9].

Steel-reinforced two-way flat slabs are popular structural systems that can simplify and accelerate on-site operations and facilitate flexible partitioning of space [10]. The two-way flat slabs are particularly efficient for constructing parking

structures. Additionally, computing the slab's resistance of shear stresses at supporting columns is a major concern in the design procedure of this structure [11]. Notably, the slab-supporting column connections have been shown to be vulnerable to high shear stresses and this might bring about brittle and sudden punching shear failures [10]. Especially when the steel reinforcements get corroded due to moisture and other hostile factors in the operational environment, punching shear failures may occur at these slab-column connections. Accordingly, these may lead to progressive collapse of the whole structure [12].

Due to such reasons, FRP bars are recently considered as effective substitutions to the traditional steel bars in concrete flat slabs [13]. Moreover, UPSC is critical factor which determines the design process of concrete slabs supported by columns. Thus, this problem is extensively studied in the literature [14]. As a consequence, various researches have been conducted to investigate the applicability of existing empirical approaches and modify them to predict the punching shear capacity of FRP-reinforced slabs [1, 10, 15, 16].

Recently, machine learning has been proved to provide a feasible alternative for modeling the punching shear capacity of FRP-reinforced slabs [6, 9, 15, 17]. The Artificial Neural Network (ANN) has been employed to predict the FRP-reinforced slab punching shear capacity [6]. The research shows that the predictive result produced by ANN is considerably more accurate than those computed by the empirical formulas. Despite the fact that ANN is a powerful method for modeling nonlinear systems [18, 19], the learning process of ANN suffers from certain challenges [20].

One major difficulty of ANN is that its model establishment stage is accomplished via a gradient descent (GD) algorithm. GD algorithm is known to be very complex and may contain many local minima [20]. Another disadvantage of the ANN approach lies in their knowledge representation [21]; the black-box nature of the method makes it difficult for structural engineers to comprehend how the ANN predicts the punching shear capacity of FRP-reinforced slabs. In addition, the ANN approach intrinsically provides no means of measuring the contribution of each input factors to the model performance.

This research aims at extending the body of knowledge by investigating a new learning alternative for modeling the punching shear capacity of FRP-reinforced slabs. The proposed approach is hybridization of an improved kernel regression and the Differential Evolution (DE) [22]. The research objective is to establish a prediction model with transparent structure, self-adaptive learning, and the capability to express the relevancy of input variables.

Notably, the kernel regression belongs to the class of instance-based regression, which is also called nonparametric regression. Nonparametric regression offers a flexible and effective way of approximating the regression function especially when the form of the regression function is inherently complex [23, 24]. The reason is that, in such circumstance, it can be difficult to construct a universal parametric model based on a limited amount of training samples. Since good performances of the nonparametric approach have been observed throughout the literature [21, 25–28], the nonparametric regression is worth being investigated in solving the problem of interest.

Furthermore, learning based on instances or examples is a common practice in construction engineering. Thus, an instance-based model for punching shear capacity of FRP-reinforced slabs can be easily perceived by practical engineers; this may facilitate the applicability of the new approach. The rest of the article is organized as follows. The second section introduces the research method. The third section describes the proposed hybrid instance-based learning, followed by the experimental results. The final section summarizes our research with several conclusions.

2. Research Methodology

2.1. A Review of Formulas for Estimating Punching Shear Capacity of FRP-Reinforced Slabs. The shear resistance of

the concrete (V_c) is known to influence the punching shear capacity of two-way reinforced concrete flat slabs. V_c acts over the area proportional to the length of a critical perimeter (b_o) multiplied by the effective depth of the section (d). Currently, there is a critical need to investigate design equations and prediction models for determining the punching shear strength of concrete slabs reinforced with FRP composite bars. The reason is that existing design equations applied for FRP-reinforced concrete sections are originated from those previously applied for steel-reinforced counterparts with certain adjustments for considering the replacement of steel by FRP. The following section reviews formula-based methods for the prediction of UPSC of FRP-reinforced slabs; it is noted that the system of units for all equations is SI.

The American Concrete Institute (ACI) Code (ACI 318-11) introduces a design formula to account for the shear transfer in two-way steel-reinforced concrete slabs:

$$V_c = 0.33\sqrt{f_c'}\,b_{0,0.5d}d, \qquad (1)$$

where f_c' denotes the specified compressive strength of the concrete (MPa), $b_{0,0.5d}$ represents the perimeter of the critical section for slabs and footings at a distance of $d/2$ away from the column face, and d is the average flexural depth of the slab.

In addition, The British Standard (BS 8110-97) suggests a formula to attain the punching shear capacity for steel-reinforced slabs as shown below:

$$V_c = 0.79\left(100\rho_s\right)^{1/3}\left(\frac{400}{d}\right)^{1/4}\left(\frac{f_{cu}}{25}\right)^{1/3}b_{0,1.5d}d, \qquad (2)$$

where f_{cu} denotes the characteristic concrete cube compressive strength (N/mm^2), ρ_s represents the steel reinforcement ratio, $b_{0,1.5d}$ is the perimeter of the critical section for slabs and footings at a distance of $1.5d/2$ away from the loaded area (mm), and d represents the average flexural depth of the slab.

On the basis of experiments, El-Ghandour et al. [29] suggested a modification to the ACI's equation by multiplying it by the term $(E_f/E_s)^{1/3}$ to account for the use of FRP bars as follows:

$$V_c = 0.33\sqrt{f_c'}\left(\frac{E_f}{E_s}\right)^{1/3}b_{0,0.5d}d, \qquad (3)$$

where E_f and E_s are Young's modulus of the FRP-reinforced slab and Young's modulus of the steel reinforcement, respectively.

El-Ghandour et al. [30] modified the BS 8110-97's design equation and suggested an alternative formula to obtain the shear strength of FRP-reinforced concrete slabs as follows:

$$V_c = 0.79\left(100\rho_s 1.8\left(\frac{E_f}{E_s}\right)\right)^{1/3}\left(\frac{400}{d}\right)^{1/4}\left(\frac{f_{cu}}{25}\right)^{1/3}$$
$$\cdot b_{0,1.5d}d. \qquad (4)$$

TABLE 1: Statistical descriptions of variables.

Input factors	Notation	Min	Average	Std. Dev.	Max
The type of column section	X_1	—	—	—	—
Section area of column (mm^2)	X_2	5027.0	76203.6	56353.8	202500.0
Effective flexural depth of slab (mm)	X_3	55.0	141.4	61.9	284.0
Compressive strength of concrete (MPa)	X_4	26.0	41.7	13.1	118.0
Young's modulus of the FRP slab (GPa)	X_5	28.4	67.4	32.8	147.6
Reinforcement ratio (%)	X_6	0.2	0.9	0.7	3.8
Punching shear capacity (kN)	Y	61.0	470.7	360.6	1600.0

Matthys and Taerwe [31] put forward an enhancement of the BS 8110-97 as follows:

$$V_c = 1.36 \left(\frac{100\rho_s \left(E_f/E_s\right) f_c'}{d^{1/4}} \right)^{1/3} b_{0,1.5d}d. \qquad (5)$$

Ospina et al. [32] introduced an improved version of the equation proposed by Matthys and Taerwe [31]; in this revision, the cube root of the modular ration is replaced by the square root. This design formula is shown as follows:

$$V_c = 2.77 \left(\rho_s f_c'\right)^{1/3} \sqrt{\frac{E_f}{E_s}} b_{0,1.5d}d. \qquad (6)$$

A design equation has been proposed by the subcommittee ACI440H [16] for calculation of steel-reinforced two-way concrete slabs. This equation has considered the influence of reinforcement stiffness to account for the shear transfer in two-way concrete slabs as follows:

$$V_c = 0.8\sqrt{f_c'}b_{0,0.5d}c, \qquad (7)$$

where $b_{0,0.5d}$ is the perimeter of the critical section for slabs and footings at a distance of $d/2$ away. And c is the cracked transformed section neutral axis depth (mm) and is calculated as follows:

$$c = k \cdot d, \qquad (8)$$

where k is defined in the following equation:

$$k = \sqrt{2\rho_f n_f + \left(\rho_f n_f\right)^2} - \rho_f n_f. \qquad (9)$$

In (9), it is noted that $n_f = E_f/E_c$ denotes modular ratio and $E_c = 4700\sqrt{f_c'}$ is the concrete modulus of elasticity.

2.2. The Collected Dataset of Punching Shear Tests.

The dataset of FRP-reinforced concrete flat slab used in this study consists of 82 tests recorded in previous research works [6, 15, 33]. As the previous work of Vu and Hoang [17], the type of column section (X_1), section area of column (X_2), effective flexural depth of slab (X_3), compressive strength of concrete (X_4), Young's modulus of the FRP-reinforced slab (X_5), and reinforcement ratio (X_6) are considered as input factors that determine the ultimate punching capacity of the FRP-reinforced concrete flat slab. The shape of the column section includes three forms: square ($X_1 = 1$), circle ($X_1 = 2$), and rectangle ($X_1 = 3$). In the dataset, the numbers of square, circle, and rectangle sections are 50, 13, and 19, respectively. The range of the punching capacity varies from 61 kN to 1600 kN. Table 1 shows the variables and their statistical descriptions. The whole dataset is provided in the Appendix.

2.3. Instance-Based Regression.

Given a set of independent observations $(x_i, y_i)_{i=1,...,N}$, where $X = \{x_i\}$ and $Y = \{y_i\}$ are called predictor variable and response variable, respectively, and N denotes the number of data points, the task of regression analysis is to construct a function $m(x)$ that provides the mapping relation between the predictor variable and the response variable:

$$y_i = m\left(x_i\right) + \varepsilon_i, \qquad (10)$$

where ε_i represents a random noise. $m(x_i)$ is generally called the regression function or regression of Y on X, which can be employed to predict the value of Y based on an unknown input variable X.

The approaches of regression analysis can be categorized into two major classes: parametric model and nonparametric model [34]. In the former class, the underlying functional form of the model is known and the model's free parameters are estimated directly from the dataset at hand. Linear/nonlinear regression models are the typically parametric and the Artificial Neural Network (ANN) can be considered as an advanced form of nonlinear parametric model. In the latter class, there is no restriction on the functional form of the regression model; the model generally stores all the collected data instances in its memory and utilizes such memory to predict unknown input data [24, 35]. Therefore, the approach of nonparametric learning is also called instance-based learning.

Previous studies found that the restriction of $m(x)$ to a certain parametric form can limit the flexibility of the learning capability. A particularly undesirable situation happens when a parametric model that is inappropriate for the dataset is chosen. In such case, the model in no way can reflect the nature of the dataset regardless of how accurately its free parameters are estimated. Furthermore, this shortcoming of parametric models can be circumvented by abandoning the restriction on the functional form of $m(x)$. This leads to the method of nonparametric learning or instance-based learning.

Instance-based learning offers an approach for constructing the mapping function with a greater degree of flexibility [24]. This approach is particularly useful when the underlying form of the regression function is very complex. In such a case, it is much more efficient to construct a series of simple local regression models instead of a complicated global regression model. Furthermore, a significant advantage of instance-based learning is that its prediction process can be easily comprehended by practical engineers; this is in contrast to the black-box learning approach used in the ANN.

In this research, the instance-based learning approach of interest is the kernel regression with the utilization of kernel smoothing. In the kernel regression, the estimated value of the response variable y is computed by a weighted average of all the data stored in the model's memory. The predicted value y of the predictor variable x, denoted as y_p, is computed as follows [36–38]:

$$y_p = \frac{\sum_{i=1}^{N} \theta_i \times y_i}{\sum_{i=1}^{N} \theta_i}, \qquad (11)$$

where y_i represents the ith data point in the memory which consists of N data points.

The Gaussian kernel is commonly selected to calculate the weight θ_i as follows:

$$\theta_i = \frac{1}{\sqrt{2\pi} \times h} \exp\left[\frac{-d(x, x_i)^2}{2 \times h^2}\right], \qquad (12)$$

where the parameter h denotes the kernel width and $d(x, x_i)$ is the similarity between the two data points x and x_i.

Herein, the Minkowski distance, a generalization of both the Euclidean distance and the Manhattan distance, is used to measure the similarity between data points:

$$d(x, x_i) = \left(\sum_{k=1}^{D} |x_k - x_{i,k}|^q\right)^{1/q}, \qquad (13)$$

where D is the data dimension and $q \in [1, \infty)$ is a scalar. It is noted that when $q = 2$ and $q = 1$, the Minkowski distance is equivalent to the Euclidean distance and Manhattan distance, respectively.

In addition, it is noted that the relevance of each input factor, or feature, can be quantified by associating it with a weighting value which varies from 0 to 1. The higher the weighting value is, the more relevant the input attribute is. The feature weights can be embedded into the distance function to measure the similarity between two data instances. The incorporation of feature weight into the instance-based regression model and more detailed explanation are discussed in Section 3 of the article.

2.4. Differential Evolution (DE). DE is an evolutionary algorithm developed by Storn and Price [22]. This metaheuristic

is a population-based stochastic approach which is very effective for global optimization in continuous domains [39, 40]. The DE algorithm relies on a novel crossover-mutation operator which is a linear combination of three different individuals and one subject-to-replacement parent (also called target vector) [41, 42]. This crossover-mutation operator of the DE algorithm aims at producing a trial vector (also called child vector) which must compete with its parent through the selection process. The selection operator of DE is a fitness based comparison between the parent and the corresponding offspring [43].

The DE algorithm [22] is unquestionably one of the most powerful approaches for solving complex optimization problems [44, 45]. Successful applications of the DE optimization algorithm as well as other metaheuristic approaches for solving complex or ill-defined engineering problems have been observed in various fields [46–51]. Given that the problem of interest is to minimize a cost function $f(\mathbf{X})$, where the number of decision variables is D, the DE algorithm can be described in Algorithm 1. In Algorithm 1, it is noted that rnd(i) denotes a random integer.

Initially, a population consisting of D-dimensional parameter vectors $X_{i,g}$ is randomly generated, where $i = 1, 2, \ldots, NP$ and g denotes the current generation number. Accordingly, a mutant vector is computed for each target vector in the following manner:

$$V_{i,g+1} = X_{r1,g} + F \times \left(X_{r2,g} - X_{r3,g}\right), \qquad (14)$$

where $r1$, $r2$, and $r3$ are random indexes lying between 1 and NP. NP represents the population size. F denotes the mutation scale factor, which controls the amplification of the differential variation. $V_{i,g+1}$ represents the newly created mutant vector.

The crossover operator of DE aims at increasing the diversity of the current population by exchanging components of the target and mutant vectors. Within the crossover phase, a trial vector is generated in the following way:

$$U_{j,i,g+1} = \begin{cases} V_{j,i,g+1}, & \text{if } \text{rand}_j \leq \text{Cr or } j = \text{rnb}(i) \\ X_{j,i,g}, & \text{if } \text{rand}_j > \text{Cr and } j \neq \text{rnb}(i), \end{cases} \qquad (15)$$

where $U_{j,i,g+1}$ represents the trial vector. j denotes the index of element for any vector. rand_j is a uniform random number lying between 0 and 1. Cr denotes the crossover probability. rnb(i) represents a randomly chosen index of $\{1, 2, \ldots, NP\}$ which guarantees that at least one parameter from the mutant vector ($V_{j,i,g+1}$) is copied to the trial vector ($U_{j,i,g+1}$).

The selection stage compares the trial vector with the target vector to identify a better solution for the optimization problem at hand. The selection operator is demonstrated as follows:

$$X_{i,g+1} = \begin{cases} U_{i,g} & \text{if } f\left(U_{i,g}\right) \leq f\left(X_{i,g}\right) \\ X_{i,g} & \text{if } f\left(U_{i,g}\right) > f\left(X_{i,g}\right). \end{cases} \qquad (16)$$

2.5. Artificial Neural Network (ANN). ANN is a soft computing method which is inspired from biological neural networks. This technique simulates the knowledge acquisition

Define the objective function $f(\mathbf{x})$, $\mathbf{x} \in R^D$
Randomly generate an initial population of **NP** vectors
Compute population fitness
Identify the best solution $\mathbf{x}_{best}$ in the current population
Define the mutation scale **F** and the crossover probability Cr
Define the maximum iteration $\mathbf{G}_{max}$
For $g = 1$ to $\mathbf{G}_{max}$
  For $i = 1$ to $\mathbf{N}$
    Generate 3 random indices r_1, r_2 and r_3
    Perform mutation: $V_{i,g+1} = X_{r1,g} + F \cdot (X_{r2,g} - X_{r3,g})$
    Perform crossover:

$$U_{j,i,g+1} = \begin{cases} V_{j,i,g+1}, & \text{if } rand_j \leq Cr \text{ or } j = rnb(i) \\ X_{j,i,g}, & \text{if } rand_j > Cr \text{ and } j \neq rnb(i) \end{cases}$$

    If $f(U_{i,g}) < f(X_{i,g})$
      $X_{i,g+1} = U_{i,g}$
      If $f(U_{i,g}) < f(x_{best})$
        $x_{best} = U_{i,g}$
      End if
    End If
  End For
End For
Return the best solution $\mathbf{x}_{best}$

Algorithm 1: Differential Evolution (DE).

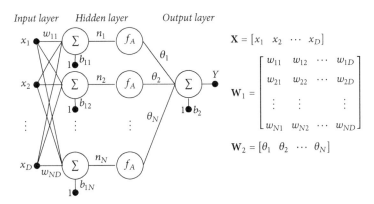

Figure 1: Artificial Neural Network structure.

and inference processes in the human brain. The advantages of the ANN can be realized by its flexibility and universal learning capability. Nevertheless, primary drawbacks of the ANN are the trial-and-error process for properly determining a network configuration and its black-box learning nature.

The learning task is to train a function $f : X \in R^D \rightarrow Y \in R^1$, where D denotes the number of input attributes. An ANN model, which includes the input, hidden, and output layers, is demonstrated in Figure 1. W_1 and W_2 represent weight matrices of the hidden layer and the output layer, respectively; N denotes the number of neurons in the hidden layer; $b_1 = [b_{11}, b_{12}, \ldots, b_{1N}]$ represents a bias vector of the hidden layer; b_2 is a bias vector of the output layer; f_A denotes an activation function (e.g., log-sigmoid).

The ANN structure used for regression analysis is shown as follows [52]:

$$f(X) = b_2 + W_2 \times (f_A(b_1 + W_1 \times X)). \qquad (17)$$

Generally, the weight matrices and the bias vectors of an ANN are trained via a process that employs the framework of error backpropagation [19]. Moreover, the Mean Square Error (MSE) is employed as the objective function for training an ANN structure for function approximation tasks [53]:

$$MSE = \min_{W_1, W_2, b_1, b_2} \frac{1}{M} \sum_{i=1}^{M} e_i^2, \qquad (18)$$

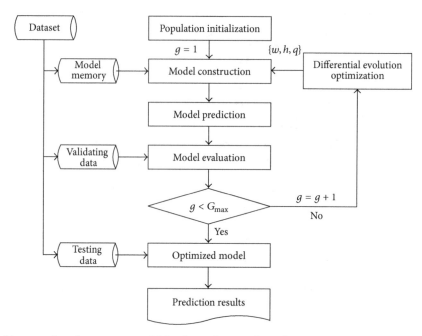

FIGURE 2: The proposed instance-based regression model for the prediction of punching shear capacity of FRP-reinforced concrete slabs.

where M represents the number of data samples and e_i is an output error. $e_i = Y_{i,P} - Y_{i,A}$ ($Y_{i,P}$ and $Y_{i,A}$ denote the predicted and actual outputs, resp.).

3. The Proposed Adaptive-Weighted Instance-Based Regression Model for the Prediction of Punching Shear Capacity of FRP-Reinforced Concrete Slabs

This section of the article describes the proposed instance-based regression model for the prediction of punching shear capacity of FRP-reinforced concrete slabs, denoted as IRM-PSC in detail. The main idea of the IRM-PSC is to employ the DE optimization algorithm to select an appropriate set of the instance-based regression model's parameters including the kernel width (h), the Minkowski distance scalar (q), and the feature weights (w_k). The proposed model consists of five major steps: data processing, model construction and model prediction, Differential Evolution optimization, model evaluation, and optimized model. Figure 2 illustrates the IRM-PSC's flowchart. In this figure, g and $G_{\max}$ represent the current generation and the maximum generation of the DE algorithm, respectively.

3.1. Data Processing.
The dataset including 82 punching tests of FRP-reinforced concrete slab collected from the literature is employed to construct and verify the prediction model. The type of column section, section area of column, effective flexural depth of slab, compressive strength of concrete, Young's modulus of the FRP-reinforced slab, and reinforcement ratio are considered as influencing factors that determine the ultimate punching capacity of the FRP-reinforced concrete flat slab. The whole dataset is randomly

separated into three sets: the training, validating, and testing sets. The training set is used to establish the model memory; the other two datasets are employed to validate and test the model performance. It is noted that, before being separated, the whole dataset has been normalized into the range of $[0, 1]$. This data normalization aspires to prevent the situation in which features with greater numeric magnitudes dominate those with smaller magnitudes.

3.2. Model Construction and Model Prediction.
At this phase, the kernel regression is utilized as the instance-based learning approach to model the mapping relation between the ultimate punching capacity of the FRP-reinforced concrete flat slab and its six influencing input variables. The model simply stores all data samples of the training set in its memory. When new input data is available, the model computes the kernel weights using this new sample and other existing samples. Accordingly, the estimated punching capacity of the new input data is calculated as a weighted average of all punching capacities of all the data in the memory.

Furthermore, it is noted that, in this study, the relevance of the input feature k is quantified by its feature weight w_k varying from 0 to 1. As mentioned earlier, a higher feature weight means that the feature of interest is more relevant for estimating the output. The feature weights are embedded into the distance measurement between two data instances. Accordingly, the modified Minkowski distance is provided as follows:

$$d(x, x_i) = \left(\sum_{k=1}^{D} w_k \times |x_k - x_{i,k}|^q \right)^{1/q}. \tag{19}$$

It is worth noticing that each data feature represents an axis in the input space. For the problem at hand, the input

TABLE 2: Prediction performance of the IRM-PSC and ANN models.

		RMSE	MAPE (%)	R^2
IRM-PSC	Training	34.62	1.22	0.99
	Testing	63.34	12.70	0.96
ANN	Training	64.29	17.14	0.97
	Testing	52.43	15.98	0.96

space is a six-dimensional space. As can be seen from (19), the introduction of the feature weight w_k can elongate or truncate the axis k in the input space. A high w_k elongates the axis k; this makes the feature k very significant for the prediction process. The reason is that when the axis is elongated, even a small difference of $|x_k - x_{i,k}|$ can result in a large kernel weight. The reversed result occurs when an axis is truncated. In the extreme case when $w_k = 0$, the quantity $|x_k - x_{i,k}|$ imposes no influence on the final kernel weight between two data instances. It is noted that the feature weight w_k used in this section is different from the Gaussian kernel weight (θ_i) defined in (11) and (12). The feature weight expresses the relevancy of input variable; meanwhile, the Gaussian kernel weight exhibits the data similarity.

3.3. Differential Evolution Optimization. The construction of the model necessitates the kernel width (h), the Minkowski distance scalar (q), and the feature weights (w_k) as hyperparameters. At each iteration, the DE algorithm guides the population of vectors to search for better solutions. Gradually, inferior solutions characterized with worse values of fitness are discarded; superior solutions with better values of fitness survive to the next iterations. The DE's search progresses until the current generation (g) exceeds the maximum generation ($G_{\max}$).

3.4. Model Evaluation. To identify an appropriate set of hyperparameters, it is necessary to define an objective function that quantifies the model performance. In this study, the model's prediction accuracy in terms of Root Mean Squared Error (RMSE) when estimating the validating dataset is employed for model evaluation:

$$f = \sqrt{\sum_{j=1}^{N} \frac{\left(Y_P^j - Y_A^j\right)^2}{N}}, \qquad (20)$$

where Y_P^j and Y_A^j denote predicted and actual value for output jth. In addition, N is the number of data samples in the validating set.

3.5. Optimized Model. When the DE based searching process terminates, the optimized prediction model, characterized by an appropriate set of hyperparameters, has been identified. The proposed IRM-PSC is ready for the prediction of UPSC of the FRP-reinforced concrete flat slab.

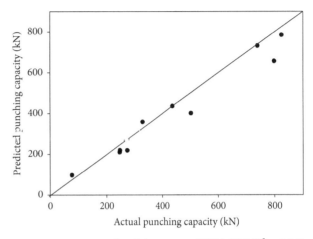

FIGURE 3: Testing results of the proposed IRM-PSC ($R^2 = 0.96$).

4. Experimental Results

When the IRM-PSC model has been constructed, the proposed model can be employed to predict the punching shear capacity of FRP-reinforced flat slab. Besides the proposed instance-based regression, previously used methods including ANN [6] and the empirical formulas are utilized as benchmark approaches. The ANN consists of 1 hidden layer with 6 neurons. The applied learning rate was 0.001 together with a number of 5000 learning epochs. The Levenberg-Marquardt algorithm is used to train the ANN model [54]. Additionally, to quantify model performance, Root Mean Squared Error (RMSE), Mean Absolute Percentage Error (MAPE), and Coefficient of Determination (R^2) are computed.

In the first experiment, the dataset has been randomly divided into two sets; the first set (Set 1) was used for model construction, while the second set (Set 2) was used for model testing. The numbers of data samples in Set 1 and Set 2 are 72 and 10, respectively. Set 1 is further divided into two subsets: subset 1 which constitutes the model memory (80%) and subset 2 (20%) which is reserved for model validating. The testing results of the IRM-PSC are illustrated in Figure 3. This figure demonstrates that the proposed approach has obtained a good fit to a straight line.

Furthermore, in this experiment, the prediction performance of the proposed instance-based model is compared to that of the ANN. The results comparison is reported in Table 2. The RMSE, MAPE, and R^2 in the testing process

TABLE 3: Result comparison.

Prediction methods	IRM-PSC	ANN	ACI 318-11	BS 8110-97	El-Ghandour et al. (1999)	El-Ghandour et al. (2000)	Matthys and Taerwe (2000)	Ospina et al. (2003)	ACI 440H
RMSE	**65.99**	**62.29**	196.61	158.38	188.94	151.27	201.58	**117.51**	342.52
MAPE	**11.81**	**12.86**	28.88	28.02	28.86	17.07	24.13	**15.48**	56.02
R^2	**0.97**	**0.96**	0.80	0.81	0.85	0.90	0.90	**0.91**	0.88

obtained from the IRM-PSC are 63.34, 12.70, and 0.96. The ANN approach yields the following results: RMSE = 52.43, MAPE = 15.98, and R^2 = 0.96. Observably, in terms of the MAPE, the new method has achieved 3.28% improvement compared with the ANN. The two prediction models obtain the same value of R^2. Nevertheless, the ANN shows better performance in terms of RMSE.

In the second experiment, a tenfold cross validation process is conducted. Because all of the subsamples are mutually exclusive, the cross validation process can accurately evaluate the model performance. The average prediction performances (measured in RMSE, MAPE, and R^2) of the IRM-PSC and the ANN are reported in Table 3. Additionally, the prediction results obtained from formula-based approaches are also provided in this table. The results of the empirical formulas are calculated using the equations (from (1) to (7)) mentioned previously in this article.

From Table 3, it is recognizable that the equation proposed by Ospina et al. [32] is the best formula-based method, and the RMSE, MAPE, and R^2 of this method are 117.51, 15.48, and 0.91, respectively. This outcome is shown to be far worse than the two machine learning approaches. RMSE, MAPE, and R^2 of the IRM-PSC are 65.99, 11.81, and 0.97, respectively. The three measurements of the ANN are 62.29, 12.86, and 0.96. Thus, the newly proposed method overcomes the ANN as measured by MAPE and R^2; meanwhile the ANN is better than the IRM-PSC in terms of RMSE. In summary, compared with the best empirical formula, the IRM-PSC has attained roughly 43% and 24% improvements in RMSE and MAPE, respectively.

Furthermore, it is beneficial to investigate the relevance of the six input features employed in this study. As mentioned earlier, the relevance of input features can be quantified by the feature weight w_k. The average feature weights of the six input attributes, obtained from the tenfold cross validation process, are as follows: w_1 = 0.63, w_2 = 0.28, w_3 = 0.81, w_4 = 0.36, w_5 = 0.26, and w_6 = 0.76. Thus, it can be seen that the type of column section (X_1), the effective flexural depth of slab (X_3), and the reinforcement ratio (X_6) are highly relevant for the prediction of UPSC of the FRP-reinforced concrete slabs. The reason is that these three features obtain the highest feature weights. Meanwhile, the other input attributes, including the section area of column (X_2), the compressive strength of concrete (X_4), and Young's modulus of the FRP slab (X_5), obtain lower values of feature weights. Nevertheless,

since all weights are greater than zero, these three features (X_2, X_4, and X_5) are still relevant for the prediction process.

5. Conclusion

This research proposed an alternative, named as IRM-PSC, for calculating the punching shear capacity of the FRP-reinforced two-way slabs. The new approach employs the kernel regression as an instance-based learning technique to infer the mapping function between the punching shear capacity and its input features. To construct the instance-based learning model, the DE is employed.

Experimental results have proved that the IRM-PSC can deliver prediction performance which is far more accurate than commonly used empirical formulas, reflected in low prediction errors (RMSE and MAPE) and a high Coefficient of Determination (R^2). The new method has also demonstrated a competitive capability compared with the ANN approach. However, as an instance-based learning method, the frameworks of learning and making predictions of the IRM-PSC are much more transparent than the black-box ANN. Furthermore, another advantage of the new method is that it can help to reveal the relevance of input features quantified by the feature weight. Thus, the new model can be better understood and easily applied by structural engineers, who may not be familiar with machine learning, to design FRP-reinforced slabs.

Thus, the applicability of the new approach may be limited to the ranges of input features recorded in the dataset. Accordingly, more slab test results should be collected both by actual experiments and by analyses via nonlinear Finite Element Method packages; these data can be incorporated into the current dataset to enhance the generalization and applicability of the IRM-PSC. These tasks can be a future direction of the current study.

Appendix

See Table 4.

Conflicts of Interest

The authors declare that there are no conflicts of interest regarding the publication of this article.

TABLE 4: The dataset of punching shear tests.

X_1	X_2 (mm²)	X_3 (mm)	X_4 (MPa)	X_5 (GPa)	X_6 (%)	Y (kN)
1	10000	55	52.9	100	0.31	61
1	10000	55	41	100	0.31	65
1	5625	61	44.6	113	0.95	78
1	5625	61	42.4	113	0.95	93
1	10000	61	39	113	0.95	96
1	10000	61	36.6	113	0.95	99
1	40000	82	37.4	46	1.1	165
1	40000	142	33.3	45	0.22	170
1	40000	112	33	46	0.81	170
1	40000	129	39	48	0.48	180
1	62500	120	37.5	28.4	0.87	206
1	62500	100	26	42	0.95	210
1	40000	82	38.2	46	1.29	210
1	40000	129	39	48	0.68	212
1	62500	120	29.5	34	0.73	217
1	62500	100	35	42	1.05	218
1	50625	110	36.3	48.2	1.18	222
1	40000	142	34.7	110	0.18	229
1	40000	82	39.7	46	1.54	230
1	62500	75	45	100	1	234
1	40000	142	30.3	45	0.47	237
1	62500	100	29	42	1.67	240
1	50625	110	36.3	48.2	2.15	246
1	50625	110	36.3	48.2	3	248
1	40000	129	39	48	0.92	248
1	62500	100	40	42	1.18	249
1	62500	120	28.9	34	1.46	260
1	40000	142	46.6	45	0.47	271
1	62500	100	71	42	1.18	275
1	40000	142	29.6	110	0.43	317
1	90000	134	34.3	48.2	0.71	329
1	90000	134	38.6	48.2	0.71	386
1	202500	134	44.9	48.2	0.71	400
1	90000	131	38.6	48.1	1.56	431
1	90000	131	37.5	64.9	1.21	438
1	90000	131	32.4	48.1	1.56	451
1	202500	131	32.4	48.1	1.56	504
1	202500	131	39.4	48.1	1.56	511
1	90000	131	75.8	57.4	1.56	547
1	90000	284	39.4	48.2	0.34	781
1	90000	284	34.3	48.2	0.34	825
1	202500	284	48.6	48.2	0.34	911
1	202500	284	32.4	48.2	0.34	1020
1	90000	281	29.6	48.1	0.73	1027
1	90000	281	39.4	48.1	0.73	1071

TABLE 4: Continued.

X_1	X_2 (mm²)	X_3 (mm)	X_4 (MPa)	X_5 (GPa)	X_6 (%)	Y (kN)
1	90000	281	46.7	48.1	0.73	1195
1	90000	281	46.7	48.1	0.73	1195
1	202500	281	29.6	48.1	0.73	1248
1	90000	275	38.2	56.7	1.61	1492
1	90000	275	75.8	56.7	1.61	1600
2	17671	95	32.6	147.6	0.19	142
2	41548	95	33.2	147.6	0.19	150
2	5027	89	35.9	40.7	3.78	171
2	17671	96	36.7	91.8	0.26	181
2	41548	96	37.3	91.8	0.26	189
2	17671	95	118	37.3	0.64	207
2	5027	122	32.1	44.8	1.21	217
2	17671	89	35.8	40.7	3.78	231
2	17671	122	32.1	44.8	1.21	237
2	17671	95	35.7	95	1.05	255
2	41548	95	36.3	95	1.05	273
2	41548	126	34.3	92	0.52	343
2	17671	126	33.8	92	0.52	347
3	150000	110	35.2	43	1.2	362
3	150000	135	35.2	43	1.2	484
3	150000	137	53.1	43	0.35	506
3	150000	140	40.3	122	0.4	530
3	37500	162	42	85	0.28	534
3	150000	135	53.1	43	0.7	549
3	37500	162	42	85	0.28	575
3	37500	162	42	85	0.28	584
3	37500	162	42	85	0.28	622
3	150750	165	49.6	122.5	0.35	674
3	37500	162	42	85	0.28	698
3	150000	135	64.8	43	1.2	704
3	150250	159	44.3	38.5	1.99	712
3	150500	156	49.2	46.5	1.21	732
3	150000	159	49.6	44.6	1	740
3	151000	165	44.3	122.5	0.69	799
3	129375	165	59	147	0.57	1000
3	129375	165	59	147	0.57	1200
3	129375	165	59	147	0.57	1328

References

[1] J. Bai, *Advanced Fibre-Reinforced Polymer (FRP) Composites for Structural Applications*, Woodhead Publishing Limited, 2013.

[2] Ç. Özes and N. Neşer, "Experimental study on steel to FRP bonded lap joints in marine applications," *Advances in Materials Science and Engineering*, vol. 2015, Article ID 164208, 6 pages, 2015.

[3] H. Fang, H. Shi, Y. Wang, Y. Qi, and W. Liu, "Experimental and theoretical study of sandwich panels with steel facesheets and

GFRP core," *Advances in Materials Science and Engineering*, vol. 2016, Article ID 7159205, 12 pages, 2016.

[4] T. Ozbakkaloglu, J.-F. Chen, S. T. Smith, and J.-G. Dai, "Applications of fiber reinforced polymer composites," *International Journal of Polymer Science*, vol. 2016, Article ID 5804145, 2016.

[5] L. Bertolini, "Steel corrosion and service life of reinforced concrete structures," *Structure and Infrastructure Engineering*, vol. 4, no. 2, pp. 123–137, 2008.

[6] I. M. Metwally, "Prediction of punching shear capacities of two-way concrete slabs reinforced with FRP bars," *HBRC Journal*, vol. 9, no. 2, pp. 125–133, 2013.

[7] E.-K. Kim, H. Oh, and J. Sim, "Semiempirical methodology for estimating the service life of concrete deck panels strengthened with fiber-reinforced polymer," *Mathematical Problems in Engineering*, vol. 2014, Article ID 273693, 13 pages, 2014.

[8] S. M. Soleimani and N. Banthia, "Shear strengthening of RC beams using sprayed glass fiber reinforced polymer," *Advances in Civil Engineering*, vol. 2012, Article ID 635176, 20 pages, 2012.

[9] M. Hassan, E. A. Ahmed, and B. Benmokrane, "Punching shear behavior of two-way slabs reinforced with FRP shear reinforcement," *Journal of Composites for Construction*, vol. 19, no. 1, Article ID 04014030, 2015.

[10] M. Hassan, E. A. Ahmed, and B. Benmokrane, "Punching shear strength of glass fiber-reinforced polymer reinforced concrete flat slabs," *Canadian Journal of Civil Engineering*, vol. 40, no. 10, pp. 951–960, 2013.

[11] M. D. E. Teixeira, J. A. O. Barros, V. M. C. F. Cunha, B. N. Moraes-Neto, and A. Ventura-Gouveia, "Numerical simulation of the punching shear behaviour of self-compacting fibre reinforced flat slabs," *Construction and Building Materials*, vol. 74, pp. 25–36, 2015.

[12] K.-K. Choi, M. M. Reda Taha, H.-G. Park, and A. K. Maji, "Punching shear strength of interior concrete slab-column connections reinforced with steel fibers," *Cement and Concrete Composites*, vol. 29, no. 5, pp. 409–420, 2007.

[13] A. W. El-Ghandour, K. Pilakoutas, and P. Waldron, "Punching shear behavior of fiber reinforced polymers reinforced concrete flat slabs: experimental study," *Journal of Composites for Construction*, vol. 7, no. 3, pp. 258–265, 2003.

[14] A. A. Elshafey, E. Rizk, H. Marzouk, and M. R. Haddara, "Prediction of punching shear strength of two-way slabs," *Engineering Structures*, vol. 33, no. 5, pp. 1742–1753, 2011.

[15] M. A. W. Hassan, *Punching shear behavior of concrete two-way slabs reinforced with Glass Fiber-Reinforced Polymer (GFRP) bars [Ph.D. thesis]*, University of Sherbrooke, 2013.

[16] A. Nanni, "Guide for the design and construction of concrete reinforced with FRP bars (ACI 440.1R-03)," in *Proceedings of the Structures Congress and the 2005 Forensic Engineering Symposium—Metropolis and Beyond*, pp. 1621–1626, New York, NY, USA, April 2005.

[17] D.-T. Vu and N.-D. Hoang, "Punching shear capacity estimation of FRP-reinforced concrete slabs using a hybrid machine learning approach," *Structure and Infrastructure Engineering*, vol. 12, no. 9, pp. 1153–1161, 2016.

[18] C.-C. Young, W.-C. Liu, and W.-L. Hsieh, "Predicting the water level fluctuation in an alpine lake using physically based, artificial neural network, and time series forecasting models," *Mathematical Problems in Engineering*, vol. 2015, Article ID 708204, 11 pages, 2015.

[19] T. Tran and N. Hoang, "Predicting colonization growth of algae on mortar surface with artificial neural network," *Journal of Computing in Civil Engineering*, vol. 30, no. 6, Article ID 04016030, 2016.

[20] A. P. Piotrowski, "Differential Evolution algorithms applied to Neural Network training suffer from stagnation," *Applied Soft Computing Journal*, vol. 21, pp. 382–406, 2014.

[21] M.-Y. Cheng and N.-D. Hoang, "Evaluating contractor financial status using a hybrid fuzzy instance based classifier: case study in the construction industry," *IEEE Transactions on Engineering Management*, vol. 62, no. 2, pp. 184–192, 2015.

[22] R. Storn and K. Price, "Differential evolution—a simple and efficient heuristic for global optimization over continuous spaces," *Journal of Global Optimization*, vol. 11, no. 4, pp. 341–359, 1997.

[23] W. Hardle, *Applied Nonparametric Regression*, vol. 19 of *Econometric Society Monographs*, Cambridge University Press, Cambridge, UK, 1990.

[24] J. Klemela, *Multivariate Nonparametric Regression and Visualization*, Wiley Series in Computational Statistics, John Wiley & Sons, Hoboken, NJ, USA, 2014.

[25] J. Wang, Y. Chen, T. Li, J. Lu, and L. Shen, "A residual-based kernel regression method for image denoising," *Mathematical Problems in Engineering*, vol. 2016, Article ID 5245948, 13 pages, 2016.

[26] D. Tien Bui, Q. P. Nguyen, N.-D. Hoang, and H. Klempe, "A novel fuzzy K-nearest neighbor inference model with differential evolution for spatial prediction of rainfall-induced shallow landslides in a tropical hilly area using GIS," *Landslides*, pp. 1–17, 2016.

[27] M.-Y. Cheng and N.-D. Hoang, "A Swarm-Optimized Fuzzy Instance-based Learning approach for predicting slope collapses in mountain roads," *Knowledge-Based Systems*, vol. 76, pp. 256–263, 2015.

[28] M. Ouassou, O. Kristiansen, J. G. O. Gjevestad, K. S. Jacobsen, and Y. L. Andalsvik, "Estimation of scintillation indices: a novel approach based on local kernel regression methods," *International Journal of Navigation and Observation*, vol. 2016, Article ID 3582176, 18 pages, 2016.

[29] A. W. El-Ghandour, K. Pilakoutas, and P. Waldron, "New approach for punching shear capacity prediction of fiber reinforced polymer reinforced concrete flat slabs," *ACI Structural Journal*, vol. 188, pp. 135–144, 1999.

[30] A. W. El-Ghandour, K. Pilakoutas, and P. Waldron, "Punching shear behavior and design of FRP RC flat slabs," in *Proceedings of the International Workshop on Punching Shear Capacity of RC Slabs, Dedicated to Professor Sven Kinnunen*, TRITA-BKN Bulletin 57, pp. 359–366, TRITA-BKN, Stockholm, Sweden, 2000.

[31] S. Matthys and L. Taerwe, "Concrete slabs reinforced with FRP grids. II: punching resistance," *Journal of Composites for Construction*, vol. 4, no. 3, pp. 154–161, 2000.

[32] C. E. Ospina, S. D. B. Alexander, and J. J. Roger Cheng, "Punching of two-way concrete slabs with fiber-reinforced polymer reinforcing bars or grids," *ACI Structural Journal*, vol. 100, no. 5, pp. 589–598, 2003.

[33] L. Nguyen-Minh and M. Rovňák, "Punching shear resistance of interior GFRP reinforced slab-column connections," *Journal of Composites for Construction*, vol. 17, no. 1, pp. 2–13, 2013.

[34] J.-S. Zhang, X.-F. Huang, and C.-H. Zhou, "An improved kernel regression method based on Taylor expansion," *Applied Mathematics and Computation*, vol. 193, no. 2, pp. 419–429, 2007.

[35] Y.-Q. Yang, J.-S. Zhang, and X.-F. Huang, "Adaptive image enhancement algorithm combining kernel regression and local homogeneity," *Mathematical Problems in Engineering*, vol. 2010, Article ID 693532, 14 pages, 2010.

[36] K. Takezawa, *Introduction to Nonparametric Regression*, Wiley Series in Probability and Statistics, John Wiley & Sons, Hoboken, NJ, USA, 2nd edition, 2006.

[37] E. A. Nadaraya, "On estimating regression," *Theory of Probability and Its Applications*, vol. 9, pp. 141–142, 1964.

[38] G. S. Watson, "Smooth regression analysis," *The Indian Journal of Statistics. Series A*, vol. 26, pp. 359–372, 1964.

[39] M. Wang, Z. Song, G. Dai, L. Peng, and C. Zheng, "Asteroids exploration trajectory optimal design with differential evolution based on mixed coding," *International Journal of Distributed Sensor Networks*, vol. 2015, Article ID 827987, 8 pages, 2015.

[40] M.-Y. Cheng and N.-D. Hoang, "Groutability estimation of grouting processes with microfine cements using an evolutionary instance-based learning approach," *Journal of Computing in Civil Engineering*, vol. 20, no. 1, Article ID 01011011, 2011.

[41] H. Peng, Z. Wu, P. Shao, and C. Deng, "Dichotomous binary differential evolution for knapsack problems," *Mathematical Problems in Engineering*, vol. 2016, Article ID 5732489, 12 pages, 2016.

[42] R. Landa Becerra and C. A. Coello, "Cultured differential evolution for constrained optimization," *Computer Methods in Applied Mechanics and Engineering*, vol. 195, no. 33–36, pp. 4303–4322, 2006.

[43] Z. Chen, F. Yan, X. Qiao, and Y. Zhao, "Sparse antenna array design for MIMO radar using multiobjective differential evolution," *International Journal of Antennas and Propagation*, vol. 2016, Article ID 1747843, 12 pages, 2016.

[44] S. K. Goudos, C. Kalialakis, and R. Mittra, "Evolutionary algorithms applied to antennas and propagation: a review of state of the art," *International Journal of Antennas and Propagation*, vol. 2016, Article ID 1010459, 12 pages, 2016.

[45] Q. Ding and G. Zheng, "The cellular differential evolution based on chaotic local search," *Mathematical Problems in Engineering*, vol. 2015, Article ID 128902, 15 pages, 2015.

[46] D. Tien Bui, B. T. Pham, Q. P. Nguyen, and N.-D. Hoang, "Spatial prediction of rainfall-induced shallow landslides using hybrid integration approach of Least-Squares Support Vector Machines and differential evolution optimization: a case study in Central Vietnam," *International Journal of Digital Earth*, vol. 9, no. 11, pp. 1077–1097, 2016.

[47] N.-D. Hoang, Q.-L. Nguyen, and Q.-N. Pham, "Optimizing construction project labor utilization using differential evolution: a comparative study of mutation strategies," *Advances in Civil Engineering*, vol. 2015, Article ID 108780, 8 pages, 2015.

[48] M.-Y. Cheng and D.-H. Tran, "Two-phase differential evolution for the multiobjective optimization of time-cost tradeoffs in resource-constrained construction projects," *IEEE Transactions on Engineering Management*, vol. 61, no. 3, pp. 450–461, 2014.

[49] A. Nasrollahi, M. Saffarzadeh, A. Isfahanian, and M. Ghayekhloo, "Application of a new binary harmony search algorithm in highway rehabilitation decision-making problems: a case study in Iran," *Civil Engineering and Environmental Systems*, vol. 32, no. 4, pp. 335–350, 2015.

[50] A. Kaveh and A. Nasrollahi, "A new hybrid meta-heuristic for structural design: ranked particles optimization," *Structural Engineering and Mechanics*, vol. 52, no. 2, pp. 405–426, 2014.

[51] A. S. Talaei, A. Nasrollahi, and M. Ghayekhloo, "An automated approach for optimal design of prestressed concrete slabs using PSOHS," *KSCE Journal of Civil Engineering*, pp. 1–10, 2016.

[52] M. H. Beale, M. T. Hagan, and H. B. Demuth, *Neural Network Toolbox User's Guide*, The MathWorks Inc, 2012.

[53] J. A. Freeman and D. M. Skapura, *Neural Networks—Algorithms, Applications, and Programming Techniques*, Addison-Wesley Publishing Company Inc, 1991.

[54] M. T. Hagan and M. B. Menhaj, "Training feedforward networks with the Marquardt algorithm," *IEEE Transactions on Neural Networks*, vol. 5, no. 6, pp. 989–993, 1994.

Permissions

All chapters in this book were first published in ACISC, by Hindawi Publishing Corporation; hereby published with permission under the Creative Commons Attribution License or equivalent. Every chapter published in this book has been scrutinized by our experts. Their significance has been extensively debated. The topics covered herein carry significant findings which will fuel the growth of the discipline. They may even be implemented as practical applications or may be referred to as a beginning point for another development.

The contributors of this book come from diverse backgrounds, making this book a truly international effort. This book will bring forth new frontiers with its revolutionizing research information and detailed analysis of the nascent developments around the world.

We would like to thank all the contributing authors for lending their expertise to make the book truly unique. They have played a crucial role in the development of this book. Without their invaluable contributions this book wouldn't have been possible. They have made vital efforts to compile up to date information on the varied aspects of this subject to make this book a valuable addition to the collection of many professionals and students.

This book was conceptualized with the vision of imparting up-to-date information and advanced data in this field. To ensure the same, a matchless editorial board was set up. Every individual on the board went through rigorous rounds of assessment to prove their worth. After which they invested a large part of their time researching and compiling the most relevant data for our readers.

The editorial board has been involved in producing this book since its inception. They have spent rigorous hours researching and exploring the diverse topics which have resulted in the successful publishing of this book. They have passed on their knowledge of decades through this book. To expedite this challenging task, the publisher supported the team at every step. A small team of assistant editors was also appointed to further simplify the editing procedure and attain best results for the readers.

Apart from the editorial board, the designing team has also invested a significant amount of their time in understanding the subject and creating the most relevant covers. They scrutinized every image to scout for the most suitable representation of the subject and create an appropriate cover for the book.

The publishing team has been an ardent support to the editorial, designing and production team. Their endless efforts to recruit the best for this project, has resulted in the accomplishment of this book. They are a veteran in the field of academics and their pool of knowledge is as vast as their experience in printing. Their expertise and guidance has proved useful at every step. Their uncompromising quality standards have made this book an exceptional effort. Their encouragement from time to time has been an inspiration for everyone.

The publisher and the editorial board hope that this book will prove to be a valuable piece of knowledge for researchers, students, practitioners and scholars across the globe.

List of Contributors

Danfeng Xie, Lei Zhang and Li Bai
Department of Electrical and Computer Engineering, Temple University, Philadelphia, PA 19121, USA

Ali Wagdy Mohamed
College of Computer and Information Systems, Al-Yamamah University, Riyadh 11512, Saudi Arabia
Operations Research Department, Institute of Statistical Studies and Research, Cairo University, Giza 12613, Egypt

Abdulaziz S. Almazyad
College of Computer and Information Systems, Al-Yamamah University, Riyadh 11512, Saudi Arabia
College of Computer and Information Sciences, King Saud University, Riyadh, Saudi Arabia

Fisnik Dalipi and Sule Yildirim Yayilgan
Faculty of Computer Science and Media Technology, Norwegian University of Science and Technology, 2815 Gjøvik, Norway

Alemayehu Gebremedhin
Faculty of Technology and Management, Norwegian University of Science and Technology, 2815 Gjøvik, Norway

Jelena Fiosina and Maksims Fiosins
Clausthal University of Technology, Clausthal-Zellerfeld, Germany

Guodong Zhang, Kazuyuki Matsumoto, Minoru Yoshida and Kenji Kita
Faculty of Engineering, Tokushima University, Tokushima 7708506, Japan

Peilin Jiang
Xian Jiao Tong University, No. 28, XianningWest Road, Xian, China

Baokai Zu, Kewen Xia, Shuidong Dai and Nelofar Aslam
School of Electronic and Information Engineering, Hebei University of Technology, Tianjin 300401, China
Key Lab of Big Data Computation of Hebei Province, Tianjin 300401, China

David M. W. Powers
College of Science and Engineering, Flinders University, Adelaide, SA, Australia

Nasim Nematzadeh
College of Science and Engineering, Flinders University, Adelaide, SA, Australia
Department of Science and Engineering, Faculty of Mechatronics, Karaj Branch, Islamic Azad University (KIAU), Karaj-Alborz, Iran

Xian-xia Zhang, Zhi-qiang Fu, Wei-lu Shan and Bing Wang
Shanghai Key Laboratory of Power Station Automation Technology, School of Mechatronics and Automation, Shanghai University, Shanghai 200072, China

Tao Zou
Shenyang Institute of Automation, Chinese Academy of Sciences, Shenyang 110016, China

Mohammed Ngadi, Aouatif Amine, Bouchra Nassih, Hanaa Hachimi and Adnane El-Attar
Systems Engineering Laboratory, National School of Applied Sciences, Ibn Tofail University, Kenitra, Morocco

Weizhen Rao
College of Economics and Management, Shandong University of Science and Technology, Qingdao 266590, China

Feng Liu
School of Management Science and Engineering, Dongbei University of Finance and Economics, Dalian 116025, China

Shengbin Wang
Department of Marketing, Transportation and Supply Chain, School of Business and Economics, North Carolina A & T State University, Greensboro, NC 27411, USA

Han Pan, Zhongliang Jing, Lingfeng Qiao and Minzhe Li
School of Aeronautics and Astronautics, Shanghai Jiao Tong University, Shanghai, China

Rui Li, Zili Zhou, Yansong Cheng and Jianqiang Wang
The Second Research Institute of CAAC, Chengdu, China

Xiaoqiang Li, Dan Wang and Yin Zhang
School of Computer Engineering and Sciences, Shanghai University, Shanghai 200444, China

Abdulkader Helwan and Dilber Uzun Ozsahin
Department of Biomedical Engineering, Near East University, Near East Boulevard, 99138 Nicosia, Northern Cyprus,Mersin 10, Turkey

Xiaoqiang Li and Yi Zhang
School of Computer Engineering and Science, Shanghai University, Shanghai, China

Dong Liao
School of Mathematic and Statistics, Nanyang Normal University, Nanyang, China

Yong Zhou, Guibin Sun, Yan Xing, Ranran Zhou and Zhixiao Wang
School of Computer Science and Technology, China University of Mining and Technology, Xuzhou 221008, China

Warapon Chinsatit and Takeshi Saitoh
Graduate School of Computer Science and Systems Engineering, Kyushu Institute of Technology, 680–4 Kawazu, Iizuka-shi, Fukuoka 820-8502, Japan

Nhat-Duc Hoang and Xuan-Linh Tran
Institute of Research and Development, Faculty of Civil Engineering, Duy Tan University, K7/25 Quang Trung, Danang, Vietnam

Duy-Thang Vu
Faculty of Architecture, Duy Tan University, K7/25 Quang Trung, Danang, Vietnam

Van-Duc Tran
International School, Duy Tan University, 254 Nguyen Van Linh, Danang 550000, Vietnam

Index

CPSIA information can be obtained
at www.ICGtesting.com
Printed in the USA
BVHW011418240519
549249BV00004B/349/P